FAMILIES LIVING WITH DRUGS AND HIV

P9-DDY-774

FAMILIES LIVING WITH DRUGS AND HIV

Intervention and Treatment Strategies

Edited by

RICHARD P. BARTH
JEANNE PIETRZAK
MALIA RAMLER

THE GUILFORD PRESS
New York   London

© 1993 The Guilford Press
A Division of Guilford Publications, Inc.
72 Spring Street, New York, NY 10012

All rights reserved

No part of this book may be reproduced, stored in a retrieval system,
or transmitted, in any form or by any means, electronic, mechanical,
photocopying, microfilming, recording, or otherwise, without written
permission from the Publisher.

Printed in the United States of America

This book is printed on acid-free paper.

Last digit is print number: 9 8 7 6 5 4 3 2 1

Library of Congress Cataloging-in-Publication Data

Families living with drugs and HIV : intervention and treatment
    strategies / edited by Richard P. Barth, Jeanne Pietrzak, Malia
    Ramler.
        p.   cm.
    Includes bibliographical references and indexes.
    ISBN 0-89862-888-1   ISBN 0-89862-150-X (pbk.)
    1. AIDS (Disease) in children—Patients—Services for—United
States.   2. Children of narcotic addicts—Services for—United
States.   3. Drug abuse in pregnancy—United States—Prevention.
4. Problem families—Services for—United States.   I. Barth,
Richard P., 1952–   .   II. Pietrzak, Jeanne.   III. Ramler, Malia.
    [DNLM: 1. Acquired Immunodeficiency Syndrome—prevention &
control.   2. Acquired Immunodeficiency Syndrome—therapy.   3. Family
Health.   4. HIV Infections—prevention & control.   5. HIV
Infections—therapy.   WD 308 F198]
RJ387 A25F36 1993
362.1′989297′9200973—dc20
DNLM/DLC
for Library of Congress   92-1693
                                                              CIP

Editors and Contributors

Richard P. Barth, Ph.D., is a Professor in the School of Social Welfare, University of California at Berkeley, where he teaches child welfare practice and policy courses, and is Co-Director of the Family Welfare Research Group, where he has led numerous studies and demonstration projects on children's services including the University of California at Berkeley study of services for Drug- and HIV-affected infants which initiated this volume. Many of these studies and projects are also related to perinatal drug and alcohol use and HIV, such as the new U.S. DHHS–funded National Abandoned Infant Assistance Resource Center for Drug-, HIV-, and Medically-Involved Children; the Caregiver Training Project; and the Child Welfare and AIDS Project. Professor Barth was Senior Fulbright Scholar to Sweden in 1990, where he studied services to drug-affected families and children. Professor Barth is also Co-Principal Investigator of the Berkeley Child Welfare Research Center. He holds the Hutto Patterson Chair in Family and Child Studies.

Jeanne Pietrzak, M.S.W., is Director of the National Abandoned Infant Assistance Resource Center. In her tenure with the University of California at Berkeley, Family Welfare Research Group, Ms. Pietrzak has directed numerous projects focusing on drug- and HIV-affected children and families, including the Child Welfare & AIDS Project, the Caregiver Training Project, the University of California at Berkeley Study of Services for Drug- and AIDS-Affected Infants, and an evaluation of the Medically Fragile Respite Care Program, an OHDS-sponsored project of Family Support Services of the Bay Area. Ms. Pietrzak has conducted workshops and training on pediatric HIV and has served as Committee Chair on the Board of the AIDS Service Providers Association of the Bay Area. She has written numerous reports and articles on drug- and AIDS-affected children and is principal author of *Practical Program Evaluation: Examples from Child Abuse Prevention* (with Ramler, Renner, Ford, and Gilbert, 1990). Ms. Pietrzak also served as a program planner, community foundation coordinator, and case manager serving families of children who were severely mentally and multiply impaired.

Malia Ramler, M.S.W., M.P.H., a senior program analyst at the Family Welfare Research Group, has been a key staff member on the Child Welfare & AIDS

86929

Project, the Caregiver Training Project, and the University of California at Berkeley Study of Services for Drug- and AIDS-Affected Families. Ms. Ramler conducted training of child welfare workers in five Bay Area counties using a curriculum she co-authored, *Children, Families & HIV: A Training Curriculum for Social Service and Health Providers* (Sokal & Ramler, 1991). She organized and chaired an interagency committee of health and social service providers from northern California that developed model policy guidelines for the case-management and care of children with HIV infection in the child welfare system, *Child Welfare Protocols for Children with HIV Infection: Guidelines for Development and Evaluation* (Ramler, 1991). Ms. Ramler has experience as a medical social worker with high-risk perinatal populations. She was a member of the Substance-Exposed Infants Task Force of the California Senate Select Committee on Children and Youth and the Assembly Committee on Human Services. In addition to presenting her work at numerous conferences, Ms. Ramler trains extensively on pediatric HIV to daycare providers in the San Francisco Bay Area. Ms. Ramler is co-author of *Practical Program Evaluation: Examples from Child Abuse Prevention* (with Pietrzak, Renner, Ford, and Gilbert, 1990), and of *Family Power: Building Skills for Families with HIV- and Drug-Affected Children* (FWRG, 1992).

Abigail English, J.D., is Project Director of the Adolescent Health Care Project and a staff attorney at the National Center for Youth Law in San Francisco, where she has worked since 1976 on health-care and foster-care issues. She has participated in major litigation affecting the legal rights of children and adolescents, has authored numerous publications, and has lectured widely to youth-serving professionals. Ms. English is a recognized expert on legal issues in adolescent health care and recently served on the Advisory Panel for the Adolescent Health Study of the Office of Technology Assessment. She is currently working on expanding access to health care for poor children and adolescents. Her work includes a special focus on problems in pediatric and adolescent AIDS.

Hope Ewing, M.D., MSEd., is a family physician and educator with a special interest in perinatal addiction. She maintains a clinical family practice with the Health Services Department of Contra Costa County and is founder and Director of the Health Department's Born Free Project, which integrates perinatal health care and intervention for women with problems of drug and alcohol dependence. The project was funded for federal demonstration under the Office of Substance Abuse Prevention in 1989 and won the 1990 Special Innovators Award of the California Association of Public Hospitals and the Public Hospitals Institute. She is on the clinical teaching faculty at the University of Southern California and the University of California at San Francisco. She is board-certified in Family Practice and certified in Addiction Medicine by the American Society on Addiction Medicine. She has a master's degree in medical education from the School of Education, University of Southern California, and a special interest in training and cross-training of health and human service providers. Much of her practice experience has been in high-risk and underserved populations in New York, Chicago, California's San Joaquin Valley, Los Angeles, Oakland, and Contra Costa County.

Mary Foran, M.P.H., is Director of the Office of Service Integration in the Contra Costa County Health Services Department, Martinez, California. She chairs the county's Alcohol, Drug Abuse and Perinatal Task Force, directs development of comprehensive perinatal care programs for low-income women, and manages the department's initiatives to integrate a wide range of services for county residents. Prior to joining the Health Services Department, Ms. Foran was responsible for initiating state-funded case management services for pregnant teens and teen parents in Alameda and Contra Costa Counties, as well as developing several prenatal care outreach and coordination projects. Other experience includes consulting in strategic planning and program development, community organizing and training, technical assistance, and evaluation for a wide range of health and social service agencies. Ms. Foran's special interest is program development with an emphasis on integrating services across disciplines and agencies. She received her Master's in Public Health in 1980 from the University of California at Berkeley.

Maria Nunes-Dinis, M.S.W., is a doctoral candidate at the School of Social Welfare, University of California, Berkeley, and a Research Assistant for the Alcohol Research Group in Berkeley and for the California State Department of Alcohol and Drug Programs. From 1981 to 1984, Ms. Nunes-Dinis worked as a social worker with alcoholics in a state mental institution and local social service agency in Azores, Portugal. While working in Portugal, Ms. Nunes-Dinis published two articles on alcohol problems and treatment in the Portugese mental health journal *Hospitalidade*. In 1989, Ms. Nunes-Dinis completed a survey of alcohol problems and solutions in Spain and Portugal, which is in press with the *International Journal of the Addictions*. The results of the survey have also been translated for publication in scientific journals in Spain and Portugal.

Diana Roberts, M.A., is the Director of the Division of Children and Family Services of the Washington State Department of Social and Health Services. Previously, she was the Regional Administrator for Oregon's Children's Services Division, Eastern Region, where she was responsible for administering social service and business operations of child welfare offices in 17 Oregon counties. She has developed her expertise in child welfare at Children's Services Division through her positions as Caseworker, Intake Supervisor, Parent Training Coordinator, Branch Manager, and Manager since she began working at the agency in 1973. She has published manuals about fatal child abuse, explanations of Oregon's child abuse and neglect laws, and most recently, a discussion of perinatal substance abuse entitled "Women, Drugs, and Babies: Born to Lose?" Ms. Roberts has appeared on television in Portland, Medford, and Eugene to discuss child abuse statistics, the problem of child maltreatment, and the incidence of child fatalities resulting from child abuse and neglect.

Nika St. Claire, M.S., is currently the program director of the Center of C.A.R.E. (Chemical Addiction Recovery Efforts) at Children's Hospital in Oakland, California. The Center of C.A.R.E. is a model infant–parent program with an array of support services for drug-affected children and their chemically dependent mothers. Ms. St. Claire has been in the field of perinatal addiction for 13 years and has worked in a variety of outpatient programs for pregnant and postpartum addicts and alcoholics and their children. She has written, directed, and produced a video presentation entitled "Treating the Pregnant Addict" for heroin addicts. She also served as a member of the steering committee for the state's task force on substance-exposed infants. Ms. St. Claire is a founder and President of California Advocates for Pregnant Women and has been active in the policy and research arena for drug-affected infants. She is a well-known lecturer in facilitating recovery services for chemically dependent women and developmental services for drug-affected children. Prior to her work in perinatal addiction, Ms. St. Claire worked as a teacher with emotionally disturbed children.

Karen Sokal-Gutierrez, M.D., M.P.H., is a private consultant on maternal and child health issues. She was the director of Maternal-Child-Adolescent Health Services for the Department of Health in Berkeley, California, as well as the medical consultant for the Child Welfare and AIDS Project and for the Caregiver Training Project at the University of California at Berkeley. Dr. Sokal-Gutierrez has worked in clinical public health practice in pediatrics, adolescent medicine, sexually transmitted diseases, and family planning. In addition, she has worked locally and internationally assisting public health and social service agencies to address the issues of AIDS and drug use in women and children. She has conducted needs assessments, drafted policies, developed educational curricula, and provided extensive training for health and social service professionals, foster parents, and childcare providers.

Laurie A. Soman, M.S.W., is a Research Policy Analyst with the Center for the Vulnerable Child at Children's Hospital, Oakland, and a consultant on perinatal alcohol and drug use to the State Department of Alcohol and Drug Programs, where she serves on the Select Committee on Perinatal Alcohol and Drug Use. She is Project Manager of the policy study "Perinatal Alcohol and Drug Use: An Analysis of Policies and Programs in California," funded by the California Policy Seminar.

Elaine Durkot Sterzin, LICSW, has developed model demonstration and outreach training programs since 1975. Currently coordinating development for the Foundation for Children with AIDS, she has designed and implemented innovative family-focused programs for children with special needs and their families. She has also developed and provided training for professionals in the transdisciplinary and transagency models of service delivery. In addition, she has written manuals for involving families in programs, implementing respite care programs for developmentally disabled children, and working with substance-dependent parents. She holds a master's degree in social work and has clinical experience in child protective services. Over the last 17 years she has worked with handicapped, drug-affected, and HIV-infected children (from birth through age 5) and their families.

Mildred Thompson, M.S.W., currently Director of Healthy Start, a federal initiative funded to reduce infant mortality by 50% in Oakland in the next 5 years, has been involved in health care for 20 years. She has an M.S.W. from New York University and a degree in nursing. Prior to her involvement in Healthy Start, Ms. Thompson was Director of San Antonio Health Clinic for 6 years and more recently was Director of the Healthy Infant Program, a case management program for drug-exposed infants based at Highland Hospital. Ms. Thompson has participated on several statewide task forces, attempting to change some of the legislative and policy barriers to service delivery. She has taught a course on ethnic diversity at San Francisco State University and worked as an independent management consultant.

Holly Vaughn-Edmonds, M.S.W., is a hospital social worker at Oregon Health Sciences University in Portland, Oregon, where she performs psychosocial assessments, crisis intervention, supportive counseling, and discharge planning to clients throughout the hospital. Previously, Ms. Vaughn-Edmonds worked as health educator in a prenatal clinic, a renal social worker, and a neonatal/pediatric social worker. She graduated from the University of California, Berkeley, School of Social Welfare with a concentration in health care settings.

Sylvia Villarreal, M.D., is Associate Clinical Professor of Pediatrics and a staff member of the Children's Health Center at San Francisco General Hospital. She is Director of the Kempe High Risk Clinic and Early Childhood Services. Her community work includes membership on the San Francisco Mayor's HIV Health Service Planning Council. She is a member of the board of directors for the California children's lobby. Dr. Villarreal has published extensively on health care issues, and her field of research is children in poverty.

Geneva Woodruff, Ph.D., is known nationally for her leadership in the field of early intervention for children with special needs and their families. For the past 14 years she has directed model demonstration and outreach training programs for children with special needs and their families. These special populations have included children with multiple handicaps and developmental delays, children born substance exposed, and children with HIV infection. Woodruff currently directs Project STAR, a home- and center-based program for HIV-infected children and their families; the Kinship Project, an intensive recovery support and developmental program for drug-exposed children and their families; and Project WIN, a national outreach program that provides training to teams interested in replicating a model of family-centered transagency services for HIV-infected children and their families.

Woodruff was one of the founders of the policy-making and advocacy group INTERACT: The National Committee for Very Young Handicapped Children and Their Families, and she is the founder of the Foundation for Children with AIDS. Currently she serves as the Executive Director of the Foundation, which is a national organization devoted to promoting and providing family-centered and community-based services for drug-affected and HIV-infected children and their families. The foundation staff publishes the *Children with AIDS Newsletter* bimonthly, sponsors conferences and training institutes, and provides onsite training and technical assistance to drug- and AIDS-affected children and their families. Dr. Woodruff holds a Ph.D. in early childhood education as well as master's degrees in special education and elementary education.

Barry Zuckerman, M.D., is Professor of Pediatrics and Public Health at the Boston University School of Medicine and Director of the Division of Developmental and Behavioral Pediatrics at Boston City Hospital. He is a member of the National Commission on Children, Chairman of the Section of Developmental and Behavioral Pediatrics of the American Academy of Pediatrics, and a member of many state and national organizations. He has conducted research and written articles on the impact of biological and environmental factors on the health and development of young children, especially those living in poverty.

Preface

While the "war on drugs" raged in the streets of the Americas, drug-affected children and families became the subject of a pitched battle among concerned professionals and policy makers. The growth of crack cocaine and the emergent realization that mothers and children were the fastest-growing group of people infected with HIV brought a stronger charge to the question of how to address this problem. Whereas service providers had long been involved with drug affected families and children in the course of their work, they were often ill-served and were not the impetus for reexamining existing services. Service providers largely worked around these families rather than with them. With the greater visibility of drug-affected children and families came an outcry for building a response that was unique to these families.

As the discovery of crack and its effects became known to local agencies and to the public through the media, panic ensued. Concerned persons rushed to develop a response. Whereas a few believed that the current period of crack use was more similar to than different from other eras of drug use and was unfairly being used again to blame the disenfranchised for their plight, many appeared to agree that the crack epidemic was unlike any other and justified more extraordinary measures. Along with calls to increase existing services were calls for discontinuing business as usual and rethinking conventional approaches. Proposals for innovative approaches to services, such as residential centers for mothers in drug treatment programs and their children, emerged simultaneously with calls for more traditional efforts, such as orphanages and early parent–child separation. This was not simply a matter of the well-informed and virtuous battling with the ill-informed and vindictive. Professionals working with families and children from many vantage points and for many years lacked the information needed to develop effective policies. Child welfare professionals lacked knowledge of the efficacy of the drug-treatment programs that they were increasingly expected to subsidize. Drug-treatment providers were unsure whether clients reported for child abuse would be fairly treated and receive sufficient benefit from child welfare services to justify the intrusion into their lives. Suddenly, even providers of intensive family preservation

services and interdisciplinary case management—among the best-regarded inno-
vations of recent years—were wondering whether the confluence of drug abuse and
HIV infection was pushing these programs beyond their limits. The discussions of
what to do were made more difficult by the limited understanding of the assumptions and outcomes of the service providers involved. The result was often as much
heat as light.

The intense concern about drug- and AIDS-affected families was the impetus
for this volume. In 1987, the Bay Area Social Services Consortium—a collaborative
effort of the University of California, local Social Service Departments, and the
Zellerbach Family Fund—identified pediatric HIV as a topic of great concern.
This began a year of fact finding and conferences that attempted to clarify the
nature of the problem and the most favorable responses to prepare the San
Francisco Bay Area for growing numbers of HIV-infected mothers and children. A
year later this effort resulted in funding of the Child Welfare & AIDS Project by a
3-year demonstration grant from the Children's Bureau, Administration on Children Youth and Families, U.S. Department of Health and Human Services. The
work of the Child Welfare & AIDS Project involves developing training, programs,
and policies to address the needs of HIV-infected children, their caregivers, and
their social workers. Work on this project included close collaboration with the
child welfare directors in the Bay Area counties, who expressed concern that the
crack epidemic was hitting them much sooner than the HIV-epidemic and that
planning was urgently needed for both. Meanwhile, the Zellerbach Family Fund,
which had been an early supporter of one of the nation's first residences for
mothers in drug recovery and their children, and the Wallace Alexander Gerbode
Foundation, which has long demonstrated its commitment to women's rights, were
also looking for ideas that would go beyond the emotionally charged and stale-
mated debates dominating the California scene. Active in both the national and
local foundation communities, Ed Nathan of Zellerbach and Tom Layton of
Gerbode knew that this challenge was not localized in California. In collaboration
with the staff of the Child Welfare & AIDS Project, their foundations helped to
conceptualize and agreed to fund this effort to analyze social and health services to
drug- and AIDS-affected families and to make that analysis available to a wider
audience.

The mechanism chosen for that analysis was a panel of local and national
experts drawn from a broad cross-section of agencies and disciplines. The Child
Welfare & AIDS Project staff served as the steering committee for the project and
began by identifying the key issues needing expert attention. We sought a broad
purview that encompassed both the decline into and the recovery from drug- and
HIV-involvement. We then began a search for panelists with disciplinary and
ethnic diversity and the potential for collaboration. We also sought a panel that
would bring salience to local issues but had substantial exposure to issues, policies,
and programs from across the country. We were fortunate to have almost everyone
we asked agree to be on the panel, and we are grateful to them for taking time from
their work and other activities to participate. We are also most appreciative of their
host agencies for allowing them release time to participate; we know that some

agencies also felt the pinch when their staff joined us for our two-day seminars, but they continued to encourage them to participate. Barry Zuckerman was gracious enough to provide a chapter on developmental considerations to round out an examination of the issues affecting children and families. Neal Halfon, former Director of the Center for the Vulnerable Child at Children's Hospital, Oakland, was particularly gracious, given that three staff members from the Center for the Vulnerable Child participated on the panel. We also invited two or three speakers to come to each day of our meetings and to provide their perspectives on research, service, and policy. These speakers included Leila Beckwith, Albione Becnel, Ric Fulroth, Dorothy Bailey, Susan Kwok, Issac Slaughter, Cynthia Hopkins, Donna Weston, Joan Henry, and Marcia Rosenbaum. Their presentations enriched our knowledge and stimulated further fact finding and discussion.

The products of this effort are three: an Executive Summary that captures the conclusions of the seminar; a videotape on drug-affected families entitled *A Season of Hope*, directed by Ashley James; and this volume, which provides a more comprehensive treatment of the salient topics by the expert panel. This volume is not a consensual document. Although the panelists met as a group for four two-day sessions and discussed their chapters on innumerable occasions in dyads and small groups, they acted as consultants to each other and not constrainers of each other. Each chapter had several readers, and the ideas in it were presented to the panel at each meeting.

We anticipate that the information available in this volume will offer a multidisciplinary audience of service providers, program developers, policy makers, and students a better opportunity to move beyond hyperbole to facts about drug- and AIDS-affected families. We have made every effort to include the most current information in a way that transcends today's newest research announcement. The authors' long experience in the research and practice of drug treatment, health care, family support services, law, and child welfare have led us to develop a framework that we believe will have continued relevance as the nature of the current epidemic changes and as other epidemics emerge.

The book is comprised of four parts. Part I, an introduction to addiction and the problems of drug- and AIDS-affected infants and their families, a framework for subsequent discussions of services. Part II addresses prevention of substance abuse and approaches to prenatal care that help prevent drug-affected childhoods. Part III considers services to families already involved with drugs. Part IV considers legal and policy initiatives.

We are grateful to Eve Vanderschmidt, Holly Vaughn-Edmonds, Rob Tufel, David Camp and Ruth Vosmek for their efforts in coordinating the activities of the seminar and the preparation of the chapters. Karen Sokal-Gutierrez was more than a chapter co-author and panelist—she also reviewed chapters for medical accuracy. Every day the editors benefit from Susan Katzenellenbogen's good humor and skill in keeping our work environment (and us) relatively sane; she was also responsible for the preparation of the final manuscript. A Lois and Samuel Silberman Senior Faculty Fellowship provided valuable support to Rick Barth, and a Senior Fulbright Fellowship allowed him a semester in Stockholm to study the

Swedish approach to work with substance-abusing families. He is grateful to his colleagues at the Family Welfare Research Group and to his co-editors for working harder than ever to take up whatever slack was left during this sojourn in Scandinavia. We appreciate the leadership of Harry Specht, Dean of the School of Social Welfare, and Neil Gilbert, Director of the Family Welfare Research Group.

Cecelia Sudia of the Children's Bureau has assisted us by ably administering our Child Welfare & AIDS Project grant. We also value the guidance of Pat Campiglia, also from the Children's Bureau, who has been our project officer for the Caregiver Training Project and the National Resource Center for Drug-, HIV-, and Medically-Involved Children funded through the Abandoned Infants Assistance Act. To our colleagues on the panel and the many clients and colleagues from whom they have learned, we are most grateful.

This project would not have occurred without the inspiration of Ed Nathan. He keeps his ear very close to the ground and hears the cries from clients and service providers, yet he finds time to develop and implement action plans. We hope this volume helps to spur the kind of thoughtful actions in many local communities that have become his trademark in the San Francisco Bay Area.

Contents

IV. LEGAL, ETHICAL, AND POLICY ISSUES

I

INTRODUCTION TO
THE PROBLEM OF DRUG-
AND AIDS-AFFECTED INFANTS

1

Rationale and Conceptual Framework

RICHARD P. BARTH

The rapid increase in the number of drug- and AIDS-affected newborns has serious consequences for health and social services providers and policy makers. Critical ethical, fiscal, and legal challenges face concerned citizens, professional and nonprofessional alike. The challenges of caring for families with multiple health, social service, financial, and educational problems has amplified the call for more integrated services. But first the challenge calls for the integration of information across the disciplines; without the integration of information, strategic planning for drug-affected families cannot occur.

The importance of this volume lies in part on its integration of information about drug- and AIDS-affected families. As the 1990s progress, the number and proportion of women and children with HIV will continue to grow. Seroprevalence rates among women approach 40% in some central African cities, and the World Health Organization indicates that several million children who are not infected with the AIDS virus are destined to become orphans in this decade. In New York City alone, experts estimate that 50,000 children will lose at least one parent to AIDS, or have already done so, by 1995 (Lambert, 1989). The percentage of children infected at birth (having received the infection from their mothers, who also have HIV) is increasing. Most HIV-infected women become infected by sharing needles during intravenous (IV) drug use or by having sex with men who are IV drug users; according to the Centers for Disease Control (1990), IV drug use is implicated in 71% of AIDS cases among women. Persistent crack use sharply increases the likelihood of HIV infection (Fullilove, Fullilove, Bowser, & Gross, 1990), at least in part due to the practice of trading unsafe sex for crack.

Yet information is not shared among the professionals who provide services to HIV-positive persons and those who treat drug-affected clients. We know few practitioners or scholars who consider themselves expert in both areas. The lack of integrated information is a grave problem in early childhood intervention, drug treatment services, social services, public health services, and health care. Analyses of graduate training programs preparing professionals to care for children from birth to age 3 who need special education have found few comprehensive programs and almost no cross-departmental training opportunities (Hanson, 1990).

This chapter identifies a range of uncertainties that face policy makers and service providers across the disciplines; it then describes guiding principles, based on what we do know, that can be used to develop responsive and responsible programs for drug- and AIDS-affected families. This will serve as a framework for the more detailed description of practices, programs, and policies in subsequent chapters.

EPIDEMIOLOGICAL UNCERTAINTY

By the yardstick of public concern, the magnitude of the impact of drugs and AIDS on family life can be easily measured; it is enormous. By any standard, the suffering of children and parents involved with drugs or AIDS, or both, is great. Practically every major periodical and network has had feature and follow-up stories on crack and AIDS and their impact on families. At the federal level, William Bennett, the first "drug czar," made public pronouncements about the need for alternative systems of care (e.g. orphanages) for children of drug users, the U.S. General Accounting Office issued a report entitled "Drug-Exposed Infants: A Generation at Risk," and the government conducted the biggest drug crackdown ever, by busting the government of Panama. A survey of legislation pertaining to drug use during pregnancy indicates that 30 states considered or passed new legislation or began implementation of a new law in the 1990 legislation session (most of the state legislatures that did not pass a law were not in session).

Public outcry and concern about the impact of HIV on families is less intense than that regarding drugs and, of late, primarily witnessed in scientific reporting. The most visible advocates for more services for HIV-affected people are gay white men, who have been hardest hit by this cruel epidemic. AIDS victims with the highest public profile are young people who were infected by transfusions; Ryan White is the best known. Yet the problem of children, especially minority children, prenatally infected with AIDS, will continue to press for the attention of the public. Within New York, Miami, and Newark, there are pockets of AIDS infection that rival rates seen in Africa, but this pattern of concentration in these three cities is shifting and now more than two-thirds of new AIDS cases occur outside of them. Women of childbearing age represent almost 10% of the nation's more than 218,000 reported AIDS cases (Centers for Disease Control, 1992) and constitute one of the fastest growing groups of newly infected adults (California AIDS

Update, 1991). One of every 150 women (.6%) who have babies in New York State is infected with the AIDS virus, and inner-city birth rates are as high as 2%–3%.

Satisfactory measures of the extent and impact of drugs and AIDS on families are not available, owing to the difficulties in measuring a private activity. There is no question, however, that the problem is great. The National Institute of Drug Abuse estimated that 5 million women of childbearing age used illicit drugs in 1988 (U.S. General Accounting Office, 1990). The percentage of children born with illegal drugs in their system may be as high as 11% (Chasnoff, 1988) or as low as 2% (Besharov, 1989); either figure represents a menace to the future of our children.

The number of children born drug-affected would not be of such great concern to the public if it were not for the great fears about the impact of drugs on children's development. Indeed, on any day more children are born alcohol exposed than drug exposed, and the consequences can be far more profound. Yet the public is less outraged about the effects of alcohol than about those of drugs. In part, this is because of a commonly held belief that children exposed to drugs fare dramatically worse than children exposed to alcohol. The concern for the future of these "drug babies" represents an opportunity for service providers and advocates, yet overreaction to the problem is a threat to mothers and children. A great part of the epidemiological uncertainty concerning drugs arises from our difficulties in accurately picturing the future of drug-affected children (see chapter 3).

The number of AIDS-affected children is more certain, and the adverse consequences of exposure to HIV better known. Current estimates are that roughly 30% of children exposed to their mother's HIV in utero will become HIV-infected. The natural history of the disease in children, now that AZT is increasingly available to them, is less predictable than before. Although most HIV-infected newborns die before reaching school age (California AIDS Update, 1991), more aggressive medical care is significantly improving their prognosis and survival.

Costs of care predictions indicate that the impact of even the lowest estimates of the number of HIV- and drug-affected births can land a staggering blow to our service delivery finances, if not our general economy. The Florida Department of Health and Rehabilitative Services estimated that the total cost of providing services to age 18 years for each drug-exposed child who shows *significant* physiologic or neurologic impairment will be $750,000. (Since those who survive adolescence become more expensive to serve as they get older, their lifetime cost could be expected to be at least twice that figure.) The Early Intervention Project at UCLA estimates that the cost of their program for drug-exposed preschoolers with mild impairment is $17,000 per year per child. In the U.S. General Accounting Office (1990) report, hospital charges for drug-exposed infants ranged from $455 to $65,325; the mean charge at three hospitals in 1989 was $7,228. Estimated costs for residential treatment for drug mothers and families are about $40,000 for MABON House in New York and Mandela House near Oakland. No estimates have been published on the minimum cost of care for less involved mothers and children.

AIDS is disproportionately a disease of women and children of color. African-American and Latino women constitute only 25% of the population nationally, yet 73% of the women with AIDS are black or Hispanic (CDC *HIV/AIDS Surveillance*). This is in apparent contrast to the case of substance abuse, where preliminary evidence indicates similar rates of illegal substance use among African-American and white women.

DEVELOPMENTAL UNCERTAINTY

Evidence on the outcomes of drug- and AIDS-exposed infants allows only the certainty that the outcomes are extremely varied. To borrow from Frank Furstenberg's study of the life course for teenage mothers, the outcomes for perinatally drug-exposed children can be described as "unpredictable and unruly" (Furstenberg, et al., 1987, p. 73). Outcomes for HIV-affected children are quite dependent on medical care: advances in medical treatment can now prevent children from dying from PCP (Pneumocystis Carinii Pneumonia) of course this advance requires that children be diagnosed, and many are not (Nicholas, 1991). Even untreated, the symptoms from one child to another can be quite different. Many AIDS-infected newborns will die within 2 years, yet some children have no symptoms until they are 5 or more years old. While there are cases reported in the literature of children remaining asymptomatic until 10 years of age, the median survival time from diagnosis to death is 6.1 months, with 75% dying within 16 months of diagnosis (California AIDS Update, 1991). More than 50% of infected children will experience neurological involvement, which may affect developmental capacity, and loss of developmental milestones with disease progression is commonly reported.

With drug-affected children, the diversity is so great that no specific syndrome has been seriously posited. For those with the most extreme levels of prenatal drug exposure there may be a common set of behaviors, but these have not yet been precisely described. Certainly, much has been written about the relationship between cocaine use and low birth weight (Petitti & Coleman, 1990), fetal growth retardation (Zuckerman et al., 1989), sudden infant death syndrome (Bauchner et al., 1988), delayed or diminished cognitive development (Chasnoff, 1987; Howard, Beckwith, Rodnig, & Kropenske, 1989), and impaired social and play skills (Howard et al., 1989). The profoundness and persistence of these affects are not fully manifest, although the most recent and defensible conclusions from existing work are reviewed in this volume.

ORGANIZATIONAL UNCERTAINTY

Service providers struggle to plan, and gain resources for, coordinated services to drug- and AIDS-affected families. Across America legislators, service providers, and advocates are seeking to determine which service providers, in which order and in which combination, should be responsible for the care of which children under which family circumstances and to which end. District attorneys, public health personnel, child welfare workers, and community groups all believe that they have the primary responsibility to protect children from the direct and indirect effects of drug exposure. District attorneys may seek to protect children from the unlawful acts of their parents, public health workers may seek to protect them from the potential disruption of family life, child welfare workers from the degradation and danger of living with parents with diminished capacity to care, and community advocates from placement outside their homes and communities.

Although it must be recognized that service integration strategies will depend on many local conditions, basic questions need to be answered regarding the appropriateness and availability of interventions from various disciplines. Much discussion has focused on the tension between criminal justice and treatment approaches to intervention (Skolnick, 1990). The argument for criminal prosecution has apparently lost some of its force (in part because prosecutors have not been very successful in their initial cases), but the debate over the optimal service approach has just begun. Significant tensions exist within the ranks of service providers. These were expressed by a panel presenting to an audience of foundation directors and officers. When faced with a question about the appropriate role of child welfare services and public health services for drug-affected newborns, I, knowing full well the shortcomings of the child welfare system, suggested that public health be the first line of response because prenatal drug exposure is a public health problem until shown otherwise through an assessment. Another panelist and health care provider, knowing full well the limitations of public health services, argued that only the child welfare system had the capacity to be the first line of response because public health nurses are not available or trained to provide 24-hour in-home assessment and referral. The obvious conclusion is the need for collaboration between professionals, but the mechanics of collaboration are unclear. Recent efforts to draft legislation in California to guide interventions on behalf of drug-affected mothers and children hinged on the debate on the appropriateness, adequacy, and timing of public health and social service responses.

Controversies about the organization of services to children and families affected by AIDS are less heated but likewise unresolved. Particular questions related to case management of health and social services have been piqued by the concern for families having as many as a dozen case managers. Julie Sarkissian (personal communication, June 8, 1989), coordinator of the Seattle–King County AIDS demonstration project, describes the way that case management can serve and disserve families:

> We are working with one family that was being served by so many different caregivers that they just closed down. The family consists of a teenage mother, who is HIV infected; her healthy toddler; her 6-month-old, who is dying from AIDS; the children's grandmother; and a 14-year-old aunt. They refused to see anyone but the staff nurse who had been going to the home daily to treat the mother's TB. She has become the central coordinating point for all of the services that this family needs. With behind-the-scenes assistance from the social worker, the nurse is arranging prenatal care for the pregnant aunt, coordinating medical and respite care, and ensuring welfare and health benefits.

Whatever the configuration, staff with both medical and social service skills must work in tandem with AIDS-involved families.

HISTORIC UNCERTAINTY

A new and different drug like crack tends, at least initially, to be treated like the first in a new class of drugs that are categorically different than all other drugs. How do recent increases in drug-exposed births fit into a theoretical, epidemiological, and historical context? That is, given that humankind has a long history of using intoxicants and that scientists have been looking at the outcomes for high-risk newborns for several decades, what is common and different about this period of time and this threat to children's well-being.

Because of its availability and intensity, crack is arguably the most destructive street drug around. The story of Lenard Hebert, a self-acknowledged expert on trends in drug abuse ("I did each drug of the decade"), captures the differences in impact of America's drugs of choice. Hebert used LSD in Vietnam, marijuana as a black militant in the seventies, cocaine for 10 years during the eighties, and then crack, which—unlike all the other drugs—turned Hebert's life upside down. He stopped dealing cocaine, turned his middle-class high-rise apartment into a crack den, and slept in abandoned cars and shelters before entering drug treatment (Hurley, 1989).

The process by which the use of new drugs expands from small cadres of avante-garde and wealthy users to the middle class is fairly well documented (Musto, 1973), but less is known about the reasons that some drugs persist and others appear to be replaced by new drugs. Crack cocaine use seems to be losing some popularity already (as have marijuana and LSD in recent years), but the future of this drug may not be predictable from examination of the history of other drugs. According to Musto, perhaps the country's foremost illicit drug historian, the recent increase in crack use is an anomaly in the country's declining interest in drugs (which began at the end of the 1970s). Certainly, the evidence is clear that high school seniors (bellwethers of the future middle class) have decreased their use of illegal drugs and any alcohol use between 1988 and 1991 but that crack cocaine use and daily alcohol use have leveled off (National Institute on Drug Abuse, 1992; U.S. DHHS, 1992). Simultaneously, hospital emergency episodes for drug-related consequences began to increase in 1991 after a decline from 1989. Also, the 1991 NIDA Household Survey on Drug Use showed that several years of downward trends were leveling off. Apparently, high school students are changing their behavior but the general public continues to use drugs and alcohol at dangerous and, again, accelerating levels. According to Musto, crack presents an opportunity to further catalyze the opposition to drugs: "Crack seemed to be the ultimate drug problem, one so frightening that it crystallized our intolerance toward all drugs. It has created a consensus in society against drugs and ended the ambivalence that had been prevalent for decades" (quoted in Hurley, 1989, p. 58). Musto views the decline as a long, gradual process that may take several decades and that will not be expedited by massive incarceration or the death penalty for drug dealing.

On the basis of the assumption that crack is more like other drugs than it is different, the middle class's distrust of the drug can be expected to eventually reduce the demand and profitability of the drug. Still, since crack has been primarily a drug of choice for low-income African-Americans, the impact of changing middle-class values is not certain to be potent. A distrust of crack is also being mobilized in the African-American community to apparently significant effect. Despite the likelihood that crack use will gradually decline, no reputable historian would argue for a laissez-faire course in addressing the current crack epidemic. Such a passive ride down the long road to reductions in American drug use will find many families stuck in roadside brambles. Recognition that other epidemics (like the early-1900s cocaine epidemic) have faded when underlying attitudes and social and economic opportunities changed may help focus the public on creating social and economic alternatives to drugs that will be useful when the next new and unprecedented drug begins to plague our families.

GUIDING PRINCIPLES

The authors of this volume, of diverse professional and institutional affiliations, have agreed upon several guiding principles for the development and reform of social and health services to drug- and AIDS-affected families, which include the following:

1. Perinatal Alcohol and Substance Abuse Are a Health Problem.
2. Drug Use Is More Than an Individual Failing.
3. Family-Focused Recovery Services Must Be Available.
4. Services Must Be Provided Voluntarily and Without Loss of Integrity.
5. Intensive Services to Parents Can Promote Family Preservation.
6. Allied Services Must Be Provided.
7. Children Have the Right to Receive Treatment.
8. Prevention Programs Should Have a Community Focus.
9. A Multidisciplinary Coordinated Continuum of Care (MCCC) Is Needed.

They are presented here for initial consideration; the authors elaborate on them in new ways and add new meaning to them in their respective chapters.

Perinatal Alcohol and Substance Abuse Are a Health Problem

Perinatal alcohol and substance abuse are first and foremost a public health issue and, secondarily, a child protective services issue; they are not a criminal justice issue.

> I see (the reclamation of neighborhoods) as a social problem and a public health challenge. A more promising national drug strategy should reflect a deeper understanding of the drug problem and its underlying causes. It would recognize,

and be responsive to, the connection between social disadvantage and street drug selling, the price we are paying for years of neglect of poor communities, and to the serious limits and support to the social and economic initiatives, not as the centerpiece for an anti-drug strategy." (Skolnick, 1990, p. 115)

Drug Use Is More Than an Individual Failing

Individual drug use is determined by social, cultural, economic, and physiological factors and should not be considered, simply, a personal failure. Drug use (and its methods, risks, and pleasures) is learned from friends, family, and the local and national culture. Within cultural and ethnic pockets of our society, individuals may "choose" to use crack or methamphetamine or PCP or vodka or a mixture of drugs and alcohol. Crack is the drug that is currently widely available and has a powerful impact on the user and is primarily smoked in the African-American community (Fullilove & Fullilove, 1990). Methamphetamine and PCP are more commonly used in white and Latino communities, respectively. Yet buyers and sellers of any of these drugs may be from any ethnic group and, across the board, the majority are certainly from the white community.

Cultural changes may result in the abandonment of drug-related lifestyles. More than one-third of the G.I.s who became addicted to drugs in Vietnam were clean by the time they returned to America. The majority of this group used the change in culture as an opportunity to cure themselves of their addictions (Special Action Office for Drug Abuse Prevention, 1973). Drug use is also different in Boston than in Buffalo and within and between social classes. Cocaine use has shifted from the middle class to the broader society. In 1983 one-half of all callers to the national cocaine hot line were college educated and 16% were unemployed; by 1987, the reverse was true and only 16% were college educated and one-half were unemployed.

The root causes of drug use are clearly greater than the individual's thoughts and behaviors and must be addressed at least at the community, economic, psychological, and medical levels. An 8-year study of the path to drug use concluded that "drug use, within its societal, as well as intrapersonal, context, is multiply determined and thus must be treated or prevented in a context involving all aspects of the environment" (Stein, Newcomb, & Bentler, 1987). This study supports, in part, a social learning model, by indicating that youth become drug users in imitation of adult or perceived adult behaviors, as well as a medical model, by positing that deviancy and pathology are the result of genetic predispositions and adverse family circumstances (Stein et al., 1987).

Addiction involves the habitual or compulsive use of drugs and is a concept that gives America fits. The legal system has held that it is not a criminal offense to be addicted to the use of narcotics in *Robinson v. California*, 370 U.S. 660 (1962: U.S. Supreme Court). The U.S. House of Representatives is on record as supporting the concept that the disabling effects of chronic alcoholism shall not be considered the result of willful misconduct. At the same time, punishment for the sale, purchase, and possession of narcotics is the centerpiece of the nation's drug control program. Whereas there is particular disagreement about how much addicts are to be held responsible for their behavior, few would argue that a person under the influence of drugs should be held inculpable for running over a pedestrian or that we should not hold an addict accountable for a crime committed under the influence of drugs.

Nevertheless, the prevailing view is that addiction is a disease—with predisposing genetic factors—and that the addict is not responsible for being unable to end the diseased state without assistance. A great appeal of the disease model is that it vividly converges with the socioecological or cultural view that drug addiction is not a moral failing but a condition determined by forces much greater than the individual. (The disease model of addiction is more fully explored in Chapter 2.) It also follows from the disease model that people should not be punished because they have a disease; after all, the insanity defense and much other legal precedent protects the victims of diseases from being further victimized by criminal sanctions. Still, there is concern about the possibility that the disease model can generate a sense of powerlessness among addicts (e.g., Peele, 1990). Also, narrow interpretations of the disease model may result in focusing prevention and treatment services "on individual vulnerability—whether genetic, biochemical, psychological, or social/cultural—. . . [with a] concomitant disregard of the social, economic, and environmental contexts of alcohol (and drug) problems" (Holder & Wallack, 1986).

Given the varied nature of substance abuse, no single model explains it precisely. Proponents of the dominant disease model and of alternative models that rely on a socioecological and learning perspective all reach the same conclusion, however, that criminal sanctions for drug addiction are not logical, fair, or effective (Marlatt & Gordon, 1989; Peele, 1990). Further, they agree that criminal interventions will not substantially reduce drug use or the development of new drug users.

Family-Focused Recovery Services Must Be Available

Recovery from addiction requires many factors but can be accomplished in many cases. A recently published evaluation, launched in 1987 by the National Institute on Drug Abuse, of programs aimed at studying and changing the behavior of intravenous drug abusers and their sex partners showed that 16%–47% of the more than 30,000 enrollees stopped all use of IV drugs (CDC, 1990). Other data from the Treatment Outcome Prospective Study (TOPS) indicates that residential treatment for cocaine users reduces its use by one-half and outpatient treatment reduces it by one-third (Hubbard et al., 1989).

Services should be family-focused, women-sensitive, culturally familiar, and developmentally appropriate. Family-focused drug treatment programs consider the drug user as a family member. Stanton and Todd's (1981) classic work with heroin addicts demonstrated that there is a slim chance of helping young addicts, who were largely male, without involving the family members who ignored, facilitated, or collaborated in their drug use or who simply did not know how to help. Reed (1987) believes that "work with the family is important and useful for men, but may be essential for women" (p. 157). Involving family members is particularly important when working with mothers. Drug abusers who are heads of families also need services (preferably during the hours of drug treatment) that address the physical care, psychological, and cognitive needs of their children, needs that result from living in a culture of substance abuse. Little has been done to develop family-centered drug dependence treatment services, although the pursuit of this goal is vastly more intense than ever before. Fatherhood has been largely ignored as a role of the drug addict, but treatment services for drug-dependent women, including mothers, are receiving new attention (Reed, 1987).

> Women-oriented drug dependence treatment services are defined as those that (a) address women's treatment needs; (b) reduce barriers to recovery from drug dependence that are more likely to occur for women; (c) are delivered in a context that is compatible with women's styles and orientations and is safe from exploitation; and (d) take into account women's roles, socialization and relative status within the larger culture. (Reed, 1987, p. 151)

A more thorough discussion of women-sensitive services is accomplished throughout this volume.

Since isolation is associated with drug use and HIV infection, whether in parent or child, family support programs are vital. HIV-infected families often decry the lack of emotional and tangible support that results from the isolation they experience because they cannot divulge their children's diagnosis for fear of discrimination and stigma. They may need assistance in communicating with significant others who could help reduce their isolation and in obtaining services, such as respite care, transportation, treatment, and financial for which they may be eligible.

While family members must be included in drug treatment so that they can best support their loved one's abstinence and learn to care for their own needs, other types of family support services may be needed. Extended family members are increasingly assuming responsibility for the care of young children when their parents are unable to, either because they are in treatment or because drug use impairs their ability to parent. Extended family caregivers (and birth parents, for that matter) need the full range of support services that would help them to care for their young, often drug-exposed relatives, including financial assistance, child care, support groups, and training to understand special care needs if the children have drug-related impairments.

Participation in Services Should Be Voluntary and Without Loss of Integrity

Drug- and AIDS-affected individuals have a right to assistance without the loss of integrity and autonomy. On principle, and because of the apparent inefficacy of coerced services, substance-abusing individuals should receive services voluntarily. Services will not always be provided unconditionally, but substance abusers have a right to enter into an agreement with service providers that clarifies the conditions of the service program. Participation in services may be conditional to achieve a desired goal, for example, to resume the care and custody of children. In these cases and all others, services must be made available in such a way that voluntary participation is facilitated. To increase the likelihood of benefit from services, necessary child care, financial assistance, and transportation must be provided to ensure that participation can result.

Confidentiality of substance abuse and HIV antibody test results should be maintained whenever possible. The limits on abridgement of this confidentiality must be only those necessary for the care and treatment of the mother and her children; the sharing of information with other service providers should be done with the consent of the mother or, at least, should be fully divulged to her. While confidentiality is an important component of any service relationship, it is of critical significance in relation to HIV antibody test results and substance toxicology screens. Service providers often struggle with the conflict between the need to share personal information about their clients in order to facilitate care and treatment for the family and the need to adhere to the legal and ethical constraints, of appropriate disclosure, not to mention the emotional responsibility they assume in divulging possibly devastating personal information to the clients themselves. The confidentiality of HIV antibody test results are under specific legal protection in all states, and it is clear that, with the exception of medical emergencies and communications to medical providers for the purposes of care and treatment, disclosure may not occur without informed consent. The issue of confidentiality of toxicology screen results is complicated by their use in child abuse reports. While service providers may abridge confidentiality if they believe that the information is critical in establishing risk of abuse or neglect to a child, toxicology screens should in general, be afforded the same protection as HIV antibody tests and should not be administered—nor should the results be disclosed (given the same caveat for medical emergencies and medical communications for the purposes of care and treatment)—without informed consent.

Intensive Services to Parents Can Promote Family Preservation

Substance-abusing and HIV-infected parents have as much right as other parents to care for their children. This right should be abridged only when parents have demonstrated an incapacity to care for their child. This incapacity should not be assumed on the basis of a positive drug or HIV antibody test. Evidence based on assessment of parent, child, and the caregiving environment (including other resources and threats to the well-being of the family) is the minimum sufficient grounds needed to make child protection decisions about abuse or neglect. Whereas the best interest of the parent and child are often inextricable—insofar as the birth family is typically the best place for the child to receive continuous and loving care—they are not indistinguishable. Conflict between the parent's desire to provide care and the child's need to receive the minimum sufficient level of care may arise when the parent is unable to provide such care. In many cases services may be able to promote the ability of the parent to do so. Recent evidence from intensive in-home service programs suggests that as many as 80% of crack-affected families may be able to resume the care of their children (perhaps in conjunction with relatives) when provided these services (Sudia, 1990). Other findings are somewhat less sanguine (e.g., Berry, 1992), but all reports indicate that the majority of parents can continue to care for their children and that the notion that the crack-using parent is certain to choose her drug lifestyle over her parenting is a myth. Substantial family-centered intervention can apparently make a critical difference.

Alternative care may be necessary if the provision of support services is not enough to ensure that a child receives adequate parental care and supervision. Relatives are given first preference to care for the child, and they deserve the same resources, training, and support that nonrelatives receive for caring for children of substance abusers or children affected by HIV. When relatives are not available, foster parents and adoptive parents should also be entitled to all necessary information and resources for the child in their care.

Allied Services Must Be Provided

Since parents involved with drugs often lack the education and skills to achieve family-supporting employment (even when they achieve abstinence), drug-affected families are likely to require considerable service beyond drug treatment. As Salvatore di Menza, special assistant to the director of National Institute on Drug Abuse, has stated: "It may be more satisfying to think mainly of residential programs because the addict is put away somewhere safe. But we're going to need a range of strategies. For many addicts, for instance, it's not rehabilitation; it's habilitation. They don't know how to read or look for work, let alone beat their addiction" (quoted in Malcolm, 1989). Dr. Molly Joel Coye, the New Jersey commissioner of health, calls for the creation of a national network of support groups with social and medical services for families afflicted by AIDS:

> The patchwork quilt of social services that today leaves too many women and children uncovered, unrecognized, and unprovided for must be improved. Our first order of business must be to develop an entire system of services to support families that have some hope of remaining functional, and to supplement families that cannot cope with surrogate families that can offer long-term comfort and care. (Children With AIDS, 1989, p. 2)

Children Have the Right to Receive Treatment

Children of all ages of substance abusers may experience many hardships and need contemporaneous services. The evidence is building that there may be a genetic predisposition to at least some types of alcoholism, and many studies suggest, whether the etiology is genetics or learned behavior, that a majority of addicts come from families where substances were abused. Working with children, then, provides an important opportunity for drug prevention by minimizing the psychological effects of life in an addictive home and by preparing children to make responsible decisions about their own use of drugs. These services can help address the psychological, physical, educational, and interpersonal difficulties that may arise from constitutional and environmental disadvantages of drug exposure.

Prevention Programs Should Have a Community Focus

Because substance abuse arises from a confluence of environmental and personal factors, prevention programs must be similarly designed. Although the risk of becoming a substance abuser cuts across all social groups and communities, that risk is not independent of culture and setting. Since many persons vulnerable to becoming substance abusers are not students, school-based programs are not sufficient. School-based programs that have been designed to prevent substance abuse, smoking, teenage pregnancy, and child abuse have often been presented to students who are at the least risk. So far, these classroom programs have shown modest impact (Barth & Derezotes, 1990; Moskowitz, 1989); therefore, we will not address them in significant detail in this volume. Prevention must address the social and physical contexts for substance abuse and provide alternative recreational and economic opportunities for high-risk communities. Prevention needs to include not only school-based programs but community redevelopment and job training.

A Multidisciplinary Coordinated Continuum of Care (MCCC) Is Needed

This chapter ends as it began, by calling for a multidisciplinary coordinated continuum of care. This concept is agreeable to most service providers but has also shown itself to be very difficult to put into practice. This volume suggests a framework for achieving a multidisciplinary coordinated continuum and provides practical and technical knowledge toward that end; it addresses a range of professional, caregiver, and client concerns, all of which constitute the continuum of care, from outreach programs to services for young pregnant women to facilitation of adoption of drug-affected children who cannot return home. Throughout the chapters and in the final chapter we discuss dimensions of the continuum of care and its accessibility, intensity, cost, and coerciveness. We present alternatives to the assumption that the farther along the continuum, the more costly and coercive the service must be. In counterpoint, we describe efforts to identify accessible, intensive, noncoercive services for all points on the continuum. The summation of this volume includes a discussion of clear, well-conceived local, state, and federal policies needed to provide efficient and effective services across a multidisciplinary coordinated continuum of care. We propose policies and programs that build upon existing community and local services and that promote the social conditions that counter drug use.

REFERENCES

Barth, R. P., & Derezotes, D. S. (1990). *Preventing adolescent abuse: Effective intervention strategies and techniques.* Lexington: Lexington Books.

Bauchner, H., Zuckerman, B., McClain, M., Frank, D., Fried, L. E., & Kayne, H. (1988, November). Risk of sudden infant death syndrome among infants with in utero exposure to cocaine. *Pediatrics, 113*(15), 831–834.

Berry, M. (1992). In-home family preservation services. *Social Work, 37,* 314–321.

Besharov, D. (1989). The children of crack: Will we protect them? *Public Welfare, 47,* 13–15, 42–43.

California AIDS Update. (1991, December). Pediatric AIDS in California. *Office of AIDS, 4*(10), 1. Sacramento, CA.

Center for Disease Control. (1990, September). *HIV/AIDS Surveillance Reports.* Atlanta, GA: Author.

Center for Disease Control. (1992, March 31). *National AIDS Hotline.* Atlanta, GA: Author.

Chasnoff, I. J. (1988). *A first: National hospital incidence study.* Chicago: National Association for Perinatal Addiction Research.

Chasnoff, I. J. (1987). Perinatal effects of cocaine. *Contemporary OB/GYN, 26*(5), 36–42.

Chirgwin, K., Dehovitz, J. A., Dillon, S., & McCormack, W. (1991). HIV infection, genital ulcer disease, and crack cocaine use among patients attending a clinic for sexually transmitted diseases. *American Journal of Public Health, 81,* 1576–1579.

Durkot Sterzin, E. (1989, November). Care and shelter for mothers and children with AIDS. *Children with AIDS, 1*(11), 1–2.

Fullilove, R., Fullilove, M., Bowser, B., & Gross, S. (1990). Crack users: The new AIDS risk group? *Cancer Report and Prevention, 14*(3), 363–368.

Furstenberg, F. F. Jr., Brooks–Gunn, J., & Morgan, S. P. (1987). *Adolescent mothers in later life.* NY: Cambridge University Press.

Hanson, M. (1990). *Evaluation of training needs for staffing PL99-457 services.* San Francisco: San Francisco State University.

Holder, H., & Wallack, L. (1986). Contemporary perspectives for preventing alcohol problems: An empirically derived model. *Journal of Public Health Policy, 7*(3), 325–339.

Howard, J., Beckwith, L., Rodnig, C., & Kropenske, V. (1989). The development of young children of substance-abusing parents: Insights from seven years of intervention and research. *Zero to Three, 9,* 8–12.

Hubbard, R. L., Marsden, M. L., Rachal, J. V., Harwood, H. J., Cavanaugh, E. R., & Ginzburg, H. M. (1989). *Drug abuse treatment: A national study of effectiveness.* Chapel Hill: The University of North Carolina Press.

Hurley, D. (1989, July/August). Cycles of craving. *Psychology Today,* pp. 54–58.

Lambert, B. (1989, July 17). AIDS abandoning growing generation of needy orphans. *New York Times,* pp. A1, A13.

Malcolm, A. H. (1989, Novermber 19). In making drug strategy, no accord on treatment. *New York Times,* pp. 1, 23.

Marlatt, G. A., & Gordon, J. R. (1980). Determinants of relapse: Implications for the maintenance of behavior change. In. P. O. Davidson & S. M. Davidson (Eds.), *Behavioral medicine: Changing health lifestyles* (pp. 410–452). New York: Brunner/Mazel.

Moskowitz, J. M. (1989). The primary prevention of alcohol problems: A critical review of the research literature. *Journal of Studies on Alcohol, 50*(1), 54–88.

Musto, D. F. (1973). *The American disease: Origins of narcotics control.* Lexington: Lexington Books.

National Institute on Drug Abuse. (1992). *National household survey on drug abuse: Highlights, 1991* (DHHS Publications No. ADM 91-1681). Rockville, MD: Author.

Nicholas, S. W. (1991). From love and mashed potatoes to clinical trials. *Pediatric AIDS Foster Care Network Bulletin, 3*(3), 1–2, 7–10.

Peele, S. (1990). *The diseasing of America: Addiction treatment out of control.* Lexington: Lexington Books.

Petitti, D. B., & Coleman, C. (1990). Cocaine and the risk of low birth weight. *American Journal of Public Health, 80,* 25–28.

Reed, B. G. (1987). Developing women–sensitive drug dependence treatment services. *Journal of Psychoactive Drugs, 19,* 151–164.

Scales, P., & Kirby, D. (1983, November). Perceived barriers to sex education: A survey of professionals. *Journal of Sex Research, 19*(4), 309–326.

Skolnick, J. H. (1990). A critical look at the national drug control strategy. *Yale Law and Policy Review, 14,* 75–116.

Stanton, M. D., & Todd, T. C. (1981). Engaging resistant "families" in treatment. *Family Process, 20,* 261–293.

Stein, J. A., Newcomb, M. D., & Bentler, P. M. (1987). An 8–year study of multiple influences on drug use and drug consequences. *Journal of Personality and Social Psychology, 53,* 1094–1105.

Sudia, C. (1990). *In-home services for crack-using mothers in Detroit, 12/26/90.* Washington, DC: Department of Health & Human Services.

U.S. General Accounting Office. (1990, June). *Drug-exposed infants: A generation at risk.* Washington, DC: Author.

Zuckerman, B., Frank, D. A., Hingson, R., Amaro, H., Levenson, S., Kayne, H., Parker, S., Vinci, R., Aboagye, K., Fried, L. E., Cabral, H., Timperi, R., & Bauchner, H. (1989). Effects of maternal cocaine use on fetal growth. *New England Journal of Medicine, 320,* 762–768.

2

Women, Addiction, and the Childbearing Family: Social Context, and Recovery Support

HOPE EWING

INTRODUCTION

This chapter will examine the interface between motherhood and the diseases of alcoholism and drug dependence. We will discuss prevalence, social and biological features, effects on family life, and recovery support, emphasizing the influence of gender.

The field of women's addiction studies is relatively new. The first wave of research and treatment demonstrations occurred in the 1970s in conjunction with Nixon's "War on Drugs" (Sutker, 1981). Increasing numbers of reviews and collections of articles appeared on the themes of women and addiction (Wilsnack & Beckman, 1984; Stimmel, 1986; Blume, 1990; Roth, 1991), and pregnancy and addiction (Chasnoff, 1991; Sonderegger, 1992). Since 1989 a new wave of pregnancy specific knowledge and services has been seen. The United States Alcohol, Drug Abuse, and Mental Health Agency has funded over 140 service demonstration projects between 1989 and 1992, accompanied by other Federal research initiatives, and state sponsored projects. In many states alcohol and drug treatment referrals are now available specifically designed to meet the needs of pregnant and parenting women.

Especially now that appropriate referrals are available, every person in the service professions and in society has a role to play in recovery support for these new mothers and their families. The role starts with becoming informed, hopeful, and supportive toward the alcohol/addict mother. The counter-therapeutic negative and punitive attitudes, which the mothers so often encounter, probably stem from the fact that core knowledge in the field of alcohol and drug dependence runs counter to common sense, and is not well taught in professional schools. Common sense would suggest that persons do not recover from alcoholism and drug dependence, and that women afflict themselves and their innocent offspring on purpose. However, alcohol and drug dependence are far from hopeless diseases. Healthy recovery is a daily reality. Furthermore, women do not choose to become alcoholic or addicted, nor do they choose to harm their unborn children. Loss of control is the key element in the definition and diagnosis of alcohol and drug dependence. The essence of recovery is acceptance of the loss of control and learning to live with such loss in a healthy abstinence-based lifestyle. This chapter will review what is being learned about childbearing women and addiction in this time of increased services and research.

The following vignette, a composite of several cases, will illustrate the sort of situation that can develop when mothers are alcohol and drug dependent, and the strong influence of gender, family, and community on this situation. Numerical figures are averages from 135 patients identified during 1990 as alcohol or drug dependent at the time of delivery, at Contra Costa County California Health Services Department's Merrithew Memorial Hospital by the Born Free Project.

Crystal

Crystal came to a nonresidential perinatal drug and alcohol treatment program at age 23, at the time of her third pregnancy. She was referred from her prenatal clinic and her caseworker in child welfare services. Fortunately, the program provided bus vouchers, as she could not afford a car or bus tickets. Members of several prior generations of her family were known to be alcoholic, including her mother, who drank while pregnant with Crystal and reputedly put alcohol in her baby bottle to keep her quiet. In childhood she was sexually abused by her mother's male partners.

Crystal was in the 6th month of an unplanned pregnancy. Both she, and this baby's father, now in jail, were dependent on cocaine and alcohol, and used illicit prescription sedatives and opioids. Chronic headaches plagued her, dating from a beating on the head by a prior boyfriend. She attempted suicide twice during her drug use.

At the time of referral, she was trying to regain custody of her 2- and 3-year old children, in foster care with her older sister. They were removed from Crystal's custody when, during an alcohol binge, she failed to return to the babysitter to pick them up as usual. The sister condemned Crystal as a loose woman, a lush, and a dope fiend and was trying to adopt her children. Despite her pregnancy, Crystal lost her Aid for Families and Dependent Children and low income housing benefits when she lost custody, so she lived in a temporary fashion with a series of friends and family members, who use drugs and drink.

In her low income community several "convenience" stores offer extended hour sales of beer, wine, liquor, and cigarettes. These items are prominently advertised on local billboards. Illicit drugs are available on the street corner.

Genetic risk, family drug and alcohol dependence, sexual abuse, violence, poverty, crime, the ready availability of alcohol and drugs, and involvement with criminal justice and social service agencies, occur with regularity in the lives of women who are using alcohol and drugs in pregnancy.

Women raising small children face major challenges in our society, even without the added liability of addiction. Increasing numbers of women are heading households without the help of a male partner (Finkelstein & Derman, 1991). These women face isolation and decreased earning power, and rarely have training, support, or recognition for doing one of the truly arduous and significant jobs in the society. They must try to meet the needs of their children without having their own most basic needs met. Providing security, consistency, and positive guidance for children is particularly demanding for poor women, who are often stressed to the maximum by the challenge of obtaining food, clothing, and shelter, and living in communities with high rates of violent crime.

Use may begin when parents offer alcohol and drugs to children, or model their use. Or it may begin as an adolescent rite of passage, a peer norm, or coping behavior. If addiction overtakes the mother and joins the family circle, denial, mood swings, and poor judgment follow. Bad company, impaired relationships, wasteful spending, and general spiritual bankruptcy further compromise her faculties and abilities. As addiction progresses, problems accumulate and life becomes a crisis of securing alcohol and drugs, coping with complications, and increasing isolation. In this chaos, most planning, including family planning, planning for safer sex, or arranging care for her children, go by the wayside. No matter how much she loves her children, pain and dysfunction follow.

Risk factors stemming from poverty and addiction cluster, and the children are set up biologically and culturally to repeat the cycle. Such women and their children have greater and more complex needs and fewer resources than almost any group the field of addictions treatment has yet encountered. This has been described as the "polyproblems" phenomenon characteristic of this group (Murphy & Rosenbaum, 1987).

INCIDENCE

Alcohol and Drug Problems in Women

Prevalence data for alcohol and drug use is available through the 1988 National Institute on Drug Abuse (NIDA) Household Survey (National Institute on Drug Abuse, 1990). According to NIDA, young adults aged 18–25 constitute the group of heaviest drug users. In this age group 27% of women admitted to using illicit drugs, 10% less than the figure reported for men. Fifty-seven percent of women and 75%

of men, age 18–25, stated that they had consumed alcohol within the past month. On a combined measure of quantity and frequency, 4% admitted that they were heavy drinkers (5 or more drinks per occasion on 5 or more of the past 30 days). The women to men ratio of heavy drinkers was approximately 1 to 4.

Reviewing the literature on drinking in adolescent girls, Thompson and Wilsnack cite abundant evidence that large numbers of high school girls at least occasionally drink in ways that lead to hazardous situations or negative consequences in their lives, such as driving under the influence or criticism from friends (Thompson & Wilsnack, 1984).

The National Institutes on Alcoholism and Alcohol Abuse (NIAAA) identified three factors as markers for high rates of alcohol and drug use in women, being between the ages of 20 and 35, having a heavy alcohol or other drug using partner, and being unemployed (NIAAA, 1990).

Prevalence of Alcohol and Drug Problems in Pregnancy

A telephone survey in 21 states between 1985 and 1988 collected data about alcohol use in pregnancy from 38,244 women aged 18–45 as part of the Behavioral Risk Factor Surveillance System of the Centers for Disease Control (Serdula, Williamson, Kendrick, Anda, & Byers, 1991). It found that pregnant women as a group report decreasing their alcohol intake during pregnancy, being only half as likely to admit taking alcohol in the past month as nonpregnant women (25.1% vs. 55.2%). Compared to nonpregnant women, pregnant women were only one-fourth as likely to admit to heavier (more than two drinks a day) drinking (0.6% vs. 2.5%) and one-fifth as likely to admit to binge drinking (2.8% vs. 11.7%). The prevalence of self-reported alcohol consumption in pregnancy declined from 32% in 1985 to 20% in 1988, but the median number of drinks per month for pregnant women who drank did not change. This could be interpreted to mean that the decrease was primarily among casual drinkers rather than women who were alcohol dependent. Unmarried status, smoking, age less than 25, and lower educational levels were associated with greater risk for continued drinking in pregnancy.

In several research populations, a minimum of 10% of pregnant women were using cocaine (Little, Shell, Palmore, & Gilstrap, 1988; Neerhof, MacGregor, Retzky, & Sullivan, 1989). Estimates of marijuana use in pregnancy range from 14% to 32%.

In looking at prevalence data, it is important to be aware that data is derived from laboratory testing or self-report, both of which underestimate the extent of actual use. Such measures also fail to distinguish between the diagnostic categories of use, abuse, and dependence.

Different sorts of intervention are called for when a pregnant woman is dependent, compared with a woman who is only using, or abusing alcohol and drugs. For users and abusers, decreased use in pregnancy is a primary goal. For drug and alcohol dependent women, decreased use in pregnancy is still an important goal, however periodic decreased use is usually already established as a coping mechanism, and maternal and family health are unlikely to improve in the long term without total abstinence and a program of comprehensive lifestyle change. We have no direct measure of the numbers of women with this degree of alcohol and drug involvement.

Often, after a brief interaction, a service provider is not clear which diagnostic category a given woman falls into. Some of the women who tell their prenatal physician, "I stopped using as soon as I found out I was pregnant", will, in fact, have stopped for good. But others will be in some stage of a long-term career in drug or alcohol use. Even for women who are alcohol and drug dependent, some will probably stop permanently when they experience or anticipate the significant life event of giving birth. Others will stop and start. Some won't miss a step in their habitual and progressive alcohol and drug use. When we are face-to-face with an individual woman in a clinical setting, neither the service provider nor the woman herself knows her future pattern. Programs of intervention have to be designed with this in mind.

THE SOCIAL CONTEXT OF ALCOHOL AND DRUG USE IN CHILDBEARING WOMEN: STEREOTYPES AND MISCONCEPTIONS

The social context of use affects every aspect of alcohol and drug use and dependence, including onset, progression, withdrawal symptoms, and recovery. These will be different for different subcultures of women; however some generalizations apply. Data often fail to confirm stereotypes of alcohol- and drug-using women. In fact characteristics that are the opposite of the stereotypes often emerge from the data.

The Using and Drinking Lifestyle: Glamorous or Difficult, and Dangerous?

Today alcohol and cigarettes are marketed to women in general, young women, and women of color as never before (Kilbourne, 1991). The suggested experience of the women in these advertisements is far more glamorous than any woman's experience of alcohol and drug use. Giant billboard images of healthy, youthful, well-dressed women who are smoking and drinking project affluence, independence, and sexual attractiveness, belying the poverty, desperation, sexual dysfunction, and violence so common in the experience of the local women with alcohol and drug problems.

Why do Pregnant Women Continue to Drink and Use?: Choice or Compulsion?

Many believe women such as Crystal choose to become pregnant, choose to become addicted, and choose to continue to use drugs and alcohol during pregnancy and childbearing, presumably because these things are fun or otherwise desirable. "If you play, you'll pay," states a newspaper editorial advocating forced sterilization for women caught using drugs in pregnancy.

The vast majority of pregnant women with alcohol and other drug use state they did not plan to get pregnant. In fact, unplanned pregnancy is often one of the first negative consequences suffered by women in conjunction with alcohol and drugs. In a recent sample, 97% of 135 women identified as having alcohol and other drug problems at delivery stated that their pregnancy was unplanned (Ewing, 1991).

In fact, alcohol and drug dependence imply loss of control by definition (American Psychiatric Association, 1987). Women with alcohol and drug dependence do have other choices, but most have lost control over drinking and using drugs. The problems that ensue are complications of loss of control, not choices. Expecting them to consistently use less or refrain altogether during pregnancy, without state-of-the-art support, is like asking someone with tuberculosis to stop coughing without offering antitubercular medications. In view of the loss of control over drinking and using drugs, chemical dependency treatment, not incarceration, is the appropriate societal response.

Mother versus Child

The interests of a fetus or child are not opposed to the interests of the alcohol- and drug-using mother. The overwhelming majority of drug- and alcohol-using women interviewed on our labor and delivery service clearly love and want their children. Finding themselves unable to stop using and drinking while carrying or parenting children leads mothers into new depths of agony and compensatory denial.

The "mother versus child" view sees women as victimizing the fetus, or "innocent addict." Hand in hand with blaming the mother goes overdramatizing the extent of risk to the fetus from in utero exposure. Although data from valid longitudinal studies is lacking, the public has been told that an entire generation of "drug babies" will swamp special education programs and create a "biological underclass" with possible criminal characteristics. The tendency to see the needs of babies as the opposite of the needs of mothers pits family member against family member, professional against professional, and agency against agency, depending upon which party is seen as the primary beneficiary of the services under consideration.

A concept that better serves both mother and child(ren) is that alcohol and other drug dependence is a generational condition, where recovery of mother and family is the primary goal. Alcohol and other drug treatment of the woman and the intact family is the most appropriate intervention once immediate child safety has been established.

Effects of Exposure in the Womb: Inevitable Fetal Damage or Potential Fetal Risk?

In fact, although there is evidence that alcohol and other drugs put the fetus at risk for a variety of problems, the idea that a baby exposed to drugs in utero is damaged is incorrect (see the detailed discussion of this in Chapter 3.)

The risk for FAS in an alcoholic pregnancy is about 1 in 10 (Rossett & Weiner, 1984; Sokol & Abel, 1992). In fact, physicians have prescribed alcohol and stimulants during pregnancy in the past for prevention of preterm labor and maternal weight gain. Opioids continue to be routinely given to laboring women for the treatment of pain. Yet these children do not carry a label such as "drug baby" with them into kindergarten. Many of todays' adults were exposed to alcohol, cigarettes, or other potentially harmful drugs in utero. Thanks to the resilience and plasticity of the developing organism, as well as to the degree and pattern of exposure, most of us cannot convincingly point to any resulting damage.

What Is the Primary Role of the Pregnant Woman with Respect to Her Baby?: Woman as Vessel or Woman as Parent?

Compared to the overreaction to maternal alcohol and drug use as threats to the fetus, the lesser concern about the effect of women's drinking and using on their parenting functions is striking. When a mother is dependent on alcohol or other drugs, a wide spectrum of risks pertain to her, her children, and her family (see Table 2.1). Many of the serious risks, and certainly the most commonly occurring ones, have to do with parenting, rather than carrying a child in the womb.

Let us compare the situation of the alcohol and drug-dependent woman engaged full time in mothering, with a woman or man employed full time in a job with the usual benefits. The work of mothering requires as much skill and effort; however, these mothers do not have training programs, a salary, vacations, and health and disability insurance plus the dignity of having a career and paying their

TABLE 2.1. Maternal Drug, Alcohol, and Cigarette Use: Summary of Risks to Family and Individual Health

Mother	Progression of chronic addictive disease with unmanageable lifestyle, violence, dysfunctional relationships, unplanned pregnancies, unsafe sex, poor living skills, impaired parenting, etc.
	Impaired health status: overdose, infectious disease, malnutrition, etc.
	Pregnancy complications: spontaneous abortion, placental accident, prematurity
Child	Congenital malformations, IUGR, FAS, fetal wastage
	Congenital and perinatal infections: HIV, syphilis, hepatitis
	Newborn syndromes: toxicity, withdrawal, neurobehavioral, impaired bonding
	Late effects of in utero substance exposure: possible hypertonicity, possible impaired visual processing, FAS, etc.
	Persistent behavioral effects of uncertain etiology (congenital vs. environmental): poor organization of behavior, problems with attachment
	Postnatal substance exposure: breast milk, passive smoking, etc.
	Unstable or dangerous environment: foster placements, neglect, abuse
	Dysfunctional adaptive personality traits and disorders
	Increased risk for development of cigarette smoking and alcohol and other drug problems
Family	Dysfunction: unstability, separations, crises, financial problems, domestic violence

own way. Mothers with emerging alcohol and drug problems have none of the health supports typically offered to chemically dependent airline employees (employee assistance programs) or nurses (diversion programs), for example. Employers see rehabilitation as more cost-effective than the replacement of such employees. Surely a child's birth mother is usually uniquely suited to parent her own child. Both ethically and economically, the same support and consideration should be given to her for her job of parenting.

Societal and Professional Attitudes:
Hopelessness or Belief in Recovery?

Another cultural belief, which is especially strong in the lore of helping professionals, is that women with severe alcohol and other drug problems cannot really be helped. The fact that women doing well in recovery are less visible than those active in their use, coupled with the chronic relapsing nature of alcohol and drug problems, leads family, friends, and professionals to experience and project a special sense of disappointment and frustration.

Treatment for alcohol and other drug dependence is at least as successful as treatment for other chronic relapsing conditions, such as diabetes and hypertension. However, even professionals seeing many alcohol- and drug-dependent persons have often had no exposure to the particular blend of cognitive, behavioral, and dynamic therapies used to support addict/alcoholics in early recovery. These include use of the family disease concept, intervention techniques, relapse prevention, and maintenance of focus on pan-abstinence.

Professionals have rarely experienced the inspirational return to health and well-being that can occur through the community self-help 12-step process in organizations such as Alcoholics Anonymous (AA), Cocaine Anonymous (CA), and Narcotics Anonymous (NA), which have guided many through the long-term inner and outer changes necessary to sustain recovery.

Family, friends, and professionals tend to want to change the alcoholic/addict, "save" the fetus, or see results in a short time frame. But these are unlikely to impossible tasks. When they grasp the real power that they do have in the situation, they can begin to project hope and acceptance, provide clarity, set limits, and give information.

THE SPECTRUM OF WOMEN WITH ALCOHOL
AND OTHER DRUG-RELATED PROBLEMS

There is a tendency to generalize results of research on pregnancy and addiction to groups of women in situations very different from those of the research cohort. For example, data gathered from inner-city populations with heavy heroin and cocaine use may generate profiles, recommendations, and ultimately policy that is unsuited or counterproductive for marijuana, methamphetamine, and alcohol addicts in rural areas. For example, inner city heroin, cocaine, and alcohol addicts may be served best in high-risk perinatal centers, while rural alcoholics and methamphetamine users may access and relate to community-based health centers more successfully.

Research on special populations of women addicts and alcoholics needs to be increased. Some populations, such as Asian-Americans and Native Americans, have been studied very little, and there is a need for more research on women in general as well as those of specific subcultures.

Ethnic and Cultural Minorities

African-American Women

African-American women in all their diversity, whether in urban, rural, or suburban lifestyles, share characteristics placing them in higher risk groups for alcohol and other drug problems than European-Americans.

The 1988 NIDA household survey showed that in the 18–25-year-old group fewer African-American women (44%) than white women (61%) used alcohol in the past month (NIDA, 1990). However, as a group African-American women are more vulnerable to alcohol- and drug-related complications when they do use drugs and drink, and these complications come sooner for them than for European-American women. They also have higher rates of heavy drinking (Gary & Gary, 1985). Today approximately 15% of African-Americans, male and female, are thought to be alcoholic (NIAAA, 1990). In pregnancy, African-American women are less likely to decrease using and drinking than are European-American women (Serdula et al., 1991).

The natural history of alcoholism seems to be telescoped for these women, progressing more rapidly and with a younger median age at entry to treatment (Amaro, Beckman, & Mays, 1987). African-American women who drink during pregnancy have 7 times the chance of comparably drinking white women to bear a child with fetal alcoholic syndrome (Sokol et al., 1986). Although African-Americans make up 12% of the population, they make up 57% of women with AIDS (Center for Disease Control, 1989), a drug-related disease.

Chasnoff, Harvey, and Barrett (1990) showed that a pregnant African-American woman was more likely to test positive for cocaine while a white woman was more likely to test positive for marijuana. An African-American pregnant woman using illicit drugs was 10 times as likely to be reported to child welfare services as a white woman.

Hispanic-Americans

Hispanic-American women, whether from Mexico, Puerto Rico, or other Central or South American countries and however different the drinking practices of their home culture may be, upon arrival in the United States tend to have the same cluster of risk factors known to be associated with alcohol and other drug problems: urban living, low income, less education, and less access to health care. Mexican-

American women also have a younger median age than the general population and have children at a younger age (Mora & Gilbert, 1991). Studies of drinking patterns have shown that as new hispanics become acculturated in the U.S. drinking increases. (Department of Health and Human Services, 1985).

NATURE AND PROGRESSION OF ALCOHOL AND OTHER DRUG PROBLEMS IN WOMEN

Physiology

The downhill course of alcohol and drug dependence in those with chronic, progressive conditions seems to be more rapid in women than in men, and although women alcoholics drink less than alcoholic men, they have more health-related consequences (Hill, 1984). These include suicide, anemia, circulatory disorders, cirrhosis of the liver, and a higher death rate. Cirrhosis of the liver and other sorts of liver damage occur after shorter drinking histories and progress faster in women than in men (Hill, 1984; Norton & Batey, 1983). Evidence is mounting that there is a direct relationship between amount of alcohol consumed and the risk of cancer of the breast (Longnecker, Berlin, Orza, & Chalmers, 1988).

Women have higher blood alcohol levels than men after intake of the same quantity of alcohol per body weight (Myeisten, Hallstedt, & Holmberg, 1978). The explanation for this is twofold: Alcohol distributes in the body water, and women have a smaller percentage of their weight in water than do men. The stomach also breaks down less of the ingested alcohol dose in women than in men; a full 30% more alcohol enters the bloodstream of a woman than of a man of the same weight drinking the same amount (Frezza et al., 1990).

The elimination from the body of alcohol, as well as many other drugs, is significantly delayed in women taking birth control pills, and this holds true for all phases of the menstrual cycle (Jones & Jones, 1984).

Alcohol, Drugs, and the Menstrual Cycle

Little research has focused on the relationship between the menstrual cycle and alcohol and drug problems in women. It is now known that the phase of a woman's menstrual cycle has important associations with ethanol metabolism, elimination, craving, and susceptibility to relapse during recovery from problem drinking. Higher rates of drinking have been noted among premenstrual women (Beckman, 1979). Women in treatment have also described increased severity of premenstrual syndrome, or PMS (Price, DiMarzio, & Eckbeil, 1987).

Reproductive System Dysfunctions

A variety of reproductive system dysfunctions are both antecedents and concomitants of heavy drinking and drug use, including infertility, menstrual abnormalities, increased rates of gynecological surgery, fetal compromise, miscarriages, pelvic pain, increased problems with pregnancy, labor, and delivery (Wilsnack, 1982). Seventy-eight percent of alcoholic women report gynecological problems as opposed to 35% of a control group (Wilsnack, 1973).

Although women have reported that alcohol intake increases sexual arousal, physiological measurements have failed to confirm this (Malatesta, Pollack, Crotty, & Peacock, 1982; Wilson & Lawson, 1976). Studies of alcoholic women report high rates of sexual dysfunction: In one study 85% of alcoholic women, as opposed to 65% of nonalcoholic women, reported drug dysfunction; 78% of alcoholic women reported sexual dysfunction before the onset of their drinking (Covington, 1986). Fear of having sex without drugs or alcohol is the most common intimacy concern expressed by women in recovery (Schaefer & Evans, 1987).

Pregnancy and Lactation

There are many serious complications associated with maternal use of alcohol and other drugs in pregnancy. Even occasional use has been associated with spontaneous abortion, high blood pressure, reduced oxygenation of fetal blood, fetal stroke, placental problems, and preterm labor. Congenital anomalies have been associated with the use of alcohol and several illicit drugs. Regular use often results in growth retardation, which, along with preterm labor, is perhaps the complication most commonly seen (for a review of the effects of drugs on pregnancy and the fetus, see Chasnoff, 1991).

There are also significant effects on the production of breast milk and on the milk ejection reflex. Drugs in breast milk have caused severe reactions in infants. Cocaine exposure from breast milk has resulted in hospitalization (Chasnoff, Lewis, & Squires, 1987). Breast-fed infants of heavily drinking mothers showed equal mental but decreased psychomotor development compared to controls at 1 year of age (Little, Anderson, Ervin, Worthington-Roberts, & Claren, 1989). Concern about toxicity for the baby in the event of relapse has led some programs to proscribe breast-feeding for recovering addicts and alcoholics. The choice to breast-feed or not should be made by the mother, with the help of education and counseling.

Psychology

There are significant differences between women and men in the psychological concomitant of alcohol and other drug problems. Women who are pregnant or who are responsible for young children are subject to even more specialized emotional patterns.

Depression

Alcoholic women are substantially more likely than alcoholic men to have an underlying primary affective disorder, particularly depression. Schuckit (1989) found a primary affective disorder to occur in 15–20% of women as an entity separate from and antecedent to the depression that is common in the practicing alcoholic. By contrast, clinical depression preceded alcoholism in only 5% of men. Another study of depression in alcoholics found that when depression and alcoholism were the only two psychiatric diagnoses, depression was antecedent to or primary in only 22% of men as opposed to 66% of women (Helzer & Pryzbeck, 1988). These very high rates of primary depression have significant implications for prevention and treatment efforts for women. They may also help to explain the apparent high relapse rate for women in the postpartum period, a time of greater vulnerability to depression.

Heavily drinking women are also more likely to attempt suicide. Among a cohort of 500 women drinking 24 or more drinks per week, 25% had attempted suicide as compared with 3% of women who drank less, 23% were regular users of tranquilizers, and 53% had major depressive episodes, compared with 10% of lighter drinkers (Wilsnack, Klassen, & Wilsnack, 1986).

Natural History of Alcohol and Other Drug Dependence in Women

Very little longitudinal prospective data is available on the natural history of alcohol and other drug use in women. Wilsnack, Klassen, Schur, and Wilsnack, (1991) conducted repeat interviews on 143 problem drinkers and 157 nonproblem drinkers who had been identified in a 1981 national survey of women's drinking. They concluded that the strongest predictors of onset of problem drinking in the 5 years between the first and second interview were younger age, cohabiting, and lifetime use of drugs other than alcohol. The most common predictors of continued chronic drinking problems over the 5 years were sexual dysfunction, part-time employment, single status, and report of recent depression. Cause and effect are not implied. Interestingly, divorce or separation predicted reduced levels of alcohol consumption.

ADDICTION AND FAMILY LIFE

Family Dysfunction

Statistics confirm that compared to the population in general, and also compared to alcoholic and drug-dependent men, women who use alcohol and drugs are more likely to have family dysfunction in their family of origin and in the family they parent. Dysfunctional family of origin, a spouse with alcohol and drug problems, a history of sexual abuse, and the status of a single head of household are more common for women than for men with alcohol and drug problems (Beckman & Amaro, 1986).

More women in treatment for addictions report they were sexually abused as children (Russell & Wilsnack, 1991). In one study a history of incest was reported by 44% of 188 patients being treated for alcoholism (Bernward & Densen-Gerber,

1975). Another study reported 39% of 100 alcohol and drug dependent women reported prior incest as opposed to 24% of controls (Schaefer, Evans, & Sterne, 1985).

Women as Single Parents

Families headed by single women make up an increasing proportion of all families today. The poverty rate of these families is 6 times greater than for male-headed single-parent families. Twelve percent of white children and 42.5% of black children are living in families with a single mother (cited in Finklestein & Derman, 1991).

Male Partners of Alcohol and Drug-Dependent Women

In our program 71% of 135 addicts and alcoholics identified at the time of delivery of a child stated that the father of the baby was a significant part of the family unit, and 45% said they lived with the baby's father. Often, the use of alcohol and other drugs is pivotal in these relationships. Enmeshment, codependency, compulsive sexuality, histories of violence, make these relationships the number one relapse trigger.

RECOVERY SUPPORT FOR CHILDBEARING WOMEN

The Institute of Medicine (1990) asserts, "Although not substantiated by research, the myth prevails that women have a poorer treatment prognosis than men" (p. 358). There has been a dearth of research on the effectiveness of treatment programs designed for women; however, outcome monitoring through the Chemical Abuse-Addiction Treatment Outcome Registry has not shown that women have better or worse outcomes than men (Blume, 1986), although statistics indicate that treatment programs are more accessible to men.

According to the Institute of Medicine (1990), the gender ratio, men to women, for alcohol and drug problems is thought to be 2:1 whereas the distribution of sexes in treatment programs is close to 4:1. The percentage of women in AA, however, has increased steadily to 34%, which is close to the percentage of alcoholics believed to be women.

For women from cultures with strong traditions of close-knit extended families, it is particularly important that explanations of alcohol and drug dependence include sociological and political aspects.

Treatment approaches that focus on individual pathology will not adequately serve groups who have an oppressed status within the society at large (Taha-Cisse, 1991). Learning about their cultural history and group survival helps remove individual guilt and empower self-esteem and motivation for recovery.

Pregnant and parenting women in recovery have many other specific treatment needs. These include access to resources and the opportunity to develop skills, which should already be the right of any member of our society. "Catch-up" skills and resources often needed by women include housing, education for literacy and other core life skills, a viable form of income maintenance, and access to child care and health care. Accessing these basic resources is a major challenge for programs offering recovery support to pregnant and parenting women. Remedial work on life skills such as budgeting, time management, clean and sober recreation, and healthy intimacy and sexuality are key (a helpful guide to setting up a women's sexuality group in a treatment setting can be found in the addendum to Schaefer and Evans, 1987). This work requires special staff training and much staff time for transportation to appointments and social service case management activities.

Appropriate therapy for the 40–50% of women addicts and alcoholics who are survivors of childhood sexual abuse and incest is another important component of treatment for women. In alcohol and drug recovery support these early events and the emotions and defenses around them sooner or later become important in therapy. A woman's risk of relapse is increased as previously hidden memories of incest and the intense feelings associated with them begin to surface; she must be helped to deal with these without the numbing effects of alcohol and drugs (Young, 1990). Most alcohol and drug treatment staff have little training or experience in the challenging area of therapy of survivors of incest and childhood sexual abuse.

Parenting education is another key component in alcohol and drug treatment of the group in question. Since many of these women were not adequately parented and suffer from guilt around their own prenatal substance use and prior parenting practices, reparenting therapy, support for perinatal mother–infant bonding, and ongoing parenting training are essentials of recovery support. Recovering women need special guidance around how parents provide primary prevention of substance abuse in their own children.

Another difference between men and women entering recovery is that when women are identified as having alcohol and drug problems at the time of prenatal care or delivery, they may find themselves parenting a newborn and undergoing the first few weeks of abstinence simultaneously. Women who have been using and drinking within the past weeks or months and who are struggling in early unstable recovery usually have limited attention spans and capacity to absorb parenting education. However, the immediacy of their need requires the development of simple methods of role modeling, role playing, and short cognitive sessions.

Addicts and alcoholics face a particularly difficult time when they report to the labor and delivery suite of a hospital for birthing, even when they are in recovery programs. They tend to arrive alone and frightened and often seem to have increased fears of the pain of labor. Nurses in labor and delivery rooms and newborn nurseries often carry anger toward alcohol- and drug-using mothers. They see the mothers briefly, often for a few hours only, but they have seen many substance-exposed newborns who were difficult to quiet.

When a mother has lost custody of her infant and/or other children and comes into drug and alcohol services with reunification as part of her motivation, anger is very often a dominant recovery issue at first. She must work through her anger at having her children taken and move from a posture of blaming others in order to extend her period of abstinence and consolidate her lifestyle changes.

Another major threat to maintenance of abstinence in early recovery tends to be the woman's relationship with her male partner, who is often an addict/alcoholic also. Dealing with this relationship is perhaps the primary relapse prevention issue in the treatment of pregnant and postpartum addicts/alcoholics. For women without a single male partner, compulsive male-seeking behavior is another common theme and relapse liability, one that often appears to be linked with her own issues as an incest survivor (Young, 1990).

Another time of increased relapse liability for pregnant or parenting women is during reunification with children who may be in out-of-home placement. Children are often angry and resentful and have multiple additional emotional issues around reunification, yet once reunification is accomplished, supports from child protective services are characteristically withdrawn, not increased.

Twelve-step programs, such as AA, NA, and CA remain key elements of ongoing recovery support. Since the 1930s the concepts of such programs have come to be used by groups dealing with personal difficulties in as many as 126 different areas. Such groups provide free nonprofessional support through creation of a caring community, the dissemination of information, role modeling, and the sharing of feelings, experiences, and solutions. Personal responsibility, service to others, and spirituality are stressed. Specialty meetings have been developed for women and for lesbians; unfortunately, they rarely provide child care. However, these invaluable organizations also tend to come from a white, middle-class, male orientation; women, particularly women of color, may have difficulty feeling at home and finding self-empowerment in them (Taha-Cisse, 1991). They also tend to be less available in poor and ethnic minority areas. Women for Sobriety, founded in 1972, brings a feminist approach to mutual self-help and is based on 13 statements of affirmation or acceptance (Covington, 1991).

CONCLUSION

Let's return to the story of Crystal, with which this chapter began. Six months after entering the program, Crystal would hold up her new baby and say, "Look at this beautiful face! If not for the help I received, my baby could have had a fetal alcohol face." Crystal was the daughter of two alcoholic parents. Musing on the future of her newborn and 3-year-old sons, she added, "There are no living adult men in my family. They are all dead from alcoholism. My sons will probably never be successful social drinkers. But at least they will have what I never had: a recovering parent as a guide and as a role model."

RECOMMENDATIONS

1. More research is needed on all aspects of alcohol and drug problems in women, including different subcultures of women.
2. Complications of maternal drug and alcohol use (neonatal withdrawal, preterm labor, etc.) should trigger a search for, and be seen in the light of,

the larger problems of individual and familial drug and alcohol dependence.
3. Agencies and funding streams should be merged or otherwise modified so that the family unit can be served as a whole.
4. A practical synthesis of state-of-the-art knowledge about parenting children of substance abusers, family building, and recovery from alcohol and drug dependence should be developed.
5. Women- and family-centered prevention efforts should be increased at all levels:
   a. Primary prevention: community education, education in schools
   b. Secondary prevention: early intervention in health care, criminal justice, welfare systems, etc.
   c. Tertiary prevention: a range of intensive nonresidential and residential treatment centers to accommodate childbearing women and their families
6. Services should be culturally appropriate, accessible, and comprehensive. Access to and coordination between health care, social services, and chemical dependency treatment are essential owing to the multiple needs of childbearing women in these areas. Child care and parent-training components must be budgeted and staffed as an integral part of any proposed alcohol or other drug prevention service.

REFERENCES

Alter-Reed, K., Gibbs, M. S., Lachenmeyer, Jr., Sigal, J., & Massoth, N. A. (1986). Sexual abuse of children: A review of the empirical findings. *Clinical Psychology Review, 76,* 249–266.

Amaro, H., Beckman, L., & Mays, V. (1987). A comparison of black and white women entering alcohol treatment. *Journal of Studies on Alcohol, 48,* 220.

American Psychiatric Association. (1987). *Diagnostic and statistical manual of mental disorders* (3rd ed., rev.). Washington, DC: Author.

Beckman, L. J. (1979). Reported effects of alcohol on the sexual feelings and behavior of women alcoholics and non-alcoholics. *Journal of Studies on Alcohol, 40,* 272–282.

Beckman, L. J., & Amaro, H. (1986). Personal and social difficulties faced by women and men entering treatment. *Journal of Studies on Alcohol, 47,* 135–145.

Bernward, J., & Densen-Gerber, J. (1975). Incest as a causative factor in antisocial behavior: An exploratory study. *Contemporary Drug Problems, 4,* 323–340.

Blume, S. B. (1986). Women and alcohol: A review. *Journal of the American Medical Association, 256,* 1467–1470.

Blume, S. B. (1990). Chemical dependency in women: Important issues. *American Journal of Drug and Alcohol Abuse, 16,* 297–307.

Chasnoff, I. J. (Ed.). (1991). *Clinics in Perinatology.* Philadelphia: Saunders.

Chasnoff, I. J., Harvey, J. L., & Barrett, M. E. (1990). The prevalence of illicit drug and alcohol use during pregnancy and discrepancies in mandatory reporting in Pinellas County, Florida. *New England Journal of Medicine, 3*(22), 1202.

Chasnoff, I., Lewis, D., & Squires, L. (1987). Cocaine intoxication in a breast-fed infant. *Pediatrics, 80,* 836.

Coleman, E. (Ed.). (1987). Chemical dependency and intimacy dysfunction. *Journal of Chemical Dependency Treatment, 1*(1).

Covington, S. (1986). Misconceptions about women's sexuality: Understanding the influence of alcoholism. *Focus on Family, 9,* 6–8.

Covington, S. S. (1991). Sororities of helping and healing women and mutual self-help groups. In P. Roth (Ed.), *Alcohol and drugs are women's issues* (pp. 85–92). Metuchen, NY: Women's Action Alliance and Scarecrow Press.

Department of Health and Human Services. (1985). *Hispanic health and nutrition examination survey* (Pub. No. ADM 89-1636). Washington, DC: Government Printing Office.

Ewing, H. (1991, April 19). *Management of the pregnant alcoholic/addict.* Paper presented at the American Society of Addiction Medicine Scientific Conference, Boston, Massachusetts.

Finkelstein, N., & Derman, L. (1991). Single-parent women: What a mother can do. In P. Roth (Ed.), *Alcohol and drugs are women's issues* (pp. 78–84). Metuchen, NY: Women's Action Alliance and Scarecrow Press.

Frezza, M., DiPodova, C., Pozzatyo, G., Terpin, M., Baraona, E., & Lieber, C. S. (1990). High blood alcohol levels in women. *New England Journal of Medicine, 322,* 95–99.

Gary, L. E., & Gary, R. B. (1985). Treatment needs of black alcoholic women. In F. Brisbane & M. Womble (Eds.), *Treatment of black alcoholics.* New York: The Haworth Press.

Helzer, J. F., & Pryzbeck, T. R. (1988). The co-occurrence of alcoholism with other psychiatric disorders in the general population and its impact on treatment. *Journal of Studies on Alcohol, 49,* 219–224.

Hill, S. Y. (1984). Vulnerability to the biomedical consequences of alcoholism and alcohol-related problems among women. In S. C. Wilsnack & L. J. Beckman (Eds.), *Alcohol problems in women* (pp. 121–154). New York: Guilford Press.

Hindman, M. (1975). Children of alcoholic parents. *Alcohol Health and Research World, 6,* 2–6.

Institute of Medicine. (1990). *Broadening the base for treatment for alcohol problems: Report of a study.* Washington, DC: National Academy Press.

Jones, M. K., & Jones, B. M. (1984). Ethanol metabolism in women taking oral contraceptives. *Alcoholism: Clinical and Experimental Research, 8,* 24–28.

Kasl, C. D. (1990, Nov./Dec.). The twelve step controversy. *Ms. Magazine,* pp. 30–31.

Kilbourne, J. (1991). The spirit of the czar: Selling addictions to women. In P. Roth (Ed.), *Alcohol and drugs are women's issues* (Vol. 1, pp. 10–22). Metuchen, NJ: Women's Action Alliance and Scarecrow Press.

Little, B. B., Shell, L., Palmore, M., & Gilstrap, L. (1988). Cocaine use in pregnant women in a large public hospital. *American Journal of Perinatology, 5*(3), 206–207.

Little, R. E., Anderson, K. W., Ervin, C. K., Worthington-Roberts, B., & Claren, S. (1989). Maternal alcohol use during breast-feeding and infant mental and motor development at one year. *New England Journal of Medicine, 321*(7), 425–430.

Longnecker, M. P., Berlin, J. A., Orza, M. J., & Chalmers, T. C. (1988). A meta-analysis of alcohol consumption in relation to risk of breast cancer. *Journal of the American Medical Association, 260,* 652–656.

Malatesta, V. J., Pollack, R. H., Crotty, I. D., & Peacock, I. J. (1982). Acute alcohol intoxication and female orgasmic response. *Journal of Sex Research, 18,* 1–17.

Mora, J., & Gilbert, M. J. (1991). Issues for Latinas: Mexican-American women. In P. Roth

(Ed.), *Alcohol and drugs are women's issues* (pp. 43–47). Metuchen, NJ: Women's Action Alliance and Scarecrow Press.

Murphy, S., & Rosenbaum, M. (1987). Editors' introduction to women and substance abuse. *Journal of Psychoactive Drugs*, (Theme Edition), *19*, 125–128.

Myersten, A. L., Hallstedt, C., & Holmberg, L. (1978). Alcohol induced changes in mood and activation in males and females as related to catecholamine excretion and blood alcohol levels. *Scandinavian Journal of Psychology*, *16*, 304–310.

National Institute of Alcoholism and Alcohol Abuse. (1990). *1990 seventh special report to the U.S. Congress on alcohol and health.* Rockville, MD: Author.

National Institute on Drug Abuse. (1990). *National household survey on drug abuse: Main findings 1988.* (DHHS Publication No. ADM 90-1682). Washington, DC: U.S. Government Printing Office.

Neerhof, M. G., MacGregor, S., Retzky, S., & Sullivan, T. (1989). Cocaine abuse during pregnancy: Peripartum prevalence and perinatal outcome. *American Journal of Obstetrics and Gynecology*, *161*(3), 633.

Norton, R., & Batey, R. (1983). Why do women appear to develop liver disease more readily than men? *Australian Alcohol/Drug Review*, *2*, 48–52.

Price, W. A., DiMarzio, L. R., & Eckbert, J. L. (1987). Correlations between PMS and alcoholism among women. *Ohio Medicine*, *83*, 201–202.

Reed, B., & Moise, R. (1980). Implications for treatment and future research. In *Addicted women: Family dynamics, self-perceptions and support systems.* Rockville, MD: The Institute.

Rosett, H., & Weiner, L. (1984). *Alcohol and the fetus: A clinical perspective.* New York: Oxford University Press.

Roth, P. (Ed.). (1991). *Alcohol and drugs are women's issues.* Metuchen, NY: Women's Action Alliance and Scarecrow Press.

Russell, D. E. H. (1983). The incidence and prevalence of intrafamilial and extrafamilial sexual abuse of female children. *Child Abuse and Neglect: The International Journal*, *7*, 133–146.

Russell, S. A., & Wilsnack, S. (1991). Adult survivors of childhood sexual abuse: Substance abuse and other consequences. In P. Roth (Ed.), *Alcohol and drugs are women's issues* (pp. 61–70). Metuchen, NJ: Women's Action Alliance and Scarecrow Press.

Schaefer, S., & Evans, S. (1987). Women, sexuality and the process of recovery. *Journal of Chemical Dependency Treatment*, *1*, 91–113.

Schaefer, S., Evans, S., & Sterne, M. (1985). Sexual victimization patterns of recovering chemically dependent women. *Proceedings of the International Institute on the Prevention and Treatment of Alcoholism.* Calgary, Alberta, Canada: August, 1985.

Schuckit, M. (1989). *Drug and alcohol abuse: A guide to diagnosis and treatment.* New York: Plenum.

Serdula, M., Williamson, D. F., Kendrick, J. S., Anda, R. F., & Byers, T. (1991). Trends in alcohol consumption by pregnant women, 1985–1988. *Journal of the American Medical Association*, *265*, 876–880.

Smith, C. G., & Asch, R. H. (1987). Drug abuse and reproduction. *Fertility and Sterility*, *48*, 3.

Sokol, R. J., & Abel, E. L. (1992). Risk factors for alcohol-related birth defects: Threshold, susceptibility, and prevention. In T. B. Sonderegger (Ed.), *Perinatal substance abuse* (pp. 90–103). Baltimore: The Johns Hopkins University Press.

Sokol, R. J., Ager, J., Martier, S., Debanne, S. Ernhart, C., Kuzma, J., & Miller, S. T. (1986). Significant determinants of susceptibility of alcohol teratogenicity. *Annals of the New York Academy of Sciences*, *477*, 87–102.

Sonderegger, T. B. (Ed.). (1986). *Perinatal substance abuse.* Baltimore: The Johns Hopkins University Press.

Stimmel, B. (Ed.). (1986). Alcohol and substance abuse in women and children (theme ed.). *Advances in Alcoholism and Substance Abuse, 5*(3).

Sutker, P. B. (1981). Drug dependent women: An overview of the literature. In G. M. Beschner, B. G. Reed, & J. Mondanaro (Eds.), *Treatment services for drug dependent women* (Vol. 1, pp. 25–51; DHHS Publication No. ADM 84-1177. Washington, DC: U.S. Government Printing Office.

Taha-Cisse, A. H. (1991). Issues for African-American women. In P. Roth (Ed.), *Alcohol and drugs are women's issues* (pp. 54–60). Metuchen, NY: Women's Action Alliance and Scarecrow Press.

Thompson, K., & Wilsnack, R. (1984). Drinking problems among female adolescents: Patterns and influences. In S. Wilsnack & L. Beckman (Eds.), *Alcohol problems in women* (pp. 37–65). New York: Guilford Press.

Vaillant, G. E. (1982). Natural history of male alcoholism. *Archives of General Psychology, 39,* 127.

Wilsnack, S. C. (1973). Sex-role identity in female alcoholism. *Journal of Abnormal Psychology, 82,* 253–261.

Wilsnack, S. C. (1982). Alcohol, sexuality, and reproductive dysfunction in women. In E. L. Abel (Ed.), *Fetal alcohol syndrome* (Vol. 2). Boca Raton, FL: CRC Press.

Wilsnack, S. C., & Beckman, L. J. (Eds.). (1984). *Alcohol problems in women.* New York: Guilford Press.

Wilsnack, S. C., Klassen, A. D., Schur, B. E., & Wilsnack, R. W. (1991). Prediction onset and chronicity of women's problem drinking: A five-year longitudinal analysis. *American Journal of Public Health, 81,* 305–318.

Wilsnack, R. W., Klassen, A. D., & Wilsnack, S. C. (1986). Retrospective analysis of lifetime changes in women's drinking behavior. *Advances in Alcohol and Substance Abuse, 5,* 9–28.

Wilson, G. T., & Lawson, D. M. (1976). Effects of alcohol on sexual arousal in women. *Journal of Abnormal Psychology, 85,* 489–497.

Young, E. B. (1990). The role of incest issues in relapse. *Journal of Psychoactive Drugs, 22,* 249–258.

3

Developmental Considerations for Drug- and AIDS-Affected Infants

BARRY ZUCKERMAN

INTRODUCTION

Substance abuse, due in part to the rapid increase in cocaine use, has become an important public health problem. Substance abusers include pregnant and parenting women, and this has raised concerns about the developmental and behavioral effects on children of prenatal drug exposure and parenting by heavy drug-using mothers.

While the concern about the outcome of drug-exposed children is great, predictions of adverse developmental outcome for these children are being made despite the lack of needed scientific information (Mayes et al., 1991). Infants exposed to cocaine prenatally are often represented in the media as severely and/or permanently brain-damaged (Toufexis, 1991; "Crack Babies," 1990), unable to ever function normally in society. Premature, unsubstantiated conclusions about the severity and universality of prenatal cocaine effects may be potentially harmful if society believes the children are beyond help (Zuckerman & Frank, 1992). If children are labeled as permanently damaged, caretakers and teachers may have lowered expectations of their performance and the label can become self-fulfilling (Rosenthal & Jacobson, 1968). This label may also result in potential foster or adoptive parents becoming reluctant to assume the care of cocaine-exposed children (Blakeslee, 1990).

Labels and underlying attitudes also carry a risk for biasing and undermining clinical decisions and scientific investigations. One study has already shown that, given an equivalent extent of use of illegal drugs by pregnant women, physicians are more likely to report to law enforcement agencies black women or women on welfare than white or middle-class women (Chasnoff, Landress & Barett, 1990). Another report indicates that scientific studies are more likely to be chosen for presentation if they report evidence of impairment due to cocaine than if they fail to show this result (Koren, Graham, Shear, & Ilnarson, 1989). These findings further suggest the potential for disseminating inaccurate information.

The development and behavior of a child affected by exposure to drugs is best understood through a multifactorial model consisting of interrelated pre- and postnatal factors. This chapter presents what is known regarding the effects of prenatal exposure to illegal drugs and emphasizes the influence of caretaking by heavy drug-using mothers. The effect of AIDS on children's development is considered separately. Most children with AIDS are exposed to drugs prenatally and dysfunctional parenting by a drug-using mother who may also be ill and dying. In addition, for some children, AIDS causes a progressive encephalopathy, leading to significant dysfunction and, ultimately, death.

A MULTIFACTORIAL DEVELOPMENTAL MODEL

The outcome for children of heavy drug-using parents depends on the dynamic interaction of the child and the social environment. The prenatal effect of drugs on the brain is seen as creating biologic vulnerability, which may be completely or partially compensated by postnatal brain growth and/or by competent caretaking (Anastasiow, 1990). This vulnerability, however, renders a child more susceptible to the effects of poor caretaking. Unless intervention is implemented, children exposed to drugs prenatally are at a double jeopardy: They suffer a biologic vulnerability due to the physiologic effects of the mother's prenatal drug use and the disadvantage of being parented by individuals whose functioning is affected by addiction or heavy drug use.

Prenatal Influences

Some drugs affect the fetus indirectly by decreasing the mother's appetite and nutrition and/or by constricting her blood vessels, resulting in decreased oxygen and nutrients to the fetus. Psychoactive substances cross the placenta and the blood-brain barrier, potentially affecting the developing fetal brain directly. A consistent, specific insult to the brain from prenatal exposure to drugs and alcohol has not been well documented, however. Prenatal cocaine and narcotic use and excessive alcohol consumption are associated with a smaller head circumference in newborns, which is thought to be associated with a smaller brain (Zuckerman & Bresnahan, 1991b). Although their clinical implications are unknown, the following specific effects have been described; neuropathologic changes associated with prenatal alcohol use, echolucencies and echodensities associated with prenatal cocaine and amphetamine use, neonatal abstinence syndrome (NAS) or withdrawal symptoms associated with heroin and methadone, and minor brain wave disturbances during sleep associated with marijuana and alcohol (Zuckerman & Bresnahan, 1991b). It is unknown whether these findings have a clinical impact on a child's late development. In addition, with the exception of NAS, these findings are from single studies and will need to be replicated before firm conclusions can be made. Neonatal neurobehavioral disturbances that may reflect direct effects on the brain are consistently found only in heroin- and methadone-exposed newborns.

The severity and types of effects produced by prenatal exposure to psychoactive drugs and alcohol depend on factors that are difficult, and sometimes impossible, to control for in clinical investigations. First, the amount, frequency, and duration of drug use are important variables. Women who discontinue drinking alcohol during pregnancy have newborns whose weight is similar to that of infants whose mothers never drank (Rosett, Werner, & Lee, 1983). Similar findings have been described for prenatal cocaine use, although newborns of mothers who stopped were more likely to have some neurobehavioral dysfunction (Chasnoff, Griffith, MacGregor, Dirkes, & Burnes, 1989).

Second, factors associated with drug and alcohol use contribute, additively or synergistically, to the drug's effect. For example, infants whose mothers had a positive urine assay for cocaine during pregnancy were approximately one pound smaller than infants whose mothers did not use cocaine, but only 25% of this weight decrement could be attributed directly to cocaine; statistical analysis indicated that the remainder was due to other factors, such as cigarette smoking, poor nutrition, and marijuana use (Zuckerman, Frank, et al., 1989) Another study suggests that prenatal exposure to both cocaine and heroin may have a synergistic, rather than an additive, effect on the severity of neonatal withdrawal syndrome (Fulroth, Phillips, & Durand, 1989).

Third, genetic factors play a role. For example, cholinesterase, the major enzyme that metabolizes cocaine, varies among individuals. While it decreases in most women during pregnancy, it remains the same or actually increases in a few women (Evans, O'Callaghan, & Norman, 1988); thus, the duration of fetal exposure to cocaine depends on levels of maternal cholinesterase. The infant's own genetic endowment may also be a factor. In one study of nonidentical twins of an alcoholic mother, for example, one twin was more adversely affected by FAS than the other (Christoffel & Salabsky, 1975).

Postnatal Influences: Parenting by Drug-Abusing Mothers

The newborn brain has a significant capacity for adaptation. Animal studies show that even though damaged nerve cells are not replaced, new connections between nerves are made and/or certain areas of the brain develop new functions to replace those lost in the damaged area (Anastasiow, 1990). Recovery of functioning is greater in the newborn than in the adult and is facilitated by a favorable caretaking environment.

Consistent with this animal research, research on humans during the past 20 years confirms the importance of the social environment and responsive caretaking in determining the developmental outcome of biologically vulnerable newborns. For example, among premature infants, IQ scores at 7 years of age were lower among those who at 1 month of age were neurophysiologically immature. However, among those infants who were immature, only those who had had less responsive caretaking in the first 2 years of life had the lower IQs; infants who were immature but had responsive caretaking developed IQs similar to those of children who were not neurologically immature (Beckwith & Parmalee, 1986). In another study the combination of high perinatal stress and low family stability impaired children's developmental functioning more severely than did the effects of perinatal stress or family instability alone (Werner, 1989).

Observations of humans also suggest that perinatal factors exert their influence primarily in early infancy, whereas social/environmental factors become predominant in subsequent development (Bee et al., 1982). Outcome of infants exposed prenatally to narcotics also appears to rely at least in part on their environment, especially as they get older. Compared with unexposed infants, methadone-exposed infants had poor motor coordination at 4 months; however, this difference almost disappeared by 12 months except among infants from families at high social risk (Marcus et al., 1982). At 2 years of age, these same infants demonstrated impaired development compared with a control group, but only when prenatal methadone exposure was combined with low social class (Hans, 1989). Finally, among infants exposed to opiates in utero, the quality of the postnatal environment and not the amount of maternal opiate use appeared to be the more important determinant of outcome (Lifschitz et al., 1983).

There is no study of the specific impact of dysfunctional parenting behavior of drug and alcohol abusers on young children's development. Heavy drug use, especially addiction, interferes with a mother's ability to provide consistent nurturing and the caretaking needed to promote children's development, self-esteem, and ability to regulate their affect and impulses. Poor or dysfunctional caretaking has been demonstrated among alcohol and narcotic abusing mothers (Bauman & Dougherty, 1983; Bernstein et al., 1984; Fiks et al., 1985). Heroin abusing mothers often demonstrate aversive interactions, characterized by commands, disapproval, provocation, and threats (Fiks et al., 1985). Addiction to both alcohol and narcotics is associated with an increased rate of child abuse and neglect (Black & Mayer, 1980; Bays, 1990; Behling, 1979; Casado-Flores et al., 1990). To best understand why heavy drug use, especially addiction, results in inadequate parenting, one must understand addiction. Addiction is a chronic, progressive disease with characteristic signs and symptoms. Central to the understanding of addiction is the idea of loss of control over the use of a substance and compulsive preoccupation despite the consequences. All aspects of the self are affected—the physical, the psychological, and the spiritual. With addicted women, their primary relationship is with their drug of choice not with their child(ren).

Interactions between drug-using mothers and their infants affect the infants' developmental functioning (Bernstein et al., 1986). And dysfunctional interactions may interfere with an infant's ability to recover from a biologic vulnerability caused by prenatal drug exposure. A common problem of infants exposed to drugs in utero is difficulty in regulating arousal. During infancy, caregivers ideally provide stimulation when infants are underaroused and reduce it when infants are overexcited, so that they develop their own capacity to control their level of alertness. Among nondrug-using mothers, those who are intrusive at 6 months and overstimulating at 3½ years are more likely to have hyperactive children compared with mothers who were not intrusive or overstimulating (Jacobvitz & Sroufe, 1987). Examples of these behaviors are seen in mothers who tickle their infants or try to get their attention when the infants are turning away, or in other ways disrupt their ongoing activity, thereby possibly impairing the infants' ability to control arousal. Such behavior seems more likely to adversely affect biologically vulnerable, drug-exposed infants. It can contribute to impulsivity, distractibility, and restlessness in these children as they get older. On the other hand, infants who have difficulty regulating themselves due to prenatal drug exposure are helped in their ability to regulate arousal by caretakers who respond to their needs in an appropriate manner.

Infants with poor arousal may not elicit sufficient caretaking from their mothers. If the mother has a drug problem, the effects of drugs, drug-seeking behavior, and withdrawal from drugs are likely to render her less sensitive to her infant's signals for stimulation and nutrition. This combination of poor arousal due to the direct effect of prenatal drugs and less sensitive caretaking may result in a cycle of neglect that leads to failure to thrive.

Among the problems associated with heavy drug use or addiction are depression and violence, which also impair parenting ability and adversely affect children. Depression may either precede or be a consequence of cocaine use. Depression itself (i.e., without drug use) has been shown to adversely affect parenting, resulting in negative consequences to children (Zuckerman & Beardslee, 1987).

Drug and alcohol use increase the likelihood that a woman will be the victim of violence (Amaro, Fried, Cabral, & Zuckerman, 1990) and that children will witness violence in their homes or be the victims of violence. There is increasing concern that this exposure to violence has serious and long-term implications for children's development, affecting their ability to function in school, emotional stability, and orientation toward the future. Symptoms that may emerge in children who witness violence include the following:

1. Diminished ability to concentrate in school because of intrusive thoughts and images
2. Persistent sleep disturbances
3. Disordered attachment behaviors with significant caretakers
4. Nihilistic, fatalistic orientation to the future, which leads to increased risk-taking behaviors

Preschoolers may be especially vulnerable to the effects of traumatic exposure to violence. They are both the most defenseless and the least able to communicate their reactions and fears. There is a tendency for adults to deny the impact of violence on young children, assuming that they will either forget or not understand.

EXAMPLES OF CARETAKING
BY COCAINE-USING MOTHERS

As part of an ongoing study of young mothers, Greer, Bauchner, and Zuckerman evaluated caretaking behaviors in the home environment of 35 mothers, two of whom used cocaine. Both mothers denied cocaine use on interview and were identified as cocaine users solely by a urine toxicology screen as part of the study. Neither mother had been referred because of a drug problem, and the individual conducting the assessment, using a structured format (Home Observation for Measurement of the Environment and Nursing Child Assessment Teaching Scale) in the mothers' home, was unaware of the mothers' drug use or other interview information. A description of one of these mothers and her child follows.

Case Example

E. J. was the 18-year-old mother of A. J., a son who was 14 months old at the time of the home visit. They lived in a two-bedroom apartment with E. J.'s 3-year-old son, her 19-year-old boyfriend (the father of both children), her mother, and four other maternal family members (three aunts and an 8-year-old cousin). The overwhelming impression upon entering the apartment was one of chaos: one person was sleeping in a room just off the kitchen, another was watching television, and two people were getting dressed in that same room. E. J. was drinking coffee out of a mayonnaise jar and arguing with her boyfriend, who was cooking breakfast. Meanwhile, the three children were running around the kitchen trying to obtain food.

E. J. appeared depressed and withdrawn, and she demonstrated little tolerance of A. J.'s behavior. At times during the session she shouted at him or appeared hostile to him. In general, her involvement and interaction with him was minimal, and the opportunity for positive stimulation appeared limited.

As part of this structured observation, E. J. was asked to teach her son to make a tower of three blocks. Her teaching consisted of saying, "Do this," building a tower of three blocks once, and then returning to her breakfast and cigarette. A. J. played idly with the blocks; after 3 or 4 minutes his 3-year-old brother and 8-year-old cousin helped him build a tower. Finally, A. J.'s father helped as well; it appeared that he wanted his son to succeed.

Two weeks after the assessment, A. J. was admitted to the hospital with second- and third-degree burns on his chin and chest; he had pulled a can filled with hot coffee from the kitchen table. Following an investigation by the State Department of Social Services, A. J. was placed in foster care because of neglect. This case description shows that the mother's interactions and ability to nurture her child was limited. However, the role of other individuals in a child's life is important. E. J.'s boyfriend, who was a member of the household, appeared to be an important figure in A. J.'s life. Unfortunately, we do not know whether he used drugs.

Thus, in the transactional model of development the developmental outcome of an infant exposed to drugs is understood to be determined by the dynamic interaction of the child and the social environment. Consider, for example, a child born at 38 weeks gestation to a cocaine-using mother who did not eat well during pregnancy and received minimal prenatal care. Following a 3-day hospitalization the infant is mildly hypotonic, has difficulty obtaining an alert state, and is minimally responsive. In the first year of life the child's passivity engenders maternal feelings of inadequacy, deepening depressive symptoms and the reliance on cocaine. The mother's positive interactions with her child are rare. The child does not look to the environment for stimulation and rarely vocalizes; the mother's feeling of inadequacy and depression increase, and her drug and alcohol use continue. In the second year of life the child's autonomy striving results in struggles for control between the mother and her toddler. The mother sets rare and inconsistent limits, and most interactions with the child are negative and involve commands. This is especially true on the days when mother stayed up late using drugs. At 2 years of age the child's language and cognitive development are delayed, and the child is hyperactive and impulsive.

What is the cause of this child's developmental and behavioral problems? Is it biologic vulnerability secondary to poor maternal nutrition and/or prenatal cocaine exposure? Or is it the mother's depression, the baby's behavior, or inadequate caretaking? A multivariate model of development considers all of these factors, each modifying and potentiating the other. Together they weave a complex pattern that cannot be understood by examining the thread of only a single risk.

COCAINE

Pharmacology

Cocaine, a stimulant similar to amphetamines, is derived from the leaves of the *Erythroxylon coca* plant, which is indigenous to the mountain slopes of Central and South America. Cocaine crosses the placenta and the blood-brain barrier and has been found in the fetal brain at high levels. It alters the brain's chemicals (i.e., dopamine and norepinephrine) that convey signals between nerve cells (Bresnahan, Brooks, & Zuckerman 1991). In adults dopamine alteration due to cocaine magnifies the pleasure response, creating a heightened sense of power, euphoria, and sexual excitement. Animal studies corroborate this finding: This augmented pleasure response initiates drug-seeking behavior that is so persistent that rats press levers to obtain cocaine until they die of overdose (Spitz & Rosecan, 1987). Chronic cocaine use results in a depletion of dopamine in the brain, a condition that is thought to cause depressive symptoms and is considered an important component of cocaine withdrawal and addiction (Gawin & Kleber, 1984). The alteration of the other brain chemical, norepinephrine, results in hyperalertness and increased heart rate and blood pressure, similar to what occurs when one is frightened.

Newborn Outcome

The increased blood pressure due to cocaine is thought to contribute to such complications as preterm labor and delivery, poor fetal growth, and congenital abnormalities. While maternal cocaine use has been associated with prematurity in some studies, this finding is not universal (Zuckerman & Bresnahan, 1991).

Numerous studies have consistently shown an association between cocaine use during pregnancy and a decrease in birth weight and head circumference (Zuckerman & Bresnahan, 1991). However, this effect on growth is probably compounded by maternal undernutrition and use of other drugs (Frank et al., 1988; Zuckerman, Frank, et al., 1989). Only one of the studies demonstrating poor fetal growth and small head circumference controlled for multiple potentially confounding variables. In this study, which is the largest one to date of prenatal cocaine exposure, 10% of infants of mothers who had a positive urine assay for cocaine during pregnancy had microcephaly or small head circumference (Zuckerman, Frank, et al., 1989); thus, some, but not all, infants prenatally exposed were affected.

Rare but serious birth defects of the kidney, arms, and heart have been described in some but not all studies. While it has not been proven that cocaine causes birth defects, this is a possible consequence since increased maternal blood pressure causes decreased blood flow to developing organs. Other studies have not shown cocaine to be independently associated with birth defects (Zuckerman, Frank, et al., 1989). A small number of case reports of children with seizures have been published, but seizures of children born to cocaine users are not commonly observed in clinical experience. Other studies report minor changes in the newborn's brain, many of which revert to normal (Zuckerman & Bresnahan, 1991).

On the assumption that cocaine would result in a withdrawal syndrome in newborns, many studies have assessed cocaine-exposed infants using the Neonatal Abstinence Scale (NAS), which was developed by Finnegan (1986) to describe withdrawal among opiate-exposed infants. One study (Fulroth et al., 1989) shows higher NAS scores for infants exposed to both cocaine and an opiate than for those exposed to cocaine or an opiate alone, suggesting a possible synergistic effect between cocaine and opiates. However, a larger study recently failed to identify any cocaine effects on the NAS scores of opiate-exposed newborns (Doberczak, Kandall & Wilets, 1991). Two other studies (Ryan, Ehrlich, & Finnegan, 1987; Hadeed & Siegel, 1989) found no differences in NAS scores between cocaine-exposed and comparison groups.

The NAS scale, designed to detect effects of opiate withdrawal, does not appear to be sensitive enough to assess potential prenatal cocaine effects. Clinically, cocaine-exposed newborns are poorly responsive and sleepy but do not show the physical signs of withdrawal (e.g., vomiting, diarrhea) that are seen among opiate-exposed infants. When alert, the former are easily overstimulated; they therefore become irritable and quickly return to sleep. A number of studies have evaluated the neurobehavioral functioning of cocaine-exposed infants using the Brazelton Neonatal Behavioral Assessment Scale (BNBAS), which is a much more sensitive assessment of newborn behavior than the NAS scale; neonatal neurobehavioral abnormalities have been reported in some, but not all, of these studies. Chasnoff, in two different reports (Chasnoff, Burns, Schnoll, & Burns, 1985; Chasnoff et al., 1986), showed that cocaine exposed newborns have increased tremulousness and startles, decreased interactive behaviors, and increased state lability. In a third report, Chasnoff (Chasnoff et al., 1989) showed that even infants whose mothers stopped using drugs in the first trimester showed impaired orientation, motor function, reflexes, and state regulation compared to infants whose mothers used no drugs. A study conducted by another research team showed impaired habituation on the BNBAS and more stress behaviors among cocaine-exposed infants than among controls (Eisen et al., 1991). Multivariate analysis showed that other factors (obstetric complications and maternal alcohol use), and not cocaine, were associated with stress behaviors. However, prenatal cocaine continued to be associated with poor habituation when these and other factors were controlled analytically. A final study showed no differences in BNBAS scores between cocaine-exposed and unexposed newborns in the first 3 days of life. While a second examination between 11 and 30 days of life showed cocaine infants had significantly lower scores in motor functioning, the magnitude of effect decreased by over 50% and the association was no longer statistically significant when confounding variables were controlled (Neuspiel, Hamel, Hochberg, Greene, & Campbell, 1990). Firm conclusions about the effect of prenatal cocaine exposure on neurobehavioral functioning cannot be drawn owing to the inconsistency of the findings.

The fact that other psychoactive substances, (and other factors, especially intrauterine growth retardation) lead to neurobehavioral dysfunction may contribute to the variability in outcomes of cocaine-exposed newborns. One study (Lester et al., 1991) using cry characteristics supports this possibility by identifying two neurobehavioral profiles among cocaine-exposed newborns. One profile, characterized as "excitable," is hypothesized to be due to the direct, primary effect of cocaine exposure. The other profile, characterized as "depressed," is thought to be due to the secondary effect of intrauterine growth retardation. Possible "opposite" effects of cocaine and undernutrition may help explain the variability in newborn behavior seen clinically and in the aforementioned studies.

Concern about sudden infant death syndrome (SIDS) was raised by an early report showing that 10 of 66 (15%) cocaine-exposed children died of SIDS (Chasnoff, Burns, & Burns, 1987). However, three subsequent and methodologically more sound studies have shown only a slightly increased rate of SIDS. Combined data from the three studies yielded a risk of SIDS of 8.5/1000 (Bauchner & Zuckerman, 1990), uncontrolled for cigarette use. Although this risk is somewhat elevated, it does not approach the level of risk found among heroin- or methadone-exposed infants (15–20/1000) and is only slightly higher than that reported for children living in poverty (4–5/1000).

Postneonatal Exposure to Cocaine

Postnatal exposure to cocaine can occur via breastfeeding and by passive inhalation. Cocaine crosses readily into breast milk; one report described an infant with hypertension and irritability associated with cocaine metabolites in breast milk after the mother used cocaine intranasally (Chasnoff, Lewis, & Squires, 1987). Prudent clinical practice suggests that women who are known active cocaine users be advised not to breast-feed to avoid the dangers of acute toxicity in their infants. However, women who stop using cocaine during pregnancy and agree to have their urine tested regularly for cocaine can be supported to breast-feed their infant if they wish to.

The number of young children at risk for postnatal cocaine exposure via passive inhalation or direct ingestion, not related to breast-feeding, is unknown. One study (Kharasch, Glotzer, Vinci, Weitzman, & Sargent, 1991) found cocaine metabolites in 2.4% of 250 urines obtained from children under 5 years of age visiting an emergency department; only one child with a urine positive for cocaine metabolites was breast-fed. Four children have been described with neurologic symptoms and cocaine metabolites in their urine following time spent in ill-ventilated rooms with adults who were smoking crack cocaine (Bateman & Heagarty, 1989).

Developmental Outcome

Some of the findings from newborns exposed to cocaine prenatally, especially small head circumference, raise concerns regarding long-term effects. On the other hand, the newborn brain may be able to adapt to and compensate for at least some of these biological changes. In one study drug-exposed (cocaine, opiates, and other drugs) toddlers had significantly greater difficulty than nonexposed toddlers in unstructured tasks, that is, tasks that require the child's initiation, goal setting, and follow-through (Rodning, Beckwith, & Howard, 1990). This type of dysfunction represents a behavioral disorganization that may not be identified in the structured settings of traditional developmental assessment tests. In another study of prenatal cocaine exposure, which excluded opiate-exposed infants, no mean differences on the Bayley Scales of Infant Development were seen at 2 years of age when cocaine-exposed children were compared to social class–matched controls (Chasnoff et al., 1992). Unfortunately, the high attrition rate of the cocaine-exposed newborns threatens the validity of the finding.

In summary, research to identify the independent effect of prenatal and postnatal cocaine on developmental outcome must control for other drugs used prenatally and for adverse circumstances in the growing child's environment, especially caretakers who abuse drugs, multiple caretakers, and adverse health effects associated with poverty. Future research must employ measures sensitive to behaviors that may not be identified by traditional structured developmental tests alone. Finally, intensive efforts to minimize attrition must be included as part of all studies.

OPIATES

Pharmacology

The opiates are a group of naturally occurring compounds obtained by drying the milky white exudate of unripe seeds from the poppy indigenous to Asia Minor. They include morphine, codeine, heroin, and meperidine hydrochloride (Demerol). The chemical structure of methadone is different from that of the opiates, but the chemical properties are similar (Zuckerman et al., 1986). These chemicals affect the brain, producing analgesia, lowered anxiety, improved mood, and drowsiness and impairing thinking. They also cause physiologic changes by slowing respiratory rate and dilating blood vessels. Tolerance (the need for an increased dose of drug to achieve the same effect) and physiological dependence, resulting in a withdrawal syndrome, occur with long-term opiate use.

In the United States as many as 10,000 infants a year may be born to women who used opiate drugs, usually heroin or methadone, during pregnancy (Hans, 1989). Opiates cross the placenta and affect the fetus directly (by causing decreased growth and neonatal abstinence syndrome). Indirect effects result from the chaotic lifestyle of the addicted mother (poor nutrition, poor self-care).

Newborn Outcome

Many studies have reported low birth weight for gestational age in infants exposed to heroin and/or methadone in utero, though this finding has not been universal. Many researchers have suggested that low birth weight is associated with poor maternal nutrition during pregnancy (Zuckerman & Bresnahan, 1991). Participation by pregnant women in a methadone maintenance treatment program during pregnancy has been associated with normal fetal growth and reduced fetal mortality as compared with continued heroin use during pregnancy (Finnegan & Fehr, 1980). These results are thought to be due to the adoption of other health behaviors such as improved nutrition and decreased use of other drugs, such as cigarettes and alcohol.

Infants exposed prenatally to opiates tend to have a smaller head circumference than infants who are not exposed (Zuckerman & Bresnahan, 1991). However, other factors, not just narcotic exposure, contribute to this finding (Lifschitz et al., 1983). By 3 years of age there was no difference in head circumference between opiate-exposed infants and controls except for heroin-exposed infants (Lifschitz, Wilson, Smith, & Desmond, 1985).

Addicted women use opiates daily because of the severe withdrawal symptoms, including sweating, headaches, abdominal pain, diarrhea, and general discomfort and agitation, they will experience if they discontinue use. Like an addict, the fetus makes a biochemical adaptation to opiates, which are bound to opiate receptors in various body tissues, including the brain. When the baby is delivered, his opiate supply ends abruptly. Symptoms of withdrawal, or Neonatal Abstinence Syndrome (NAS), are seen when low opiate levels are reached. Recovery occurs when the infant's metabolism adjusts to the absence of the opiate (Finnegan, 1986). Opiates are excreted in small amounts in breast milk, so babies who are breast-fed by opiate-using mothers continue to receive opiates and maintain an opiate dependence (Ananth, 1978).

NAS consists of physiologic symptoms such as sweating, stuffy nose, diarrhea, and vomiting. Behaviorally, infants with NAS are very irritable, jittery, and difficult to alert. They have difficulty habituating to a light; with repeated light stimulation, they usually become overstimulated and inconsolable. These infants cannot get comfortable and frequently have abrasions on their elbows and knees because of their continual movement.

The timing and duration of withdrawal effects from heroin and methadone differ owing to the different half-lives of each drug. In adults the half-life of heroin is 4 hours, of methadone 23 hours. The half-life of methadone in newborns is 32 hours (Brown & Zuckerman, 1991). Withdrawal from heroin usually starts within the first 24 hours and lasts approximately 10 days. Withdrawal from methadone starts between 2 and 7 days postpartum and lasts 3 to 8 weeks (Brown & Zuckerman, 1991). Approximately 40%–50% of heroin-exposed and 70%–90% of methadone-exposed infants display NAS. Use of both drugs by the mother results in a more variable withdrawal pattern. A subacute withdrawal syndrome involving restlessness, poor sleep patterns, and vomiting may continue for up to 6 months but does not require drug treatment. These neurobehavioral abnormalities do not appear to persist or to predict future developmental outcome.

Morbidity related to the NAS may be decreased by pharmacologic management of very symptomatic infants. Finnegan (1986) developed an NAS scoring system of infant behaviors to identify withdrawal and to monitor the progress and effectiveness of treatment. The abstinence score includes 21 symptoms, which are usually evaluated at 4-hour intervals. When the score is 8 or higher for three consecutive screenings, pharmacologic intervention is used. The most commonly used drugs are paregoric (tincture of opium) or phenobarbital. Paregoric is the drug of choice for symptoms due exclusively to narcotic use (Finnegan, 1986). If pharmacologic intervention is required, scoring is continued throughout the therapy; dosage is increased if scores go above 10 and is decreased daily if scores stay below 8. Once therapy is discontinued, scoring is continued for 3–5 days to ensure that symptoms will not reappear when the baby is at home.

Some infants have a milder withdrawal syndrome, maintaining scores below 8, and do not require drug therapy. They are hypersensitive to stimulation, however, and are helped by an environment in which stimulation is reduced. Lights and noise are kept low, touching and handling are minimized, and the baby is swaddled (wrapped tightly in a blanket) to keep his or her extremities contained and quiet.

Later Developmental Outcome

Opiates affect the central nervous system (CNS) as well as somatic growth and thus threaten postnatal development. Studies on the cognitive development of opiate-exposed infants generally show normal scores on the mental development index (MDI) of the Bayley Scale of Infant Development (Kaltenbach & Finnegan, 1984; Brown & Zuckerman, 1991). However, while the scores are normal, two points are important: First, in some but not all studies, scores from social class–matched controls are higher. In these studies it is difficult to separate a prenatal drug effect from a postnatal environmental effect even when infants are matched with a control infant of the same socioeconomic status. Children of addicted mothers have a high incidence of behavioral and school-related problems whether they were exposed to drugs prenatally or just raised in an environment shaped by drug use (Brown & Zuckerman, 1991). Second, infants who can be found and tested at 1 to 2 years postpartum probably have mothers who have remained in a service system. Thus, the infants' normal outcome scores may represent the effect af intervention; it is likely that infants lost to follow-up would have worse outcomes.

Reports of hyperactivity and inattention have been conflicting. One preliminary study showed no difference in attention or school performance between school-aged children exposed to opiates prenatally and controls. However, the children had some impairment of visual motor perception and motor incoordination (Wilson, 1989). Another preliminary report found increased activity and inattention, poor fine and gross motor coordination, and speech and language delays in 6-year-olds exposed to methadone in utero (Rosen & Johnson, 1985). In both of these long-term follow-up studies, loss of study and comparison subjects was high, preventing valid conclusions. It is also difficult to separate the biological vulnerability due to prenatal drug exposure from the environmental vulnerability due to caretaking by drug-using parents. Thus, the long-term outcome (i.e., during the school years) of children exposed to opiates in utero is unknown.

MARIJUANA

Pharmacology

Marijuana use is most common among individuals in their late teens and early twenties. The range of women reported to use marijuana during pregnancy varies from 5% to 34%. The principle psychoactive chemical of marijuana is 1-delta-9-tetrahydrocannabinol (THC). Approximately one half of the THC present in a marijuana cigarette is absorbed following inhalation. THC is stored in fatty tissues of the body, and a single dose of cannabis has a half-life in humans of 7 days and may take up to 30 days to be completely excreted. For this reason, marijuana accumulates in the body during chronic use (Parker & Zuckerman, 1991).

Like all psychoactive drugs, marijuana crosses the placenta. Placental transfer is highest early in gestation and diminishes as pregnancy progresses. Marijuana decreases the amount of oxygen getting to the fetus by its effect on the lung. Decreased oxygen to the fetus also results from inhalation of carbon monoxide, which is present at higher levels in marijuana smoke than in cigarette smoke (Zuckerman & Bresnahan, 1991). How the decreased oxygen affects the fetus is unknown. Since cigarettes, marijuana, and cocaine all decrease oxygen to the fetus, it is possible that potential harm occurs when a women uses any of these three drugs. Thus, the cumulative adverse effect of polydrug use and the influence of parental lifestyle may be critical in understanding the effect of drugs on the fetus.

Newborn Outcomes

Only seven studies with large enough sample sizes to control for confounding variables have investigated the effects of marijuana on human fetal growth, and their results are conflicting (Zuckerman, 1988). The best study to date (because it used urine assays to determine marijuana use) showed a small decrement in birth weight (79 grams) and length in newborns of users compared to those of nonusers.

Studies of neurobehavioral functions of newborns exposed prenatally to marijuana have been few. One research group showed that moderate and heavy maternal marijuana use during pregnancy was associated with infants who had increased tremors, decreased responsiveness to visual stimuli during sleep, and a higher pitched cry (Fried & Makin, 1987), but another research group found no such correlation (Tennes et al., 1985). Heavy marijuana smoking during pregnancy altered the computer-measured acoustic characteristics of the newborn cry; this altered cry was consistent with patterns that were related in other studies to perinatal risk factors and to later poor develpmental outcome (Lester & Dreher, 1989). Another study showed marijuana to alter slightly one specific brain wave pattern during sleep (Scher et al., 1988). The implications of these findings are unknown.

Later Developmental Outcome

Only two studies have evaluated developmental and behavioral functioning among children exposed prenatally to marijuana. In one study no independent association was seen between prenatal marijuana use and developmental scores at 12 and 24 months (Fried & Watkinson, 1988). However, heavy prenatal marijuana use (more than 6 joints per week) during pregnancy was associated with scores earned by 4-year-olds on memory and verbal subscales of the McCarthy Test that were below those earned by children of mothers who did not smoke marijuana. This finding remained after controlling for confounding variables, including the home environment (Fried & Watkinson, 1990). The other study found no effect of prenatal marijuana use on IQ at age 4 (Streissguth et al., 1989). Thus, firm conclusions are lacking.

AIDS

AIDS affects children's development by a number of mechanisms, either directly by infection with HIV or indirectly through medical complications such as brain tumor, stroke, and infection. Studies suggest that anywhere from 9% to 60% of children with symptomatic HIV infection have some involvement of their central nervous system (Brouwers, Belman, & Epstein, 1991). Malnutrition and general malaise due to illness can also affect children's development. These problems occur in addition to the effects of prenatal drug exposure and caretaking dysfunction.

The mechanism and timing of HIV entering the brain or central nervous system is unknown. Brain dysfunction in HIV-infected children includes a progressive disorder that involves the loss of previous acquired language, cognitive skills, and motor functions. The head circumference for some of the children does not change, indicating lack of brain growth, and adverse changes on computerized tomography (CT) examinations are seen. Approximately 25% of children with symptomatic HIV will have static encephalopathy, which is seen as a slower rate of acquisition of developmental skills (Brouwers et al., 1991). These children have a low IQ but continue to acquire developmental skills at a slower than normal rate. Other confounding factors, such as prenatal exposure to drugs, dysfunctional parenting, and undernutrition, contribute to impaired development.

Central nervous system dysfunction can also be caused by complications of HIV infection. Tumors in the brain, while rare among children, are more commonly seen among children with AIDS. Some children may suffer strokes owing to the destruction of platelets that is part of the immunologic disorder associated with HIV infection. Strokes may result in a hemiparesis, which is increased muscle weakness or spasticity on one side of the body. Owing to immunosuppression, infections of the brain, such as toxoplasmosis or cytomeglovirus (CMV) are more common in HIV-infected children. These infections have a direct destructive effect on the brain and can cause significant developmental problems.

Since most HIV-infected newborns have also been drug exposed, they suffer from the potential adverse consequences of prenatal drug exposure and a drug-using caretaking environment. The most distinctive aspect of children with AIDS compared to those exposed prenatally to drugs is the progressive brain dysfunction, which is usually associated with general progressive disease.

CLINICAL IMPLICATIONS

Special Considerations for Drug-Using Mothers and Their Infants

The number of treatment facilities available for substance abusers is inadequate, and there are special barriers to treatment for drug-using women, especially pregnant and parenting women. Treatment programs were designed initially by and for men, with little attention to the emotional, social, and economic realities of women's lives, especially their interest in and responsibilities for their children. Mothers may feel stigmatized by attending drug treatment programs. Many mothers do not come into residential treatment because they do not wish to put their children in foster care or because they are fearful of losing custody of the children. The lack of child care may even interfere with participation in outpatient treatment. Treatment programs for women and their children need to integrate addiction treatment principles with care for the child and mother.

More treatment and family support resources are needed to ensure the children's health, safety, and well-being. For the infants, services must include adequate nutrition, health care, and early intervention programs, for the mothers, drug treatment, health care, and family support assistance. The availability of these services is surely important, but their effectiveness will depend on the organization and coordination of the services. It is difficult for any parent to go to multiple facilities with multiple appointment systems and multiple professionals. It is especially difficult for someone who is a heavy drug user or addicted. Treatment and service programs need to be set up for the whole child and the whole family.

Parent- and Child-Focused Treatment
in the Pediatric Primary Care Clinic

The Women and Infants' Clinic at Boston City Hospital was developed in 1989 as a small model pilot program based on our clinical experience that the best way to help the children of drug-using mothers is to help the mothers themselves. The primary goal was to determine if drug treatment could be provided in a pediatric primary care facility. By combining pediatric care, child development services, and drug treatment, the women and infants' clinic is an example of "one-stop shopping," an integration and coordination of services that was recommended by the National Commission on Infant Mortality as a mechanism to increase compliance and effectiveness. The pediatric primary care clinic was chosen as a setting because it was nonstigmatizing and supported the mothers' interest in their children. In addition to the weekly clinic session, a relapse prevention group and a mother and child group were implemented on another half day.

Thirteen mothers who used crack cocaine three or more times a week during pregnancy were initially enrolled following the birth of their infants. Eight reported alcohol consumption, three used marijuana, and none of the mothers used opiates. Twelve had a history of physical or sexual abuse or witnessing a shooting. Four were homeless, and three were HIV positive.

The drug therapist played an important role in these women's lives, emphasizing care for their babies as well as for themselves. Key aspects of drug therapy included breaking the mother's denial that she had an addiction and helping her to identify the triggers to her drug use; alternative responses to these triggers were identified. For example, if a mother said she took drugs when she experienced a certain feeling, heard a certain song, or received money, other responses (such as calling a friend or a sponsor, calling a drug therapist, speaking to a relative, going to church, etc.) were suggested. The drug therapist also provided case management by acting as a liaison with the Department of Social Services (DSS) and welfare services, making other medical appointments and reminding the mother of them, identifying agencies that distribute free food, helping the mother obtain the Special Supplemental Food Program for Women, Infants & Children (WIC) and identifying non–drug-using family members to help the mother and her child. Community resources such as Narcotics Anonymous (NA) and AA were recommended. A weekly relapse prevention group was an important part of the treatment program.

The pediatrician provided preventive health services and monitored the child's health and growth. In addition, the pediatrician helped the mother better understand her infant's behavior and development while supporting the mother's maternal self-image and competency. This was done by asking questions and making observations about the child's behavior and by emphasizing the infant's competencies and responses to the mother. The pediatrician modeled interactive behavior with the infant and identified and acknowledged positive caretaking responses of the mother.

The weekly mother and child group focused on mother–infant interaction with the goal of strengthening parental attachment and awareness of the infant's needs. By identifying developmentally appropriate interactive behaviors and play, by commenting on the children's play with toys and each other, and by modeling language expansion and limit setting, the early childhood educators who ran the group helped the mothers understand the developmental skills, needs, and concerns of the infants as they grew and changed. Parents were encouraged to discuss their child's behavior and to enjoy books with their children. Birthdays and holidays were celebrated by the group. As these group experiences grew, the early childhood educators took mothers on field trips to a children's museum, a zoo, and a farm.

The women and infants' clinic successfully delivered key services (pediatric care, child development support, and drug treatment) to mothers and children in one place. Our impression is that this small pilot program has had a significant positive impact on the lives of the mothers and their infants. Eleven of the thirteen children are still being cared for by their mothers. After more than a year, all children have received regular pediatric checkups, preventive care, and immunizations. There have been no injuries requiring the care of a doctor or reports of child abuse. Three children, two of them HIV positive, were hospitalized, but because they and their mothers were involved in the program and assured of good medical and social follow-up, the hospitalizations were shorter than they would have otherwise been. Only one child, who is HIV positive, appears to have a developmental delay. Of the mothers, two have totally abstained from cocaine, nine have had 30- to 90-day periods of abstinence, and two have continued to have uncontrolled drug use. These two women were referred for residential placement, and the children are still being followed by program staff.

The apparent short-term success of this program is due to many factors. First, we used the "one stop shopping" model, collocating key services so that the mothers were not overwhelmed by having to make and keep multiple appointments in different locations with different staff. On the basis of our experience, we believe that combining drug treatment and maternal and child health services in one setting is critical. Second, the emphasis on the children and support of each mother's interest in her child helped to keep the mothers in the drug treatment aspect of the program. More than one mother said, "I am doing this for my baby." The healthiest part of these mothers appears to be their interest in their children. If programs support and emphasize mothers' interest in caring for their children, the mothers will also benefit. The birth of a baby provides a special window of opportunity because the mothers feel guilty and want better lives for themselves and their children. That is, mothers reach the bottom following the birth of their child, a circumstance that can facilitate their involvement in drug treatment. Third, the pediatric primary care clinic is a nonstigmatizing setting, which made it easy for the mothers to come for care. Many drug treatment settings are stigmatizing to women and thus discourage attendance. Fourth, a relatively small number of professionals provided services so that the mothers were not overwhelmed by having to deal with many subspecialty individuals. By combining the roles of case manager, drug therapist, and pediatric nurse in our personnel, we made it easier for the women to feel connected to the program.

Even if the model proves to be successful after replication and systematic evaluation, this type of outpatient program will not meet the needs of all mothers. Some will need more intensive treatment, such as day or residential treatment. However, a program similar to the women and infants' clinic can be considered the first level (least intensive and least expensive) of a community-based program to help drug-using mothers and their infants. Such a program retains children and their mothers in the health-care system following the birth of an infant. It provides an opportunity for an extended evaluation and initial treatment for their drug use. While outpatient treatment may be successful for many mothers, those who need more intensive treatment can be identified and referred.

In order to replicate such a program, service providers may have to give up some of their turf. Service systems, whether health care, early childhood education, mental health, social welfare, or drug treatment, have developed over time a system of care that better meets the needs of the providers, not the clients. These specialty programs need to be recombined to form a system that meets the needs of the whole child and whole family.

Barriers that will need to be overcome include traditional specialty orientations, and categorical funding streams. For example, drug treatment programs discharge clients who don't fully comply with all the rules involved in the treatment program. This contrasts to professionals who care for children, who are legally and ethically obligated to protect all children at all times. Thus, if a drug treatment program refuses to allow a mother to continue drug treatment because of a violation of one of its rules, a dilemma is created for the child-oriented professional. These professionals need to decide whether to remove the child from the mother since the child remaining in the care of the mother was predicated on the mother being in treatment. Programs need guidelines and collaborative working relationships to support family preservation efforts when these are appropriate.

The second barrier to family support involves separate eligibility criteria and other rules for maternal and child health services, drug treatment services, early intervention services, and welfare. Decategorization means that traditional categories through which funds are spent will be dissolved in order to provide greater flexibility of spending. For example, a mother who has her child removed until she has three "clean" urines does not have the money or health insurance for drug treatment or urine tests since both welfare payments and Medicaid are discontinued when the child is removed.

Decategorization of funding will optimally occur with an incentive to local communities of receiving additional funds only when they demonstrate that all identified families receive all services that they are eligible for. Thus, the burden will be on the community or local provider to develop the system that will effectively meet this goal. This should result in single-site programs that will be more user friendly than our present patchwork of categorical programs located at different sites with different eligibility criteria and different staff. This is an important step in improving the health and well-being of drug- and HIV-exposed infants.

Acknowledgment

This work was supported by grants from the Harris Foundation, Bureau of Health Care Delivery and Assistance, Maternal and Child Health Branch (MCJ 009094), and National Institute for Drug Abuse (RO1-DA 06532-01). We thank Jeanne McCarthy for her help in preparing the manuscript.

REFERENCES

Amaro, H., Fried, L. E., Cabral, H., & Zuckerman, B. (1990). Violence during pregnancy and substance use. *American Journal of Public Health, 80,* 575–579.

Ananth, J. (1978). Side effects from psychotropic agents excreted through breast-feeding. *American Journal of Psychology, 135,* 801–809.

Anastasiow, N. J. (1990). Implications of the neurological model for early intervention. In S. J. Meisels & J. P. Shonkoff (Eds.), *Handbook of early childhood intervention* (pp. 196–216). New York: Cambridge University Press.

Bateman, D. A., & Heagarty, M. C. (1989). Passive freebase cocaine ("crack") inhalation by infants and toddlers. *American Journal of Development of Children, 143,* 25.

Bauchner, H., & Zuckerman, B. (1990). Cocaine, sudden infant death syndrome, and home monitoring. *Journal of Pediatrics, 117,* 904–906.

Bauman, P., & Dougherty, F. (1983). Drug addicted mothers; Parenting and their children's development. *International Journal of Addictions, 18,* 291–302.

Bays, J. (1990). Substance abuse and child abuse: Impact of addiction on the child. *Pediatric Clinics of North America, 37*(4), 881–904.

Beckwith, L., & Parmalee, A. (1986). EEG patterns in preterm infants, home environment, and later I.Q. *Child Development, 57,* 777–789.

Bee, H. C., Barnard, K. E., Ayres, S. J., Gray, C. A., Hammond, M. A., Spietz, A. L., Snyder, C., & Clark, B. (1982). Prediction of IQ and language skill from perinatal status, child performance, family characteristics, and mother–infant interaction. *Child Development, 53,* 1134–1156.

Behling, D. W. (1979). Alcohol abuse as encountered in 51 instances of reported child abuse. *Clinical Pediatrics, 2,* 87–91.

Bernstein, V., Jeremy, R. J., Hans, S., & Marcus, J. (1984). A longitudinal study of offspring born to methadone-maintained women: II. Dyadic interaction and infant behavior at four months. *American Journal of Drug and Alcohol Abuse, 10,* 161–193.

Bernstein, V. J., Jeremy, R. J., & Marcus, J. (1986). Mother–infant interaction in multiproblem families: Finding those at risk. *Journal of American Academy of Child Psychiatry, 5,* 631–640.

Black, R., & Mayer, J. (1980). Parents with special problems: Alcoholism and opiate addiction. *Child Abuse and Neglect, 4,* 45.

Blakeslee, S. (1990, May 19). Parents fight for a future for infants born to drugs. *The New York Times,* p. l.

Bresnahan, K., Brooks, C., & Zuckerman, B. (1991). Prenatal cocaine use: Impact on infants and mothers. *Pediatric Nursing, 17,* 123–129.

Brouwers, P., Belman, A., & Epstein, L. (1991). Central nervous system involvement. In P. Pizzo & C. Wilfret (Eds.), *Pediatric AIDS* (pp. 318–335). Baltimore: Williams & Wilkens.

Brown, E. & Zuckerman, B. (1991). Infants of drug abusing mothers. *Pediatric Annals, 20,* 555–561.

Casado-Flores, J., Bano-Rodrigo, A., & Romero, E. (1990). Social and medical problems in children of heroin-addicted parents. *American Journal of Development of Children, 144,* 977–982.

Chasnoff, I. J., Burns, K. A., & Burns, W. J. (1987). Cocaine use in pregnancy: Perinatal morbidity and mortality. *Neurotoxicology and Teratology, 9,* 291–293.

Chasnoff I. J., Burns, K. A., & Burns, W. J. (1986). Prenatal drug exposure: Effects on neonatal and infant growth and development. *Neurotoxicology and Teratology, 8,* 357–362.

Chasnoff, I. J., Burns, W. J., Schnoll, S. H., & Burns, K. A. (1985). Cocaine use in pregnancy. *New England Journal of Medicine, 313,* 666–669.

Chasnoff, I. J. , Griffith, P. R., Freier, C., & Murra, J. (1992). Cocaine polydrug use in pregnancy: Two year follow-up. *Pediatrics, 89,* 284–289.

Chasnoff, I. J., Griffith, D. R., MacGregor, S., Dirkes, D., & Burnes, K. A. (1989). Temporal patterns of cocaine use in pregnancy. *Journal of the American Medical Association, 261,* 1741–1744.

Chasnoff, I. J., Landress, H., & Barett, M. (1990). The prevalence of illict-drug or alcohol use during pregnancy and discrepancies in mandatory reporting in Pinellas County, Florida. *New England Journal of Medicine, 332,* 1202–1206.

Chasnoff, I. J., Lewis, D. E., & Squires, L. (1987). Cocaine intoxication in a breast-fed infant. *Pediatrics, 80,* 836–838.

Christoffel, K. K., & Salabsky, T. (1975). Fetal alcohol syndrome in dyzgotic twins. *Journal of Pediatrics, 87,* 963–965.

"Crack Babies." (1990, October 18). *Rolling Stone,* p. 68.

Doberczak, T. M., Kandall, S. R., & Wilets, I. (1991). Neonatal opiate abstinence syndrome in term and preterm infants. *Journal of Pediatrics, 118,* 933–937.

Eisen, L. N., Field, T. M., Bandstra, E. S., Roberts, J. P., Morrow, C., & Larson, S. K. (1991). Perinatal cocaine effects on neonatal stress behavior and performance on the Brazelton Scale. *Pediatrics, 88,* 477–480.

Evans, R. T., O'Callaghan, F., & Norman, A. (1988). A longitudinal study of cholinesterase changes in pregnancy. *Clinical Chemistry, 34,* 2249–2252.

Fiks, K., Johnson, H., & Rosen, T. (1985). Methadone-maintained mothers: Three-year follow-up of parental functioning. *International Journal of Addictions, 20,* 651–660.

Finnegan, L. P. (1986). Neonatal abstinence syndrome: Assessment and pharmacotherapy. In F. F. Frubaltelli & B. Granati (Eds.), *Neonatal therapy: An update* (pp. 123–146). New York: Elsevier.

Finnegan, L. P., & Fehr, K. O. (1980). The effects of opiates, sedative-hypnotics, amphetamines, cannabis, and other psychoactive drugs on the fetus and newborn. In O. Kalant (Ed.), *Research advances in alcohol and drug problems* (Vol. 5, pp. 653–723). New York: Plenum.

Frank, D., Zuckerman, B., Amaro, H., Aboagye, K., Bauchner, H., Cabral, H., Fried, L., Hingson, R., Kayne, H., Levenson, S. M., Parker, S., Reece, H., & Vinci, R. (1988). Cocaine use during pregnancy: Prevalence and correlates. *Pediatrics, 82,* 888–895.

Fried, P. A., & Makin, J. E. (1987). Neonatal behavioral correlates of prenatal exposure to marijuana, cigarettes, and alcohol in a low risk population. *Neurobehavioral Toxicology Teratology, 9,* 1–7.

Fried, P. A., & Watkinson, B. (1988). 12- and 24-month neurobehavioral follow-up of children prenatally exposed to marihuana, cigarettes and alcohol. *Neurotoxicology and Teratology, 10,* 305–313.

Fried, P. A., & Watkinson, B. (1990). 36- and 48-month neurobehavioral follow-up of children prenatally exposed to marijuana, cigarettes, and alcohol. *Journal of Developmental and Behavioral Pediatrics, 11,* 4958.

Fulroth, R., Phillips, B., & Durand, D. J. (1989). Perinatal outcome of infants exposed to cocaine and/or heroin in utero. *American Journal of Disabled Children, 143,* 905–910.

Gawin, F. H., & Kleber, H. D. (1984). Cocaine abuse treatment. *Archives of General Psychiatry, 41,* 903–909.

Hadeed, A. J., & Siegel, S. R. (1989). Maternal cocaine use during pregnancy: Effect on the newborn infant. *Pediatrics, 84,* 205–210.

Hans, S. L. (1989). Developmental consequences of prenatal exposure to methadone. *Annals of the New York Academy of Sciences, 562,* 195–207.

Jacobvitz, D., & Sroufe, L. A. (1987). The early caregiver–child relationship and attention-deficit disorder with hyperactivity in kindergarten: A prospective study. *Child Development, 58,* 1488–1495.

Kaltenbach, K., & Finnegan, L. P. (1984). Developmental outcome of children born to methadone maintained women: A review of longitudinal studies. *Neurotoxicology and Teratology, 6,* 271–275.

Kharasch, S. J., Glotzer, D., Vinci, R., Weitzman, M., & Sargent, J. (1991). Unsuspected cocaine exposure in young children. *American Journal of the Development of Children, 145,* 204–206.

Koren, G., Graham, K., Shear, H., & Ilnarson, T. (1989). Bias against null hypothesis: The reproductive hazards of cocaine. *Lancet,* 1440–1442.

Lester, B. M., Corwin, M. J., Sepkoski, C., Seifer, R., Peucker, M., McLaughlin, S., & Golub, H. (1991) Neurobehavioral syndrome in cocaine exposed newborn infants. *Child Development, 62,* 694–705.

Lester, B. M., & Dreher, M. (1989). Effects of marijuana use during pregnancy on newborn cry. *Child Development, 60,* 765–771.

Lifschitz, M. H., Wilson, G. S., Smith, E. O., & Desmond, M. M., (1983). Fetal and postnatal growth of children born to narcotic-dependent woman. *Journal of Pediatrics, 102,* 686.

Lifschitz, M. H., Wilson, G. S., Smith, E. O., & Desmond, M. M. (1985). Factors affecting head growth and intellectual function in children of drug addicts. *Pediatrics, 75,* 269–274.

Marcus, J., Hans, S. L., & Jeremy, R. J. (1982). Differential motor and state functioning in newborns of women on methadone. *Neurotoxicology and Teratology, 4,* 459–462.

Mayes, L. C., Granger, R. H., Bornslein, M. H., & Zuckerman, B. (1992). The problem of prenatal cocaine exposure: A rush to judgement. *Journal of the American Medical Association, 267,* 406–408.

Neuspiel, D. R., Hamel, S. C., Hochberg, E., Greene, J., & Campbell, D. (1990). Maternal cocaine use and infant behavior. *Neurotoxicology and Teratology, 13,* 229–233.

Parker, S., & Zuckerman, B. (1991). The effects of maternal marijuana use during pregnancy and fetal growth. In G. G. Nahas & C. Latour (Eds.), *Advances in Biosciences* (Vol. 80, pp. 55–63). New York: Plenum.

Rodning, C., Beckwith, L., & Howard, J. (1990). Characteristics of attachment organization and play organization in prenatally drug-exposed toddlers. *Development and Psychopathology, 1,* 277–289.

Rosen, T. S., & Johnson, H. L. (1985). Long-term effects of prenatal methadone maintenance. *National Institute of Drug Abuse Research Monograph Series, 59,* 73–83.

Rosenthal, R., & Jacobson, L. (1968). *Pygmalion in the classroom: Teacher expectation and pupils' intellectual development.* New York: Holt, Rinehart & Winston.

Rosett, H. L. Werner, L., Lee, A., Zuckerman, B., Dooling, E., & Oppenheimer, E. (1983). Patterns of alcohol consumption and fetal development. *Obstetrical Gynecology, 61,* 539.

Ryan, L., Ehrlich, S., & Finnegan, L. (1987). Cocaine abuse in pregnancy: Effects on the fetus and newborn. *Neurotoxicology and Teratology, 2,* 295-299.

Scher, M. S., Richardson, G. A., Coble, P. A., Day, N. L., & Stoffer, D. S. (1988). The effects of prenatal alcohol and marijuana exposure: Disturbances in neonatal sleepcycling and arousal. *Pediatric Research, 24,* 101-105.

Spitz, H. I., & Rosecan, J. S. (1987). *Cocaine abuse: New directions in treatment and research.* New York: Brunner/Mazel.

Streissguth, A. P., Barr, H. M., Sampson, P., Darby, B. L., & Martin, D. C. (1989). IQ at age 4 in relation to maternal alcohol use and smoking during pregnancy. *Developmental Psycholoy, 25,* 3-11.

Tennes, K., Avitable, N., Blackard, C., et al. (1985). Marijuana: Prenatal and postnatal exposure in the human infant. In T. M. Pinkert (Ed.), *Current research on the consequences of maternal drug abuse, NIDA research monograph* (pp. 48-60). Rockville, MD: NIDA.

Toufexis, A. (1991, May 13). Innocent victims. *Time Magazine,* pp. 56-63.

Werner, E. (1989). Children of the Garden Island. *Scientific American, 106,* 111.

Wilson, G. S. (1989). Clinical studies of infants and children exposed prenatally to heroin. *Annals of the New York Academy of Sciences, 562,* 183-194.

Zuckerman, B. (1988). Marijuana and cigarette smoking during pregnancy: Neonatal effects. In I. Chasnoff (Ed.), *Drugs alcohol, pregnancy and parenting* (p. 73). London: Kluwer Academic.

Zuckerman, B., Amaro, H., & Bauchner, H. (1989). Depressive symptoms during pregnancy: Relationship to poor health behaviors. *American Journal of Obstetrics and Gynecology, 160,* 1107-1111.

Zuckerman, B., & Beardslee, W. (1987). Maternal depression: A concern for pediatricians. *Pediatrics, 79,* 110-117.

Zuckerman, B., & Bresnahan, K. (1991). Developmental and behavioral consequences of prenatal drug and alcohol exposure. *Pediatric Clinics of North America, 38,* 1387-1406.

Zuckerman, B., & Frank, D. (1992). "Crack Kids": Not broken. *Pediatrics, 89,* 337-339.

Zuckerman, B., & Frank, D. (in press). Prenatal cocaine and marijuana exposure: Research and clinical implications. In *Maternal substance abuse and the developing nervous system.* San Diego, CA: Academic Press.

Zuckerman, B., Frank, D., Hingson, R., Amaro, H., Levenson, S. M., Kayne, H., Parker, S., Vinci, R., Aboagye, K., Fried, L. E., Cabral, H., Timperi, R., & Bauchner, H. (1989). Effects of maternal marijuana and cocaine use on fetal growth. *New England Journal of Medicine, 320,* 762-768.

Zuckerman, B., Parker, S. J., Hingson, R., Mitchell, J., & Alpert, J. (1986). Maternal psychoactive substance use and its effect on the neonate. In A. Milunksy, E. A. Friedman, & L. Gluck (Eds.), *Advances in prenatal medicine* (5th ed., pp. 125-170). New York: Plenum.

II

PREVENTION

4

Perinatal Alcohol and Drug Use: Community-Based Prevention Strategies

LAURIE A. SOMAN

THE CONCEPT OF PREVENTION

When we hear the word *prevention* in a health context, most of us imagine it quite literally as activities that keep something dangerous or undesirable to our health from happening. The public health model assumes a much broader, and ultimately more realistic, view of prevention, recognizing it as a continuum rather than a single category. In this continuum view of prevention are included three basic types: primary, secondary, and tertiary.

Primary prevention conforms to our simple view of prevention: the design and implementation of processes and activities that will reduce the incidence of a health problem. The concept of secondary prevention is based on the assumption that some people will either not respond to or will fail to be exposed to our primary prevention and will go on to develop health problems. Secondary prevention, then, includes the provision of early identification and intervention services to reduce initial problems and prevent the appearance of more serious consequences. Tertiary prevention is often called treatment; it includes those activities designed to treat more severe health problems and to prevent further deterioration or death. Under the public health model it is never too late for prevention; the goal is always to ameliorate whatever problems might exist while striving to prevent them from worsening.

Just as the basic concept of prevention is broader than it might seem, the approaches to implementing prevention activities are more con often assumed. Prevention, from primary to tertiary, is sometimes thought to be an individual solution, even by those in the public health field. Individuals are at risk for certain health problems; they avoid behaviors that increase their risk or they obtain early intervention services to mitigate the impact or they receive the appropriate services to treat their problems. A community-based view of prevention assumes that health risks are complex combinations of multiple factors, only some of which at any given time will be purely individual. For example, while personal behavior plays a major role in alcohol and drug use, many other factors in our cultural environment influence individual actions. These factors include intangibles such as social values and attitudes, public policies that either promote or discourage drinking or drug-using behavior, and the accessibility of appropriate intervention and treatment. The public health model of prevention stresses that individual behavior is profoundly influenced by community norms and behavior as well as by public policies and the environment in which alcohol and drug use takes place. Therefore, the strategies employed by this model are multilevel, with activities at the community and environmental, or public policy, levels as well as at the individual level.

FACTORS INFLUENCING WOMEN'S ALCOHOL AND DRUG USE

To effectively address the prevention of perinatal alcohol and drug use, we must first understand why women drink or use drugs, particularly during pregnancy. There are a number of factors that influence women's drinking and drug-using behavior in the first place, including individual characteristics, social and family norms and attitudes, and environmental factors. In addition, there are powerful forces that affect women's access to treatment and recovery once they are drinking or using drugs, such as treatment barriers, financial barriers, and public policy barriers.

Individual Characteristics

Research has shown that there are several important commonalities among women who drink or use drugs, regardless of their race, class, age, or ethnicity. A number of studies have reported that women alcoholics and addicts have low self-esteem and that this poor self-concept is also associated with feelings of alienation, social isolation, anxiety, and depression (Beckman, 1984; Reed, 1985). In one study comparing women alcoholics with nonalcoholic women, women alcoholics were more likely to report drinking for escapist reasons; they were also more likely to report that they felt powerless and inadequate before drinking. The study concluded that heavy alcohol consumption is a coping mechanism for women, which they perceive as helping to relieve their feelings of helplessness, powerlessness, ineffectiveness, and poor self-concept (Beckman, 1984). These patterns are similar in women who use drugs other than or in addition to alcohol. The psychological and behavior patterns of these women resemble the learned helplessness observed in battered women. All too often, drug-dependent women have been battered as adults or physically and sexually abused as children (Amaro, Fried, Cabral, & Zuckerman, 1990; Harrison & Belille, 1987; Reed, 1985, 1987). In general, chemically dependent women are likely to have come from disturbed families with a history of drug or alcohol dependency, mental illness, family violence, and suicide (Burns, 1986; Harrison & Belille, 1987; Mondanaro, 1977; Regan, Leifer, & Finnegan, 1982; Unger, 1988). They also have less education, fewer financial resources, and fewer life options than non-drug-dependent women (Reed, 1985; Unger, 1985). While these characteristics obviously affect women on an individual basis, in the aggregate they suggest that, ultimately, addiction may be a concomitant of oppression and poverty.

Social and Family Norms and Attitudes

Norms and attitudes toward women's use of alcohol and drugs, both within their families and in society at large, can play an enormous role in individual behavior, yet relatively little has been said or published about addiction and women until fairly recently. Prior to the 1960s, addiction was viewed as a predominantly male disease, and its presence in women was regarded as rare (Unger, 1988; Wilsnack, Wilsnack, & Klassen, 1987). The entire research literature published in English between 1929 and 1970 contained only 28 studies of alcoholic women (Wilsnack et al., 1987). With the advent of the second wave of the women's movement, activists, treatment professionals, and researchers began to pay more attention to women's drug and alcohol use as well as to their treatment needs. The identification of Fetal Alcohol Syndrome in the literature in 1973 (Jones, Smith, Ulleland, & Streissguth, 1973) focused serious attention on women's drinking behavior for the first time, albeit less for its impact on women than for its potential damage to the fetus. Some research on women and opiate use, primarily heroin, also appeared in the 1960s and 1970s. However, 30 years after publication of some of these studies, the research world still lacks comprehensive information on the impact of alcohol and drugs on women and specifically on pregnant women. More important, women themselves, as well as the families, partners, and community who all influence their behavior, also lack this information. Until fairly recently, alcohol use during pregnancy was not recognized as risky by either the general population or health professionals; indeed, many people still believe that it is harmless to drink moderately during pregnancy. Despite the U.S. Surgeon General's advisory in 1981 that pregnant women or women considering pregnancy abstain, some health organizations maintain a different opinion (Blume, 1986). Some physicians and other health care practitioners even recommend a glass of wine to pregnant women to help them relax. The alcohol beverage industry has made a major campaign of challenging the alleged risk of any alcohol consumption other than "abusive" or "excessive" drinking (Wine Institute, 1991); such drinking has been defined by the National Institute on Alcohol Abuse and Alcoholism as more than two "standard" (containing 1 ounce of alcohol) drinks per day (Blume, 1986). At the same time, we know from recent studies that one to two drinks per day have demonstrated health and developmental consequences for children, including decreased birth weight, growth abnormalities, and behavioral impairment (Cook, Peterson, & Moore, 1990; Little & Erving, 1984; Wright, Barrison, Toplis, & Waterson, 1984).

Nor has the use of other drugs by women, whether pregnant or not, been a major topic in either the research or public education worlds until recently. Most research, education, and treatment has been directed toward men. This lack of information has left women unaware or unsure of the risks of alcohol and drug consumption during pregnancy. In addition, the mixed messages resulting from the current debate on alcohol consumption (How much is too much?) can confuse women and prompt them to view all similar health warnings with skepticism.

Family members and partners also play a significant role in influencing women's drinking and drug-using behavior. In fact, partners often introduce alcohol and drugs to women, and addicted women are far more likely than addicted men to be married or attached to other addicts (Frakas, 1976; O'Donnell, Besteman, & Jones, 1967; Reed, 1985). In a 1986 survey of women callers to the 800-COCAINE hotline, 87% said they had been introduced to cocaine use by men (Washton, 1986).

This influence carries over to the attitudes of family and partners should women seek treatment for their drug use. Two studies have found that the family and friends of women alcoholics were more likely to oppose their entry into treatment than were the family and friends of men alcoholics, with approximately one quarter of all women reporting opposition (Beckman, 1984). Such opposition was rare for men alcoholics. Women also reported more negative consequences for seeking treatment, including disruptions in family relations, loneliness, avoidance by friends and coworkers, loss of friends, and anger of spouse. In the words of one researcher: "These results provide perhaps the first evidence that women experience greater social stigma because of their drinking problems than do men" (Beckman, 1984, p. 104). This stigma is even stronger when the drug consumed is illicit, rather than the legal alcohol, and when the woman is pregnant. These attitudes are often held by alcohol and drug treatment counselors and health care providers as well (Reed, 1987). Thus, women often not only lack access to reliable information from trusted sources on the risks of alcohol and drug consumption during pregnancy but also face serious stigma, social isolation, and other negative consequences if they recognize their dependency and seek help.

Environmental Factors

Environmental factors in perinatal alcohol and drug use are most readily apparent with regard to alcohol, the legal drug. Mosher and Jernigan (1988) assert that individual-focused prevention efforts alone will fail because the social environment surrounding alcohol use does not support prevention or recovery. Instead, such social institutions as government; advertising; the media; the medical, mental health, and legal professions; religious organizations; industry; and business all promote inaccurate information about alcohol and the risks it poses to health (Mosher & Jernigan, 1988). Numerous studies have documented the role of television in particular in glorifying alcohol consumption (often heavy consumption), linking it with physical attractiveness and sexual success (National Institute on Alcohol Abuse and Alcoholism, 1990). Several popular television programs, among them "Dallas" and "Cheers," have specifically presented pregnant women consuming alcohol with no apparent negative consequences for themselves or their children.

Recently the alcohol beverage industry has turned its $2 billion annual advertising budget to youth and women, particularly women aged 18 to 44, the childbearing years. This advertising promotes alcohol as an acceptable, even healthful, beverage that poses no risks to health or development. Distillers advise retailers on how to appeal to women as a market; the beverage industry targets women as a "growth market" for advertising and promotions; and the industry aggressively seeks to expand sale of alcoholic beverages to grocery stores and supermarkets as a convenience for women buyers. In addition, in-room self-service refrigerator bars are marketed to hotels with the argument that the increasing numbers of women business clients prefer to drink in their rooms rather than in the hotel bar (Blume, 1986).

Both media depictions and alcoholic beverage advertising have served to fuel an existing cultural attitude of "better living through chemistry," that is, the belief that good times are made even better and bad times can be made tolerable through alcohol and other drugs. At the same time, alcohol and drugs of all kinds are easily available to everyone, including children, adolescents, women of childbearing age, pregnant women, and their partners. Many alcoholic beverages, such as beer and wine coolers, are priced to compete with soft drinks; some illegal drugs, such as crack cocaine, are extraordinarily cheap per dose. As is true of the current promotion of alcoholic beverages and tobacco, there is some evidence that drug dealers now are specifically marketing certain drugs, crack cocaine among them, to women.

BARRIERS TO DRUG AND ALCOHOL TREATMENT FOR WOMEN

Treatment Barriers

Historically, few services have focused on the treatment of chemical dependency in women. Many programs are still heavily oriented toward men, and some studies have reported that men outnumber women in treatment facilities at ratios higher than 4:1 (Harrison & Belille, 1987). In a 1987 study of state-funded alcohol and drug programs across the nation, fewer than 20% of all admissions in that year were for women. Approximately 64% of these women were in the 18–44 age range (Butynski & Canova, 1988).

Alcohol and drug use is now believed to occur in women at much higher rates than previously thought. The National Institute on Drug Abuse (NIDA) 1988

National Household Survey reported that 60% of all women of childbearing age drink alcoholic beverages. During their peak reproductive years (ages 18–34) 10% of all women consume an average of two or more drinks per day, or 14 or more drinks per week, an amount that poses risks to a pregnant woman and her fetus. NIDA's survey also found that nearly 10% of all women of childbearing age acknowledged using an illegal drug in the month before the survey. Women's use of cocaine, in contrast to other illicit drugs, had increased markedly since the previous survey in 1985 (Cook et al., 1990). The Institute of Medicine estimates, using the NIDA data, that approximately 10% of all past-month drug users clearly need treatment and another 20% probably need treatment (Gerstein & Harwood, 1990).

Given the increases in women's use of alcohol and other drugs, the national admissions data mentioned above indicate a significant underserving of women, including women of childbearing age and women who may be pregnant. A number of barriers block women's access to the treatment and recovery services they need.

The evidence is strong that there is an absolute lack of services available to women, particularly pregnant women. Too many facilities, still operating on the "male disease" model, offer services that were designed originally for a male population. As a consequence, many programs either do not admit women or treat them in far smaller numbers than men (Blume, 1986; Reed, 1987). Many treatment facilities that do accept women, including publicly funded ones, are reluctant to accept pregnant women, believing that pregnancy is a medical condition that the program is unequipped to handle, particularly given the current climate of fear of liability for obstetrical problems. A 1990 survey conducted by the National Association of State Alcohol and Drug Abuse Directors estimated that 280,000 pregnant women nationwide are in need of drug treatment, yet fewer than 11% of them receive care. Women, including pregnant women, routinely wait weeks, even months, for entry into treatment (U.S. General Accounting Office, 1990).

Women's access to and use of services are also affected by the types of services offered. A study of 53 alcohol and drug treatment facilities in two California counties looked at the relationship between structural variables in the agency (such as services offered and staffing patterns) and the percentage of women in the client population. This study identified factors that either inhibit or promote women's participation in treatment and reached the following conclusions:

- Women need access to recovery homes with accommodations for their children; the two counties studied had *no* facilities with live-in child care, leaving foster care as perhaps the only, and often unacceptable, option.
- Women clients prefer and benefit from having women staff members at treatment facilities.
- Women are more likely to use agencies that provide after-care services and treatment for children, including child care while in the program. Child-related services were of paramount importance for women in the facilities surveyed.

- Women overall prefer programs with a greater number of support services, including transportation, vocational counseling, and legal aid.

These results were valid for all the agencies surveyed, that is, rural and urban, public and private, and those offering alcohol and alcohol/drug services (Beckman & Kocel, 1982).

Another study asked women in treatment directly about their needs. The women surveyed were three times as likely as men to report that they needed child care, were more likely to say they needed health care, and were somewhat more likely to report needing legal help. The unprovided services most frequently reported as needed by women included women's support groups, legal services, organized recreation, and health care (Beckman, 1984). Employment-related services have also been noted as important to women, many of whom enter treatment with few economic resources (Reed, 1985).

While other factors that serve as barriers blocking access to treatment services often affect men, they exert even greater impact on women. These factors include geographic inaccessibility (i.e., counties and regions have no alcohol/drug treatment facilities), cultural and linguistic barriers (i.e., services are not culturally sensitive to women of color or those whose primary language is not English), homophobia (i.e., programs are not open to accepting lesbians as clients), and inaccessibility for women with disabilities (including women with mobility limitations; wheelchair users; and deaf, blind, or mentally retarded women).

Financial Barriers

Financial barriers to treatment, although still strong for both sexes, are even more powerful for women. While a number of states do mandate insurance coverage of alcohol/drug treatment, women are more likely than men to be uninsured because they are less likely to be employed full-time and more likely to work in industries with poor or no health insurance. Even women with health insurance may not have third-party coverage specifically for alcohol/drug treatment (Blume, 1986). Alcohol and other drug detoxification and treatment are currently optional services under the federal Medicaid program and therefore not available through many states' Medicaid plans (Gerstein & Harwood, 1990). In states that do have Medicaid coverage, many programs do not accept Medicaid clients (Chavkin, 1990).

Many alcohol- or drug-using women also lack access to adequate prenatal and other health care. Major funding cuts at the federal level over the last 10 years have diminished maternal and child health care, family planning services, and primary health care for women. In many areas pregnant women may find it impossible to find a private physician who accepts Medicaid (McNulty, 1990). Approximately 25% of all women in the United States fail to begin prenatal care early in pregnancy, and more than 5% receive little or no care at all (Brown, 1988).

These financial barriers, plus publicly and privately funded programs' bias against admitting women, particularly pregnant women, clearly play a major role in limiting women's access to care. Chavkin's (1990) survey of drug treatment facilities in New York City paints a chilling picture of the impact of these barriers: 54% of all programs surveyed categorically do not accept pregnant women as clients; 67% do not accept pregnant women on Medicaid; and 87% would not accept a pregnant woman on Medicaid who was addicted to crack cocaine. Thus, the women with the fewest options and probably the greatest need have the least access to treatment.

Public Policy Barriers

The impact of federal, state, and local policies on women's access to care begins where barriers in treatment facilities and financing leave off. Policies can either encourage women to seek and complete treatment or they can deter and frighten them from treatment. As Blume (1986) states: "Since women constitute the overwhelming majority of single parents in contemporary society, policies on abuse, neglect, custody, and child care are of special relevance to women. . . . Legal definitions of abuse and neglect can act as important treatment barriers" (p. 305). In some states prenatal alcohol or drug use is now defined as child abuse or neglect, and in other states legislation is pending to define prenatal alcohol and drug use as fetal abuse (Moore, 1990). Increasingly, states are attempting to criminalize a woman's use of alcohol or other drugs during her pregnancy. There have been at least 50 cases of prosecution of women for prenatal alcohol or drug use, with two convictions (Chavkin, 1991). Many public hospitals have instituted mandatory toxicological screening (primarily for illicit drugs, although occasionally for alcohol or prescription drugs as well) of women or infants during labor or on delivery and are reporting positive screens to child welfare services. Currently, in 11 states these reports are mandatory (Moore, 1990); in some areas, positive screen reports are automatically followed by removal of children for dependency hearings. Some pregnant women who have been found to use alcohol or drugs have been jailed for the duration of their pregnancies, ostensibly to protect the fetus (Galbraith, 1990; Jessup & Roth, 1988; McNulty, 1987–1988). New coercive approaches include attempts to legally mandate that women enter treatment under civil commitment statutes for the duration of their pregnancies and to require implants of the long-term contraceptive Norplant. Yet there is evidence that all of these policies serve as barriers by deterring women from seeking either prenatal care or alcohol/drug treatment (Chavkin, 1990, 1991; Jessup & Roth, 1988; McNulty, 1987–1988).

DOES PREVENTION WORK?

Despite the historical lack of research attention paid to women's alcohol and drug treatment needs, there is a growing body of knowledge regarding the kinds of services that women, particularly pregnant and parenting women, require for successful prevention, intervention, treatment, and recovery (Beckman, 1984; Beckman & Kocel, 1982; Harrison & Belille, 1987; Jessup, 1990; Jessup & Roth, 1988;

Kronstadt, 1989; Lawson & Wilson, 1979; Marsh, 1982; Mondanaro, 1977; Reed, 1985; Russell, 1985; Tittle & St. Claire, 1989; Unger, 1988; Weiner, Rosett, & Mason, 1985).

Primary prevention strategies for women include broad-based health education and promotion campaigns that address individual behavior and environmentally based strategies that address the availability of and general attitudes toward alcohol and other drugs. As Mosher and Jernigan (1988) suggest, in order to increase the chances for success, prevention efforts must target both the individual and the community levels and must create and support an environment that is conducive to prevention.

Primary and Secondary Prevention: Successful Program Models

There are examples of successful primary and secondary prevention programs targeted to pregnant women and women of childbearing age. One program, the Fetal Alcohol Education Program at the Boston University School of Medicine, aims to improve the skills of health professionals in assessing and intervening in women's drinking during the prenatal period. The program reports that counseling at the prenatal clinic, even among women identified as heavy drinkers, resulted in approximately two-thirds of the women abstaining or significantly reducing their alcohol consumption prior to the third trimester. The program trains physicians, nurses, social workers, dieticians, and alcohol counselors in identification of and intervention with pregnant women with alcohol problems, paying careful attention to assessment through use of a drinking history questionnaire (Weiner et al., 1985).

The Pregnancy and Health Program, a 2-year demonstration project conducted at the University of Washington, also reported significant decreases in alcohol use among the two-thirds of clients identified with "slight" alcohol problems. This program used a five-component strategy: public education, professional training, a telephone information service (which brought in referrals as well), screening and counseling services for pregnant women, and pregnancy outcome assessment (Little et al., 1985).

The Fetal Alcohol Syndrome Project of the Indian Health Service was created to address perinatal alcohol use among Native Americans in a huge geographic area covering New Mexico, southern Colorado, southern Utah, and northern Arizona and including four major tribes. This program strongly stresses a broad-based, culturally appropriate community approach to the problem. A major component is the training of clinicians and outreach workers in identification and referral of suspected fetal alcohol syndrome (FAS) in children and in prevention counseling with women. Primary prevention efforts involve tribal councils, schools, and local government in targeted community training sessions. In a 2-year period 232 training sessions were held for more than 11,000 people. The majority (almost 64%) of those trained were community members, primarily school-aged children, clinical staff, and outreach workers. Education includes films, posters, and pamphlets that build on Native American themes and motifs appropriate to the individual tribes targeted by the program. The program also has a research component designed to develop incidence and prevalence figures for FAS in the geographic area and for individual tribes, to identify the factors underlying perinatal alcohol use, and to use this information to design appropriate prevention strategies (May & Hymbaugh, 1982–1983).

The Women's Alcohol and Drug Education Project is a model program designed for national replication that is now being tested in community- or campus-based women's centers in New York City, Buffalo, Ann Arbor, El Paso, and Fort Wayne. The women served are low-income displaced homemakers, welfare recipients, and single parents. Many are teens and women of color, primarily African-American and those of Hispanic origin. The model stresses the infusion of alcohol- and drug-oriented services into the centers' ongoing activities, including hiring of alcohol/drug educators; alcohol- and drug-related information, referral, and intervention services and support groups; community liaison; and advocacy to assist women in empowering themselves. The program was created in 1987 by the Women's Action Alliance of New York to counter the lack of services specifically designed to reach women with alcohol and drug information. In its first year the program provided direct services to 3,200 women in three pilot test sites. An additional 13,500 people received education, referral, and training services. The project includes a strong evaluation component and has developed a guide that explains how to establish a similar program in women's centers and other women's organizations (Office for Substance Abuse Prevention, 1989a).

Professional Education

A number of programs emphasize professional education on perinatal alcohol and drug use. While there is little research on the effectiveness of these campaigns, there is evidence that advice from physicians and other primary health care providers is the strongest factor in women's decisions to reduce drinking and drug use, followed by advice from family members and female friends (Weiner et al., 1985). At the same time, studies demonstrate weak diagnostic and referral skills by providers, including obstetricians. One study found that the involvement of key alcohol research staff or a department chair in the clinical setting encouraged the use of assessment tools (such as a 10-question drinking history) and the inclusion of a diagnosis of alcohol use in the prenatal medical record (Blume, 1986).

Lessons from Primary Prevention with School Children

A great body of prevention literature is amassing on programs aimed at preventing alcohol and other drug use in children and youth. Since adolescence is the beginning of the childbearing years and a critical time to conduct primary prevention, evaluations of these programs are useful in gauging the effectiveness of prevention approaches. Most prevention programs that stress knowledge and changing attitudes in adolescents are very effective at increasing knowledge but report limited or no impact on adolescents' actual alcohol and drug use. Analysis of study data indicates that the variables most often addressed in these programs (knowledge, attitudes about alcohol and other drugs, decision-making skills, and self-esteem) have limited influence on the drinking and drug-using behavior of students whereas factors related to students' relationships with their parents, peers, and their community demonstrate greater influence. Data from successful smoking prevention programs for youth suggest that for adolescents changes in the current social climate about smoking and newly held general beliefs that people should not smoke underlie program success (National Institute on Alcohol Abuse and Alcoholism, 1990).

Other researchers report similar findings on the critical role of community-based efforts in reinforcing school-based prevention efforts (Benard, 1988). For example, the University of Southern California Comprehensive Drug Abuse Program model combines two approaches: resistance skills training for prevention of alcohol and other drug use in the middle school transition time and a community organizing planning process that involves many sectors of the community— families, schools, media, workplaces, and local government, among others. This model has been implemented as Project Star in Kansas City, Missouri, in 15 school districts and in 1988 as Project I-Star in Indianapolis, Indiana. Both projects are comprehensive, emphasize a community-wide program development process, collaborate with other community agencies and programs, use long-term intervention (5 to 6 years), and have ongoing process and impact evaluation components (Benard, 1988). The latest evaluation data from these unique projects show "significant promise in reducing adolescent drug use," including use of alcohol, cigarettes, marijuana, and cocaine (Office for Substance Abuse Prevention, 1991).

The Exemplary Alcohol and Other Drug Prevention Programs of the Office for Substance Abuse Prevention (OSAP), many of which address youth, demonstrate that effective prevention programs use multiple strategies that recognize the unique characteristics, cultural diversity, and structure of individual communities. These model programs use community-based prevention planning and community organizing approaches and are coordinated with existing community programs, services, and traditional institutions such as schools and religious organizations. Effective programs also develop culturally specific services that reflect and strengthen the ethnic identities of the youth and families targeted (OSAP, 1990). The impact of these programs buttresses arguments that in order to have real impact on drinking and drug-using behavior, individual prevention approaches must be accompanied by community-based activities that address the larger social, economic, and political climate in which alcohol and other drug use occurs.

Prevention Through Environmental Change

The San Diego County Alcohol Program in San Diego County, California, focuses on preventing alcohol problems through environmental strategies that seek to decrease both alcohol availability (through ordinances controlling consumption, increasing enforcement of existing law, and server training) and alcohol demand (through community education on fetal alcohol syndrome and alcohol-related birth defects). The program responds to the community and its concerns about alcohol use by providing information, education, and technical assistance through contracts with outside organizations, including neighborhood recovery centers, the University of California at San Diego, and prevention research groups (OSAP, 1989a).

Many other communities have adopted strategies that target the environment for change, such as passing ordinances requiring warning signs on the consumption of alcohol during pregnancy, demanding more responsible alcohol advertising by local media, and challenging billboards promoting tobacco products and alcoholic beverages, particularly those targeting youth, women, and communities of color.

Public Education and Media

Public education and mass media campaigns represent a prevention approach that can serve to reinforce prevention messages delivered in other settings. Mass media campaigns by themselves do not change behavior, but they can be instrumental in increasing knowledge, changing social norms and attitudes, and altering the social climate in which behavioral choices, including the choice to drink or use drugs, are made. A number of sources emphasize the importance of linking media campaigns with local advocacy groups and community-based programs, ideally with a common strategy (National Institute on Alcohol Abuse and Alcoholism, 1990). Approaches that have proven successful in reaching women at risk for perinatal alcohol and drug use are both comprehensive and implemented at the community level and do not use fear or guilt tactics, in part because guilt appears to increase stress and may actually encourage alcohol and drug use (DeJong & Winsten, 1990; Funkhauser & Denniston, 1985).

Characteristics of Successful Prevention Programs

In sum, effective primary and secondary community-based prevention strategies for women at risk for perinatal alcohol and drug use exhibit the following characteristics:

• They reflect a solid knowledge of the community and sensitivity to its ethnic, cultural, and linguistic composition. They also reflect an understanding of urban and rural differences and consider the differing strategies required for small neighborhood projects versus large regional programs.

• They design materials that recognize differences in education and reading level.

• They recognize the special prevention needs of adolescent women and young girls and design specific approaches for them.

• They reflect a grasp of the psychology of women and of the need to build women's self-esteem and deliver positive messages of prevention rather than threats or guilt-inducing pronouncements.

• Programs are truly community based, involving community members, service consumers, local government, health and other service providers, the religious community, and others in both design and implementation.

• Since women trust information received from physicians and other health care providers, programs emphasize training these professionals to assess, diagnose, counsel, treat, and refer women at risk for perinatal alcohol and drug use.

• All education provided has a clear, consistent, and simple message that is shared and reinforced by all components of the community-based effort.

• Programs recognize and consider targeting particular groups of women at high risk: women living in a chemically dependent environment (children or partners of a chemically dependent person); survivors of incest, sexual assault, or other violence; women in transition (e.g., those who are newly divorced, returning to the work force, pregnant, or newly parenting); and adolescents.

• Programs use outreach strategies that reach women where they can be found: health and mental health services, child care centers, women's centers and other women-oriented services, supermarkets, beauty parlors, churches, workplaces that employ primarily women, welfare and social service programs, including domestic violence and homeless shelters, family planning clinics, and jails.

• Programs recognize the strong influence of male partners on women's drinking and drug use and direct prevention efforts at these partners as well.

• Programs are innovative and flexible, creating and using their own evaluation process to guide them to adapt strategies to keep them current, interesting, and effective.

• Programs recognize the role of larger social policy issues in order to begin to address underlying causes of alcohol and other drug use. They coordinate their activities with other community groups organized to fight for social and economic justice.

Tertiary Prevention: Successful Treatment Approaches

The evidence is strong that comprehensive, community-based primary and secondary prevention strategies can and do work. At the same time, many women continue to use alcohol and other drugs during pregnancy and require treatment. For these women, pregnancy may be an excellent time for intervention, since a woman's pregnancy or concern for her newborn often provides compelling motivation for her to seek treatment for her alcohol and other drug use (Jessup, 1990; Weiner et al., 1985). This fact makes it all the more important that appropriate services be available and accessible, overcoming the barriers described earlier, once a woman is drinking or using drugs during pregnancy. There is general agreement in the field on the nature of appropriate services for this group of women, as well as evidence that provision of woman-oriented services increases both entry into and completion of programs (Reed, 1985; Beckman & Kocel, 1982).

A Formula for Successful Treatment Programs for Women

The elements most often cited in successful treatment programs include the following:

1. Programs are comprehensive, with as many services as possible offered on-site or easily available to the woman client. Comprehensive services include perinatal care for the woman; pediatric care for the infant; alcohol/drug treatment and recovery services for the woman; coordination of social services; family services to address the woman's partner and family as a whole; counseling services addressing battering and sexuality issues such as incest, rape, and self-image; and parenting skills support and training.

2. Programs are confidential and accessible and avoid intensifying women's fear of abuse, neglect, or criminal charges or loss of their children to child protective services.

3. Programs are collaborative and coordinated, with case management (including service linkage, therapeutic support, and advocacy) as the means of ensuring true coordination of services.

4. Services are intensive, including home visits, drop-in services, 24-hour telephone hotlines, and related services that address the social and emotional needs of women as well as their medical needs.

5. Programs have a supportive orientation toward women, address women's need for support and building self-esteem, and include support groups for women in treatment and counseling that focus on self-image and identity issues. Most treatment experts recommend women-only programs.

6. Day treatment, residential treatment, and drug-free housing options are available for all women, including pregnant women and women with children.

7. Programs have strong parent education, child care, and child development components (Beckman, 1984; Beckman and Kocel, 1982; Kronstadt, 1989; Lawson & Wilson, 1979; Reed, 1985, 1987; Rogan, 1985; Tittle & St. Claire, 1989).

CALIFORNIA'S STATE PERINATAL ALCOHOL AND DRUG USE PREVENTION EFFORT: A CASE STUDY

Since the evidence points to the importance of community-wide social and environmental prevention as the means for altering alcohol and drug use patterns, it is important to ask what the role of the state should be in promoting such broad-based prevention efforts. California's experience with this issue illustrates what a state—in this case, the state's department charged with alcohol and drug issues—can initiate to prevent and mitigate perinatal alcohol and drug use.

California historically has had a system of community-based alcohol and drug treatment and recovery services. Unlike many other states, California has many public treatment and recovery services that operate on a social model, offering outpatient or residential counseling and 12-step model support groups, whether provided directly by county alcohol/drug program staff or through contracts with community-based organizations. This service system has a strong philosophical commitment to the concept of prevention, to the concept of social and environmental, as well as individual, roots of alcohol and drug use, and to the public health model that stresses intervention at all levels. The system provides a context and fertile ground for community based prevention and intervention efforts.

In 1986 California's State Department of Alcohol and Drug Programs (ADP) created a Select Committee for the Prevention of Alcohol-Related Birth Defects to develop concrete recommendations that would provide the basis for a state plan for the prevention of alcohol-related birth defects. This committee, later renamed the Select Committee on Perinatal Alcohol and Drug Use, was composed of appointed representatives from state and local health care, social service, and educational organizations, county alcohol program administrators, and staff from other state departments, including the departments of health services, developmental services, social services, and education. This membership was intended to form the basis for planning and policy development through a state and local partnership. To develop the state plan the Select Committee convened a Forum on Issues and Priorities for the Prevention of Alcohol-Related Birth Defects. This invitational forum, held in 1988, brought together more than 100 people from around the state, including educators, maternal and child health care providers, alcohol and drug treatment and recovery providers, policy analysts, and representatives of state and local agencies. Their task was to agree on a set of recommendations that would serve as the foundation for the state prevention plan. Many of these participants had not previously worked together, nor did they know much about each other's fields. In this way the forum was a unique opportunity to collect a multidisciplinary group of people, all concerned with perinatal alcohol use, to discuss, debate, and ultimately come to a consensus on concrete recommendations to prevent or reduce the impact of alcohol-related birth defects. The philosophical heart of the forum was recognition that because the problem of perinatal alcohol use is broad and systemic in scope, it must be addressed as a public health and social problem and not simply as an issue of individual behavior. The strength of the forum's recommendations, therefore, lay in their comprehensive, systemic approach to a complex, multifaceted problem.

Recommendations of the Select Committee

Forum participants developed a package of goals and more than 50 specific strategies that addressed the total context in which decisions about drinking are made. These strategies were designed to be implemented at the state and local levels by state departments, by publicly funded county alcohol/drug and health services, by private programs, and by community organizations and coalitions. The recommendations were organized in nine broad subject areas:

1. *Interagency cooperation and collaboration*, addressing the need for state and local agencies and organizations to coordinate their activities and to engage in interdisciplinary initiatives, including joint funding.
2. *Access to care*, with specific recommendations to address the need for pregnant women, women with children, and women of childbearing age, including

adolescents, to have access to comprehensive and coordinated health, social, and alcohol- and drug-related services.

3. *Children- and youth-oriented services*, with proposed strategies for primary prevention of alcohol use by children and youth.

4. *Media and communications*, presenting a plan for a statewide public information program on the risks of perinatal alcohol use, including electronic and print media, a planning and oversight committee, strong local community involvement, and a clear, consistent overall message.

5. *Education and training*, addressing the training and education of service providers and others concerned with perinatal alcohol use, including a recommendation for the development of multidisciplinary cross-training programs.

6. *Networking and support groups*, with recommendations to support the creation and maintenance of local prevention networks, coalitions, and support groups involved with issues related to alcohol-related birth defects.

7. *Public policy*, with recommendations for actions that ultimately have systemic impact on alcohol consumption and access to services (including broadened Medicaid eligibility; increased alcohol excise taxes; state-mandated rotating warning messages on all alcoholic beverage containers; limitations on alcohol advertising aimed at youth and at women of childbearing age; and a strong policy statement that alcohol use during pregnancy is a health issue, not a criminal justice issue, based on recognition that punitive approaches toward a woman's alcohol use based on her pregnancy alone are both inappropriate and ineffective).

8. *Research needs*, with recommendations for specific research initiatives on drinking and pregnancy.

9. *Funding opportunities*, calling for the identification of new funding sources for perinatal alcohol use, such as earmarked alcohol excise taxes, as well as additional funding from the state general fund.

Impact of the Select Committee Recommendations

More than 800 copies of the Select Committee report were distributed following its release in 1989, often to local communities looking for ideas to pursue to address alcohol and drug problems at the local level. Four major strategies recommended by the Select Committee report have been implemented at the state or local level:

1. *Pilot Projects for Comprehensive, Coordinated Services.* Seven pilot projects in the state now provide comprehensive, coordinated services for chemically dependent pregnant and parenting women and their children. The services were funded through the federal Alcohol, Drug Abuse, and Mental Health Services Block Grant (at about $1.5 million each), with contributions from the California state departments of social services and health services. The pilot projects bring together the state departments of alcohol and drug programs, health services, social services, and developmental services to coordinate policy and program development at the state level through a State Interagency Task Force. Pilot project services are coordinated at the local level through perinatal coalitions that oversee

the pilots and provide planning and policy development. Services through the pilot projects include outpatient and residential care for women and their children, case management for the women, linkage with perinatal and pediatric care and social services, child care, and, for those cases where children are removed to protective custody, foster parent recruitment, training, and respite care. ADP has also funded planning grants to assist other counties and regions to plan similar comprehensive services.

2. *Statewide Media Campaign on Perinatal Alcohol and Drug Use.* ADP funded a $450,000 statewide public education project on the risks of perinatal alcohol and drug use. Initiated in May 1991, the campaign included television, radio, and print media spots, a media guide for local communities, and linkage with activities at the local level.

3. *Local Coalitions for Prevention of Perinatal Alcohol and Drug Use.* To date, 29 county or regional coalitions concerned with perinatal alcohol and drug use have been funded by ADP. The $10,000 grants are designed to assist these groups in launching activities such as prevention education and service coordination efforts. This funding has proven a very effective investment of state dollars, since the coalitions have often been extremely successful at bringing together service providers, administrators, and consumers who have never before worked together. A number of coalitions have developed or are now developing interagency agreements and protocols, and several have submitted grants to foundations and to the federal Office for Substance Abuse Prevention to fund comprehensive service programs and other activities. In addition, many of the coalitions worked with the statewide media campaign to provide coordinated prevention education in their communities.

4. *Cross Training of Health and Social Service Providers.* Four cross-trainings have been held in different geographic areas of the state to educate health and social service providers on the nature of chemical dependency, its impact on pregnancy, and its treatment, as well as on how the disciplines can work together to serve chemically dependent women and drug-affected children. ADP also provided follow-up technical assistance to programs on request. (Educators, judges, police, and district attorneys were largely absent from the trainings, leaving a major gap to be filled in future training efforts.) As with the Forum, these cross-trainings brought together a multidisciplinary group of workers who often had little previous contact with each other or knowledge of each other's work.

The Select Committee report was issued at a time when both the state and local communities were ready to act, and many of the recommended strategies had been implemented or were on their way to implementation within the year after the report appeared. The Select Committee and ADP convened a follow-up forum in 1990 with an expanded list of 170 participants, including representation from drug-related services, social services such as child welfare programs, and law enforcement. The charge to this group was to look at the entire spectrum of services and policies related to perinatal alcohol and drug use, building upon the experience of the 2 years since the issuing of the original report. The second report, with updated and new prevention strategies, was released by ADP in December 1991.

TRANSLATING CALIFORNIA'S EXPERIENCE
TO OTHER STATES

California's experience holds some interesting lessons for other regions. There were two major factors that clearly contributed to the state's ability to launch community prevention activities aimed at perinatal alcohol and drug use: (1) a local network of community-based programs with an already existing commitment to community prevention that provided a healthy growth environment for these activities; and (2) a state department dedicated specifically to alcohol and drug issues that exercised leadership and served as the coordinator/convener of activities both at the local level and with other relevant state departments.

The state's community prevention activities reflect what the literature and community experience demonstrate are effective approaches to prevent and mitigate perinatal alcohol and drug use. The state has implemented new and innovative treatment initiatives, a public education media campaign, cross-disciplinary training and education, and, most recently, an increase in alcohol taxes. Local communities have responded with multidisciplinary prevention coalitions, service coordination efforts, and community-based education and activism such as challenging alcohol product billboards and advertising. Together, the state and local groups have succeeded in raising the consciousness of California's residents about the risks of alcohol and drug use during pregnancy and in setting a prevention and treatment agenda for the state.

Challenges in Implementing Prevention Approaches

Some of the difficulties inherent in California's experience may also be instructive. For example, the so-called maternal versus fetal rights split, between those considering themselves child advocates and those labeled women's advocates, surfaced during the development of the state prevention plan, with some participants supporting criminal prosecution or civil commitment of chemically dependent pregnant women and removal of their children to protective custody. This split is a common phenomenon across the nation and must be addressed directly if we are to foster a supportive environment for prevention, intervention, and treatment. The experience in California suggests that an important first step is to draw together players in all the relevant fields—alcohol/drug treatment, prenatal and pediatric health care, social services, child welfare, education, and law enforcement—as soon as possible to educate each other on their specialties and on the nature of perinatal addiction in order to surmount turf and disciplinary barriers and to develop strategies for working together to achieve the best possible outcomes for both mother and child. Incorporating social services and law enforcement into state policy bodies such as California's Select Committee and cross-trainings are two possible strategies to defuse this conflict. Attention to the issue is critical; the lack of communication between the specialties that allows the mother–child dyad to be split into two adversarial camps is extremely dangerous, both for community prevention activities and for chemically dependent women and their children.

Coordination of services remains an unmet goal. Achieving comprehensive prevention and treatment approaches requires a great deal of coordination at the state and local levels. This coordination is not free; it must be nurtured through staff time, funding, and a strong commitment to bridging the gulfs—and sometimes antagonisms—between programs and disciplines. Despite the push for coordination in California, fragmentation among state departments and local services is still experienced. This fragmentation at both levels reflects territorialism and residual antagonism on the part of agencies, as well as a lack of financial and staff support for coordination activities.

Finally, California's enormous budget deficit, a problem common to other states, endangers its ability to provide even basic health, social, and financial services to the poorest and most vulnerable residents. At the same time, it is clear that these basic services are a vital part of effective alcohol and drug prevention.

CONCLUSION

Despite problems and barriers, experience demonstrates that community-based prevention activities can have an impact on perinatal alcohol and drug use. Broad-based prevention approaches can create and nurture an environment in which people make informed choices about drinking and drug use, supported by a broad array of economic, social, and health policies and services that address the multiple factors that underlie alcohol and drug use.

REFERENCES

Amaro, H., Fried, L. E., Cabral, H., & Zuckerman, B. (1990). Violence during pregnancy and substance abuse. *American Journal of Public Health, 80,* 575–579.

Beckman, L. J. (1984). Treatment needs of women alcoholics. *Alcoholism Treatment Quarterly, 1,* 101–114.

Beckman, L. J., & Kocel, K. M. (1982). Treatment-delivery system and alcohol abuse in women: Social policy implications. *Journal of Social Issues, 38,* 139–151.

Benard, B. (1988). An overview of community-based prevention. In K. H. Rey, C. L. Faegre, & P. Lowery (Eds.), *Prevention research findings: 1988* (pp. 126–147) . Rockville, MD: Office for Substance Abuse Prevention.

Blume, S. B. (1986). Women and alcohol: Public policy issues. In *Women and alcohol: Health-related issues* (pp. 294–311, Research Monograph No. 16). Washington, DC: National Institute on Alcohol Abuse and Alcoholism.

Brown, S. S. (1988). Preventing low birth weight. In H. M. Wallace, G. Ryan, Jr., & A. C. Oglesby (Eds.), *Maternal and child health practices* (pp. 307–324). Oakland, CA: Third Party.

Burns, W. (1986). Psychopathology of mother–infant interaction. In I. J. Chasnoff (Ed.), *Drug use in pregnancy: Mother and child* (pp. 106–116). Lancaster, UK: MTP Press.

Butynski, W., & Canova, D. M. (1988). Alcohol problem resources and services in state-supported programs, Fiscal year 1987. *Public Health Reports, 103,* 611–620.

Chavkin, W. (1990). Drug addiction and pregnancy: Policy crossroads. *American Journal of Public Health*, 80, 483–487.

Chavkin, W. (1991). Mandatory treatment for drug use during pregnancy. *Journal of the American Medical Association*, 266, 1556–1561.

Cook, P. S., Peterson, R. C., & Moore, D. T. (1990). *Alcohol, tobacco, and other drugs may harm the unborn.* Rockville, MD: Office for Substance Abuse Prevention.

DeJong, W., & Winsten, J. A. (1990, Summer). The use of mass media in substance abuse prevention. *Health Affairs*, 9(2), 30–46.

Frakas, M. I. (1976). The addicted couple. *Drug Forum*, 5, 81–87.

Funkhauser, J. E., & Denniston, R. W. (1985). Preventing alcohol-related birth defects: Suggestions for action. *Alcohol Health and Research World*, 10(1), 54–59.

Galbraith, S. (1990, May 17). *Law and policy affecting addicted women and their children.* Testimony before the House Select Committee on children, Youth, and Families.

Gerstein, D. R., & Harwood, H. J. (Eds.). (1990). *Treating Drug Problems* (Vol. 1). Washington, DC: National Academy Press.

Harrison, P. A., & Belille, C. A. (1987). Women in treatment: Beyond the stereotype. *Journal of Studies on Alcohol*, 48, 574–578.

Jessup, M. (1990). The treatment of perinatal addiction. *Western Journal of Medicine*, 152, 553–558.

Jessup, M., & Roth, R. (1988). Clinical and legal perspectives on prenatal drug and alcohol use: Guidelines for individual and community response. *Medicine and Law*, 7, 377–389.

Jones, K. L., Smith, D. W., Ulleland, C. N., & Streissguth, A. P. (1973, June 9). Pattern of malformation in offspring of chronic alcoholic mothers. *Lancet*, 1267–1271.

Kronstadt, D. (1989). *Pregnancy and cocaine addiction: An overview of impact and treatment.* San Francisco: Far West Laboratory for Educational Research and Development, Drug Free Pregnancy Project.

Lawson, M. S., & Wilson, G. S. (1979). Addiction and pregnancy: Two lives in crisis. *Social Work in Health Care*, 4, 445–457.

Little, R. E., & Erving, C. H. (1984). Alcohol use and reproduction. In S. C. Wilsnack & L. J. Beckman (Eds.), *Alcohol problems in women* (pp. 155–188). New York: Guilford Press.

Little, R. E., Streissguth, A. P., Guzinski, G. M., Uhl, C. N., Paulozzi, L., Mann, S. L., Young, A., Clarren, S. K., & Grathwohl, H. L. (1985). An evaluation of the Pregnancy and Health Program. *Alcohol Health and Research World*, 10(1), 44–53.

Marsh, J. C. (1982). Public issues and private problems: Women and drug use. *Journal of Social Issues*, 38, 153–165.

May, P. A., & Hymbaugh, K. J. (1982–1983). A pilot project on fetal alcohol syndrome among American Indians. *Alcohol Health and Research World*, 10(2), 3–9.

McNulty, M. (1987–1988). Pregnancy police: The health policy and legal implications of punishing pregnant women for harm to their fetuses. *Review of Law and Social Change*, 16, 277–319.

McNulty, M. (1990). Pregnancy police: Implications of criminalizing fetal abuse. *Youth Law News*, 11(1), 33–36.

Mondanaro, J. (1977). Women: Pregnancy, children, and addiction. *Journal of Psychoactive Drugs*, 9(1), 59–68.

Moore, K. G. (1990). Substance abuse and pregnancy: State lawmakers respond with punitive and public health measures. *American College of Obstetrics & Gynecology Legisletter*, 9(3), 3–7.

Mosher, J. F., & Jernigan, D. H. (1988, Spring). Public action and awareness to reduce alcohol-related problems: A plan of action. *Journal of Public Health Policy, 9*(1), 17–41.

National Institute on Alcohol Abuse and Alcoholism. (1990). *Alcohol and health: Seventh special report to the U.S. Congress.* Rockville, MD: Author.

O'Donnell, J. A., Besteman, K. J., & Jones, J. P. (1967). Marital history of narcotic addicts. *International Journal of the Addictions, 2,* 21–38.

Office for Substance Abuse Prevention. (1989a). *Prevention plus: II. Tool for creating and sustaining drug-free communities.* Rockville, MD: Author.

Office for Substance Abuse Prevention. (1990). *Communities creating change: Exemplary alcohol and other drug prevention programs.* Rockville, MD: Author.

Office for Substance Abuse Prevention. (1991). Ongoing evaluation of Midwest projects provides promising data. *Prevention Pipeline, 4*(1), 5–6.

Reed, B. G. (1985). Drug misuse and dependency in women: The meaning and implications of being considered a special population or minority group. *International Journal of the Addictions, 20*(1), 13–62.

Reed, B. G. (1987). Developing women-sensitive drug dependency treatment services: Why so difficult? *Journal of Psychoactive Drugs, 19*(2), 151–164.

Regan, D. O., Leifer, B., & Finnegan, L. P. (1982). Generations at risk: Violence in the lives of pregnant drug-abusing women. *Pediatric Research, 16,* 91.

Rogan, A. (1985). Issues in the early identification, assessment, and management of children with fetal alcohol effects. *Alcohol Health and Research World, 10*(1), 66–67.

Russell, M. (1985). Alcohol abuse and alcoholism in the pregnant woman. *Alcohol Health and Research World, 10*(1), 28–31.

Tittle, B., & St. Claire, N. (1989). Promoting the health and development of drug-exposed infants through a comprehensive clinic model. *Zero to Three, 9*(5), 18–20.

Unger, K. B. (1988). Chemical dependency in women: Meeting the challenges of accurate diagnosis and effective treatment. *Western Journal of Medicine, 149,* 746–750.

U.S. General Accounting Office. (1990). *Drug-exposed infants: A generation at risk.* Washington, DC: Author.

Washton, A. M. (1986). Special report: Women and cocaine. *Medical Aspects of Human Sexuality, 20,* 128–132.

Weiner, L., Rosett, H. L., & Mason, E. A. (1985). Training professionals to identify and treat pregnant women who drink heavily. *Alcohol Health and Research World, 10*(1), 32–35.

Wilsnack, R. W., Wilsnack, S. C., & Klassen, A. D. (1987). Antecedents and consequences of drinking and drinking problems in women: Patterns from a U.S. national survey. In P. C. Rivers (Ed.), *Alcohol and addictive behavior* (pp. 85–158). Lincoln, NE: University of Nebraska Press.

Wine Institute. (1991, August). No negative effects detected from moderate consumption of alcohol during pregnancy. *Health and Social Issues Newsline.*

Wright, J. T., Barrison, I., Toplis, P. J., & Waterson, J. (1984). Alcohol and the fetus. *British Journal of Hospital Medicine, 29,* 260–264.

5

The Role of Prenatal Care
Services in Assisting Families
Affected by Drugs, Alcohol,
and AIDS

HOPE EWING
MARY FORAN

INTRODUCTION

Today we live in a social and professional climate that first promotes and condones and then stigmatizes and even criminalizes the use of alcohol and other drugs, especially by pregnant women.

What would happen if the dangers of substances such as alcohol, tobacco, and prescription and illicit drugs were exposed in our media, educational institutions, churches, and political arenas? What if cigarette smoking and alcohol consumption were portrayed as expensive, risky, and unglamorous? What if health and medical professionals received routine training in the diagnosis of drug and alcohol use, abuse, and dependence and frequent updates on state-of-the-art intervention and treatment approaches? What if those who became dependent on substances were viewed with compassion and offered immediate enrollment in a treatment program appropriate to their needs? What if all women, men, and children were taught how family life can be harmed by a family member's use of drugs, alcohol, and tobacco? What if they were taught how to distinguish problem from nonproblem use and knew help was available when smoking, drinking, and drug use continued despite evidence of harm?

The short answer is that if all these things were to come to pass, those of us working in prenatal care would find our jobs enormously easier.

If all these things were to come to pass, addicts and alcoholics would be seen by health professionals as human beings in the grip of a powerful and frightening process, biologically comparable to other chronic diseases but with particularly pronounced psychological and social dimensions. If the percent of prenatal patients known to be using harmful substances continues at the present figure of 10%–30%, public clinics and private obstetrical practices would, hire or develop experts in perinatal substance abuse counseling. These counselors would provide interventions consisting of assessment, education, motivational counseling, and referral to recovery resources as part of routine prenatal care, and these services would be fully reimbursable. Providers of prenatal care would realize their power to offer clarity, hope, and guidance to patients with alcohol and other drug problems while accepting their powerlessness to change or save them. There would be an array of treatment modalities to choose from, matched to the multiple special needs of families with young children. Waiting times for services would be limited. All services would be financially accessible and comprehensive. Pregnant women would receive special support, not special censure.

We are a long way from achieving these ideals. Alcohol and drug dependence is misunderstood, leaving the majority of professionals feeling hopeless, helpless and angry, especially toward alcoholics and addicts who are pregnant.

Distinguishing among use, abuse, and dependence and matching patients to appropriate recovery support are skills that are inadequately taught to health professionals. Counseling interventions in prenatal clinics are not reimbursable under most insurance plans. Addiction is still viewed as a moral weakness; hence the efficacy of treatment is still questioned. Funding for treatment resources is subordinated to fire power for police actions. Alcohol and cigarette companies increasingly target youth, women, and minority communities in their marketing strategies. Prevention programs focus on education and individual behavior change while activities that address the social milieu and media images are limited to infrequent public service announcements.

The "high cost of child care" and "prohibitive liability issues" are cited as justifiable reasons for the failure to provide treatment for pregnant women and women with young children. Pregnant and newly delivered women with alcohol and other drug problems are greeted with loss of custody and criminal prosecution on such charges as felony possession, drug dealing, and child endangerment, rather than diagnosis, education, intervention, and appropriate treatment.

All fertile women, particularly those who are indigent or less educated, are at risk for being caught in this scenario. Poor and minority women are more likely to bear the brunt of such approaches than are white and more affluent women, despite comparable rates of use of drugs and alcohol during pregnancy (Chasnoff, Landress, & Barrett, 1990). They are also at the greatest risk for developing medical complications. Inadequate education and low income are the best predictors of excess morbidity and mortality for all health conditions in the United States. Access to health care, including prenatal care, is constrained by financial status.

Publicly funded health care and public health agencies strive to conduct prevention programs and provide care for ever-increasing numbers of uninsured or publicly insured patients with ever-dwindling resources. Proposals that seek to address circumstances which increase the risk for addiction—especially poverty, lack of economic opportunity, and disintegrating social structures, whether in poor or wealthier families—are judged too expensive, grandiose, and idealistic. Finally, poor and minority women and their offspring are also the populations into which the HIV virus is spreading the most rapidly. The mode of transmission to mothers is largely through sharing needles and sex with infected partners. It is against this larger backdrop that our chapter turns to address the questions of how prenatal care services can and should assist families affected by drugs, alcohol, and AIDS.

PRENATAL CARE PROVIDES A GOLDEN OPPORTUNITY FOR INTERVENTION

The condition of pregnancy provides a unique window of opportunity for prevention of and early intervention in hidden disease processes. Our prenatal care systems are an ideal arena for primary and secondary prevention activities for women and their families. Pregnancy brings a woman and her family into contact with health and social services at a time when she may be as yet unaware of or in denial about the existence, nature, and consequences of alcohol and other drug problems or HIV infection.

While addicts and alcoholics are overrepresented in the group of women with little or no prenatal care, a study at Merrithew Memorial Hospital (Contra Costa County) in 1989 (Ewing, 1991) showed fully half of 135 addicts and alcoholics identified at delivery had four or more prenatal visits beginning before the third trimester of pregnancy. Sensitively trained prenatal staff have a major public health role to play in identifying and referring afflicted women. Pregnancy creates a situation of intrinsic change and hope for the mother, making it a time when she tends to be receptive to such referrals.

The whole family is affected when the mother is in the grip of alcohol and drug problems. At the time of childbirth family members tend to come together to welcome the new baby. When an alcohol- or drug-exposed newborn is removed from the parents' custody, he or she is often placed with family members. Thus, the family as a whole may be more available for therapy at the time of a birth than at any other time.

HOW COMMON IS ALCOHOL AND OTHER DRUG USE DURING PREGNANCY?

Determining the number of pregnant women who continue to use alcohol or drugs during pregnancy is difficult, as estimates from different sources are based on very different populations and use different methods, including self-report, clinical assessment, and onetime toxicology screening (usually urine). A urine screening provides no information about the extent of the disease process, and alcohol is rarely included. All these methods are likely to miss a significant number of pregnant women with alcohol and other drug problems. Bias may be introduced by the fact that hospitals and prenatal care providers with large numbers of low-income and minority patients have adopted history and toxicology screening more readily than have institutions serving privately insured patients. Nonetheless, some consistency in findings has emerged.

Estimates of alcohol consumption by pregnant women are as high as 20% (Serdula, Williamson, Kendrick, & Byers, 1991), with 5% of pregnant women taking at least two drinks daily (Sokol, Miller, & Reed, 1980), and 6% of women of childbearing age deemed alcoholic (Clark & Midanik, 1982).

Studies focusing on the use of illicit drugs during pregnancy estimate prevalences of 10%–15% (Little, Snell, Palmore, & Gilstrap, 1988; Chasnoff, 1988; Neershof, McGregor, Petzky, & Sullivan, 1989). A widely quoted study conducted in Pinellas County, Florida, found that for the 14.8% of prenatal patients testing positive on urine toxicology screens, there were no significant differences in rates of use between public clinic and private physician patients or between African-American and white patients. Drug of choice, however, differed by race, with African-American women more likely to use cocaine and white women more likely to use cannabinoids (Chasnoff, Landress, & Barrett, 1990).

These estimates are consistent with the results of the 1985 National Institute on Drug Abuse (NIDA) National Household Survey on Drug Abuse (National Institute on Drug Abuse, 1989), which indicates that 8 million women of childbearing age, representing 15% of that population, use illicit drugs and that use of cocaine among women over 18 increased 59% from 1982 to 1985 (Jones & Lopez, 1990). NIDA's 1988 national household survey shows that the use of illicit drugs continues to increase among women of childbearing age (National Institute on Drug Abuse, 1989).

WHO ARE HIV-POSITIVE WOMEN?

Drinking and drug use during pregnancy occurs among all racial, ethnic, and socioeconomic groups. There appear to be differences in drugs of choice for different racial groups, and there are local variations, with certain drugs being popular in some areas and rarely seen in others. In contrast, HIV-positive women are currently concentrated within low-income and minority groups. Among women diagnosed with AIDS (21,225 as of December, 1991) 52% are African-American women and 21% are Hispanic women; 50% contracted HIV through IV drug use and 34% through heterosexual contact, presumably with male IV drug users or bisexual men (Centers for Disease Control, 1992).

Drug use in childbearing women is a key factor in the spread of pediatric AIDS. The Centers for Disease Control estimate that 75% of infants diagnosed with AIDS are born to women who are IV drug users themselves or the sexual partners of IV drug users. Another powerful link between drug use and perinatal HIV infection is the sex-for-drugs trade, especially common in crack houses and among crack cocaine users. Unprotected intercourse with multiple partners, carried out under the influence of the drug, leads to multiple risks, including pregnancy and exposure to sexually transmitted diseases such as syphilis and AIDS.

PRENATAL CARE IN THE UNITED STATES

If we are to harness the potential for prevention of alcohol and other drug problems in childbearing women, we need to understand the current structure of prenatal care services in our country. The following questions are key:

- When do women begin prenatal care?
- Who provides prenatal care services?
- What services are provided?

The Institute of Medicine's report *Prenatal Care: Reaching Mothers, Reaching Infants* (1988) described the U.S. maternity care system as "fundamentally flawed, fragmented and overly complex" (p. 12). The report concluded that efforts to draw women into care must be based on making prenatal care more responsive to the needs of the women who enroll. The report goes on to enumerate the many stubborn and powerful barriers that limit access to prenatal care for those most in need of it.

It has become a truism that prenatal care is an effective means to reduce infant mortality and its precursors, especially low birthweight. Questions remain about which specific elements of prenatal care promote better birth outcomes. However, it is clear that the provision of medical monitoring along with health education and social support during pregnancy do increase rates of infant survival. Despite these findings, the women most likely to have sickly babies are those least likely to receive sufficient prenatal care or any care at all.

When Do Women Begin Prenatal Care?

The American College of Obstetricians and Gynecologists recommends that all women begin prenatal care within the first 3 months of pregnancy. By 1985, 76% of all women giving birth in the United States reported starting prenatal care in the first 3 months of pregnancy; this represents about 2.8 million births. Approximately 211,000 women, or 5.7%, had no prenatal care at all or delayed care until the last 3 months of pregnancy (U.S. Department of Health and Human Services, 1986).

Poverty and lack of private health insurance are by far the strongest predictors of late or no prenatal care. A number of other important factors affect the likelihood that a woman will have prenatal care, notably, whether the pregnancy was intended, the woman's perception of the value and acceptability of care, and whether the woman has a regular source of health care.

Women involved in drug- and alcohol-using lifestyles are among those most likely to enter prenatal care after the first trimester. This means that outreach activities need to be developed for these women. Strategies need to be developed to promote the perception of prenatal care as a safe place to discuss alcohol and drug use. Fears about criminalization and loss of custody need to be seen as important deterrents to a woman's seeking prenatal care. A spirit of acceptance, advocacy, and expertise toward women with alcohol and drug problems needs to be promoted and projected by prenatal care providers.

Where Do Women Obtain Prenatal Care?

In 1982, 83% of nonpoor women and 54% of poor women received their prenatal care from private physicians (National Survey of Family Growth, as quoted in Institute of Medicine, 1988). However, two powerful trends in recent years are changing that picture. A decreasing number of physicians accept Medicaid patients for obstetrical care, the key deterrents being low rates of reimbursement, delays in receiving reimbursement, and rising malpractice costs. Medical malpractice insurance costs for obstetrical providers doubled between 1982 and 1985 and have continued to rise since then. These rising costs, as well as fears of malpractice litigation, have lead to a reduced number of physicians practicing obstetrics, as well as to the practice of screening out from care those pregnant women who appear to be at high risk for pregnancy complications or who cannot pay for the full cost of care. Women who are obviously alcohol or drug dependent and those who are HIV positive or at high risk of HIV exposure are disproportionately represented in these groups.

The alternative for women without access to private physicians is to seek clinic-based prenatal care provided by a range of organizations, including public health departments, community health centers, migrant health centers, and hospital outpatient departments. Most of these organizations rely on public sources of funding, either through direct subsidy or collection of Medicaid reimbursement. Referring again to 1982 data, 39% of poor women (compared to 12% of nonpoor women) and 60% of women on Medicaid received their prenatal care in clinics (Institute of Medicine, 1988).

Clinic-based prenatal care can offer a number of benefits not found in private physician offices, especially for women with special needs for education, support, or referral. Clinics often have nonphysician professionals on staff, such as nutritionists, social workers, and public health nurses, to provide more comprehensive care. The staff of these large organizations specializing in serving lower income women are more likely to have good knowledge of other social and economic assistance programs in the community that pregnant women may need. They have the patient volume that permits them to hire an alcohol and drug counselor as part of the prenatal care team. However, there are several important disadvantages to the current array of most clinic-based prenatal care programs.

Long waits for appointments and long waits once the women arrive at the clinic to see the medical staff are common. Large systems are impersonal and difficult to negotiate. Clinic staff are often overworked, leading to rudeness and impatience with patients, who in turn feel they have been treated with disrespect and are therefore disinclined to be compliant. The clinic environment is often noisy and unattractive. Physicians are rushed and women often do not see the same physician at each visit, resulting in poor communication and little opportunity to build trust.

There is ample evidence that the demand for publicly funded maternity services will continue to increase as the crisis of escalating health care costs continues. Only 73% of women of childbearing age are covered by private health plans. Nearly 15 million women in the childbearing years have no insurance for maternity care; of these, about 9.5 million have no health insurance at all (Alan Guttmacher Institute, 1987).

For poor women the insurance picture is even more distressing. In 1985, while 17% of deliveries were paid for by Medicaid, another 15% of deliveries had no source of insurance coverage at all (Gold, Kenney, & Singh, 1987). Medicaid eligibility for pregnant women has been expanded significantly during the last 5 years. By 1990 all states were required to provide Medicaid coverage for all pregnant women (and children up to age 5) who have incomes up to 100% of the federal poverty level, even if they do not qualify for Aid to Families with Dependent Children (AFDC). In 1988, the average income eligibility cutoff for Medicaid was only 49% of the federal poverty level. Despite this expansion and the promise of others to come (as of 1990, 18 states had adopted the federal option of providing Medicaid coverage for pregnant women and infants up to age 1 with incomes up to 185% of the federal poverty level), delays in obtaining Medicaid eligibility and lack of public awareness of the availability of coverage for new groups leads to low enrollment rates by pregnant women, especially during the early months of pregnancy (Institute of Medicine, 1988).

Women living the chaotic life of addiction often seek prenatal care later in pregnancy and participate irregularly. However, their entrance and participation in care is compromised as well by the state of the system as just described. Financial and other access barriers make the provision of effective care a questionable proposition for women affected by drugs, alcohol, and HIV even when they reach out for it.

What Services Are Included in Prenatal Care?

"No single specification of the content of prenatal care is unanimously accepted by public health authorities, health care providers or researchers" (Institute of Medicine, 1988). However, various groups issue recommendations to guide the provision of care. In 1989 the Public Health Service, through its Expert Panel on the Content of Prenatal Care, issued *Caring for Our Future: The Content of Prenatal Care*. This report recommends major changes in current patterns of prenatal care on the basis of a review of the research literature for evidence of the efficacy and effectiveness of the components of care currently being provided.

Since the 1950s, physician-dominated prenatal care provided in medical settings has become the norm (Thompson, Walsh, & Merkatz, 1990). The neonatal mortality rate has declined greatly in the United States during the past 20 years, attributed primarily to improved survival of low birthweight infants through neonatal intensive care (Institute of Medicine, 1985). However, at the same time that these technological achievements have taken place, patient education and psychosocial support have been deemphasized as prenatal care components. The most recent guidelines from the American College of Obstetricians and Gynecologists (ACOG) and the American Academy of Pediatrics (AAP), recommend that all three functions be included in prenatal care, namely, "serial surveillance . . . to identify risk factors or abnormalities and to determine uterine size; patient education to foster optimal health, good dietary habits and proper hygiene; and appropriate psychosocial support" (American Academy of Pediatrics and American College of Obstetricians and Gynecologists, 1988, p. 51). The guidelines state that initial history should include assessing the pregnant woman's use of cigarettes, alcohol, and drugs. They also urge that counseling and HIV antibody testing occur "in any medical care setting in which women at risk of infection are encountered" (p. 155). Unlike the Institute of Medicine's recommendations, these stop short of recommending HIV risk assessment of all prenatal patients, despite the fact that it is difficult to know which settings include clients at risk without conducting universal risk assessment.

While the medical profession's guidelines acknowledge the potential impact of drugs, alcohol, and HIV infection on pregnancy, they offer little information about how to intervene effectively. The focus is on frequency of visits, laboratory tests, uterine measurements, blood pressure readings, and management of labor and delivery. Education and psychosocial issues are to be attended to largely through written materials and referral. Medical prenatal care has become much more sophisticated during the past 40 years, but the primary focus remains oriented toward preventing, detecting, and treating problems that occur in the third trimester of pregnancy, particularly preeclampsia and preterm birth.

This approach may be a reasonable one for low-risk women, but women with risks that are evident early in pregnancy, including poor nutrition, smoking, and alcohol or drug use, need extra attention and services during the first and second trimesters. The traditional pattern of visits—every 4 weeks unti the 28th week of pregnancy, then every 2 to 3 weeks until the 36th week, and then weekly thereafter—requires modification, especially when behavioral risk factors, rather than medical risk factors, are present. Not only should women at risk for alcohol and drug problems be the subjects of outreach and be made to feel accepted in prenatal care, but visits early in pregnancy should be frequent.

There is increasing recognition of the need for prenatal care to respond to new challenges. One of the recommendations of the Institute of Medicine's *Preventing Low Birthweight* (1985) was to study the content of prenatal care so that it might become more effective. The Public Health Service Expert Panel on the Content of Prenatal Care (1989) proposed some major shifts in emphasis. Specifically, the panel recommended increasing attention to preconception care and early pregnancy along with enriching care throughout pregnancy. It recommended three components of care: "(1) early and continuing risk assessment, (2) health promotion, and (3) medical and psychosocial interventions and follow-up" (p. 2). In its formulation of the components of the care the panel advocates a change from a medical model of care to one that places equal emphasis on medical and psycho-social concerns, since "medical, psychological and social risks often interact with each other and consequently require a multi-disciplinary strategy for success" (p. 3). Specific recommendations with respect to drug, alcohol, and HIV issues suggest that health care providers offer tests for HIV and drug toxicology to *all women*, educate *all women* on the risks of drug and alcohol use, advise abstinence from alcohol and drugs during pregnancy, increase the ability of professionals to recognize drug and alcohol use, and assure that referrals are made to recovery resources when appropriate. Throughout its report the panel underscores the necessity to have a "risk-responsive" approach to the provision of care.

During the last two decades, in response to consumer demand, the birthing process in hospitals and under the direction of physicians has become more humane and inclusive of other family members. The father of the baby who was once relegated to the waiting room, has participated as the childbirth coach in the labor room. Hospitals offer childbirth preparation classes at reasonable rates for middle and upper income families, although such services for users of public services are less readily available. In addition, the level of participation by the baby's father and other family members depends largely on their interest. There are few institutional structures to encourage or require such participation.

Although pregnancy care continues to focus almost exclusively on the pregnant woman and the developing fetus, the woman's partner and her family and family situation play critical roles in the pregnancy. Prenatal care recommendations about diet, exercise, rest, and the use of cigarettes, drugs, or alcohol may be followed or rejected depending on the opinion of significant others in a woman's life. A woman's partner or other family members may all be in the drug culture themselves, or a woman may be codependent to a degree that sabotages her movement toward a clean and sober pregnancy, delivery, and subsequent family life. For example, crack smoke in the ambient air has been associated with increased risk for cocaine intoxication (Chasnoff, Lewis, & Squires, 1987). Obviously, it is vitally important to include family members and significant others in the health education and psychosocial support components of prenatal care, particularly those designed to change behavior.

HOW SHOULD PRENATAL CARE SERVE WOMEN WITH ALCOHOL AND OTHER DRUG RISK?

In the next two sections we discuss how the prenatal care system just described can incorporate specific services appropriate to the needs of women who use alcohol and other drugs and women with or at risk for HIV infection. (Similar approaches can be applied to prenatal use of cigarettes, perhaps the most commonly abused substance, but tobacco is not addressed in this chapter.)

We propose a generic model for integrating recognition and referral of women affected by HIV or alcohol and other drug use into prenatal care and show how such services are consistent with the recommendations of ACOG/AAP and the Public Health Service Expert Panel described earlier. Examples are given from the experience of the Born Free Project of Contra Costa County, California, particularly as it relates to Healthy Start, the comprehensive prenatal care program of the county Health Services Department.

Contra Costa County is a part-urban, part-suburban, part-rural county of 800,000 in the East San Francisco Bay area. The county's Health Services Department operates the 179-bed Merrithew Memorial Hospital, which delivers 1,700 women a year and serves as home base for a family practice residency affiliated with the University of California at Davis. The Health Services Department also maintains five comprehensive family practice health centers, which provide prenatal care to the majority of low-income women in the county.

The Born Free Project is a demonstration project funded by the United States Office of Substance Abuse Prevention. The Project has developed a model for drug and alcohol intervention in pre- and perinatal health services, consisting of three components: (1) education and training; (2) alcohol and other drug intervention in pre- and perinatal health services, and (3) a 3-year, four-phase nonresidential recovery program.

Two thousand pregnant women enter this integrated prenatal and substance abuse intervention system yearly. At the time of intake to prenatal care, all two thousand receive special screening to determine those who may be at risk for alcohol or other drug problems. Approximately 800 a year, or 40% are deemed at increased risk, and 250, or 12.5% of all prenatal patients, agree to an intervention by a substance abuse counselor who is integrated into the prenatal care team. About 60 women a year participate in the in-house nonresidential recovery program, which is located at the site of prenatal care in each region of the county. Community self-help, intensive day, and residential recovery services are also available to prenatal patients by referral.

Creating an integrated service system legitimizes alcohol and drug problems as a medical risk factor similar to diabetes or hypertension. Integration responds directly to the Institute of Medicine's concerns about lack of access and fragmentation of services for poor women. As an increasing number of women receive prenatal care in high-volume clinics, it becomes more feasible to bring alcohol and drug experts on staff as part of the prenatal care team and to support these positions through funding sources such as Medicaid. For smaller practices, this expertise may be obtained on a consultant basis or developed from existing prenatal staff.

In our experience, four specific drug and alcohol prevention activities can and should be incorporated into routine prenatal care, whether in clinics or private offices:

ALL PATIENTS

1. *Education* on
   a. Effects of alcohol and other drug use on pregnancy and fetus
   b. The nature of alcohol and other drug dependence

2. *Screening* for alcohol and other drugs
   a. Use
   b. Dependence
      PATIENTS AT INCREASED RISK (positive on screening)
3. *Intervention,* when risk for alcohol and other drug problems is suspected: a focused alcohol and other drug specialty interview that includes
   a. In-depth assessment
   b. In-depth education
   c. Motivational counseling
   d. Referral to appropriate local programs for treatment
4. *Recovery support and coordination* with other services to which women have been referred.

Figure 5.1 illustrates the relationship of the four elements to prenatal care and community recovery support programs, with percentage estimates based on the Born Free/Healthy Start experience.

The First Component: Education

Primary prevention efforts center around core patient education aimed at all prenatal patients and include the following elements:

1. Education on dangers of alcohol and other drugs and cigarettes in pregnancy and lactation
2. Recommendation to cease all use of alcohol and other drugs and cigarettes during pregnancy and lactation
3. Education on the signs and symptoms of alcohol and other drug dependence and on local recovery resources

Core prenatal patient education can be done by any member of the health care team on an individual or group basis with the use of such modalities as lectures, pamphlets, and videos. A written protocol for health education is helpful.

The Second Component: Screening for Alcohol and Other Drug Problems in Prenatal Care

Screening is designed to designate patients at risk for the broad spectrum of individual and family problems associated with use of, abuse of, and dependence on substances (as described in Chapter 2).

Screening is designed to indicate *any* level of involvement with alcohol and drugs in pregnancy. The extent and character of a given woman's involvement with alcohol and drugs can be assessed in a thorough manner in subsequent encounters.

Many modalities are in use today for determining the subgroup in need of further investigation and services. These include the same methods we use for determining other sorts of prenatal risk, laboratory testing, history taking (with

PRENATAL CARE

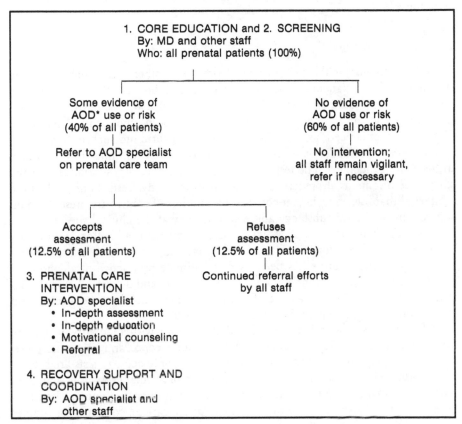

FIGURE 5.1. The four basic components of alcohol/drug prevention services added to comprehensive prenatal care. *AOD = alcohol and other drugs; **Model demonstration projects are collocating some of these AOD treatment services with prenatal care. Percentages are from preliminary data, Contra Costa County, CA., Health Services Department, Born Free Project.

questions being self- or staff-administered), and observation of physical signs and symptoms.

Laboratory Testing

Chemical screens for the presence of alcohol and other drugs include testing specimens of the patient's urine, hair, blood, and breath. A mother's use of chemicals in the days prior to delivery can be assessed by testing the newborn; newborn urine, hair, blood, and meconium (newborn stool) have been used. Complex issues concerning civil rights and consent surround such testing.

As with other laboratory tests, results from toxicology tests must be interpreted in their clinical context. The tests show only the presence of a substance over the short time it remains at predetermined levels in the body. Tests do not tell us the context of that use, and whether compulsion and loss of control are present. To do this requires specialist substance abuse competency at the clinical site.

There has been a tendency in the field of perinatal addiction to attribute significance to laboratory results beyond what they can really tell us. Blind laboratory testing of urine has been used to estimate prevalence of alcohol and other drug use in populations coming for prenatal care and delivery. These studies underestimate the true prevalence of use during pregnancy because alcohol and the majority of drugs remain in urine only hours to days.

There are several other problems that crop up with regularity when the laboratory is used to screen pregnant women for alcohol and other drug use. Selection of patients to be tested and interpretation of toxicology tests are subject to the personal and cultural biases of health care providers. Addiction is an area where professional training is rarely extensive, and stigma abounds. Issues of consent and confidentiality are often unclear, and legal consequences for mother and child can be major. Compared with tests for alcohol, tests for illicit drugs are performed more often and the results are taken more seriously, despite the fact that the data on alcohol effects during pregnancy are far more substantial and show more serious impairment in offspring.

As with all laboratory tests there are both false positives and false negatives in toxicology testing. This is especially true since many clinical sites do not feel they can afford the more expensive and specific confirmatory test of the two-stage preliminary/confirmatory process that is often used.

Thus, laboratory testing, has some value for case finding, prevalence studies, and as a part of alcohol and other drug treatment, however this modality should be used for screening with care and with all results interpreted in their clinical context.

Screening by History

Historical screening will take different forms appropriate to different populations and prenatal care systems. In some systems health aides, social workers, nurses, or nutritionists do the screening. In others the physician performs this as part of the first medical visit.

Brief self-administered questionnaires have identified 20% of the total prenatal care population as at risk during 1991 at Kaiser Permanente Hospital in Oakland, California (A. Boddum, personal communication, 1991). The Born Free screening tool administered by the intake social worker, Public Health Nurse (PHN), or nutritionist identified 25% also in 1991 of the prenatal patients as at risk in the Born Free/Healthy Start services.

The Born Free Screening Tool (see Fig. 5.2) is a quick four-point screen designed to be nonthreatening for both intake worker and patient (Ewing, 1991). It differs from other published tools in that it focuses on chronicity and the family nature of alcohol and drug problems to identify a broad group at increased risk. Parent and partner use of alcohol and drugs are used as markers for increased risk of substance use by the pregnant woman and as liabilities justifying counseling during pregnancy even when the woman herself is not using or drinking. When the screen is positive, a full interview is arranged as part of routine comprehensive prenatal care. The tool is designed to reflect self-reporting only, and any positive answer generates a positive screen. The word *problem* on the screening tool means continued use of alcohol or drugs despite adverse consequences. The screen is designed to identify patients in need of further education, assessment, motivational counseling, and referral.

The commitment of the members of the prenatal care team to the screening process must be sought, and protocols must be accepted by all. Providers need to believe that intervention can positively affect family health, agree about legal and ethical aspects of screening, and accept addicts and alcoholics as patients with a health problem rather than a moral weakness. Programs failing to lay this groundwork have had problems screening effectively. It is helpful for staff to appreciate that they are not being asked to diagnose or label women as alcohol or drug dependent. Rather, they are assigning increased risk to these patients, who will then be offered an intervention interview.

The Third Component: Perinatal Alcohol and Other Drug Intervention

The intervention interview has four different functions: (1) assessment, (2) in-depth education, (3) motivational counseling, and (4) referral. One-half hour to 1 hour is usually required for the counselor to perform these functions and develop a relationship of acceptance and advocacy. The interview becomes one additional component of comprehesive prenatal care, alongside the physician, public health

yes ___ no ___ 1. Parent who is an alcoholic or addict
yes ___ no ___ 2. Partner with problem
yes ___ no ___ 3. Past problem
yes ___ no ___ 4. Pregnancy use of drugs or alcohol

FIGURE 5.2. The born free screening tool.

nurse, social worker, and nutritionist visits. In the Born Free/Healthy Start model we make treatment referrals both to our own nonresidential recovery program, in each major prenatal clinic, and to outside services such as 12-step meetings, intensive day treatment, and residential facilities.

Ideally, an experienced alcohol and drug counselor should be hired to do intervention interviews. It is generally easier to train such a counselor in pertinent aspects of pregnancy, than to try to train a nurse, social worker, or other prenatal provider knowledgeable about pregnancy to do alcohol and drug counseling. Many members of the penatal care staff will not be able to acquire the necessary skills to persistently offer hope and guidence to patients with the denial, manipulations, and antisocial behavior that characterize drug and alcohol dependent individuals. Motivational drug and alcohol counceling is directive, while nurses and social workers are usually more comfortable with nondirective psychotherapeutic approaches. To perform alcohol and other drug interventions well, a counselor needs both training and a calling to the work.

In our experience about half of the patients identified as at risk at intake to prenatal care agree to at least one counselor interview. In this interview we have found that questions about the family and significant other's alcohol and drug use are less threatening to the pregnant woman than questions about her own use. This indirect line of questioning can get her attention, establish concern, support basic education, and develop further insight into the patient's own use and drinking. The genetic, generational, and family nature of addictions provides a rational basis for this approach. The interview might proceed as follows:

> Would you say that one of your parents had a problem with alcohol or other drugs? (65% answer yes). If so, did you know that there is evidence that alcoholism, at least, may have a genetic component? The baby in your womb has half its genes from you, and you got half from the parent you are telling me about. You might like to learn more about alcohol and other drug problems so you can teach your child when he (she) reaches adolescence.
>
> Whether you or your parents ever had a problem, your baby has half its genes from its own father. Do you consider that the baby's father has had problems with alcohol or other drugs? This will help you know if your baby is at risk for these problems.

If the patient denies problems in her generation but identifies problems in a parent, she will still benefit from a counseling session and a referral to resources for recovery for family members.

As the interview proceeds care is taken to decrease the common barrier to acceptance of recovery services. Assurances of confidentiality are also given. Education about the disease concept of alcohol and drug dependence helps relieve guilt and shame. Dangers to the pergnancy and fetus are mentioned in a way that is without blame. Local practices with regard to loss of custody are discussed in a spirit of reassurance and advocacy, since this is an area of extreme anxiety for many women using alcohol and drugs in pregnancy.

There are patterns in the responses of women identified in prenatal care as at risk for chemical use, abuse, and dependence (Ewing, 1991). They occur with enough frequency to examine in detail and discuss at staff trainings. Such responses include the following:

1. I use, but it's not a problem.
2. I had a problem in the past, but I have stopped using/drinking.
3. I have a problem, but I have to solve it on my own.
4. I have a problem, and I just don't care (whether the baby or I live or die).
5. I have a problem, and need help, but I can't accept help because . . .
6. It would be a problem, but (my parents, my boyfriend, etc.) always take(s) care of everything.
7. I wish I could tell you about my problem, but I'm afraid of what it will mean for me and my children.
8. I have a problem, and I want help now.

It is important for the counselor to accept and respect where the patient may be in her process of disease and recovery, and to step outside her framework and offer a reality check on what may be happening. In Vaillant's (1982) research with male alcoholics up to one-third eventually went into long-term abstinence without intervention or a recovery program, usually citing health problems or spiritual experiences as the trigger for their changes. A given woman who states that she stopped drinking/using for good when she found out she was pregnant may, in fact, have done so. On the other hand, it is also likely that she is now, or will soon be, using again since alcohol and other drug dependence is chronic and relapsing and denial is a cardinal symptom of the process. Dependence is usually characterized by episodes of use interspersed by periods of control. Whatever her responses and despite uncertainty as to her true level of involvement with alcohol and drugs, the counselor offers education and discusses recovery support should she decide she needs it.

The issue of appropriate referrals to treatment can be another powerful barrier to effective prenatal clinic intervention. Health and social service providers sometimes despair of finding drug/alcohol treatment services that are appropriate and accessible for women who are pregnant or responsible for small children. Drug and alcohol recovery support specifically designed for this population is slowly becoming available. Communities are beginning to find solutions to the special treatment issues involved, such as medical linkages, liability considerations, child care, transportation, parenting, housing, women's sexuality, generational family dysfunction, and a drug/alcohol-using partner. Meanwhile, health care and social service providers must increase referrals to existing recovery resources. A motivated woman will find support in services without special components. Existing referrals, such as Alcoholics Anonymous (AA) and Narcotics Anonymous (NA), or Cocaine Anonymous (CA), residential and outpatient treatment programs (usually found inthe local phone directory), are still underused by health and social service professionals. We must forge ahead and not despair of making referrals because ultimately referrals may generate services.

Intervention in prenatal care can be seen as a modification of the concept of alcohol and other drug intervention. Recent years have seen the rapid development of chemical dependence intervention efforts in the workplace, within professional societies, and through community treatment centers. Chemical dependence intervention is a technique pioneered by the Johnson Institute in Minnesota. The basic concept is that the addict/alcoholic need not wait to "hit bottom" to change, as there is too much to lose. In this model concerned family, friends, colleagues, and employers meet together, learn about the disease, and develop a strategy of confrontation with the drinker/user that provides a coherent assault on the latter's denial system and offers recovery services. Sometimes there are consequences for failure to comply. Traditionally, the consequences included firing, divorce, or separation.

Perinatal and drug/alcohol services can work together in a partnership to provide a system-wide chemical dependence intervention program for childbearing women and their families. Other services or agencies involved in the family's care, including child protective services can participate when appropriate. Together they can provide affected women with a structured pathway into recovery for themselves and their families. Women in prenatal care are looking for help, are at a time of intrinsic change, are focused on family issues, and are in contact with services over many months. The prenatal clinic is an ideal place for intervention to take place.

The Fourth Component: Coordination and Ongoing Recovery Support

The fourth responsibility of prenatal care toward women with alcohol and other drug problems applies to women who have chosen to actively participate in recovery resources while continuing in prenatal care. Perinatal staff need to distinguish these women from those who have not been ready to avail themselves of support services, appreciate them, and learn from them. Prenatal patients in active recovery are powerful educators and motivators of prenatal care staff. Staff need to understand that relapse is often part of the natural history of recovery and need to maintain contact with recovery services, as with any other service or agency that is serving a prenatal patient. They must understand the special constraints around confidentiality and consent and be avid in securing the necessary signed releases before sharing information within the service network. Coordination activities should promote feedback to the whole prenatal care team about a given woman's progress in recovery so that each caregiver can be more effective in providing ongoing support for the patient.

TREATMENT OF ESTABLISHED ADDICTIVE DISEASE IN PREGNANT WOMEN

At the Born Free Project a nonresidential recovery program has been established at each of three principle sites of prenatal care delivery in the county health system.

In our experience the closer recovery services are to prenatal care services, the easier it is to recruit and retain pregnant women. The physician or a staff member from the prenatal clinic can walk a patient from her medical or social service visit down the hall for a face-to-face introduction or reintroduction to the substance abuse counselor. Substance abuse counselors have become integrated into the prenatal care team of public health nurses, physicians, nutritionists, and educators and into the network of internal referrals, case conferences, and charting. They are responsible for the prenatal substance abuse intervention component and run the recovery program.

The 2-year recovery program is a conventional nonresidential program. Three to four group, individual, or family sessions occur weekly. Structure, incentives, sanctions, sequential phases, and outside 12-step program attendance are key program features. Integrated into the work on denial, abstinence, and lifestyle recovery are issues specific to pregnant and parenting women, such as bonding, parenting, women's sexuality, intimacy, family-of-origin issues, child abuse prevention, choosing and using child care, family planning, literacy, clean and sober recreation, basic life skills, economic survival, housing, and cultural empowerment. Parenting and life skills consultants assist the counselors by teaching classes and going into the home. Child care coverage is provided for group times.

Predictably, women receiving services in the prenatal clinic after a process of screening and motivational counseling in prenatal care are often less ready to accept recovery resources wholeheartedly than the clients counselors are accustomed to serving. Most are not at their "bottom," have not yet experienced multiple losses, and are young and resilient. This is true early intervention and has the potential to save these families years of dysfunction, danger, and despair. However, it requires a counseling approach that can accommodate "prerecovery" behavior, including what may be a prolonged initial continued use and drinking, and multiple lapses and relapses. During transition to stable abstinence the counselor must maintain an abstinence and recovery focus and avoid abetting the patient's denial system, or scaring her out of prenatal care altogether.

For those women who are not ready to take steps leading to abstinence and a recovery lifestyle, prenatal care providers need to continue with medical monitoring and informal motivational counseling in the context of regular prenatal visits. Staff need to project acceptance of the patient while gently mirroring the dangers in her situation.

Training Prenatal Providers and Staff

To create an effective intervention system, prenatal care providers need basic training in perinatal addiction followed by continuing education. Cross-training with providers from collaborating agencies, particularly alcohol and other drug treatment programs and child protective services, is also helpful in providing integrated, consistent services. Training should include learning the interview techniques for patients in denial, a core knowledge about alcoholism and addiction and the medical consequences of drug use and drinking in pregnancy. Exercises that help staff clarify their own values are also helpful.

Because addiction is a stigmatized condition, and professional training in addictions is scanty, common misconceptions should be addressed directly. These misconceptions include the following:

- The alcoholic or addict *chooses* to behave as she does: for example, to become pregnant, to harm her baby, to continue to use.
- Her alcohol or other drug problem is only a symptom of underlying problems that must be solved first.
- Addicts and alcoholics do not recover, so why bother?
- My job is to change this woman and/or protect this fetus. If a patient continues to use or drink, I have failed.
- We need to teach her how to control her level and time of use. Abstinence from all mind-altering drugs is not necessary for lasting lifestyle recovery.
- A woman who is abstinent is in recovery.

The standard diagnostic criteria for use, abuse, and dependence on alcohol and other drugs should be taught (American Psychiatric Association, 1987). However, diagnosis is often uncertain even after multiple visits.

The responsibility of prenatal care staff is not to make a firm diagnoses. Instead, it is to accomplish these 3 tasks: (1) to identify risk; (2) to project a therapeutic posture of acceptance, hope, and advocacy; and (3) to continue to refer the patient to a designated team member with special substance abuse expertise. Staff training needs to emphasize and reemphasize that when any member of the prenatal care team has done these three things, he or she has succeeded in his or her professional responsibility to patients with alcohol and other drug problems. The staff member has succeeded whether or not the patient's attitude or behavior seems to change as a result.

SPECIAL MEDICAL NEEDS
OF THE PREGNANT ADDICT/ALCOHOLIC

Pregnant women present the disease of drug and alcohol dependence within a wide spectrum of severity. Many are early on in their disease. For many the inability to stop in pregnancy is the first visible sign that they are out of control and using compulsively. Others may stop successfully in pregnancy only to return to use, or progress in their disease, postpartum. Some have full-blown disease with multiple obvious life consequences such as arrests, loss of custody of children, and prior participation in recovery support systems.

For most of our patients the acuity of their drug and alcohol dependence is such that prenatal care per se need be little different for them than for women who are not addicts/alcoholics. Neighborhood health centers, family practice clinics, methadone treatment systems, private physicians, and other community-based health care settings can serve this population, many of whom will be far more likely to use local prenatal care than a high-risk perinatal center. If medical problems emerge, patients can be referred to a high-risk center following the same procedures used with other prenatal patients.

There are a few modifications of routine prenatal care that apply to all women thought to be using alcohol and other drugs. They should be scheduled for more frequent prenatal visits than other patients. Hypertension, poor weight gain, spontaneous abortion, placental accidents, fundus small for gestational age, maternal or fetal tachycardia, miscarriage, and preterm labor all increase in frequency in polydrug-using women. Screening for infectious disease should be intensified, with heptatitis B surface antigen and screening tests for tuberculosis done routinely. Syphilis screening should be done twice and HIV testing vigorously promoted. Endocarditis, skin abscesses, pneumonia, and sexually transmitted diseases in addition to those just mentioned should be expected in increased frequency. IV drug users should receive tetanus immunications if they have not been immunized in the past 5 years.

In addition high-risk urban centers where all patients have more risk, also include ultrasound at 20 weeks to evaluate anatomic anomalies (Evans & Gillogley, 1991) and nonstress tests, with biophysical profiles weekly, beginning at 32 weeks (M. Lee, personal communication, 1991; L. Yonekura, personal communication, 1991). When either hypertension or seizures are present, they may be drug related, rather than pregnancy induced (Goodlin, 1991).

Medical detoxification is needed only for two groups of pregnant women. In the first group are women currently dependent on opioids, for whom methadone substitution is the standard of care. In the second group are current sedative addicts (alcohol, valium-type drugs, etc.) with severe histories and apparent danger of seizures or vascular collapse.

Effective use of family planning modalities is especially difficult for the addicted and alcoholic woman, both during her using phase and during early recovery. Many women wish to have a child later in recovery and resent innuendos that they should be sterilized because of their substance abuse. A particularly important time for family planning is when women make the change from use of street heroin to use of a methadone maintenance clinic. At this time the menstrual cycle, and many other aspects of life, tends to regularize and pregnancy often results. Education about and specific referrals for family planning services should be part of prenatal care for all women, especially those with alcohol and drug problems.

HOW SHOULD PRENATAL CARE SERVE HIV-INFECTED WOMEN?

The same model of primary and secondary prevention and referral to and coordination with treatment services is applicable to pregnant women with HIV infection. Primary prevention includes providing for all women entering prenatal care routine education on how HIV is (and is not) spread and on how to reduce the risk of infection. Because the image still prevails that HIV infection and AIDS are limited to gay men, many women do not consider themselves to be at risk. Educational messages must be personalized as much as possible. More and more educational pamphlets, videos, and tools about HIV infection are being developed for women. Prenatal providers need to find materials that will communicate *as specifically as possible* to the patients they serve. The message about HIV and AIDS is so emotional and frightening that it can be obscured and misunderstood very easily. Language, educational level, socioeconomic status, and degree of acculturation all affect understanding. An integral part of primary prevention is follow-up by the prenatal care provider with specific questions to assess whether the information has been understood.

Risk reduction education for women of childbearing age must include discussion of safer sex practices, which includes helping the woman communicate with her partner about condom use. This communication requires women to act assertively about sexual matters, something many women are not used to doing and something many men do not welcome. Effective ways to develop women's safer sex negotiation skills include one-to-one counseling and safer sex workshops and support groups, where women can express their feelings, fears, thoughts, and beliefs and help each other develop confidence and ease in discussing safer sex practices with their partners (Kanuha, 1990).

At a minimum, all prenatal service providers should obtain in-service training on HIV risk assessment and risk reduction counseling and should have appropriate educational materials on site. Large clinic programs and prenatal service providers that serve women from the groups that are currently hardest hit by HIV infection may be able to have specialized HIV/AIDS educators/counselors on staff to provide the basic risk assessment and risk reduction education. However, even when a separate HIV/AIDS counselor is available, training for all prenatal staff in HIV/AIDS awareness and issues is highly recommended. Only with such training will a consistent message about the importance of HIV risk assessment and risk reduction be communicated to patients.

Secondary prevention includes offering HIV antibody testing (either on site or by referral) and special counseling for women who have identified HIV risks. If local prevalence of HIV infection is high, the recommendation of routine testing of all pregnant women may be warranted. If not, the appropriate presentation of HIV risk information should help identify women with risks. Those with risks should be encouraged strongly to have an HIV antibody test. Although the test will not predict whether the infection will be transmitted perinatally, several factors support the importance of testing. Specialized care and counseling can be provided for the woman if she is identified as HIV positive, which may include treatment for HIV infection and special monitoring. If it is early enough in the pregnancy, termination can be considered, although many HIV-infected women will not choose to abort (Hauer, 1989). In addition, special precautions to prevent spread of infection to the fetus at delivery may be taken, and preparation for special infant care and follow-up can be made. Finally, test results, whether positive or negative, are an opportunity for intense risk reduction counseling not only about sexual practices, as mentioned earlier, but also about needle sharing, needle cleaning, and contraception. If women are using drugs, HIV testing is an opportunity to facilitate enrollment into drug recovery services.

Because many prenatal care providers will not have the desire or resources to work intensively with women who are at risk of HIV infection or who are infected, it is imperative that they know the local AIDS/HIV resources. Some practices may choose to have HIV testing and follow-up provided by staff from a local AIDS/ HIV program (whether on-site or elsewhere), in which case procedures for effective referral, such as offering the referral or asking permission of the woman to have the referral agency contact her, must be established.

Issues related to the course of prenatal care for HIV-infected women include consideration of special medical care needs as well as attention to the mental and emotional needs of the women and their families. Because of the severe emotional response to a diagnosis of HIV infection and the rapid rate of change in management of HIV infection and AIDS, prenatal practices should work closely with local HIV/AIDS resources to ensure that adequate emotional and practical support is provided. Consultation with or referral to HIV/AIDS specialists for medical needs should be sought.

CHANGING PRENATAL CARE PRACTICE: WHAT WILL IT TAKE?

It is crucial that prenatal care providers take the lead in educating, identifying, and referring pregnant women who use drugs and alcohol and those at risk of or affected by HIV infection. Prenatal care is a critical but time-limited part of the continuum of services that families affected by drugs, alcohol, and HIV infection need. The prenatal service provider focuses on the health and behavior of the pregnant woman and, through the woman, tries to promote the health of the fetus. It is essential that the basic unity of the fetus with the pregnant woman is not overlooked. Oftentimes, there's a tendency to separate the fetus from the woman.

There are several different ways in which the appropriate counseling expertise for HIV, alcohol, and other drugs can be secured for a given system of prenatal care delivery:

- Obtain intensive training for existing staff, either through national training and technical assistance resources such as the March of Dimes, the Office of Substance Abuse Prevention, the Department of Health and Human Services, and appropriate professional associations, or through the local HIV, drug, and alcohol programs.
- Arrange with local resources to assign staff to provide services at your site.
- Become part of a local demonstration effort.

Another approach is to refer women who are found by history to require further assessment to a program outside of the prenatal site. The success of such a referral depends on excellent communication and coordination with the outside agency. Unfortunately, many women will not follow through on such a referral because it requires them to take direct action. One way to make the referral system more effective is to ask the prenatal patient if the referral program may contact her.

Some prenatal service providers are located in areas characterized by high levels of substance abuse and HIV infection. These private practices and clinics have the opportunity to extend their basic education, screening, and intervention activities to include more intensive collaboration with recovery or HIV/AIDS resources by incorporating these special programs into their prenatal services. In this instance, prenatal care (and, often, ongoing medical and pediatric care) is integrated with drug and alcohol recovery services or the HIV/AIDS service at one site. One way to create this "one-stop shopping" approach is for prenatal service providers to identify the substance abuse treatment and HIV services for women that already exist in the community and to link with them and work together to strengthen and increase what services exist. Collaborative planning can help ensure efficient use of resources and avoid duplication of effort. Participation of prenatal care providers in local coalition efforts can help direct community resources toward intervening during pregnancy and avoid adding another drug- or alcohol-exposed or HIV-infected infant to the overburdened child welfare system. Growing attention to the general problems of stalled or increasing rates of late or no prenatal care, low birthweight, and infant mortality have sparked various local, state, and national initiatives to improve birth outcomes. These efforts can be a source of support for developing perinatal substance abuse and HIV services that are linked to prenatal care or provided at the same site in an integrated manner.

Whether a prenatal service provider is offering drug and alcohol and HIV/AIDS services at the same site or integrating the recommended elements of primary and secondary prevention into the practice and whether the practice is a private physician's office, a large group practice, or an overburdened public clinic, it is essential to address the following issues administratively if these pregnant women are to be served well:

- Outreach (bringing women into care and helping them to stay)
- Personnel attitudes (selecting, training, supervising and supporting staff to work effectively with pregnant women who have special needs)
- Clear policies and procedures regarding education, assessments, referral, toxicology testing, informed consent, and confidentiality
- Resources adequate to support the required services

Outreach

Outreach includes a number of interrelated activities designed to encourage women to begin and continue in prenatal care. Women affected by drugs, alcohol, or HIV have many reasons to avoid prenatal care: fear of censure; desire to continue current behaviors; shame, guilt, and anger about previous negative experiences; and lack of insurance or other means to pay for care. Prenatal care practices that desire to be effective will consider what outreach they can do. One of the most powerful outreach tools is the provision of quality care in a respectful manner. Word of mouth travels fast. If prenatal staff are rude, rushed, condescending, or punitive, the word will spread quickly. On the other hand, if staff are compassionate yet firm in offering clear information about risks, support, and referral for identified problems, they will extend the availability and effectiveness of care.

There are numerous local projects that seek to address the worsening rates of infant mortality and low birthweights by deploying staff and volunteers to find pregnant women and bring them into care. It is essential for prenatal practices to become part of the local outreach and referral networks. One very simple way is to accept traditionally underserved women into care. Local and state health agencies are hungry for prenatal service providers to participate in the outreach and referral projects. In many cases the success of information campaigns and outreach workers is compromised by a serious lack of places to refer women once they express a desire to find prenatal care.

For women affected by drugs, alcohol, or HIV, successful outreach is enhanced significantly when outreach staff address their particular concerns. For example, in Contra Costa County, the prenatal service outreach projects provide regular training for staff on drug, alcohol, and HIV issues, as well as on available treatment and support resources. The outreach staff, who are drawn from the communities they serve, are intimately familiar with the prenatal service programs and other needed resources. They provide personal support to women, first by finding them at the shelters, soup kitchens, welfare offices, housing projects, and even street corners. Then they make appointments, remind the women of the appointments, discuss transportation and child care arrangements, and, if necessary, go out to find the women again when they miss appointments. A personal connection is established so that follow-up on referrals is assured.

One of the programs, Healthy Tomorrows, a project to reach African-American women, brought a drug and alcohol counselor onto the staff because so many of the women reached by the project were using alcohol and other drugs. The counselor provides recovery support to women who are being followed by the community health outreach workers. This model is proving to be a valuable way to support the early recovery of women who might otherwise have remained without care until delivery of an infant affected by drugs, alcohol, or HIV.

Successful outreach projects depend on the personal connections that the staff are able to make, both with the women they meet and between the women and the care providers. Outreach staff can be an essential ingredient to extending the effectiveness of the prenatal practice.

Personnel Attitudes

Prenatal care practitioners who wish to provide high-quality care will seek training for themselves and their staff in perinatal drug, alcohol, and HIV issues. As noted earlier, they need to know the nature of the diseases, the risks during pregnancy, the modes of screening and prenatal intervention, and the local referrals for treatment or higher risk care. If the office or clinic is seeing more than an occasional woman affected by drugs, alcohol, or AIDS, there should be ongoing staff support activities such as regular discussions and further training and participation in mutual support group meetings such as Al-Anon, Co-Dependents Anonymous, and AIDS support groups.

When selecting office staff, care should be taken to assess the applicant's attitudes about perinatal substance abuse and AIDS. Even the most caring person can have blind spots. These issues can turn kind, understanding professionals into critical, punitive, or excessively co-dependent persons who make excuses for clients and cover up for their dangerous addictive behaviors. Unless one has experienced it firsthand, it is hard to believe the power of addiction to distort the reality of each person caught up in it. Similarly, until one has experienced it firsthand, it is impossible to imagine the degree of health and well-being that can result from recovery activities. Supervision needs to include attention to the way each member of the prenatal care team functions around women who are affected by drugs, alcohol, or HIV. Do staff project acceptance and hope, or do they project judgment and anger?

Prenatal care providers should attend open meetings to become familiar with the principles and operating procedures of 12-step recovery programs so that they can make knowledgeable referrals. Prenatal service providers can join with others to bring to the attention of the public, other providers and policymakers the necessity for programs specific to women and to pregnant women.

As the perinatal HIV problem is concentrated currently in urban areas, virtually any provider who identifies an HIV-positive woman should be able to link, at the very least, with the local public health agency for assistance in finding HIV support services. The same agency can be a resource for continuing professional education and patient education materials.

One of the greatest challenges for prenatal care providers who are caring for addicts, alcoholics, or HIV-affected women is maintaining staff effectiveness. Staff (including physicians) need continuing training and specific structures for developing their resiliency and avoiding burnout. Chemical dependency and HIV/AIDS are devastating diseases that can sap the strength of even the most optimistic personnel. We cannot stress enough the importance of recognizing and combating staff co-dependency and burnout in an ongoing fashion.

Policies and Procedures

It is important to acknowledge the complexity of providing effective education, screening, intervention, and ongoing recovery and support coordination for women affected by alcohol, drugs, or HIV as an integral part of prenatal care. That is why each setting needs to adopt clear policies and procedures for carrying out the additional services. Unless there is consensus developed among staff and consistent use of the policies and procedures, many women in need of services will be missed and the stereotypes about who uses during pregnancy and who gets HIV disease will be reinforced. It is necessary to agree on the selection and update of educational materials; teaching guides for patient education (content and methods); a screening tool or list of questions to conduct basic screening; assessment protocols; up-to-date contact information for drug, alcohol, and HIV referral resources; a protocol for drug testing women in care; and procedures for coordinating the various elements of care, including adequate training on informed consent and patient confidentiality.

Coordination of Services

Coordination of care when women are referred out for assessment and/or recovery or HIV services presents a number of challenges. Coordinating prenatal services with the other crucial care elements of substance abuse treatment and HIV/AIDS support/intervention both eases the burden of responsibility on the prenatal caregiver and makes it more complicated. The situation becomes particularly complicated when issues of protection of confidentiality conflict with the need for communication and coordination between services. In some parts of the United States health care professionals are required to report alcohol- and drug-using pregnant patients to child protective services or law enforcement. Caregivers recognizing perinatal alcohol and drug problems as health problems are reluctant to communicate and coordinate with other services when this may lead to civil or criminal legal proceedings.

In addition, manipulation is one hallmark of the disease of chemical dependency. When a patient is receiving services from a number of different people at the same time, attempts to split the various professionals so that they argue with one another are common, especially if the patient is in denial, early recovery, or relapse. Prenatal care providers need to know this, see it for what it is—a symptom of the disease—and not be fooled by it. To avoid being fooled requires a willingness to learn the principles and languages of the coordinating services, especially the chemical dependency treatment and recovery field, which is probably the one that is most foreign to the prenatal care practice.

Coordination with treatment programs eases the burden for the prenatal care provider by offering the pregnant woman more specific expertise to guide recovery. However, a key function remains with the prenatal care provider: supporting and encouraging the recovery process. This means that when the patient appears intoxicated, the physician or other care provider confronts the patient about her behavior rather than acting on his or her preference not to discuss it. When the patient who has previously admitted to a serious substance abuse problem later denies it or states that she has it under control now and does not need any help, the physician confronts the denial and urges acceptance of assistance rather than colluding in the denial.

Regular communication among members of the treatment team needs to occur on at least two levels. Caregivers who are providing different services for the patient need to hold case conferences and formally coordinate their plans and strategies. Case conference time for all those involved needs to be a regular part of the job and valued as such. Case conferences are not only a time to agree on interventions but also a time to share information and perspectives across disciplines and to remain up-to-date about community resources.

Another level of regular communication to promote service coordination is on the agency-to-agency level. Woodruff and Sterzin (Chapter 9) describe the "transagency board," which supports "advocating on families' behalf in the larger society." In California 22 local coalitions have been funded to promote the development of interdisciplinary approaches to perinatal substance abuse. Participation by prenatal physicians and clinics in local boards and coalitions can promote shared understanding of local perinatal needs and resources, as well as cross-training among prenatal, substance abuse, and AIDS professionals. Coalition work is time consuming, but it is required in order to pool the resources and specialties that chemically dependent and HIV-affected women need. If interagency meetings to address these complicated issues serve only to inform participants of the various resources in their communities and to foster interaction among professionals from different disciplines who are concerned about the same women, albeit from different perspectives, they are a success. Often, interagency meetings go much further to advocate for the comprehensive prenatal services crucial to meeting identified local needs.

Confidentiality and Consent

The need to coordinate services presents a challenge to the issues of confidentiality and consent. Abigail English (Chapter 13) discusses with great clarity and depth the legal and ethical issues surrounding services for families affected by drugs, alcohol, and HIV. In prenatal services these issues relate to securing informed consent for tests and treatments and protection of confidentiality. As a general rule for promoting quality physician–patient relationships, prenatal service providers should obtain informed consent for all tests and treatments and should maintain the confidentiality of all test results and services provided. Yet possible exceptions to this rule immediately come to mind. Blind screening without obtaining informed consent is permitted when a protection of human subjects committee agrees the testing is for a legitimate purpose and when parallel services are available and offered to the patients being tested. For example, blind HIV testing of populations to develop prevalence rates for HIV infection is permitted as long as HIV education and testing is made available at the same time to the groups being tested blindly.

A clear exception to the rule of confidentiality is the requirement of all health, education, and social service professionals to report suspected child abuse to the proper agencies, even when the suspicion arises from information disclosed in confidential sessions. Professionals with this responsibility usually are careful to alert clients to this rule and certainly inform them when such a report becomes necessary. Both of these exceptions to the general rule of obtaining informed consent and maintaining confidentiality are granted because of the presumed greater good to be achieved. More knowledge of HIV infection prevalence is necessary to assist those at risk. Notification of suspected child abuse is critical for protecting child welfare.

Are there other circumstances that support exceptions? One common response of prenatal care providers to the challenge of identifying perinatal substance abuse or HIV infection is to propose testing without consent as part of routine prenatal care. State and federal laws and regulations strictly govern the processes for obtaining consent and maintaining confidentiality of HIV tests. However, rules for drug testing in prenatal settings are not as clearly defined. A key question to ask is whether testing without consent is the only way to assess drug use or HIV risks. Clearly, the answer is no. There are many historical, behavioral, and physical characteristics that can be assessed in order to assemble evidence of substance use, as well as HIV risk. This information can be summarized and presented to the client as part of an intervention, as described earlier (it is well to remember, however, that a positive toxicology screen test result only indicates use at a single point in time and is not by itself, useful in defining the pattern of use). Finally, a practice of testing without consent betrays the trust that should exist and be cultivated between caregiver and client. The very practical result of testing without consent may be decreased attendance at the prenatal care facility.

Random urine screening as part of an intervention process or ongoing treatment program is often a useful and effective tool for supporting recovery. However, women enrolled in the program should be informed of the program's testing intentions and should give their consent before testing is initiated.

The requirements for informed consent and protection of confidential information are designed to protect both parties; that is, to protect prenatal care practitioners from censure should tests or procedures cause unforeseen harm, and clients from physical or emotional invasion that they have not consented to ahead of time. These requirements are also necessary to protect clients from discrimination and other social consequences of their medical conditions. Addiction and HIV infection evoke fear and negative judgment from others. Loss of housing, employment, insurance benefits, and relationships with friends and relatives can result from the inappropriate disclosure of information.

Federal regulations governing drug and alcohol treatment programs that receive federal funds strictly prohibit the disclosure of even the fact of drug or alcohol treatment unless the client has given specific written consent describing what information can be disclosed and to whom. The client is permitted to revoke consent for disclosure at any time. These drug and alcohol confidentiality protections pose some specific challenges for projects that seek to coordinate a range of services for the prenatal patient. If the service components to be coordinated are different parts of one agency, information may be shared. However, if the program elements are drawn from different agencies—for example, a freestanding community prenatal clinic and a nonprofit drug and alcohol treatment agency—specific consent to share information across agencies must be given by the client. Federal drug and alcohol regulations require this specific consent, and the importance of creating a partnership with the client makes it highly advisable.

The difficulties are that alcohol and other drug dependence is a chronic condition characterized by continued use despite adverse consequences and recovery is a long process characterized by periods of relapse. Recovery is in the client's hands, not the caregivers. The client at any time may (and does) withhold or revoke consent to share information. If agencies take seriously the provisions of the confidentiality rules (and drug and alcohol agencies must because they risk severe penalties if they do not), a free exchange of information designed to assist the client may be stopped suddenly or prohibited from starting.

In Chapter 9 Geneva Woodruff and Elaine Durkot Sterzin argue eloquently for a transdisciplinary, family-centered community-based approach to serving multiple need families. They underscore the critical element of family involvement in the development and implementation of "a coordinated, cross-agency family service plan." Should a third exception to the general rule of maintaining confidentiality be sought in order to support the development and implementation of transagency service plans in the absence of client consent?

It is tempting to say yes. It is tempting to argue that the denial and manipulation inherent in chemical dependency require professionals to act for the client when the client refuses consent. But if client involvement is key to designing and implementing successful plans and if recovery resides only in the one who is recovering, then it seems that confidentiality rules and the limits clients may introduce into the process of interagency collaboration serve to remind us of the primary role the client plays in the collaborative effort.

Instead of decrying the rules, perhaps we can be inspired by them to build mutually respectful relationships with the pregnant woman for whom we wish to coordinate services. It then becomes vital for providers to involve patients in designing care plans for them. If the plans are the clients' own, then consent to share information is fairly well assured. And when progress slows and relapse occurs, even if consent to communicate across agencies is withdrawn, the task is to reestablish the relationship with the client so that progress and cross-agency communication can begin again. This approach requires prenatal care professionals to recognize our essential powerlessness in the face of the diseases of chemical dependency and HIV infection. It also highlights the potential power of collaborating with, rather then planning for, the pregnant woman we have chosen to serve.

RESOURCES

The activities that we suggest be added to prenatal care so that families affected by alcohol, drugs, and AIDS will be better served require additional financial resources. We have suggested some ways that these resources can be created: through sharing or borrowing staff, through building advocacy coalitions, and through additional training of existing staff. However, in the long run, financing mechanisms that support comprehensive prenatal services are necessary. Education, screening, prenatal intervention, referral, and coordination must become reimbursable activities.

There is growing recognition that prenatal education and support services are appropriate items for reimbursement. In California, MediCal (Medicaid) will pay for nutrition, health education, and psychosocial services during pregnancy. This policy change came about (in large measure) because a cost–benefit study was able to show how much money was saved from the decrease in the number of low birth-weight births when such services were provided (California Department of Health Services, 1984).

Numerous reports underscore the high costs of treating sick babies, costs that could be eliminated if preventive care were provided. The costs of caring for drug- or alcohol-exposed infants and HIV-infected infants are astronomical, in both human and financial terms. The medical, child welfare, child development, and educational systems all participate in caring for these children. Their parents often are supported by the public medical and welfare systems, and by the criminal justice system as well. Our economic system is bearing the cost of not addressing the needs of our most vulnerable families. How much better it would be if the preventive services we are advocating for were provided.

Within the past 3 years there has been tremendous growth in the number of demonstration projects developed to serve pregnant and postpartum women with alcohol and other drug problems and their infants. However, there has not been nearly the same response to the needs of HIV-infected women.

The danger is that after 3 to 5 years the demonstration projects will end and the enhanced services will disappear. One way to prevent this scenario is for prenatal service providers to advocate for their importance and for the importance of incorporating these services into regular or standard prenatal practice. An alliance among the worlds of prenatal care, HIV services, social services, and drug and alcohol programs could be powerful enough to make a difference.

A VISION FOR THE FUTURE

Caring for substance-abusing and HIV-infected women is not easy. It is, however, a tremendous opportunity to enlarge one's understanding of human nature and to be challenged to be more creative than one ever thought possible. Confronting the forces of infectious disease, addiction, and co-dependency demands compassion for oneself as well as others and humility in large doses. Many things are needed: training, outreach, advocacy, referrals, and perinatal-specific recovery and support services. But what is needed most is an unshakable belief in the ability and right of every pregnant woman to care for herself and her fetus when she is given the tools and assistance if need be, to do so. Our job as prenatal caregivers is to make sure that the tools are available to her, namely, access to care, education about risks, identification of problems, and support to find new, healthier ways to live.

RECOMMENDATIONS

We have divided our recommendations into three categories: policy, training, and services and resources.

Policy

Prenatal care in a form that meets the different needs of each pregnant woman is a necessary service for all women in order to promote the health of the fetus, infant, woman, and family. Women who have special risks due to drug or alcohol use or HIV infection are in particular need of prenatal care. State, federal, and local governments, the insurance industry, health maintenance organizations, foundations, and other policy research organizations all have a role to play in achieving the following policy goals:

- Guarantee all women financial access to prenatal care through such avenues as continuous and presumptive eligibility for Medicaid and expansion of insurance coverage (public and private) to include families without maternity benefits.
- Include reimbursement for the full range of drug and alcohol intervention and recovery services in new proposals for structural changes in our health care delivery systems.
- In proposed new reimbursement packages for health services include costs for the women-specific services that make participation in prenatal and recovery programs possible, including child care, transportation, parenting and child development classes, home visits, outreach, and case management.
- Continue research to map the nature, character, and extent of drug and alcohol use during pregnancy and of HIV risk.

Training

In order for prenatal care to meet the various needs of pregnant women for education, referral, and support, physicians, nurses, midwives, and other health professionals should receive training in drug and alcohol issues as well as in HIV and AIDS treatment.

- Professional schools and licensing boards should require initial and continuing education in the disease concept; the life cycle of treatment and recovery; the nature of resources for treatment and recovery; HIV risks; risk reduction education techniques; drug, alcohol, and HIV risk screening; and intervention methods.
- Professional organizations should work together to develop a standard of care that incorporates education, screening, intervention, and referral for drug and alcohol use and HIV risk into all services that reach women of

childbearing age (including adolescents). These services include family planning; school health; obstetrics–gynecology; pediatric; family practice; and sexually transmitted disease programs.

Services and Resources

Reaching women when they are pregnant about drug and alcohol issues and HIV risks requires that services be different. Prenatal care must change, drug and alcohol programs must be modified, and HIV services must reorient themselves to serve new groups. There are not enough services to meet these women's needs, and most are just beginning to learn how to respond. Special resources are needed to support the changes that are necessary. All the aforementioned groups should participate in the following activities:

- Continue research and demonstration projects designed to develop and refine effective services for families affected by drugs, alcohol, and AIDS.
- Disseminate research and demonstration results through nationwide training and technical assistance efforts.
- Create special outreach projects to find high-risk pregnant women, bring them into care, and then continue to follow them to encourage continued care. HIV, drug and alcohol, maternal and child health, and prenatal care projects should pool resources through jointly designed projects that cross-train staff and assure cross-referrals when women do seek care.
- Develop and make available to professionals in the fields of prenatal care, family planning, school health, pediatric care, family practice, obstetrical and gynecological practice, and sexually transmitted disease low-cost patient education materials in a range of languages, materials that are culturally and educationally appropriate and coupled with guidelines for their use.
- Implement as core components of prenatal care—HIV and alcohol and other drug education, screening, intervention, and referral coordination— and provide reimbursement for them. Use trained counselors on site in high-volume practices.
- Develop effective media messages, with well-funded campaigns, to inform the public of the risks and dangers of HIV infection, as well as drug, alcohol and tobacco use during pregnancy, with emphasis on including men as well as women as the targets for information. Media messages should consider the entire family as the recipient of this education.

Acknowledgments

The authors wish to thank Leslie Lieberman, MSW, and Jeffrey Gould, MD, MPH, for manuscript review; Katherine van Leuwen for research assistance; and Barbara Tarango and Collette Schulte for manuscript preparation. In addition, we are grateful to the Contra Costa County Health Services Department for additional financial support during the preparation of this chapter. The views expressed are solely the responsibility of the authors.

REFERENCES

Alan Guttmacher Institute. (1987). *Blessed events and the bottom line: Financing maternity care in the United States.* New York: Author.

American Academy of Pediatrics and American College of Obstetricians and Gynecologists. (1988). *Guidelines for perinatal care* (2nd ed.). Washington, DC: Author.

American Psychiatric Association. (1987). Diagnostic and statistical manual of mental disorders (3rd ed., rev.). Washington, DC: Author.

California Department of Health Services. (1984). *Final evaluation of the obstetrical access pilot project: July 1979–June 1982.* Sacramento, CA: Author.

Centers for Disease Control. (1992, January). *HIV/AIDS Surveillance Report.* Washington, DC: Public Health Service.

Chasnoff, I. J. (1988). A first national hospital incidence survey. *NAPARE Update Newsletter,* pp. 4–5.

Chasnoff, I. J., Lewis, D. E., & Squires, L. (1987). Cocaine intoxication in a breast-fed infant. *Pediatrics, 80*(6), 836–838.

Chasnoff, I. J., Landress, H. J., & Barrett, M. E. (1990). The prevalence of illicit drug or alcohol use during pregnancy and discrepancies in mandatory reporting in Pinellas County, Florida. *New England Journal of Medicine, 322*(17), 1202–1206.

Clark, W., & Midanik, L. (1982). *Alcohol use and alcohol problems among U.S. adults* (DHSS Publication No. ADM 82–1190). Washington, DC: U.S. Government Printing Office.

Evans, A. T., & Gillogley, K. (1991). Drug use in pregnancy: Obstetrical perspectives. *Clinics in Perinatology, 18,* 23.

Ewing, H. (1991, March). *Intervention in health services with alcoholic and addicted women.* Paper presented at the American Society of Addiction Medicine, Boston, Massachusetts.

Ewing, H. (1991). Care of women and children in the perinatal period. In M. Flemming (Ed.), *Addictive disorders: A practical guide* (Chap. 11, Mosby Year Book). St Louis: Mosby.

Gold, R. B., Kenney, A. M., & Singh, S. (1987). Paying for maternity care in the United States. *Family Planning Perspectives, 19*(5), 190–206.

Goodlin, R. C. (1991). Preeclampsia as the great imposter. *American Journal of Obstetrics and Gynecology, 164,* 1577–1581.

Hauer, L. B. (1989). Pregnancy and HIV infection. *Focus: A Guide to AIDS Research and Counseling, 4*(11), 1–2.

Institute of Medicine. (1985). *Preventing low birthweight.* Washington, DC: National Academy Press.

Institute of Medicine, Division of Health Promotion and Disease Prevention (1988). In S. S. Brown (Ed.), *Prenatal care: Reaching mothers, reaching infants.* Washington, DC: National Academy Press.

Jones, C. L., & Lopez, R. E. (1990). Drug abuse and pregnancy. In I. R. Merkatz, J. E. Thompson, P. D. Mullen, & R. L. Goldenberg (Eds.), *New perspectives on prenatal care* (pp. 273–318). New York: Elsevier.

Kanuha, V. (1990). Women and AIDS: Considerations for effective HIV and AIDS education. *California AIDS Clearinghouse Review, 2*(2), 1–5.

Little, B. B., Snell, L. M., Palmore, M. K., & Gilstrap, L. C. (1988). Cocaine use in pregnant women in a large public hospital. *American Journal of Perinatology, 5,* 206–207.

Malloy, K. (1990). [Anonymous perinatal drug prevalence study]. Unpublished data.

National Institute on Drug Abuse. (1989). *National Household Survey on Drug Abuse 1988 Population Estimates.* Washington, DC: Department of Health and Human Services.

Neerhof, M. G., McGregor, S. N., Retzky, S. S., & Sullivan, T. P. (1989). Cocaine abuse during pregnancy: Peripartum prevalence and perinatal outcome. *American Journal of Obstetrics and Gynecology, 161,* 633.

Public Health Service Expert Panel on the Content of Prenatal care. (1989). *Caring for our future: The content of prenatal care.* Washington, DC: Public Health Serivce.

Serdula, M., Williamson, D. F., Kendrick, J. S., Anda, R. F., & Byers, T. (1991). Trends in alcohol consumption by pregnant women 1985 through 1988. *Journal of the American Medical Association, 265*(7), 876–880.

Sokol, R. J., Miller, S. I., & Reed, G. (1980). Alcohol abuse during pregnancy: An epidemiologic study. *Alcoholism.*

Thompson, J. E., Walsh, L. V., & Merkatz, I. R. (1990). The history of prenatal care: Cultural, social and medical contexts. In I. R. Merkatz, J. E. Thompson, P. D. Mullen, & R. L. Goldenberg (Eds.), *New Perspectives on prenatal care* (pp. 9–30). New York: Elsevier.

U.S. Department of Health and Human Services. (1986). *The 1990 health objectives for the nation: A midcourse review.* Washington, DC: Author.

Vaillant, G. E. (1982). Natural history of male alcoholism. *Archives of General Psychology, 39,* 127.

III

SERVICES TO PARENTS OF DRUG- AND AIDS-AFFECTED INFANTS

6

Health Care Services for Children and Families

KAREN SOKAL-GUTIERREZ
HOLLY VAUGHN-EDMONDS
SYLVIA VILLARREAL

INTRODUCTION

Prenatal exposure to drugs, alcohol, and HIV infection can have a significant impact on a child's health and development and on the well-being of the family. While there are differences in the effects of substance exposure and HIV infection, there are many similarities in the special needs of the children and the services that might benefit their families. In addition, due to the strong association between pediatric HIV infection and parental substance abuse, many children and their families suffer from both problems.

The role of health care services is to promote healthy lifestyles for children and families, promptly identify health problems, and provide treatment and services that help families to optimize the health and development of their children. Services aim to assist all children, including those with special medical and developmental needs, to enjoy a normal and active life, living at home, playing, and going to school.

HEALTH EFFECTS OF PRENATAL DRUG AND ALCOHOL EXPOSURE AND HIV INFECTION ON CHILDREN

Prenatal Drug and Alcohol Exposure

When a pregnant woman uses drugs or alcohol, these substances circulate in fetal tissues and can disrupt almost any aspect of fetal growth or development. The effects of prenatal exposure to drugs and alcohol vary depending upon the particular substances used, the amount, the frequency, the timing during pregnancy, and other metabolic characteristics of the individual (Finnegan, Mellott, Ryan, & Wapner, 1989; Kaltenbach & Finnegan, 1989).

Substance-exposed children can experience a variety of effects with a wide range of severity, from little or no symptoms to disability or fatality. Symptoms can be short-term or long-term; they may be apparent at birth or not revealed until later in infancy or childhood. While few prospective studies have reliably detailed outcomes for drug-exposed children, many experts predict that the range of effects follow a normal distribution, in which the majority of children experience mild to moderate effects and a small number of children experience either no apparent effects or severe effects (Chasnoff, Hatcher, & Burns, 1982; Finnegan et al., 1989; Rodning, Beckwith, & Howard, 1989).

Prenatal drug or alcohol use commonly causes failure of the fetus to grow properly (intrauterine growth retardation), with stunting of weight gain, length, and sometimes head growth (microcephaly). Prenatal substance exposure can also cause premature birth of the baby. These babies may be born up to 4 months early, weigh as little as 1 pound, and require months of hospitalization and intensive care. Premature and substance-exposed babies commonly suffer from breathing problems (respiratory distress syndrome) that might necessitate ventilator support and from feeding problems for which nasogastric or intravenous nutrition may be necessary. They can experience sudden stoppage of breathing (apnea), requiring monitoring and cardiopulmonary resuscitation (CPR), and are at greater risk for sudden infant death syndrome (SIDS). These babies are susceptible to infections in the bloodstream (sepsis), pneumonia, and meningitis, which often necessitate treatment with intravenous antibiotics and can be fatal. They may suffer neurological problems such as strokes and seizures. In addition, prenatal substance exposure can cause congenital or birth defects, such as fetal alcohol syndrome (FAS), which can involve heart, facial, limb, growth, and developmental abnormalities (Bauchner, Brown, & Peskin, 1988; Chasnoff, 1988; Oro & Dixon, 1987; Ryan, Ehrlich, & Finnegan, 1987).

In addition to the toxic effects of drugs and alcohol on fetal development, these substances can cause addiction in the fetus and withdrawal in the newborn. The newborn may experience symptoms of drug withdrawal at birth, although symptoms have been reported to be delayed for up to 1–2 weeks and may last for months (Finnegan & Ehrlich, 1990). Symptoms of withdrawal include irritability, prolonged and inconsolable crying, tremulous and jerky movements, seizures, respiratory and gastrointestinal distress, difficulty feeding, difficulty sleeping, and increased sleepiness and lethargy (Collins, Hardwick, & Jeffrey, 1989; Finnegan & Ehrlich, 1990; Strauss, Lessen-Firestone, Stair, & Ostrea, 1975).

Information is limited regarding long-term outcomes for substance-exposed children. Beyond the newborn period the infant may continue to experience floppiness (hypotonicity), muscular stiffness (hypertonicity), and spasticity (cerebral palsy). In addition, many caregivers report persistent difficulty feeding and calming the infant. Some studies have also demonstrated poor growth and developmental delay (Finnegan & Ehrlich, 1990; Strauss et al., 1975; Collins et al., 1989). Some studies have reported that substance-exposed toddlers and young children may demonstrate difficulty concentrating, diminished creative play and spontaneity, poor impulse control, language and learning difficulties, and decreased fine and gross motor coordination (Chasnoff, 1988; Howard & Kropenske, 1990; Rodning et al., 1989).

While numerous studies demonstrate that substance-exposed children may experience health and developmental problems, most studies do not clearly delineate the effects of prenatal drug exposure from the effects of other prenatal and postnatal factors. In many cases substance-exposed children are also exposed to such other environmental factors as poor prenatal and postnatal nutrition, ongoing parental drug use, neglect, abuse, and lack of health care—all of which can also adversely affect the child's health and development. Experts agree, however, that whereas environmental hardships can exacerbate a substance-exposed child's condition, excellent care can make great strides in ameliorating the child's health and developmental problems (Beckwith, 1988; Chasnoff, 1988; Escalona, 1982; Lifschitz, Wilson, Smith, & Desmond, 1985; Regan, Ehrlich, & Finnegan, 1987; Rosen & Johnson, 1984).

HIV Infection

Over 80% of children with AIDS, to date, were infected with HIV from perinatal transmission from their mothers during pregnancy. The majority of these women were infected with HIV in association with drug use, either through their own intravenous drug use or through sex with a drug-using partner (Center for Disease Control, 1990).

HIV infection begins with an asymptomatic period in which the child appears healthy. Over time, the virus can damage the body's immune defenses and other organs and make the child symptomatic with a variety of illnesses. If the child experiences a certain combination of diseases associated with HIV, a diagnosis of AIDS may be made. Children with HIV/AIDS may experience growth problems or weight loss, developmental delay or loss of skills, and neurologic problems such as seizures, weakness, or blindness. In addition, they commonly develop swollen lymph nodes (lymphadenopathy), enlarged liver and spleen (hepatosplenomegaly), chronic cough, diarrhea, skin rashes, anemia, and recurrent infections, including thrush and pneumonia.

Children with HIV/AIDS can alternate between healthy and sick periods; between care at home and need for hospitalization; between mild effects and severe, disabling complications. Although acute illnesses may remit, the general course of HIV disease involves progressive disability (Hauger & Powell, 1990; Oleske, Connor, & Boland, 1988; Scott, 1991). The time course for HIV disease is variable: In some children the disease may progress quickly with severe illnesses; others may be healthy for years and deteriorate slowly with milder illnesses. In general, perinatal HIV infection is asymptomatic at birth, although the newborn may demonstrate symptoms of other problems such as prenatal drug exposure or prematurity. Symptoms may begin to develop over the first few months of life. A recent prospective study showed that 50% of HIV-infected babies experienced symptoms by 12 months of age, 78% were diagnosed with AIDS by 2 years of age, and 50% died by 3 years of age. Although the prognosis for many children with HIV is poor, some perinatally infected children have lived to 12 years of age (Scott et al., 1989).

Recent studies have shown that early identification of HIV-infected children and extensive care including meticulous home care, close medical follow-up, antibiotics and new antiviral treatments can significantly improve the health and survival of children with HIV. Experts hope that, with improved care, HIV disease will be increasingly regarded as a chronic, rather than a terminal, illness (Boland, 1987; Oleske, 1990).

PSYCHOSOCIAL ISSUES FOR DRUG- AND HIV-AFFECTED FAMILIES

Substance abuse and AIDS are diseases of the family; when a child is affected with these conditions, it usually indicates that other family members have problems as well. If the child was prenatally exposed to drugs, then the mother (and often her partner) has drug problems and other siblings may also be drug-affected. If the child was perinatally infected with HIV, then the mother (and often her partner) has HIV infection or AIDS and other siblings may also be HIV-infected.

Families of both drug- and HIV-affected children commonly face many psychosocial difficulties. Some of these problems may be long-standing, such as poverty, poor education, substance abuse, and parental HIV disease. Other problems may result from the stress of caring for a child with chronic health and developmental problems, terminal illness, and the stigma of AIDS. Families often struggle with guilt for having exposed or infected their child, depression, grief, anxiety, isolation, and anger. They must deal with logistical problems such as multiple clinic visits, transportation, and child care arrangements for their other children. They often struggle with financial problems, which may be long-standing or the result of expenses incurred and the difficulty of maintaining a job while caring for a sick child or other family member. They may have to deal with ongoing drug use, mental illness, violence, or marital problems, which are often aggravated by the stresses of chronic illness. Finally, they may also have to deal with legal problems associated with drug use, family violence, or discrimination as a result of AIDS. Experts agree that drug- and HIV-affected families often need considerable psychosocial support in caring for their children (Kazak, 1989; Lawson & Wilson, 1979; Septimus, 1990).

THE PHILOSOPHY OF HEALTH CARE
FOR CHILDREN AND FAMILIES

Preventive Care

Children's health services have been strongly focused on *primary care, health maintenance,* and the *prevention* of adverse health outcomes. Each family should choose a primary medical care provider for the child, either a physician or a nurse practitioner, whom they can trust. The primary provider should be available to see the child for routine checks and sick visits and to coordinate the child's health care with other specialists who may see the child. This model of health care has been proven to be more cost-effective and humane than episodic sick care and crisis management (Wise & Richmond, 1988).

In recent years the philosophy of health care for children has been redefined as a *partnership* between the child's medical providers and the family based on mutual respect and concern for the welfare of the child (Shelton, Jeppson, & Johnson, 1989). Medical professionals assume responsibility for periodically assessing the child's condition, recommending appropriate treatment and follow-up, educating the family about caring for the child, and helping parents to make significant decisions about the child's care. The family is responsible for the day-to-day care and nurturing of the child, early identification of illnesses, taking the child to the physician for evaluation, making informed decisions about the care of the child, following the recommended treatment regimens, and being the ultimate advocate for the welfare of the child. While drug-affected families often experience difficulties in caring for their children, most demonstrate concern for the welfare of their children, and the model of partnership is considered to be an effective approach to care (Lief, 1985; Woodruff & Hanson, 1990; Zankowski, 1987). Health and social service providers can best help high-risk families by carefully assessing them and gearing services toward each family's particular problems, needs, capabilities, and resources. Providers' efforts should focus on building on each family's strengths and facilitating the additional assistance that may be necessary, such as financial and social support, health education, or case management.

Comprehensive Services

The physical and psychosocial health of children are inextricably interwoven. Particularly for drug- and HIV-affected children, optimizing the child's health requires close attention to emotional nurturing and developmental stimulation as well as to the child's medical condition (Howard & Kropenske, 1990; Septimus, 1990). Accordingly, the model for health care for these children involves *comprehensive services* for the child, including medical care, developmental assessment and early intervention, physical therapy, and mental health assessment and counseling.

Comprehensive children's health services usually involve a *multidisciplinary team* with on-site physicians, nurse practitioners, registered nurses, social workers, and health educators. Many programs also refer patients to developmental specialists, nutritionists, occupational and physical therapists, and other specialists for services that may be needed. In addition to clinic-based staff, most programs rely on community health workers and public health nurses to provide intensive in-home follow-up for families. Periodic case conferences are helpful so that key staff members can share their assessments of the child and family and develop a coordinated plan for intervention.

Health providers value the multidisciplinary team approach for several reasons. First, owing to the complexity of the medical and psychosocial problems of the child and family, individual providers may feel unqualified or lack the sufficient time to address all of the child's needs. Second, since many drug-involved families are distrustful of "the system," it often requires several different providers to engage the family's trust in order to elicit the entire history and develop effective collaboration with the family. Finally, because of the many difficult ethical and legal decisions, such as referral to child protective services (CPS) for suspected child neglect or abuse or determining a do-not-resuscitate order for a terminally ill child with AIDS, providers find it helpful to confer among themselves (Allbritten, 1990; de Yanez, 1988; Howard & Kropenske, 1990; Seibert, Garcia, Kaplan, & Septimus, 1989).

Since few programs have the capacity to address all of the child's needs, most families are involved with a variety of agencies, including medical care; social services; early intervention programs; the Women, Infant, and Children (WIC) supplemental food program; and crippled children's services (CCS). In order to avoid overwhelming the family and needlessly duplicating services, it is essential that care be *coordinated* among the various providers. Either the primary care provider, a case manager, or an interagency council can serve this purpose (Woodruff & Hanson, 1990).

Family-Centered Care

A child's health and the family's well-being have a profound impact on each other. For this reason, health services for children have been found to be most effective when they care for the child in the context of the family. In recent years services have developed a *family-centered* focus, addressing the health and psychosocial needs of the key family members involved in the care of the child (Shelton et al., 1989). Health providers have tailored their services to address the diverse and often changing array of caregivers who may be responsible for the child, including birth parents, extended family members, and foster or adoptive parents. Although children are often cared for by single mothers, the involvement of other family members, especially fathers, should be strongly encouraged.

Programs have found that ancillary services for caregivers help to maintain the continuity and cooperation of high-risk families in the care of their children. Caregivers report that they have benefited from services such as drug treatment, parenting education, support groups, and family planning (Boland, 1990; Howard & Kropenske, 1990; Pietrangelo, 1990). There is preliminary evidence that teaching caregivers specific child care skills can improve the child's health outcomes, such as growth, development, and immunizations, and can decrease rates of neglect, abuse, and out-of-home placement (M. Sorenson and A. Septimus, personal communication, August 1990).

Community-Based Services

Some programs have extended the responsibility for partnership in the care of children to the community. Substance abuse and AIDS are, in many cases, enmeshed with poverty and lack of education, and ethnic minorities have been disproportionately affected (Escamilla-Mondanaro, 1977; Regan et al., 1987; CDC, 1990; United States General Accounting Office, 1990). Some successful programs have developed a *community-based* approach, using paraprofessional health workers to do outreach, enroll high-risk families, and provide prevention education within at-risk neighborhoods. Programs emphasize *culturally sensitive* services, incorporating staff from the same ethnic background as clients and providing cultural awareness training for staff from all backgrounds. These staff members are able to address clients in their native language, at an appropriate educational level, and with consideration for their particular cultural values. Many programs also utilize staff who are recovering addicts or alcoholics or people with AIDS who are "graduates" or current users of the program. These staff members often have a particular sensitivity to the needs of the clients, carry some credibility for "having been there," and may serve as role models for their clients (Stein & Jessop, 1985; Woodruff & Hanson, 1990).

THE SCOPE OF HEALTH CARE SERVICES FOR CHILDREN AND FAMILIES

Prenatal Care and Delivery

Based on the maternal–child health model, many programs aim to follow the substance- and HIV-exposed child from prenatal care through infancy. The *prenatal* component includes the usual obstetric care plus intensive assessment, education and counseling, testing, and treatment, if necessary, for drug use and HIV. If the pregnant woman is using drugs or alcohol, it is important to identify the problem and refer her to a recovery program as early as possible. If the woman is at risk for HIV, testing is also recommended as early as possible during pregnancy in order to facilitate decisions about the pregnancy and treatment for the mother and baby. Special attention must be paid to informed consent for HIV and drug testing and to ensuring the confidentiality of test results and other sensitive patient information. If disclosure of confidential medical information to other health or social service providers is necessary, it should be done with the patient's consent (Chasnoff, 1988; Minkoff & Feinkind, 1989). A prenatal visit to a pediatrician is highly recommended. This visit can begin to establish trust and to address any concerns such as the schedule for well-baby visits or follow-up for possible drug effects or HIV infection in the infant.

Labor and delivery involves close monitoring by the perinatal team of obstetrician, neonatologist, and pediatrician. Toxicology screening of the mother and baby may be helpful, primarily in order to identify any drugs that might acutely affect the newborn and to prepare for possible interventions to treat drug effects (Silver, Wapner, Loriz-Vega, & Finnegan, 1987). In addition, most programs maintain toxicology screens to provide evidence that may be necessary to use later in cases of suspected child neglect or abuse.

On the *postpartum* ward attention should be paid to the woman's physical and emotional condition. Efforts should be made to encourage bonding with the baby, such as arranging for rooming-in for babies who are healthy or facilitating visits to the baby in the nursery. Breast-feeding should be strongly encouraged except if the mother is HIV-infected or using drugs postpartum, since both the virus and drugs can pass to the baby through the breast milk (Chasnoff, 1988; Minkoff & Feinkind, 1989). The woman should have a postpartum clinic visit scheduled for 6 weeks after the delivery. If a woman is at high risk for medical or psychosocial problems, it can be helpful to schedule an earlier follow-up appointment. The physical and emotional health of the mother and baby should be thoroughly addressed; problems identified and interventions begun during the prenatal period need follow-up. In addition, family planning should be discussed and contraceptive supplies dispensed.

Neonatal Care

Neonatal services involve the usual newborn care with special focus on the assessment and management of drug effects, including withdrawal, as well as of other possible perinatal complications such as prematurity or respiratory distress. The severity of the baby's drug withdrawal is rated on a standard scale and periodically reevaluated over the course of the baby's stay in the nursery. This helps to determine what treatment might be necessary, to follow the course of withdrawal in the newborn, and to decide when the baby is ready to be discharged to home (Finnegan & Ehrlich, 1990).

If the baby requires intensive care, this can be very stressful for the infant and family. Staff should make efforts to minimize invasive interventions, provide nurturing physical contact for the newborn, and facilitate involvement and support of the family (Bauchner et al., 1988). If the baby is at risk for HIV infection, prompt testing should be done in order to plan for follow-up care and treatment. Informed consent to test the child should be obtained from the parent or legal guardian; a court order is necessary to test a court-dependent child. Again, special attention should be paid to ensuring confidentiality (Minkoff & Feinkind, 1989). A *discharge plan* is made, with input from the physician, nursing staff, and social worker. This plan outlines the newborn's condition, the standard and special care needs, the home placement of the child, and the recommended well-baby follow-up. A multidisciplinary assessment of the family's ability to meet the child's needs serves a dual purpose. The primary purpose is to determine and obtain the additional support services needed, such as baby formula, clothes, car seat, or more intensive education to facilitate the family's ability to care for the child. A second purpose is to determine the likelihood that, even with some added supports, the family may not be able to adequately care for the child's needs. This assessment of the child's risk for neglect and abuse informs decisions to refer the family to CPS for investigation, services, and consideration of out-of-home placement in order to protect the child.

The hospital staff educates the family about standard infant care, including feeding, sleeping, diaper changing, clothing, umbilical cord and circumcision care, car seat safety, well-baby visits, recognizing signs of illness, and taking a temperature. If the child has special care needs, the staff also educates the family, as needed, about drug effects and withdrawal, calming and feeding the baby, infection control, special equipment or medications, emergency measures, and follow-up visits (Schneider & Chasnoff, 1987).

Infant and Toddler Services

Well-baby health care visits are scheduled periodically according to standards promulgated by the American Academy of Pediatrics and the federal and state-supported program Early Periodic Screening Diagnosis and Treatment (EPSDT). Well-visits for infants and toddlers are scheduled for 2 weeks and for 2, 4, 6, 9, 12, 15, 18, and 24 months of age. For children with special care needs, health providers recommend more frequent or "interperiodic" well-visits (de Yancz, 1988, Mendez, 1990). In order to maximize continuity in health care for the family, it is preferable that the family receive well-baby health services from a provider associated with the perinatal services for the family, ideally the provider seen on the pediatric visit prior to the birth of the child. It is important that the health providers be familiar with the special needs of substance- and HIV-affected children and families. In general, however, it is not necessary to treat the children in segregated programs (e.g., for "crack babies"), which may be viewed as stigmatizing and may not address their particular needs.

At the first well-baby visit, a thorough *medical history* is obtained from the family, as well as the hospital records concerning the prenatal course, birth history, and family history. The prenatal history may include complications such as sexually transmitted diseases, drug use, and preterm labor; the birth history includes gestational age, birth weight, drug effects, and other medical complications and interventions; and the family history documents the health and illness of family members and pertinent features of the child's home environment, such as who the caregivers are, the ages of other children at home, the languages spoken, and whether there are any drug or mental health problems in the family. It is useful to inquire whether the family is involved with other specialists or agencies, such as public health nursing, a developmental center, CCS, and CPS. Finally, the discussion focuses on how the caregiver and child have been adjusting since discharge from the hospital, with the health care provider paying particular attention to the baby's general state; his or her pattern of feeding, sleeping, and elimination; and other concerns expressed by the parents. At subsequent visits the history focuses on the child's health since the last visit and on new developmental skills, behaviors, and relationships with caregivers and siblings.

At every visit the medical provider carefully observes the *caregiver–child interaction*, particularly noting the caregiver's degree of physical contact with the child and attention and responsiveness to the child's needs, as well as the child's response to the caregiver. The child has a complete *physical exam* for growth, including measurements of height, weight, and head circumference. Careful examination is made of the child's general appearance and the condition of the skin, eyes, ears, mouth, lymph nodes, heart, lungs, abdomen, and limbs. A detailed *developmental exam* is performed in order to assess the child's progress in gross and fine motor skills, social interaction, and language. Developmental screening can be carried out using a variety of instruments, including the Denver, Brazelton, or Bayley scales (Bayley, 1969; Brazelton, 1973). Pediatricians and developmental specialists generally agree that each screening test has areas of greater and lesser sensitivity in detecting the child's strengths and deficits and that no single test is perfectly adapted for working with drug-exposed children (Schneider & Chasnoff, 1987). Health providers can use the physical and developmental exam both to assess the child and to teach the caregiver about the child's responses (Griffith, 1988; Lief, 1985). *Laboratory tests* may also be done, including routine screening of blood for anemia and tests specific to the child's medical condition, such as HIV testing and measures of immune function.

In addition, other team members might evaluate the child and the family. For example, the social worker might take a more extensive psychosocial history concerning the family's basic needs, such as for money, housing, and food; any ongoing drug use or family violence; special areas of stress; and the family's sources of emotional and practical support. The nursing staff often has the opportunity to engage the caregiver in a more intimate discussion of her concerns and to observe caregiver–child interactions more closely.

On the basis of the history and observations of all team members, the physical exam, and the laboratory tests, the primary provider makes an assessment of the child's condition and *a plan* for the family to follow regarding the child's care. *Treatments* may be planned, such as the routine series of childhood immunizations at 2, 4, 6, 15, and 18 months of age. While immunizations are important for all children, they are especially critical for children with HIV infection or drug and alcohol effects, who may be particularly susceptible to illnesses (Hauger & Powell, 1990). Providers must be aware that children with HIV should receive special immunizations such as inactivated polio vaccine (IPV), instead of live oral polio vaccine (OPV); pneumococcal and influenza vaccines; and gamma globulin upon exposure to measles or chicken pox (Center for Disease Control, 1988). In addition, other medications, such as antibiotics to prevent HIV-related infections, may be prescribed, depending upon the medical needs of the child. Since new treatments for HIV are constantly being developed and the process of governmental approval of new drugs is slow, the prime opportunity for children to obtain special treatment may be through enrolling in clinical experimental trials run by a pediatric AIDS medical center (American Foundation of AIDS Research, 1990).

Extensive *health education* is provided for each family; the child's condition is described in detail, and the caregiver's questions are answered. Depending upon the needs of the child and the family, information is given on drug effects, bonding, calming, feeding, and stimulating the baby. The provider may demonstrate, for example, how to calm the baby by avoiding direct face-to-face contact, gently rocking the baby, and talking in a soothing voice. The parent can be encouraged to practice the skill under the guidance of the provider. All families are given information about concerns they should anticipate in the upcoming months, including developmental issues such as crawling, temper tantrums, and toilet training and the prevention of child abuse and injuries such as choking, falls, and poisoning (Howard & Kropenske, 1990; Ross, 1984; Schneider & Chasnoff, 1987).

In addition, depending upon the child's particular medical and developmental problems, *referrals* are made to clinical specialists such as an HIV program, pulmonologist, neurologist, nutritionist, or physical therapist. The child may also be referred to local programs such as CCS for medical case management and payment of services; a regional center for developmental evaluation, early intervention, and case management; and public health nursing for home visits. Maximal efforts should be made to help the family care for the child at home and avoid hospitalization or institutionalization. If hospitalization for acute illness is necessary, efforts should be made to involve the family and primary medical care provider with inpatient management and to facilitate a smooth transition back to home and outpatient care.

Children's and Teens' Services

While most programs for drug-affected families follow the children only through infancy, experts agree that longer follow-up is better for the child's health and development (Shelton et al., 1989). Whereas the standard schedule for health visits for well children is extended to every 1–3 years during childhood, children with special health or developmental needs, such as drug and alcohol effects or HIV/ AIDS, should be seen more frequently, depending upon their particular health status (Howard & Kropenske, 1990; Mendez, 1990). Health care follow-up for older children should be similar to that for infants and toddlers, involving a complete history of how the child has been and the concerns that the caregivers might have, staff observations of child–caregiver interactions, physical exam of the child, selected laboratory tests, and, if necessary, treatment. Health education should be provided for the child as well as the caregivers, and special attention should be paid to addressing the child at his or her developmental level.

As with caregivers of infants and toddlers, staff should explain the child's condition to the caregiver and answer any questions. They should also discuss upcoming developmental or behavioral issues, such as school, sexuality, and drug use, and focus on the prevention of child abuse and injuries, such as pedestrian and car accidents, falls, and drowning. Education for teens should focus on the prevention of unwanted pregnancies, drug and alcohol use, and violence. Referrals should be made to other services, as needed, especially for early intervention or special education if the child is found to have developmental delay.

Family Services

Since substance use and HIV are diseases of the family, parents and other siblings are often affected and all family members need to receive primary health care. It can be preferable for continuity to have one program treat the entire family. If family members cannot be treated by the program, they can then be referred to another health care provider (Woodruff & Hanson, 1990). In addition to primary health care, parents may also need treatment for substance abuse, HIV infection, and mental health problems. Postpartum follow-up should be provided for the mother, as well as sex education and family planning services, which are particularly important in order to prevent the unintended birth of another drug- or HIV-affected child and exacerbate the already difficult task of caring for a child with special needs (Howard & Kropenske, 1990; Kronstadt, 1989; Lambert, 1990).

Services offered to the family should provide both practical and emotional support. Services should focus on building upon the family's particular strengths and minimizing the difficulties of caring for the child's special needs in order to maximize the quality of life for the child and the family. Support groups are often of great benefit to families, providing an empathetic community and a forum for sharing coping strategies. Parenting classes, family therapy, 12-step recovery groups, respite care, and homemaker services are often helpful as well. Anticipatory grief and bereavement counseling should be available to help caregivers deal with the loss of the child, either through a change in placement or death (Howard & Kropenske, 1990; Boland, 1990; Pietrangelo, 1990; Doka, 1990).

It can be especially challenging for providers to work with drug- and alcohol-involved families. These families may exhibit inconsistent follow-up with treatment and hostile behavior. Providers should try to maintain the hope of helping each family but must also understand the chronic nature of drug addiction and resist interpreting a setback in treatment as a personal failure. It is helpful for the provider to establish reasonable goals for treatment and a clear plan of action with each family. In addition, it is important to set limits, such as refusing to see a client if he or she comes to an appointment intoxicated. Other helpful strategies include offering money or gifts, such as baby clothes and car seats, as incentives for follow-up. Some programs also use elaborate ceremonies to celebrate a family's successful completion of the program (Lawson & Wilson, 1979).

Child Protective Services

Due to their special care needs and the psychosocial difficulties that their families often experience, drug- and HIV-affected children are at particular risk for neglect and abuse (Regan et al., 1987). The health providers for all children, from neonates to teens, must pay special attention to assessing the adequacy of care of the child at each visit and refer the family for additional support services, if needed. Providers must always be alert to the possibility that even with additional assistance the family may not be able to adequately care for the child. In that case, the health provider is obligated by law to report the family to CPS for assessment.

In the perinatal setting the family should be assessed for the potential for child neglect or abuse as part of the process of discharge planning. Factors to consider include the family's previous history of child abuse, CPS involvement, and out-of-home placement of children; the family's current functional status and compliance with prenatal care visits; evidence of perinatal substance abuse, including toxicology screens; the family's shelter, social supports, and preparedness for baby care; and the family's desire and intention to keep the baby, their interactions with the baby in the nursery, and their ability to learn to care for the child's special care needs. Some delivery hospitals consider a positive toxicology screen sufficient evidence of potential for child neglect or abuse to warrant a referral to CPS; other programs require that additional poor prognostic factors be present in order to make the referral. Once a referral has been made, CPS standards usually require other significant evidence of neglect or abuse in order to justify removal of the child from parental custody. In California only 27% of infants referred to CPS are placed in out-of-home care (Senate Office of Research, 1990).

Providers of health services to infants and children must also be aware of evidence of child neglect or abuse. Warning signs include missed appointments, observations that the parent appears high on drugs, failure of the parent to touch the child or respond quickly to his or her cries, poor hygiene of the child, and evidence of multiple bruises or injuries. In addition, failure to thrive or inadequate weight gain or growth of the child can be a significant sign of neglect or abuse (Edwards & Gil, 1986). In HIV-infected children, however, failure to thrive is often part of the disease itself and does not necessarily indicate inadequate care of the child. The presence of a combination of the aforementioned factors should lead to intensive intervention on the part of clinic staff. The staff should have a case conference to assess the child's health and safety and determine a plan of action. The primary provider should discuss the concerns directly with the caregiver. Maximal efforts should be made to provide the family with specific education, supplies, and resources to help redress the problems. The parent should understand that the staff needs to have close follow-up with the family and must observe improvement in the care of the child over a certain period of time. If the signs of neglect or abuse are severe, the child appears to be in imminent danger, or the caregiver fails to comply with the agreement with the health providers, a referral to CPS should be made.

While families usually regard CPS involvement as a threat to their custody of the child, CPS referral should be considered part of the parent–provider partnership devoted to ensuring the welfare of the child. CPS policies require that "reasonable efforts" be made to support placement of the child with his or her natural parents, and health providers can provide encouragement and services to support parental custody. If, however, the safety of the child is in serious question, the child's health providers may be called to provide testimony and evidence supporting a recommendation for out-of-home placement. During a specified period of time the natural parents can be working toward reunification with the child. In many cases drug-using parents acknowledge that the desire to maintain or regain custody of their children provided the motivation necessary to break their drug habit and establish a healthier lifestyle for themselves and their family.

The possibility of criminal prosecution of a woman for using drugs during pregnancy poses a grave threat to a woman's life and liberty, beyond the threat of loss of custody of her children. This issue has generated enormous controversy and fear among patients, health providers, and legal advocates. Most health providers support public health nursing and CPS intervention to assist drug-using families and adamantly oppose criminal sanctions (Jessop & Roth, 1988; McNulty, 1987–1988).

MODEL HEALTH PROGRAMS FOR DRUG- AND HIV-AFFECTED CHILDREN AND FAMILIES

Many programs around the country have pioneered the model of comprehensive family-centered, community-based health care for drug- and HIV-affected children and their families. Several exemplary programs will serve as illustrations.

Kempe Clinic, San Francisco General Hospital

The Kempe Clinic in the Children's Health Center at San Francisco General Hospital was established to address the needs of teen mothers, infants with failure to thrive, and chemically dependent women and their children. The clinic's major objective is to encourage comprehensive health care and to prevent physical, sexual, and emotional abuse in high-risk families. Children and families are referred to the Kempe Clinic either prenatally, at birth, or upon identification of risk factors. Infants prenatally exposed to drugs or alcohol are identified by maternal history, toxicology screening, or withdrawal behavior in the nursery. The clinic has followed 150 drug-exposed infants and their families for 3 years. Medical conditions of these children include failure to thrive (15%), neurologic or developmental compromise (15%), and HIV seropositivity (2%). All family configurations are represented: 60% of the children are with their birth parents, 25% are living with extended family, 13% are in foster care, and 2% are in adoptive homes.

The clinic provides comprehensive primary care pediatrics in a team approach involving a pediatrician, neonatologist, nurse practitioner, social worker or counselor, nutritionist, masseur, and community advocate. The clinic staff is multicultural and bilingual. Routine health maintenance visits are scheduled in accordance with standard guidelines. Health and developmental screening, immunizations, treatment of problems, and referral to specialists are subsidized by the EPSDT program. Prevention education about drug and alcohol use, and HIV and sexually transmitted diseases is provided to parents. Confidential HIV testing with informed consent and counseling is offered to families at risk. The clinic encourages families' participation in parenting classes, support groups, infant–parent mental health treatment, and drug and alcohol rehabilitation. Housing problems are addressed, and enrollment of the child in special day care or Head Start is encouraged. In the event of suspected child neglect or abuse, CPS is notified and the family is assessed for their ability to adequately care for the child. Most infants and families are referred to public health nursing for in-home follow-up.

Longitudinal follow-up is planned for the children as they reach school age. Psychological and developmental testing of the children has been arranged, and evaluation of the clinic is in progress. Preliminary results indicate that the majority of the substance-exposed children are on developmental track and that their families are coping with the challenge of meeting the children's needs.

UCLA Department of Pediatrics Prevention/Intervention Model for Chemically Dependent Parents and Their Offspring

The UCLA program was developed in 1985 under a 3-year grant from the Department of Education to serve pregnant drug-using women and their families. Most families are referred to the program following the infant's birth. Key services include prenatal and infant health care; psychosocial, medical, and developmental assessments for the mother, infant, and siblings, case management; and intra-agency coordination. In addition, parents and foster parents are provided education regarding infant development, safety, and nutrition. Special attention is paid to assessing each infant's neurobehavioral status at 4, 9, and 18 months of age.

Three primary team members—a social worker, public health nurse, and pediatrician—assess each family and coordinate their treatment through frequent clinic and home visits. Staff are bilingual and receive ongoing training on a variety of topics from neurochemistry to drug treatment. The staff works closely with CPS, regional developmental centers, Visiting Nurses Association, the WIC supplemental food program, drug treatment programs, and CCS. The family's case manager initiates case conferences when needed. Staff case conferences are held once a week whereas interagency conferences average two per year per family. During a 12-month period the staff works with an average of five agencies per family and contacts each family an average of once a week (Howard, 1988). Staff have also conducted trainings for child welfare workers and public health nurses, both locally and statewide, to promote interdisciplinary teams of professionals working with families.

The UCLA program cites success in maintaining a consistent staff, coordinating care for their families, and reducing the number of foster placements for drug-affected infants. Success is attributed to extensive interdisciplinary staff training, intensive case management, and education for all family members.

Children's Hospital AIDS Program of Newark, New Jersey

The Children's Hospital AIDS Program (CHAP) of Newark, New Jersey, is an outpatient and inpatient hospital-based program designed to provide medical care and to promote the social and emotional development of children with HIV. The program's services are focused on keeping the HIV-infected child at home and assisting the family in coping with the medical and psychological aspects of HIV infection. It is estimated that 80% of the clients are seen on an outpatient basis (including home-based care) and 20% of the clients are being hospitalized at any one time.

The CHAP program is staffed by multidisciplinary teams of social workers, nurses, and physicians. Children with special needs are also referred to hospital subspecialists, including neurologists, child development specialists, radiologists, pathologists, hematologists, surgeons, and gastroenterologists. Nurses, some of whom are bilingual and bicultural, work closely with social workers to provide case management for each child. Case conferences are held weekly and care plans are reviewed. Once a month, a CHAP team assesses each child's course of illness, the home environment, familial coping, and the adequacy of home-based services such as speech and occupational therapy.

Children receive periodic developmental assessment at the hospital's child development center. The hospital's early intervention program is staffed by speech therapists, physical therapists, occupational therapists, and early childhood education specialists who assist the children in developing their speech and motor skills in order to enhance their learning capacities. For the families of these children, CHAP offers support groups and opportunities for education within the hospital and through community agencies. The program has collaborated with the state Department of Human Services Division of Youth and Family Services (DYFS) to develop case management and provide training for community agencies such as protective services, homemaking agencies, and transportation companies who serve HIV-infected children and their families. CHAP strongly supports maintaining clients in their homes, an arrangement that promotes a more individualized approach and is more cost-effective than foster care placement or institutionalization. Finally, CHAP has incorporated a component for staff support that includes monthly staff meetings to allow staff to vent their frustrations, grief, and despair. The program also offers continuing education to promote staff career development.

Weiler Hospital of the Albert Einstein College of Medicine Comprehensive AIDS Family Center

The Comprehensive AIDS Family Center of Weiler Hospital of the Albert Einstein College of Medicine (WHAECOM) is an outpatient and inpatient program initiated in 1984 to address the medical and psychosocial needs of the HIV-infected families in New York City. The Family Center serves over 300 children and their families, 60% of which include extended family members. Weekly clinics are run by a multidisciplinary team consisting of a social worker, nurse, and physician. A clinical psychologist is available to administer psychological tests, and consultation is frequently sought from occupational therapy, physical therapy, speech therapy, neurology, psychiatry, and dentistry. WHAECOM also provides extensive services to family members, including information and referral, medical care, psychosocial assessment, crisis intervention, family therapy, grief counseling, and support groups.

The Comprehensive AIDS Family Center works closely with several local agencies. These include the Bronx AIDS Task Force, foster care and adoptive services, and Birch Children Services, which is a transitional facility where children live prior to foster care placement. In addition, WHAECOM works with a medical assistance program of the Human Resource Administration that can provide a case worker, nurse, and homemaker for the family. WHAECOM staff participate in the Case Management Task Force for AIDS, which meets once a month. Other task force participants include administrators from the Human Resource Administration, local hospitals, and service providers. Members attempt to coordinate programs and policies to provide services in the most efficient manner for their clients.

WHAECOM staff believe that the strength of their program lies in the "one-stop shopping" approach, where all family members can receive treatment at the same site on the same day. In addition, staff is accessible by phone 24 hours a day. Staff are also given a considerable amount of independence and responsibility for their work with families. Monthly staff meetings are held to promote staff support and elicit ideas for improving the program.

FUNDING FOR PROGRAMS

Health care programs for drug- and HIV-affected families have utilized a wide variety of funding sources in order to support the extensive array of services that they provide. Most programs rely upon reimbursement for clinical services from private insurance and from federal and state statutory programs.

The Medicaid program, which is supported by both federal and state funds, pays for medical services for low-income families. States have established different financial eligibility levels, however, and some fail to cover a substantial proportion of poor families. The federal EPSDT program pays for periodic health assessments of Medicaid-eligible, as well as some other low-income, children from birth through age 18. It also funds community outreach to identify children who need preschool exams and immunizations, as well as follow-up for health or dental programs. It is designed, however, for preventive screening of healthy children and will generally not cover the intensive and frequent follow-up that may be needed for children with special needs.

CCS pays for medical services and limited case management for children with serious health problems such as AIDS or severe neurological sequelae of prenatal drug exposure. In addition, regional developmental programs may be available to pay for developmental services and case management for children with severe developmental disabilities.

Since the model programs for drug- and HIV-affected children also provide an extensive array of nonmedical services that are generally nonreimbursable, they must often rely on other sources of funding. Many programs have applied for funding from federal, state, or local grants. Some funding has been available for demonstration projects through the Department of Health and Human Services Maternal–Child Health Branch, Office of Human Development Services, National Institutes of Health, Centers for Disease Control, Alcohol Drug and Mental Health Administration, Office of Substance Abuse Prevention, and Department of Social Services. Most recently, the Ryan White Care Bill has made additional funding available for services for HIV-affected children and families. Private foundations, such as the Robert Wood Johnson Foundation, have also been an important source of funding. In addition, many programs utilize staff from county health departments and facilities as well as from university medical centers. Other programs rely on volunteers to provide some services.

PROGRAM EVALUATION

In order to determine the effective components of health care services, rigorous evaluations of the programs are needed. To date, however, few programs have undergone evaluation, and most definitions of success are based on the clinical impressions of health care providers. All of the programs contacted stated that their evaluation results were pending and that more evaluation of health services for drug- and HIV-affected families was needed (personal communication; E. Gross, August 1990; M. Sorenson, August 1990; A. Septimus, September 1990).

A number of factors are responsible for the minimal attention to program evaluation. When most clinical programs were developed, little attention was devoted to evaluation. Since many programs are financed by reimbursement for clinical services, it is difficult to devote resources to research, and most of the programs that are grant-funded are on such tight budgets that they have had to prioritize clinical services over research (A. Septimus, personal communication, September 1990). Many of those programs that conduct evaluations are run by clinicians who may lack technical expertise in evaluation research. Furthermore, it is difficult to evaluate clinical services, especially when it might be unethical or unfeasible to establish an experimental study in which a control group of families receives no services. In addition, significant controversy exists regarding the definition of a successful outcome and whether abstinence from drug use is a reasonable goal to expect with a disease that, by nature, is recidivistic. Other difficulties in evaluating programs include the small numbers of patients served, the short follow-up time, and the high dropout rate for many families.

Most of the measures used to evaluate programs focus on patient outcomes. Parental factors assessed include attendance at a prenatal clinic or a drug treatment center, decreased drug use or abstinence, prenatal weight gain, results of toxicology screens, parenting skills, provision of a safe and adequate home environment, and subsequent unwanted pregnancies. Child factors assessed include gestational age, birth weight, birth complications including drug withdrawal, results of neonatal toxicology screen, well-baby and specialty clinic visits, adequate hygiene and nutrition, growth, development, immunizations, incidence of child abuse reports, and out-of-home placement. Other evaluation measures involve outcomes for program administration. Factors that can be assessed include the number of clients served, client retention rate, the cost per client served, patient and staff satisfaction, and staff turnover.

BARRIERS TO CARE

The model of comprehensive, family-centered, community-based health services has held considerable promise for improving the health of high-risk families. The patchwork of services currently available, however, has had serious drawbacks. The fact that, for example, nearly 60% of California children and 75% of Blacks and Latinos failed to receive the appropriate immunizations by age 2 indicates that significant barriers exist to families obtaining appropriate health care (Scheiber & Halfon, 1990).

Lack of Access to Care

In many rural areas, in particular, clinic services are simply unavailable or inaccessible. For example, a typical rural clinic may be 1 or 2 hours' drive away, but with no public transportation available a family without a car would be unable to attend regular clinic visits. Major financial barriers exist to families obtaining needed health services (Miller, Margolis, Schwethelm, & Smith, 1989). The charge for a typical clinic visit—ranging from approximately $30 to $100 with some basic laboratory tests, immunizations, or treatments—would equal 1 to 4 days' salary for a parent working at minimum wage. Completing the standard schedule of six well-visits in an infant's first year of life often presents serious financial hardship for families. While many families get health services paid for by medical insurance subsidized by their employer or by Medicaid, it is estimated that at least 15% of all Americans (33% of them children) are uninsured—not poor enough to qualify for Medicaid in their state and yet too poor to afford basic health care (Davis & Rowland, 1990).

Exacerbating the financial crisis for families, many health providers throughout the country refuse to accept payment from Medicaid. Providers claim that Medicaid reimburses at such low rates (e.g., 46% of charges in California) that they cannot afford to accept Medicaid (Romney, 1990). In rural areas there are often no providers who accept Medicaid; in urban areas there are often only a handful of providers. The services that do accept Medicaid, usually county public health clinics and hospitals, are often severely overcrowded. Getting an appointment for a clinic visit usually entails a 1–3-month delay, which can seriously hamper attempts to obtain immunizations for a child's school entry, timely contraception, or early prenatal care. Clinic visits themselves often require the patient to spend nearly the entire day at the clinic, which is difficult for families that have other child care or job responsibilities (Miller et al., 1989; Romney, 1990).

Lack of Information

Many families are unaware of the importance of regular health care. In particular, immigrants from developing countries where children commonly become disabled from hearing, developmental, or orthopedic defects are often unaware that health care in this country can often prevent or ameliorate such disabilities. Whereas most illegal immigrants assume that they would not qualify for any public assistance, there are, in fact, health programs—such as WIC, EPSDT, and CCS—for which they may qualify. Even though illegal immigrants may qualify for some services, they often avoid using them for fear of being reported to Immigration and Naturalization and being deported.

Another problem, especially for ethnic minorities and non-English speakers, is that many services are not appropriately adapted to a family's particular cultural background. Patients may feel alienated by clinics where no staff member speaks their language or where they feel that medical personnel fail to understand their problems and "talk over their heads."

Special Problems for Drug-Affected Families

Many drug users miss clinic appointments and can be lost to follow-up for extended periods of time. There are a variety of reasons for this problem, including the transiency of the life of poverty and crime; the necessity of giving precedence to meeting the basic needs of shelter, food, or child care; and the decision to procure drugs over health care. In addition, drug users may not understand the importance of clinic visits or may be incapacitated by intoxication or mental illness. Many drug users also distrust "the system" and may avoid medical visits because of their fears of being reported to child protection or law enforcement agencies.

Many health and social service providers have negative attitudes toward drug users, which can set up barriers to care. Providers commonly experience anger and frustration toward drug-using parents. Child health providers often regard themselves as advocates for the child victim and may blame the parents for causing the child's suffering. Health providers may interpret a family's lack of compliance as a lack of concern for the child's welfare or as a rejection of their services. It is easy for health providers to feel overwhelmed by the extent of a family's problems and to avoid actively encouraging them to return for further care.

The unfortunate result of all of these barriers to care is that families often avoid bringing their children for regular health maintenance visits and come to medical attention only after a mild illness has progressed to a more severe one or to a chronic, disabling condition. Moreover, these families often see a variety of providers who are unfamiliar with the child's history, resulting in a lack of continuity of care.

RECOMMENDATIONS

Research

Further research is necessary to define the barriers to care and the interventions that are effective in improving outcomes for drug- and HIV-affected children and families. Some important research questions include the following:

- What are the features in prenatal care that motivate pregnant drug and alcohol users to recover from their addiction?
- For pregnant women who continue to use drugs and alcohol, do prenatal health services reduce morbidity and mortality in the infant?
- What are the features in well-baby care that motivate families to comply with recommended follow-up and care?
- Is education to prevent injuries and child abuse actually effective?
- Do home visits by public health nurses or community outreach workers reduce morbidity and mortality in children?
- Is CPS intervention effective in preventing morbidity and mortality in children?
- What is the minimum staffing and cost per patient required to provide comprehensive, effective health services for high-risk children and their families?
- Is funding by reimbursement for clinical services by Medicaid and EPSDT sufficient to provide comprehensive care for high-risk families?

Legislation and Policy

It is generally agreed that there are several barriers to care that could be alleviated by legislation and policy changes (Davis & Rowland, 1990; Jessop & Roth, 1988). Financial barriers to health care should be removed, ideally by legislating and funding universal health care coverage. Short of major health care reform, minor revisions that could be made include increasing Medicaid appropriations to expand eligibility to uninsured families; expanding coverage for transportation to medical visits, respite care, and home health aide services; and increasing reimbursement to providers. Additional public and private funding should be encouraged to support demonstration projects in drug and HIV prevention and treatment. In addition, since many families avoid necessary health services because of their fears of legal repercussions, these barriers need to be removed. Prenatal drug use should not be considered a criminal offense, and immigrants should not be deported for appropriately seeking care. Finally, confidentiality and antidiscrimination statutes should be strengthened and enforced to protect drug- and HIV-affected families.

Program Development

The results of evaluation research should guide the development and revision of health programs in order to maximize their effectiveness in serving high-risk populations. Successful models such as the comprehensive, family-centered, community-based health centers should be replicated. In addition, programs should be encouraged to develop other innovative models, such as clinics that unify health care, social services, and child care.

Training

Since the problems of drug use and AIDS cut across ethnic, neighborhood, and socioeconomic boundaries, all health providers need to maximize their ability to care for drug- and HIV-affected families. All health professionals—as well as social service, education, and legal professionals—need training on substance abuse and AIDS. They need to be prepared to identify families at risk, provide appropriate prevention education and services, and refer families to other community resources that might be of assistance.

Community Awareness

The prevention and treatment of substance abuse and AIDS must not simply be regarded as the burden of the health care system. Rather, what is needed is an affirmative and coordinated approach by health, social service, education, and legal professionals and, above all, the community-at-large in order to optimize the health and welfare of children and families in the face of this epidemic.

REFERENCES

American Foundation of AIDS Research. (1990). *AIDS/HIV Treatment Directory*, 4(1), 3–25.

Anderson, G. (1990). Children and AIDS: Crisis for caregivers. In G. Anderson (Ed.), *Courage to care: Responding to the crisis of children with AIDS* (pp. 1–16). Washington, DC: Child Welfare League of America.

Bauchner, H., Brown, E., & Peskin, J. (1988). Premature graduates of the NICU: A guide to follow-up. *The Pediatric Clinics of North America*, 35(6), 1207–1227.

Bayley, N. (1969). *The Bayley Scales of Infant Development*. New York: Psychological Corporation.

Beckwith, L. (1988). Intervention with disadvantaged parents of sick preterm infants. *Psychiatry*, 51(3), 242–247.

Boland, M. (1987, April). Management of the child with HIV infection: Implications for service delivery. In B. K. Silverman & A. Waddell (Eds.), *Report of the Surgeon General's Workshop on Children with HIV Infection and their Families* (DHHS Publication No. HRS D-MC 87-1). Rockville, MD: Department of Health and Human Services.

Boland, M. (1990). Supporting families caring for children with HIV infection. In G. Anderson (Ed.), *Courage to Care: Responding to the crisis of children with AIDS* (pp. 65–76). Washington, DC: Child Welfare League of America.

Brazelton, T. (1973). *Neonatal Behavioral Assessment Scale*. Philadelphia: Lippincott.

Center for Disease Control. (1988, April). Immunization of children infected with human immunodeficiency virus. *Morbidity and Mortality Weekly Report* 37, 181.

Center for Disease Control. (1990, October). *Center for Disease Control HIV/AIDS Surveillance Report.* (p. 8). Atlanta, GA: Author.

Chasnoff, I. (1988). Drug use in pregnancy: Parameters of risk. *The Pediatric Clinics of North America, 35*(6), 1403–1412.

Chasnoff, I., Hatcher, R., & Burns, W. (1982). Polydrug and methadone addicted newborns: A continuum of impairment? *Pediatrics, 70*(2), 210–213.

Collins, E., Hardwick, R., & Jeffrey, H. (1989). Perinatal cocaine intoxication. *The Medical Journal of Australia, 150,* 331–333.

Connor, K. (1990, July). *California's drug-exposed babies: Undiscovered, unreported, underserved: A county-by-county survey* (Report for Senator Diane Watson). Sacramento, CA: Senate Office of Research.

Davis, K., & Rowland, D. (1990). Uninsured and underserved: Inequities in health care in the United States. In P. Conrad & R. Kern (Eds.), *Sociology of health and illness: Critical perspectives* (pp. 249–263). New York: St. Martin's Press.

de Yanez, N. (1988). A multidisciplinary approach to developmental delay in high risk infants. *Delaware Medical Journal, 60*(3), 159–163.

Doka, K. (1990). Grief education: Education about death for life. In G. Anderson (Ed.), *Courage to care: Responding to the crisis of children with AIDS* (pp. 285–293). Washington, DC: Child Welfare League of America.

Edwards, D., Gill E. (1986). *Breaking the Cycle.* Santa Monica, CA: Association for Advanced Training in the Behavioral Sciences.

Escalona, S. (1982). Babies at double hazard: Early development of infants at biologic and social risk. *Pediatrics, 70,* 670–676.

Escamilla-Mondanaro, J. (1977). Women: Pregnancy, children and addiction. *Journal of Psychedelic Drugs, 9*(1), 59–67.

Finnegan, L., & Ehrlich, S. (1990). Maternal drug abuse during pregnancy: Evaluation and pharmacotherapy for neonatal abstinence. *Modern Methods in Pharmacology, 6,* 255–263.

Finnegan, L., Mellott, J., Williams, L. & Wapner, R. (1989). Perinatal e posure to cocaine: Human studies. In J. Lakoski, M. Galloway & White (Ed.), *Cocaine: Pharmacology, physiology and clinical strategies* (pp. 391–409). Boca Raton, FL: CRC Press

Griffith, D. (1988). The effects of perinatal cocaine exposure on infant neurobehavior and early maternal–infant interaction. In I. J. Chasnoff (Ed.), *Drugs, alcohol, and pregnancy and parenting* (pp. 105–115). Lancaster, UK: Kluwer Academic.

Hauger, S., & Powell, K. (1990). Infectious complications in children with HIV infection. *Pediatric Annals, 19*(7), 421–436.

Howard, J. (1988). *Project TEAMS (training, education, and management skills): Final Report: Meeting the needs of infants exposed prenatally to drugs.* Los Angeles: University of California.

Howard, J., & Kropenske, V. (1990). A prevention intervention model for chemically dependent parents. In S. E. Goldston, C. W. Albee, B. L. Bloom, E. L. Cohen, M. Swift, & T. P. Gullotta (Eds.), *Preventing mental health disturbances in childhood* (pp. 71–84). New York: American Psychiatric Press.

Human Resources Division, United States General Accounting Office. (June, 1990). *Drug-exposed infants: A generation at risk.* (Report to the Chairman, Committee on Finance, U.S. Senate, GAO Publication No. HRD-90-138). Gathersburg, MD: Author.

Jessop, M., & Roth, R. (1988). Clinical and legal perspectives on prenatal drug and alcohol use: Guidelines for individual and community response. *Medicine and Law, 7*, 377–389.

Kaltenbach, K., & Finnegan, L. (1989). Prenatal narcotic exposure: Perinatal and developmental effects. *Neurotoxicology, 10,* 597–604.

Kazak, A. (1989). Families of chronically ill children: A systems and ecological model of adaptation and change. *Journal of Consulting Psychology, 57*(1), 25–30.

Kronstadt, D. (1989). *Pregnancy and cocaine addiction: An overview of impact and treatment.* San Francisco: Center for Child and Family Studies, Drug Free Pregnancy Project.

Lambert, J. (1990). Maternal and perinatal issues regarding HIV infection. *Pediatric Annals, 19*(8), 468–472.

Lawson, M., & Wilson, G. (1979). Addiction and pregnancy: Two lives in crisis. *Social Work in Health Care, 4*(4), 445–447.

Lief, N. (1985). The drug user as a parent. *The International Journal of the Addictions, 20*(1), 63–97.

Lifschitz, M., Wilson, G., Smith, E., & Desmond, M. (1985). Factors affecting head growth and intellectual function in children of drug addicts. *Pediatrics, 75*(2), 269–274.

McNulty, M. (1988). Pregnancy police: The health policy and legal implications of punishing pregnant women for harm to their fetuses. *N.Y.U. Review of Law and Social Change, 16,* 277–319.

Mendez, H. (1990). Ambulatory care of infants and children born to HIV-infected mothers. *Pediatric Annals, 19*(7), 439–448.

Miller, C., Margolis, L., Schwethelm, B., & Smith, S. (1989). Barriers to implementation of a prenatal care program for low income women. *American Journal of Public Health, 79*(1), 62–64.

Minkoff, H., & Feinkind, L. (1989). Management of pregnancies of HIV-infected women. *Clinical Obstetrics and Gynecology, 32*(3), 467–475.

Oleske, J. (1990). The medical management of pediatric AIDS: Intervening in behalf of children and families. In G. Anderson (Ed.), *Courage to care: Responding to the crisis of children with AIDS* (pp. 27–40). Washington, DC: Child Welfare League of America.

Oleske, J., Connor, E., & Boland, M. (1988). A perspective on pediatric AIDS. *Pediatric Annals, 17*(5), 319–321.

Oro, A., & Dixon, S. (1987). Perinatal cocaine and methamphetamine exposure: Maternal and neonatal correlates. *Journal of Pediatrics, 111,* 571–578.

Pietrangelo, J. (1990). Caregiver support groups for foster and adoptive parents. In G. Anerson (Ed.), *Courage to care: Responding to the crisis of children with AIDS* (pp. 229–245). Washington, DC: Child Welfare League of America.

Regan, D., Ehrlich, S., & Finnegan, L. (1987). Infants of drug addicts: At risk for child abuse, neglect, and placement in foster care. *Neurotoxicology and teratology, 9,* 315–319.

Rodning, C., Beckwith, L., & Howard, J. (1989). Prenatal exposure to drugs: Behavioral distortions reflecting CNS impairment. *Neurotoxicology, 10,* 629–634.

Romney, B. (1990). *Code blue: The Medi-Cal emergency.* San Francisco: West Coast Office of Consumers Union.

Rosen, T., & Johnson, H. (1984). Children of methadone-maintained mothers: Follow-up to 18 months of age. *Journal of Pediatrics, 101*(2), 192–196.

Ross, G. (1984). Home interventions for premature infants of low income families. *American Journal of Orthopsychiatry, 54*(2), 263–270.

Ryan, L., Ehrlich, S., & Finnegan, L. (1987). Cocaine abuse in pregnancy: Effects on the fetus and newborn. *Neurotoxicology and Teratology, 9,* 295–299.

Scheiber, M., & Halfon, N. (1990). Immunizing California's children: Effects of current policies on immunization levels. *The Western Journal of Medicine, 153,* 400–405.

Schneider, J., & Chasnoff, I. (1987). Cocaine abuse during pregnancy: Its effects on infant motor development: A clinical perspective. *Top Acute Care Trauma Rehabilitation,* 2(1), 59–69.

Scott, G. (1989). Perinatal HIV-1 Infection: Diagnosis and management. *Clinical Obstetrics and Gynecology, 32*(3), 477–483.

Scott, G. (1991). HIV infection in children: Clinical features and management. *Journal of Acquired Immune Deficiency Syndrome, 4*(2), 109–115.

Scott, G., Hutto, C., Makuch, R., Mastrucci, M., O'Connor, T., Mitchell, C., Trapido, E., & Parks, W. (1989). Survival in children with human Immunodeficiency Virus type-1 infection. *The New England Journal of Medicine, 321*(26), 1791–1795.

Seibert, J., Garcia, A., Kaplan, M., & Septimus, A. (1989). Three model pediatric AIDS programs: Meeting the needs of children, families and communities. In J. Seibert & R. Olson (Eds.), *Children, adolescents, and AIDS* (pp. 25–60). Lincoln: University of Nebraska.

Septimus, A. (1989). Psychosocial aspects of caring for families of infants infected with HIV. *Seminars in Perinatology, 13*(1), 49–53.

Septimus, A. (1990). Caring for HIV-infected children and their families: Psychosocial ramifications. In G. Anderson (Ed.), *Courage to care: Responding to the crisis of children with AIDS* (pp. 91–106). Washington, DC: Child Welfare League of America.

Shelton, T., Jeppson, E., & Johnson, B. (1989). *Family-centered care for children with special health care needs.* Washington, DC: Association for Care of Children's Health.

Silver, H., Wapner, R., Loriz-Vega, M., & Finnegan, L. (1987). Addiction in pregnancy: High risk intrapartum management and outcome. *Journal of Perinatology, 7*(3), 178–184.

Stein, R., & Jessop, D. (1985). Delivery of care to inner-city children with chronic conditions. In N. Hobbs & H. Perrin (Eds.), *Issues in the care of children with chronic illness* (pp. 382–401). San Francisco: Jossey-Bass.

Strauss, M., Lessen-Firestone, J., Stair, R., & Ostrea, E. (1975). Behavior of narcotic addicted newborns. *Child Development, 46,* 887–893.

Wise, P., & Richmond, J. (1988). Preventive services in maternal and child health. In H. Wallace, G. Ryan, & A. Oglesby (Eds.), *Maternal and child health practices* (3rd ed., pp. 217–226). Oakland, CA: Third Party.

Woodruff, G., & Hanson, C. (1990). *Community-based services for children with HIV infection and their families: A manual for planners, service providers, families and advocates.* Quincy, MA: South Shore Mental Health Center.

Zankowski, G. (1987). Responsive programming: Meeting the needs of chemically dependent women. *Alcoholism Treatment Quarterly, 4*(4), 53–66.

7

Drug and Alcohol Misuse: Treatment Outcomes and Services for Women

MARIA NUNES-DINIS

While women drink less than men and consume fewer illicit drugs, their problems related to the use of alcohol and drugs are an important concern to public health officials and to those delivering a variety of public services. Specifically, the birth of drug-affected children has prompted many strong reactions on the part of officials and professionals delivering services. Drug misuse among pregnant women cuts across all racial and socioeconomic groups. Greater access to effective drug treatment is needed to reduce the creation of drug-affected infants. This chapter presents up-to-date information on philosophies, models, and effectiveness of treatment for cocaine, heroin, and alcohol use. When available, information specific to women is presented. Innovative and emerging programs for pregnant and postpartum women are also detailed.

The need for effective treatment remains great. In 1974, for example, 3% of all U.S. households reported cocaine use during a particular month. This usage tripled to 9% by 1979 and then leveled off to 7% in 1985 for persons 18–25 years of age (National Institute on Drug Abuse, 1988). Recent estimates from the 1988 national household survey by the National Institute on Drug Abuse suggest that the United States has 4 million drug addicts (Malcolm, 1989). Among clients admitted to federally funded treatment programs in 1981, 6% reported cocaine as their primary drug of misuse; 11% reported that it was the secondary drug and 3% the tertiary drug. Between 1970 and 1981 cocaine use doubled among methadone clients (Hubbard et al., 1989).

As cocaine use has grown, heroin use—especially heroin use alone—has dropped. Between 1969 and 1974, 82% of clients entering Drug Abuse Reporting

Programs (DARP) used heroin in the previous 2 months and 73% used it daily. However, the percentage of heroin users admitted to programs that were part of the Client Oriented Data Acquisition Process (CODAP) decreased from 61% in 1976 to 36% in 1981. Recent heroin users are more likely to use a variety of drugs, such as cocaine, marijuana, and alcohol (Hubbard et al., 1989).

Although alcohol use receives less public attention than drug use, it is a more prevalent problem. The prevalence of alcohol use in the month prior to report by all respondents between 18 and 34 years of age was about 70% (National Institute on Drug Abuse, 1988). While the difference in alcohol use between males (78%) and females (64%) aged 18–25 was not very large, a greater percentage of males (67%) than females (48%) over 35 reported alcohol use in the month prior to report.

Consumption patterns also differ between males and females. From the 1979 national survey of alcohol use and alcohol problems, Clark and Midanik (1982) reported the following differences between males and females for all ages: (1) 25% of the males were abstainers while 40% of the females abstained; (2) 20% of the men and 31% of the women were light drinkers; (3) 44% of the males and 27% of the females were moderate drinkers; and (4) 12% of the men and 3% of the women were heavy drinkers. Hilton (1987) reported similar findings with data from the 1984 general population survey.

There were also differences in alcohol use reported by the National Institute on Drug Abuse (NIDA, 1988) on other demographic variables such as race, education, and employment. For instance, more 18–25-year-old whites (75%) than Hispanics (58%) or blacks (57%) reported alcohol use in the month prior to report. More college graduates (82%) reported alcohol use, followed by those with some college (74%), high school graduates (71%), and those with less than a high school education (61%). Those employed full-time (76%) and the unemployed (70%) reported alcohol use more often than those employed part-time (66%).

While the demographics of persons in drug and alcohol treatment programs and callers to the national cocaine hotline should not be viewed as representative of the characteristics of users in the general population, the profiles of these two groups are, nonetheless, of interest. Those seeking help for cocaine use have traditionally been white, male, single, well educated, and employed. Public and private inpatient and outpatient treatment facilities manifest different client demographics. Public-funded drug outpatient clinics generally attract a client population with fewer economic resources than those using private inpatient hospital-based programs (Clayton, 1985; Means et al., 1989; Schnoll, Karrigan, Kitchen, Daghestani, & Hansen, 1985).

Findings from the National Drug and Alcoholism Treatment Unit Survey (National Institute on Drug Abuse, 1989) of clients in treatment in the fall of 1987 show that white males were the predominant clients in the 6,671 drug and alcohol treatment units in inpatient and outpatient settings. The treatment units reported having almost twice as many alcoholics (1,430,034) as drug addicts (834,077). Calls to the national cocaine hotline have shifted markedly in recent years and are now typically from less educated, lower income users (Hurley, 1989).

Highlights from NIDA's 1988 national household survey of 8,814 people aged 12 and older, a more representative sample of the general population, yielded the following results: Males represented 65% of the cocaine users, females 34%; and cocaine users were primarily white (69%), with blacks constituting 15% and Hispanics 13% of users. The prevalence of lifetime crack cocaine use in the U.S. population was 1% (2.5 million persons), while prior month use was less than half of 1% (half a million persons). Among heroin users, the lifetime rates were approximately 2% for those aged 26–34. Prior year rates were less than half of 1% and prior month rates were so low that the National Institute on Drug Abuse (1990) found it impossible to estimate the rates reliably. The proportions of demographic groups reporting any alcohol use in the past month were males (58%), whites (53%), blacks (41%), and Hispanics (46%). The proportions reporting heavy alcohol use in the past month, however, were males (8%), females (1%), whites (4%), blacks (3%), and Hispanics (5%). These estimates of drug and alcohol use are conservative because the 2% of the U.S. population who are apt to have heavy drug and alcohol habits, such as residents of military installations, correctional institutions, college dormitories, hospitals, single occupancy hotel rooms, and the homeless, were not part of the household survey.

In the following sections of this chapter treatment models and findings of cocaine, heroin, and alcohol treatment effectiveness and outcome are presented. Since treatments can differ from drug to drug, this chapter primarily addresses what is known about cocaine, heroin, and alcohol treatment efficacy. Although there is greater recognition of the need for more women-sensitive treatment approaches (Reed, 1987), treatment models that have been developed or evaluated have not been gender specific. The majority of clients in these studies are male. Hence, the generality of these findings on treatment effectiveness and outcome await confirmation with female subjects.

TREATMENT PERSPECTIVES

Drug treatment approaches derive from three perspectives: the biological, the psychological, and the sociocultural. Each perspective has generated different models. The medical model has developed from the biological perspective, the psychological perspective has inspired psychological and social learning models, and the sociocultural perspective focuses on persons in their social and physical environment. Finally, the biopsychosocial is an integrative model of the three perspectives (Institute of Medicine, 1990a).

Medical

In the medical model of treatment, addiction to drugs or alcohol has been described as a progressive disease requiring treatment and/or supervision by a physician. In this model the person is not responsible for such physical vulnerabilities as craving but is responsible for seeking treatment and preventing relapse. Drug treatment programs that include methadone or medications (e.g., antidepressants) are medical model programs. The clients in outpatient clinics may also receive counseling (Hubbard et al., 1989). Generally, the staff employed in methadone clinics are doctors, nurses, social workers, and counselors. Blockers such as naltrexone may be used to reduce craving of opiates. The medical treatment for cocaine addiction may include medications like tricyclic antidepressants and even bromocriptine (a blocker). Antidepressants may assist the powder cocaine or crack cocaine user during the period of neurotransmitter depletion. Thus far, however, there are no effective blockers for cocaine users that are equivalent to methadone for heroin users (A. Stalcup, personal communication, January 2, 1990).

Psychological

From the psychological perspective, drug or alcohol problems in people originate from motivational, learning, or emotional dysfunctions. Addiction problems may be seen as symptoms of psychopathology (intrapsychic conflicts) or the results of social learning (the behavioral model). For example, Khantzian (1985) argues that addicts do not choose drugs randomly but that their choice of drug is the result of the way the drug reduces their personal distress; cocaine has its appeal because of its ability to relieve distress associated with depression, hyperactivity, restlessness, and bipolar illness.

Social learning–based models closely follow from a psychological perspective: Persons who use drugs are considered to have deficits in social and cognitive coping skills that lead to an inability to manage everyday stress and that make them vulnerable to relying on substances in order to function. The social learning model may inform individual psychotherapeutic relationships, adjunctive psychotherapies (i.e., group therapy), and behavior therapy techniques (Institute of Medicine, 1990a; Marlatt & Gordon, 1980).

Sociocultural

In the sociocultural perspective, addiction problems result from lifelong socialization processes in social and cultural environments. The treatment strategy may include environmental restructuring such as alternative living arrangements and involvement with self-help groups. Social groups like family, church, Narcotics Anonymous (NA) and Alcoholics Anonymous (AA) are considered important influences on the person's drinking behavior, response to treatment, and resistance or susceptibility to relapse.

Biopsychosocial

The biopsychosocial orientation model integrates biological, psychological, and social factors in assessment and treatment of drug problems. There is recognition in this approach that problems are determined by multiple factors. This model recognizes that one or a combination of these factors may determine individual outcomes (Institute of Medicine, 1990a).

Even though treatment may be individualized in some places, programs that mix treatment models are uncommon. Treatment strategies are generally not individualized since it is practically impossible to operate a completely individualized program given the current system and its funding (A. Stalcup, personal communication, January 2, 1990). Within the same physical clinic, social model programs may operate alongside medical approaches without any integration of methods (Cynthia Hopkins, director of nursing at Haight Ashbury Clinic, personal communication, January 12, 1990). Typically, treatment counselors try to fit the client to the program rather than the program to the client. The most individualized drug treatment components are psychotherapeutic and pharmacologic treatments, which address unique client characteristics and personal triggers to drug use.

Until recently, treatment methodology was the same regardless of the drug used, with the primary focus being on the problem of addiction during treatment (Schnoll et al., 1985). The treatment community is increasingly endeavoring to apply different treatment models and approaches that are specific to the type of drug used (A. Stalcup, personal communication, October 30, 1989).

TREATMENT EFFECTIVENESS AND OUTCOMES

The Drug Abuse Reporting Program (DARP) was the first comprehensive nationally based evaluation of drug treatment effectiveness of community-based treatment systems from 1969 to 1974 (Hubbard et al., 1989). DARP evaluated primarily public-funded outpatient methadone, residential, and outpatient drug-free programs. There were no significant differences in outcomes (e.g., changes in drug use and criminal activity) among the treatment models. The main distinguishing factor of positive outcomes was not program type but length of treatment. For instance, 3 months was found to be the minimum time necessary to produce positive change, but additional positive outcomes resulted from increased time spent in treatment, up to a year. Hence, duration of treatment and program completion appear to be better predictors of positive outcome than other client and treatment characteristics. However, many of the findings of positive treatment outcomes have not been replicated.

The Treatment Outcome Prospective Study (TOPS) was the second large-scale study that described clients, programs, and outcomes of treatment (Hubbard et al., 1989); it covered the years from 1979 to 1981. A review of the TOPS literature indicates that for clients treated for at least 3 months, methadone maintenance and drug-free approaches were effective for up to 5 years at reducing overall drug use (heroin, cocaine, and nonmedical use of psychotherapeutic drugs) and effective in reducing criminal activity. For example, after the first year of treatment, regular heroin use for methadone clients was one-fourth of the pretreatment rate, regular cocaine use was halved, and regular nonmedical use of psychotherapeutic drugs was reduced by one-third. For residential clients, the posttreatment prevalence of regular heroin use was one-third of the pretreatment rate, regular cocaine use was halved, and nonmedical use of psychotherapeutic drugs was one-fifth. For outpatient drug-free clients, regular use of heroin and nonmedical psychotherapeutic drugs was halved, and cocaine treatment, though less effective, still decreased use by one-third. While use of most street drugs has been shown to decrease during and after treatment, alcohol and marijuana use tends to increase; relapse may occur within 5 years after treatment, but less than 20% of former clients in any given year treated by any modality were regular users of any street drug except for alcohol or marijuana. Clients in residential treatment for 1 year or more and those with at least 6 months in outpatient drug-free treatment were, however, twice as likely to have full-time jobs as those who remained less than 1 week in residential treatment.

Criminal activity was reduced considerably for clients in both outpatient and inpatient programs, especially while they were in treatment (Hubbard et al., 1989). Residential clients, compared to outpatient methadone and outpatient drug-free clients, had the highest crime-related costs before treatment in dollars per person per day because of their higher rates of criminal activity in the year before treatment and the higher proportion of criminal justice referrals (outpatient drug-free clients had the lowest costs in the year before treatment); the lower crime-related costs during treatment are largely attributed to the restrictive nature of residential treatment. Posttreatment costs for outpatient methadone clients were higher than pretreatment costs; this increase may be an artifact, since those heavily involved in drug use may not have reported criminal activities, thus resulting in an underestimation of costs prior to treatment. These clients may also have been in other restrictive environments (jail, prison, medical services, or other treatment programs) in the year before entering the TOPS program. In general, restrictive environments limit clients' ability to incur crime-related costs during treatment; therefore, such costs were lowest during treatment for all modalities (Hubbard et al., 1989).

The costs of drug treatment can be compared to the savings associated with lower crime rates of drug users during and after treatment. The greater economic benefits to society from residential treatment for drug users result from decreased criminal activity rather than from increased economic productivity from these individuals.

Reviewers of the TOPS program (Hubbard et al., 1989) note that longer-term impact of treatment was not examined and that differences in client populations across the modalities were not controlled for. Still, these findings indicate that drug treatment yields economic gains to citizens and to society from crime reduction. Related social benefits from gains in family stability and reduced foster care use by children of successful clients are also likely to be great.

Research Limitations

The generalizability of positive findings of drug treatment from both studies (DARP and TOPS) to current drug users is uncertain owing to changes in current patterns of drug use and in treatment programs. The methodological problems of these two studies, such as the absence of control groups and the lack of randomized clinical trials, makes it difficult to draw sound conclusions. Other factors, like older subjects, could account for the improvement in treatment outcomes (General Accounting Office, 1990; Institute of Medicine, 1990b).

Most of what is known across the major drug treatment modalities is based on data collected from DARP and TOPS between 1969 and 1981. In the last 10 years knowledge about treatment effectiveness has not grown rapidly since federal support for drug treatment research declined during the 1980s. Although federal support for this research has increased since the Anti-Drug Abuse Acts of 1986 and 1988, the number of researchers and centers has declined considerably since the late 1970s. For instance, there were approximately two dozen centers in treatment-oriented research on drug use in the early 1970s around the country whereas now there are merely a handful in a few major metropolitan areas. Research done from 1969 to 1981 on the effectiveness of the different drug treatment modalities shows that some modalities have been studied far more than others (see Table 7.1). According to the Institute of Medicine (1990b), the methadone maintenance treatment modality has been evaluated only in a few randomized clinical trials and quasi-experimental studies (e.g., when introducing a new treatment modality or closing a program or in an incompletely randomized trial using multivariate analysis). However, methadone maintenance has been assessed in numerous controlled-observation studies (i.e., studies of treatment cohorts that usually include the treatment refusals and have used multivariate analysis) and in simple observation studies (i.e., single studies of treatment cohorts without nontreatment comparisons and using only univariate or bivariate analyses). Therapeutic communities have not been evaluated in randomized clinical trials but have been assessed in a

TABLE 7.1. Research Techniques, Admissions, and Revenues across Drug Treatment Modalities from 1969 to 1981

	Methadone maintenance	Therapeutic communities	Outpatient (nonmethadone)	Chemical dependency treatment centers
Randomized clinical trials	Few	None	None	None
Quasi-experimental studies	Few	One	None	None
Controlled observations	Many	Many	Few	None
Simple observations	Many	Many	Many	Few
Annual admissions in 1987 (in thousands)	130	110	430	140
Annual revenues in 1987 (in millions of dollars)	200	200	300	500

From *Treating Drug Problems: Vol. 1. A Study of the Evolution, Effectiveness, and Financing of Public and Private Drug Treatment Systems* (p. 186) by Institute of Medicine, 1990b, Washington, DC: National Academy Press. Copyright 1990b by the National Academy Press. Adapted by permission.

single quasi-experimental study and in many controlled and simple observation studies. Outpatient nonmethadone programs have not been assessed with randomized clinical trials or quasi-experimental studies but have been evaluated in a few controlled observation and in many simple observation studies. The chemical dependency modality (which involves a 28-day stay in a treatment center) has not been evaluated on randomized clinical trials, quasi-experimental, or controlled observation studies; it has been assessed in a few simple observation studies. In Table 7.1, however, the total annual number of admissions and the annual revenues for methadone maintenance, therapeutic communities, outpatient non-methadone, and chemical dependency modalities show that the order of expenditure for the various modalities is the reverse of the order of knowledge about their effectiveness (Institute of Medicine, 1990b).

Drug and alcohol studies have had research limitations. Also, studies have primarily been organized under a single type of drug (i.e., the client's principal drug of choice). Nevertheless, reliance must be placed on this body of research to understand the usefulness of drug treatment for clients affected primarily by cocaine, heroin, or alcohol.

ASSESSING TREATMENT EFFECTIVENESS BY MEDICAL AND NONMEDICAL APPROACHES

The results of treatment effectiveness and outcomes from both drug and alcohol studies have been divided between medical and nonmedical approaches. The distinction used in this chapter is between those approaches that use medications as part of the treatment program and those that do not use any medications. The therapy techniques used with the clients may or may not be different between the two approaches and vary across programs within each approach. For instance, in so-called adaptive outpatient methadone and outpatient drug-free programs (e.g., DARP and TOPS), drug misuse is considered a "metabolic disease" that reflects a physical or biochemical deficit (Hubbard et al., 1989); abstinence is not the major goal of treatment. The symptom of craving is corrected by administering a daily dose of methadone, and clients are expected to remain on methadone indefinitely. Clients are also expected to develop vocational skills to hold a job. Counseling and supportive services are provided and viewed as adjuncts, and there are no provisions for withdrawal or aftercare. In contrast, drug misuse is seen in the change-oriented programs based on the psychotherapeutic model as a symptom of emotional disorder and methadone is seen as an adjunct to psychotherapy. The goal of change-oriented outpatient methadone and outpatient drug-free programs is to achieve drug-free living by prescribing the lowest level of methadone possible, resocializing clients back to the community and their families, and providing therapeutic activities along with services for withdrawal and aftercare. The two major beliefs of residential programs (e.g., therapeutic communities) are the following: (1) addiction cannot be cured but can be placed in remission by relying on self-help and support from other addicts, and (2) all aspects of lifestyle, attitudes, and behavior contributing to drug misuse must be changed in order to achieve remission. Residential programs rely on a self-help approach and on the use of program graduates as peer counselors. Group counseling or therapy sessions are usually confrontive and emphasize openness and honesty. The goal of treatment in residential programs is to change the addict's lifestyle completely, including the achievement of abstinence from drugs, the elimination of criminal behavior, and the development of vocational skills, self-reliance, and honesty (Hubbard et al., 1989).

The search for new medications to treat drug addiction in a controlled manner may have important ramifications. The current cocaine problem, for instance, is the fifth epidemic of stimulant misuse in our history (Gawin & Ellinwood, 1988). The first epidemic of cocaine misuse was in the 1890s, the second in the 1920s. In the epidemics of the early 1950s and the late 1960s amphetamine and methamphetamine, respectively, were the stimulants misused. Now it is powder and crack cocaine. Even if a new medication were discovered that could treat or control cocaine addiction, new street drugs would appear and would require yet other medications to treat or control them. Also, the problem with a medication that would treat cocaine addiction is that is is never a substitute for services that are often needed by users, including housing, job training, social services, counseling, child care, health services, transportation, financial assistance, educational services, and so on. Programs that incorporate social services assist users in developing rewarding new lifestyles to compete with their current drug-using activities (Reed, 1987; Sutker, 1987; Hubbard et al., 1989; E. Rahdert, personal communication, January 10, 1990). Hence, developing a medication every time there is a new drug epidemic merely substitutes drugs instead of addressing the social contexts and lifestyles that generate substance misuse.

In the following section, treatment effectiveness and outcomes are presented for cocaine, heroin, and alcohol. The literature on treatment effectiveness for these substances has been divided along the lines of medical and nonmedical approaches. Since problems with cocaine are more recent than those with heroin or alcohol, the development of medical and nonmedical approaches to cocaine-related treatment encompass more contemporary approaches.

Cocaine

Medical

While methadone is a substitute drug used to treat withdrawal from heroin, there is no similar substitute available to treat cocaine withdrawal. Extensive crack cocaine and methamphetamine use may create delusions, which can be treated with antipsychotic agents (e.g., Haldol, or haloperidol). For milder anxiety, mild tranquilizers (e.g., Valium, or diazepam) are used. Beta-blockers (e.g., Inderal, or propranolol), which lower blood pressure and heart rate, have been used to treat cocaine-induced anxiety states, hypertensive crisis, and/or other cardiovascular dysfunctions (Gawin & Ellinwood, 1988; Wesson & Smith, 1985).

Cocaine users have had some clinical trials with tricyclic antidepressants, such as desipramine. Gawin and Ellinwood (1988) reported an abstinence rate of about 90% for cocaine users treated with tricyclic antidepressants, compared to less than 50% for patients who were given lithium or methylphenidate antidepressants or who were treated in psychotherapy without medication. Gawin and Kleber (1984) reported that anhedonia (a limited ability to experience pleasure in life, which increases with cocaine use) diminishes with long-term treatment with desipramine. Clinical consensus indicates that the anhedonia of stimulant withdrawal usually resolves over time. However, anecdotal reports from Scandinavia and Japan and rare reports in the United States have described long-term, high-dose stimulant users with anhedonia, anergia, and a craving for stimulants even after 10 years of abstinence. It is possible that severe misusers may continue stimulant misuse to compensate stimulant-induced neurotoxic deficits (Gawin & Ellinwood, 1988). Tennant and Tarver (1984) point out that short-term treatment with desipramine does not assist in achieving abstinence from cocaine, a conclusion that is consistent with the physiological findings of Charney, Menkes, and Heninger (1981). Rosecan (1983) reports similar results from another tricyclic antidepressant, imipramine. However, Gawin, Byck, and Kleber (1985) and O'Brien (1987) report initial data from double-blind, placebo-controlled studies in which imipramine increased abstinence rates and decreased cocaine use, craving, and withdrawal symptoms. Golwyn (1988) reports successful results in treating 26 cocaine users with phenelzine, an antidepressant antianxiety drug that boosts the production of neurotransmitters (dopamine, serotonin, and norepinephrine) and that may also reduce craving. However, there is limited use of the drug because of its severe side effects and because of the danger attached to phenelzine-cocaine reactions (headaches, increase in blood pressure, fever, seizures, coma, or death). The risks attached to phenelzine limit its use to those patients who are not likely to relapse to cocaine use and require these patients to give informed consent to its use.

The effectiveness of medical cocaine treatments has not been conclusively demonstrated, and there is debate about some of the treatment approaches. However, professionals agree that dual users of cocaine (a stimulant) and heroin (an opiate) should not be placed in a methadone treatment program unless a physician determines that the person is addicted to heroin. If a person is not addicted to an opiate, methadone treatment may result in addicting the person to methadone.

Nonmedical

In the TOPS study, 1-year abstinence rates for cocaine useres who stayed in treatment for at least 3 months were slightly higher if they were treated residentially than by other treatment modalities (47% for residential, 40% for outpatient methadone, and 42% for outpatient drug-free treatment). The 1-year improvement rates for subjects in this study (defined as reduced or ceased cocaine use) in the year after treatment in outpatient drug-free programs was 77%; this exceeds the improvement rates of outpatient methadone clients (70%) or residential clients (68%). Hence, the most effective modality to reduce cocaine use depends somewhat on whether abstinence or improvement rates are used. Overall, treatments of equal length appear to yield equivalent results (Hubbard et al., 1989). These comparisons do not control for differences in client population across the treatment modalities, a variable that may result in different effectiveness rates. Changes in the use of one drug also may be tied to changes in the use of another drug; for example, abstaining from heroin during treatment may increase alcohol use or restrict cocaine use.

A review of cocaine treatment, which draws on clinical consensus rather than systematic data, reports that 30% to 90% of users in outpatient programs stop using stimulants (cocaine and amphetamines) while in treatment (Gawin & Ellinwood, 1988). Some studies have found that outpatient treatment is less effective than residential treatment in reducing cocaine use (Hubbard et al., 1989). However, most studies to date lack (1) comparable samples across treatment programs, (2) rigorous study designs, (3) follow-up on program dropouts, and (4) data indicating that one treatment approach is superior or even that specific patients should be matched to particular psychotherapies.

Heroin

Medical

The first methadone maintenance program was opened at Beth Israel Hospital in New York after Dole and Nyswander (1965) and Dole, Nyswander, and Warner (1968) demonstrated that opiate addiction could be treated with a daily dose of methadone. This mode of treatment for opiate use became accepted by the early 1970s, and the number of methadone clinics increased rapidly in that decade. By the late 1970s there were over 75,000 heroin users being treated in outpatient methadone maintenance treatment programs. In 1982, 41% (71,000) of the total clients in drug treatment were being treated in outpatient methadone programs alone (Hubbard et al., 1983; Hubbard et al., 1989).

The clients in the TOPS sample who were served in the outpatient methadone treatment programs in 1979 and 1980 differed from those in the DARP sample of 1969–1973. The TOPS sample had a higher proportion of females (31% vs. 22% in DARP), more clients over age 25 (76% vs. 52%), more non-Hispanic whites (43% vs. 16%), more persons with prior treatment experiences (73% vs. 49%), more clients with no involvement in the legal system (83% vs. 70%), and more clients using a variety of other nonopiate drugs like alcohol, marijuana, and cocaine. Assessment of drug use for those in the TOPS sample was more comprehensive than for those in DARP. Nevertheless, a higher proportion of TOPS clients appear to have used a large variety of drugs and used them more frequently. In TOPS, for example, over a quarter of the methadone clients had used cocaine and minor tranquilizers in addition to heroin. Marijuana was used weekly or more often by over half of the clients. More than half the clients in TOPS were classified as moderate or heavy drinkers. In fact, in the year prior to treatment, few clients were found to use heroin exclusively (Hubbard et al., 1983).

Outpatient program clients from TOPS (1979-1980) showed improvements after the first 3 months in treatment and through the second 3 months in the use of the primary drug on a weekly basis, drug-related problems, indicators of depression, commission of serious crimes, and full-time employment: There was a drop in the use of the primary drug from 80% before entering drug treatment to slightly over 13%, drug-related problems decreased from 79% to 18%, reports of depression dropped from 59% to 30%, commission of crimes was reduced from 26% to 12%, and full-time employment increased from 20% to 22% (Hubbard et al., 1983).

Tricyclic antidepressants have been used to assist patients with depression in methadone maintenance programs. Liu and Wang (1986) found that tricyclic antidepressants improved the therapeutic effects of methadone maintenance by reducing the need for methadone and the use of illicit drugs. Their study investigated the pharmacological basis of amitriptyline (an antidepressant), since it was reported to be widely used among drug patients. The results suggest that amitriptyline treatment prolonged methadone maintenance analgesia because it increased the sensitivity of the central nervous system to methadone rather than changed methadone maintenance metabolism.

Another medical treatment for heroin is levo-alpha acetyl methodol (LAAM). Zangwell, McGahan, Dorozynsky, and McLellan (1986) compared the effectiveness of LAAM with methadone. Their study compared patients who had been stabilized on LAAM but had stayed in treatment less than 6 months with other LAAM patients who stayed in treatment for at least 6 months. Although both groups showed improvements in the seven areas of adjustment (medical status, employment, alcohol use, drug use, legal status, family relations, and psychiatric status), the long-term group showed greater improvement in drug use, alcohol use, employment, legal status, and family relations. However, the long-term patients did not show improvement in the psychiatric area; instead, they reported increases in anxiety and tension. Long-term LAAM patients were then matched with methadone-maintained patients of similar background status who were on medical treatment for their addiction for the same length of time as the LAAM patients. The results were similar in most areas for both groups except in the area of general psychiatric status: The methadone group showed significantly fewer psychiatric symptoms than the LAAM group during the treatment period, which lasted for at least 6 months. For heroin users unable to maintain with high dosages of methadone, Tennant (1988) found that 9 out of 10 were able to maintain with LAAM, probably because the drugs involve different metabolic reactions.

Nonmedical

In the TOPS sample, for regular heroin users in the year before treatment, 1-year abstinence rates showed that over half of outpatient methadone clients and residential clients who stayed in treatment at least 3 months did not use heroin with any frequency in the year after treatment. One-year improvement rates showed that 7 out of 10 outpatient methadone clients and residential clients decreased or ceased heroin use in the year after treatment. Because of the small percentage of regular heroin users entering outpatient drug-free programs, abstinence and improvement rates were not calculated for this group (Hubbard et al., 1989).

Alcohol

Medical

Pharmacotherapies used to treat alcohol misuse include the following: antidipsotropic medications (which cause adverse results when alcohol is consumed), effect-altering medications (which are intended to diminish the intoxicating properties of alcohol), and psychotropic medications (which are used to treat depression, psychosis, or anxiety).

Disulfiram (Antabuse) is an antidipsotropic agent. Controlled trials in recent years have shown no differences in treatment outcomes between those receiving Antabuse and those receiving placebo. Findings indicate that the effectiveness of Antabuse is largely based on patient or client compliance. Compliance with taking Antabuse (or even vitamin supplements) was highly associated with abstinence rather than with specific medication effects. Motivational strategies to increase compliance (i.e., the presence of a spouse who provides praise and support) resulted in better treatment outcomes at 6-month follow-up. Moreover, there are side effects (i.e., increased sexual dysfunction or craving for alcohol) associated with long-term use of disulfiram that must be taken into consideration, given the lack of evidence of its effectiveness (Institute of Medicine, 1990a).

Effect-altering medications like zimelidine, citalopram, fluoxetine, indalpine, viqualine, fluvoxamine, alaproclate, and norzimelidine are serotonin uptake inhibitors that reduce the intoxicating effects of alcohol without producing illness. Alcohol intake has been reduced in animals taking these medications. Humans taking zimelidine and citalopram also reduce alcohol intake. For heavy drinkers, zimelidine was found to increase the number of abstinent days. However, because zimelidine produces flu-like symptoms and neuropathy, it has been removed from human use. At this time in the United States, only fluoxetine is approved for treatment of depressive disorders; it has been tested only among heavy drinkers. Fluoxetine does not increase blood alcohol levels, but rather seems to affect the initiation of drinking rather than moderating it, and does not synergistically with alcohol on physiologic, psychometric, and psychomotor activity (Institute of Medicine, 1990a).

Psychotropic medications are used for detoxification, to decrease the desire for alcohol, and in treatment of "dual diagnosis" patients (individuals with both alcohol problems and psychopathology). There were no significant treatment differences found between alcoholics who were given lithium and those who received a placebo. Compliance with either lithium or a placebo was highly associated with abstinence. Alcoholics with a dual diagnosis have a poor prognosis and a high rate of treatment dropout. Although it has not been conclusively demonstrated that treating alcoholics with a dual diagnosis produces positive treatment results, it is logical to assume that treating both problems simultaneously is likely to improve outcomes. However, it is important that sufficient time pass for complete withdrawal from misused substances and that a diagnosis be established before psychotropic medications are prescribed (Institute of Medicine, 1990a).

Currently, there is no medication that cures alcohol misuse. Pharmacotherapy is an adjunct treatment to be used with other strategies; medications are not a "cure" for alcohol problems but are considered aids to recovery (Institute of Medicine, 1990a).

Nonmedical

The Institute of Medicine (1990a) recently reported several conclusions about alcohol treatment outcome:

1. In controlled studies a variety of specific treatment methods, including pharmacotherapy, aversion therapy (a method that employs imagery and covert sensitization), conjoint therapies with couples and families, and broad-spectrum treatment strategies such as social skills training and stress management, have been associated with improved treatment outcome when compared to no treatment or alternative treatments.

2. There is no single approach that is more effective than any other. While there are several available treatment alternatives, different treatments may be optimal for different types of individuals. Thus, studies have found that matching individuals to specific treatments on such variables as demographic factors (e.g., marital status), psychiatric diagnoses (e.g., depression), personality factors (e.g., locus of control, self-image), severity of alcohol problem (e.g., Jellinek classification, alcohol dependence), and antecedents to drinking (e.g., anxiety related to drinking, situational factors) may improve treatment outcome.

3. Therapist skills and characteristics appear to influence treatment outcome.

4. There are no major differences found in treatment outcome studies between residential and outpatient programs or between longer versus shorter inpatient programs. Residential programs are considered more appropriate for the homeless, the unemployed, and those with severe levels of alcohol dependence and psychopathology.

5. Treatment cost is greater for residential or inpatient programs.

6. Treating other life problems related to drinking can improve outcome in persons with alcohol problems.

7. Treatment process factors, posttreatment adjustment factors, the character-

istics of individuals seeking treatment, the characteristics of their problems, and interactions among all these factors determine treatment outcome.

DRUG AND ALCOHOL TREATMENT FOR WOMEN

Very little is known about drug and alcohol treatment outcomes of women-sensitive or women-oriented services because drug treatment programs offer few alternatives that could be evaluated for women (Reed, 1987). Treatment outcome measures often include activities, like violent crime, that are more common for men than for women. (On the other hand, the ability to care for children, which is considered a critical outcome indicator for women, is rarely assessed in men. Skill and participation as parents and family members and interpersonal relationships are important outcome indicators for all clients.)

There are treatments (family therapy, group therapy) and treatment conditions (separate treatment for men and women; use of female therapists) that have been endorsed for women with alcohol problems. Studies have generally supported the following conclusions with respect to women: Group therapy is more effective than individual therapy, family therapy is more effective than other modalities, the sexes should be treated separately, and female therapists are more effective than male therapists. However, there is very little evidence to show that one treatment modality is more effective than another for women (Institute of Medicine, 1990a).

Clinical data suggest different treatment program considerations for female versus male alcoholics. Findings indicate that female alcoholics are more likely than male alcoholics to have (1) a primary affective disorder (depressed or sad mood states), (2) liver disease, (3) marital instability, (4) family-of-origin instability, (5) a spouse or partner with alcohol problems, (6) low self-esteem, (7) drinking as a response to major life crises, (8) a history of sexual abuse, (9) family and friends opposing treatment, and (10) child care responsibilities, reflecting the fact that many are divorced or single heads of households (Institute of Medicine, 1990a). These differences between men and women with alcohol problems seem to indicate that better treatment outcomes for women could be obtained with treatment programs offering child care, assessment of psychiatric and medical disorders, treatment for depression, methods to build self-esteem (e.g., skills training), support and education for family and friends, staff to work with families, and the teaching of coping strategies to deal with stress. The value of these recommendations for women, however, remains speculative without further controlled studies. Also, these services may be just as important in improving outcome for those men who do not do well in standard treatment (Institute of Medicine, 1990a).

According to the 1987 National Drug and Alcoholism Treatment Unit Survey (National Institute on Drug Abuse, 1989), approximately 85% of persons in public and private alcohol and drug treatment were in outpatient/nonresidential care; this percentage includes those in aftercare. There are some residential programs around the country that are tailored specifically to treat women with drug and/or alcohol problems and that allow their children to live with them. One example is MABON (Mother and Babies Off Narcotics), located on Wards Island, New York, and run by Odyssey House ("Crack Mothers," 1989). At one time the residents were primarily in treatment for heroin; today they are being treated for crack cocaine. Currently, there are 20 women and 23 children enrolled in the program. The average age of the women in the program is 29. With the children in nurseries or preschool, the women participate in group therapy, encounter groups, or individual therapy; work toward their G.E.D.'s; and take vocational training courses. The program is supported by public funds and costs between $30,000 and $40,000 per family unit per year. MABON reports that about 48% of their enrollees graduate, as compared to 25%–30% for other residential drug treatment programs. The Rectory in Vallejo, California, a similar program that treats women with drug and alcohol problems, reports that the method of entry affects outcome; 8 of 13 graduates (or 2%) who entered the program voluntarily were "clean and sober" 1 year later whereas only 1 of 5 women (or 20%) who entered the program because of a child protective service referral was sober and drug-free at 1-year follow-up (A. Becnel, director of the Rectory, personal communication, January 12, 1990).

Services for Pregnant and Postpartum Women Using Drugs

Estimates of the percentage of infants exposed to illicit drugs during gestation range from 2% to 11% (California State Department of Alcohol and Drug Programs, 1989; "Many Unborn," 1988). The estimated number of babies born in New York, for instance, to substance-abusing mothers in 1989 was 10,000. If even one quarter of the mothers of these babies were treated at residential centers, at $30,000–$40,000 per family unit, the cost of their treatment would range up to 100 million dollars. Residential programs of alternative lengths and formats are clearly needed to provide reasonable cost alternatives. Given the additional incentives for recovery in women who wish to give birth to drug-free children and maintain the care of their children, women-centered approaches have particular promise.

To build on the little that is known about the efficacy of drug treatment for women, the National Institute on Drug Abuse (NIDA) has recently funded 20 programs (10 programs were funded in October 1989 and 10 in October 1990) as demonstration projects to study polydrug treatment outcome among women and their infants. These projects are 5-year demonstration research projects. The effectiveness of the programs will be assessed not only on the basis of the physical and mental health of the mother but on their impact on the baby as well. Measures of treatment effectiveness will include determinations of each woman's communication skills; relationship with her spouse and child; ability to handle her infant; psychological, medical, and nutritional status; progress in vocational training; and performance in the parenting class, as well as assessment of the neonate's health and development. The program will also measure drug treatment outcomes, educational pursuits, reduction in criminal activity, and, if appropriate, increased vocational study (E. Rahdert, personal communication, December 5, 1989, and October 2, 1990).

The Office for Substance Abuse Prevention (OSAP) has also recently funded demonstration projects for 3–5 years to provide services and study polydrug treatment outcome among women and their infants. While these demonstration projects are primarily providing services to pregnant and postpartum women and their infants, some of them are planning an evaluation component that will assess the efficacy of the services.

Drug Treatment Program Elements Sensitive to Women's Needs

Conventional drug treatment services have been designed and evaluated for men, the largest group of consumers. Although studies of women in treatment may have methodological problems due to their small numbers, thereby preventing us from generalizing the results, there are program elements, from the standpoint of practitioners, that are considered sensitive to women's needs.

Practitioners serving pregnant drug-using women and their children have recommended a variety of intervention strategies. Kronstadt (1989) reports on the intervention strategies recommended by practitioners from some of the major programs currently serving pregnant drug-using women. These recommendations include the following:

1. Programs should be comprehensive, with as many services as possible offered at one site (e.g., prenatal care, pediatric care, chemical dependency treatment, and service coordination.
2. Programs should offer confidentiality to women fearing criminal reprisals, moral judgments, and the loss of their child to protective services.
3. Programs should be made more accessible by offering child care and transportation.
4. Programs should provide case management to clients and avoid fragmentation of services by collaborating and coordinating with other agencies.
5. Interventions should be intensive and include home visits, drop-in centers, and 24-hour crisis phone lines.
6. Programs should provide a supportive psychotherapeutic model, featuring support groups that encourage interaction and peer support and that focus on common problems, rather than the confrontational group technique used successfully with men.
7. Programs should provide residential treatment and drug-free housing.
8. Programs should offer parent education and quality child care.

Reed (1987) also recommends that women's services include vocational training, training in self-esteem and coping skills and on sexuality and intimacy issues, legal assistance, and education on chemical dependency.

OSAP will attempt to integrate and examine the usefulness of some of these intervention recommendations with the prevention, education, and treatment demonstration projects it sponsors. OSAP demonstration programs, serving alcohol- and drug-using pregnant and postpartum women and their infants, generally have 3–5-year grants ranging from $172,000 to $475,000 each. Many of the programs were funded to coordinate and enhance existing treatment services rather than provide direct treatment services. In some of the programs women are referred for treatment within the same service agency, although the treatment is underwritten by other funding sources.

OSAP Programs

Goals of OSAP Programs

The information in this section is based on a telephone survey conducted by the author with 46 OSAP programs located across the continental United States during the summer of 1990, with 72% (or 33 programs) of the sample participating in the interview. Selection of the programs was based on their locations, that is, programs were selected from all the states where they were available. Directors of OSAP demonstration programs for pregnant and postpartum women were asked questions about the range of services for women, as well as about licensing, certification, and fiscal matters.

The goals of the OSAP programs are broad and address areas such as service development and provision, treatment, prevention, outreach, skills building, and staff training. The main goals identified are the following:

- Reduce drug-addicted deliveries, infant mortality, and low birth weight.
- Increase the availability and accessibility of early intervention and treatment services.
- Give women parenting skills to improve infant–parent relationships.
- Reduce stressors that lead to drug use (e.g., peer pressure, lack of support system, unemployment) and teach anger management.
- Prevent adverse birth outcomes and defects in babies born to alcohol- and drug-addicted mothers.
- Intervene early in the pregnancy of addicted women and assist them in staying drug-free.
- Prevent relapse during pregnancy and after delivery.
- Conduct extensive outreach and education in the community regarding substance misuse during pregnancy.

Approaches of OSAP Programs

Approaches of 33 of the OSAP programs are shown in Table 7.2. Nonmedical approaches are used more frequently than the more costly medical approaches

TABLE 7.2. Approaches Used by a Selection of OSAP Programs

Approach	Frequency	Percentage
Medical	5	15
Nonmedical	11	33
Combined (medical and nonmedical)	14	43
Programs not providing direct services	3	9
TOTAL	33	100

(33% vs. 15%). About 43% of the programs use a combination of medical and nonmedical approaches. Three programs do not provide direct treatment services.

OSAP Program Settings and Treatment

Twenty-six of the 33 OSAP programs (79%) use an outpatient model, three use a combination of residential and outpatient services, one uses short-term (3 days) medical detoxification in an outpatient service, and three do not use either model since they are not providing direct services. One outpatient program is in the process of acquiring spaces for clients in a few residential facilities. Another program is located in a health center prevention clinic that provides education and counseling in substance misuse.

In-home services, a relatively uncommon treatment alternative, are provided to persons who are homebound because of pregnancy complications or disability. Although they do not directly provide in-home services, 61% of the programs are able to refer to those providing such treatment if necessary. Nine programs of the 33 in total provide in-home services directly, while four programs neither provide nor refer for this service.

The types of treatment provided by the selection of OSAP programs studied are presented in Table 7.3. Thirty programs (91%) provide on-site identification and treatment. The availability of residential treatment programs for women and children is limited; only one program provides residential treatment that includes children. Of the 18 states included in the OSAP sample, 5 states (Massachusetts, Wisconsin, Pennsylvania, Oklahoma, and Washington) have very few on-site residential treatment programs for women with children. Seven programs provide on-site day treatment, while twenty-one of them will refer for those services when necessary. Day treatment programs are not available in three states (Massachusetts, Florida, or Pennsylvania). Counseling is offered by perinatal addiction counselors on-site, who are employed by OSAP, or elsewhere by drug treatment counselors under contract with other agencies. Only one program offers adolescent services.

Twenty-six programs (79%) refer clients to other agencies for other types of services such as neighborhood recovery programs, alternative programs, drop-in centers, and aftercare; five programs provide aftercare; and three programs provide

TABLE 7.3. Treatment Types by Number of Programs Reporting ($N = 33$)

Treatment types	On-site	By referral
Identification and intervention	30	5
Chemical dependency treatment	14	20
Partner/family involvement	11	20
12-step groups	10	21
Residential treatment	2	29
With children	1	25
Without children	2	29
Partner/family involvement	2	29
Day treatment (chemical dependency)	7	22
With children	7	19
Without children	7	21
Partner/family involvement	7	22
Individual counseling	26	10
Group counseling (Facilitated by therapist)	25	11
Confrontational/encounter groups	16	16
Branch (sharing) groups	17	16
Family counseling	20	18
Family counseling including the individual	20	15
Peer discussion groups	21	12

a drop-in center for mother and children, one of which also provides aftercare. Another program provides a support group. One program is developing a neighborhood recovery program. Another program refers clients to Alcoholics Anonymous and Cocaine Anonymous.

Adjuncts to Treatment in OSAP Programs

OSAP programs have a strong commitment to providing a range of services in support of drug treatment. The services provided by programs as adjuncts to treatment are listed in Table 7.4. In one program, housing assistance (the first month's rent) was available to women who came out of a residential program; another provided assistance with the first and the last month's rent. Two programs mentioned that they provide health and developmental assessments of children and assessments of parent–child interaction. For the therapeutic child care component, four programs offer either education, special education, child development intervention, or occupational and speech therapy. Two programs use neighborhood advocates, social workers, nurses, or recovering addicts as home health visitors. Two programs are developing a hot line to provide specific information on education, services, and care, while another program has a hot line by a contract agency to deal with behavioral and medical problems. To help clients with

TABLE 7.4. Adjuncts to OSAP Treatment by Number of Programs Reporting (N = 33)

Adjunct services	Prenatal	Postnatal	Services by referral
Outreach	24	24	NA
Prenatal medical services	16	NA	16
Pediatric medical care	NA	12	20
Maternal medical care	1,515	15	16
Developmental assessment (infant)	NA	26	5
Psychosocial assessment/counseling	NA	24	7
Nutrition assessment/counseling (WIC)	23	23	8
Emergency resources (food, shelter, clothing)	15	15	18
Case management/social services liaison	28	28	4
Child care	22	22	6
Therapeutic	10	10	8
Nontherapeutic	20	20	7
Home health visitor	26	26	2
Parenting and child development education	25	26	3
Parenting support group	25	26	3
Pregnancy support group	23	23	3
AIDS education/HIV prevention and treatment	27	27	4
Chemical dependency education	29	29	4
Services intended to support family maintenance or family reunification efforts	22	22	10
Job training/educational	10	10	23
Housing assistance	16	16	15
Drop-in center	6	5	18
Hot line	6	6	19
Respite care for child/parent	5	5	20
Transportation (bus tickets)	28	28	1
Aftercare component for women and children	19	19	11

transportation, programs have cars or vans (often driven by volunteers) or provide bus tokens, bus tickets, or taxi vouchers. With respect to psychotherapeutic services, two programs offer self-esteem groups; one of these programs also offers special services to adolescents (e.g., groups devoted to self-empowerment and decision making). One offers training in providing care to drug-exposed children to staff, probation officers, child protective service workers, nurses, and foster parents. Case managers in all of the OSAP programs (i.e., social workers, public health nurses, or perinatal addiction counselors) provide ancillary services, such as counseling on parenting and home visiting.

Coordination of Services in OSAP Programs

All 33 OSAP programs coordinate services for clients through social workers, counselors, and case managers whose function is a "linkage-brokerage function." The services are coordinated case by case through participation in task forces, consortiums, and coalitions, with some activities accomplished by telephone. These programs use a variety of formal and informal agreements to coordinate services with and between hospitals, clinics, courts, and children's services.

Service agreements are an important part of providing or coordinating services in some OSAP programs. Seven programs have service agreements and/or coordinate services on a referral basis. One program contracts with two perinatal care hospitals and one outpatient center, while another makes appointments and escorts women to their appointments. Another program has the drug specialist work with other agencies in the community. One program has a contact person within those organizations that have been assigned to it; having a contact person in each outside agency with which a service agreement has been made facilitates access to information and resources. Another program contracts for medical services that are provided at the OSAP program's own facility.

Two programs have developed a perinatal coalition and one participates in countywide perinatal coalitions. Two programs have a community advisory board: One is composed of supervisors, managers of child protective services (CPS), the urban league, the housing authority, adult and family services, and children's services while the other is composed of 10 community agencies. The mix of agencies represented in coalitions and advisory boards facilitates communications and referrals of clients between agencies. An example of state-level coordination is found in Oklahoma where the health department (maternal and child health), CPS, the legislature, and the departments of mental health, alcohol, and corrections are coordinating services. This program intends to prepare a position paper on the prevalence problem of drug-exposed infants in that state. Another program in Massachusetts collaborates with five other agencies (research agency, education program, a children's hospital, and two residential treatment facilities); this program informs clients of the services, gives them contacts, and connects clients with those programs or services.

Two programs reported on their special efforts to share information and resources with related programs. One program has weekly team meetings that include staff from a jail and social service agencies, a health nurse, and drug and alcohol treatment providers. Another program has established a consortium of 15 organizations to meet monthly to discuss perinatal topics and resources (although from October to June the consortium is comprised of 35 to 40 members).

A majority of the programs (76%) coordinate services throughout the case, as needed. The remainder of programs coordinate services at specific times or in specific ways. Thus, coordination may occur

- Throughout the case as needed (25 programs)
- When the case manager determines it is appropriate

- Until 1 year postpartum (3 programs)
- During weekly conferences
- At the time of referrals from other agencies
- At initial intake (3 programs)

Benefits of and Obstacles to Coordinating Services

The benefits of coordinating services are summarized in Table 7.5. Identifying service gaps, leading to better access to services, was the most frequently mentioned benefit (64%), followed by improved service delivery (42%).

Other benefits anticipated from coordinating services include the following:

- Reducing treatment gaps and increasing services for women
- Identifying and obtaining more appropriate services
- Informal feedback to the client from the service providers to whom he/she was referred
- Better compliance from clients because of the trust relationships that are built
- Ability to provide services, by using case management, to women who would otherwise "slip through the cracks"
- Development of a holistic integrated service plan
- Improved client referral system
- Ability to track women at intake and discharge
- Development of a resource manual of services
- Improved ability to obtain ancillary services (e.g., housing)

However, the programs also identified multiple and varied obstacles to coordination, including (1) communication problems, (2) political and fiscal tensions, (3) lack of time, and (4) tensions related to the provider–client relationship.

TABLE 7.5. Number of OSAP Programs Reporting Various Types of Benefits from Coordinating Services ($N = 33$)

Benefits	Number	Percent*
Improved service delivery	14	42
Cost savings	9	27
Not duplicating services	10	30
Identifying service gaps (leading to better access to services)	21	64
Better treatment outcomes	4	12
Too early to tell	5	15

*Percentages do not sum to 100% because of multiple responses.

Program Outcomes: Coercing Women into Treatment

Due to the brief existence of the OSAP projects, the information provided here is based on prior experiences of project staff rather than on specific outcome information from the OSAP programs. The information that follows is primarily on program outcomes with coerced clients (i.e., those ordered by a court or by CPS) rather than with voluntary clients.

Like men, women may be coerced into treatment through civil commitments, criminal justice referrals (particularly from drunk driving), and employee assistance programs (Weisner, 1990). In addition, women are increasingly being coerced into drug treatment by courts and children's agencies (i.e., CPS) if they are pregnant and using drugs. The policy of coercing drug-using pregnant women into treatment is quite controversial. Some public health treatment professionals believe that coercing pregnant women into drug treatment will improve positive treatment outcomes for them and their infants while other treatment professionals believe that coercing them is likely to reduce the number of women who come in for services (e.g., prenatal care or drug treatment services) because of their fear of criminal prosecution and losing custody of their children. Different states have tended to take either a medical or a legal approach to drug abuse by pregnant women.

Only one OSAP program had experience, most of which was negative, working with pregnant women who were coerced into services. The program found that coerced clients are more likely to avoid active participation and more likely to drop out of services; these clients may not do well in treatment since their motivation is related to an avoidance of negative sanctions rather than to a striving toward recovery.

Factors associated with treatment philosophies and child custody regulations further reduce the chances of a mother's success in treatment. For example, the children's services agency may not tolerate drug use by the mother and may remove the children, and conflicting regulations may impede the return of children to their mothers (e.g., mothers cannot get housing unless they have custody of their children and they cannot have their children until they get housing).

While eight of the programs said that they accepted only voluntary clients, the rest had to deal with the issue of coercing clients, revealing contrasting beliefs about this issue. In one program, CPS clients were retained for longer periods of time than were other clients because the women wanted to get their babies back. However, according to two program administrators, coerced clients were not necessarily more likely to complete treatment or more likely to stay abstinent longer. A staff person at one program observed that coerced clients are more likely to come to treatment but are not more likely to stay abstinent longer. The ideal scenario of forcing a woman to begin treatment, which she may subsequently realize is in her best interests, occasionally works but not always. A staff member in one program observed, "People tend to dig in their heels when forced into treatment and often go out to use again, and then go back to treatment to prove that they do what they want." A worker in another program, in a state where treatment is mandated, reported that coerced clients are more likely to comply with the treatment plan and more likely to complete treatment while a program in a state where there is no mandate to treatment indicated no difference in improvement between coerced and noncoerced patients.

Administrative Aspects in OSAP Programs

The intent to provide women-sensitive drug treatment services can be preempted by administrative difficulties. Licensing and certification in alcohol and drug treatment programs (done by the state) are important because they generally raise the standards of residential treatment facilities and access other services for the client. Licensed programs have increased health and safety requirements. Certified programs can access third-party payments, and their participants are eligible to receive general assistance and state disability insurance benefits.

Licensing and Certification in OSAP Programs

Few programs were found to be licensed (30%) or certified (27%) for drug and alcohol treatment because many were not providing direct treatment services (e.g., education-oriented programs). Increased health and safety requirements (e.g., TB tests, health screening, proper food storage, fire safety) were the benefits found in eight licensed programs. One program in New York has found that CPS is less likely to remove babies from their homes if the mothers are in a licensed program. A worker in another program stated that the benefit package and work safety requirements were good for employees and the varied services offered by the hospital were good for the clients.

With respect to the liabilities of licensing, workers in one program in Oregon mentioned that they cannot receive third-party payments because of the hospital's decision to accept only welfare clients. Those in another program in Florida mentioned that space regulations in their day care center make it difficult to operate a program. A worker in one program described the lack of flexibility that exists when a program is licensed: for example, a client may want to be in treatment right away but the paperwork required because the program is licensed can lose the client in the process.

With regard to certification, access to additional funding sources is a benefit of certification. Benefits for being certified are listed in Table 7.6. Third-party payments are the major benefit of certification. Participants are also eligible to receive General Assistance (GA) or State Disability Insurance (SDI) benefits. Only two programs mentioned liabilities of certification: fire marshal requirements and the diversion of money for expenses related to the physical facility instead of to service delivery.

Fiscal Matters in OSAP Programs

Source of Payment. The source of payment for these 33 OSAP programs draws on a combination of funding resources (Table 7.7). In two programs the counties have

TABLE 7.6. Number of OSAP Programs Reporting Various
Certification Benefits (N = 33)

Benefits	Number	Percent
Third-party payments	9	27
Eligible to receive GA or SDI	4	12
Eligible to receive food stamps	3	9
Increased credentialed staff	5	15
Staff evaluated annually	1	3
Additional services provided	1	3

assistance from general funds. One program stated that if they are certified they are eligible to bill Title 19 (Medicaid). In another program, the State Office of Child Abuse Prevention (OCAP) has joined funds with OSAP to pay for speech and hearing problems of the developmentally disabled drug-exposed children from the 6-month follow-up until 5 years of age. One program has OSAP funds for the family recovery component and Maternal Child Health (MCH) money for outreach services. In Florida one program has funds from the Juvenile Welfare Board (a state-supported agency since 1948), which has the ability to tax for the welfare of the children. In one program there are client copayments when services exceed what the county is able to pay. While OSAP pays for outreach and case management services, in Pennsylvania private funding through a foundation pays for the therapeutic direct services portion of the program. In one California program, the OSAP grant pays for 95% of the cost and 5% comes from the county alcohol and drug misuse mental health administration.

Client Fees. The vast majority of the 33 OSAP programs studied (61%) do not charge clients for services; however, eight (24%) programs have sliding fee scales and two additional programs are developing a scale. Two other programs charge no fees for the OSAP services but have a sliding fee scale for health clinic services.

TABLE 7.7. Source of Payment for the 33 OSAP Programs

Sources	Number	Percent
Third-party reimbursements (private insurance)	5	15
Medicare	NA	NA
Medicaid	17	52
Other government assistance	3	9
Client fees	4	12
Donations	4	12
United Way	2	6
March of Dimes	1	3

Summary of Findings from OSAP Programs

OSAP programs, with their combined medical and nonmedical treatment models, are utilizing approaches that differ from traditional drug treatment programs. Nearly three-quarters of the programs are using an outpatient model. Programs generally conduct an assessment of the drug problem and provide and/or coordinate services for the client, making use of project case managers. Services for clients have moved beyond traditional drug counseling to include an array of health and social services (e.g., medical care, education, vocational training, child care, transportation). Given their funding limitations, OSAP programs cannot provide comprehensive services but do provide various services in-house and then refer clients out to other programs considered sensitive to women's treatment needs. Hopefully, outcome evaluation studies of the innovative ideas included in the OSAP programs, such as combining program approaches, coordination of services, case management approaches, and providing habilitative services, will expand our drug treatment knowledge of women and assist us to develop more effective treatment models.

RECOMMENDED TREATMENT APPROACHES FOR DRUG MISUSERS

Comprehensive drug treatment approaches are more frequently described than offered. Comprehensive outpatient treatment programs include weekly contacts with peer support groups, family or couples therapy, the use of treatment contracts, with corresponding contingencies for completing activities related to abstinence, urine monitoring, education sessions, and individual psychotherapy.

The first goal of cocaine treatment is withdrawal from the stimulant. Measures to achieve this goal, which are often added to conventional detoxification approaches (Gawin & Ellinwood, 1988), include a range of ways to help clients avoid environmental triggers for drug-using behavior, such as providing an alternative residence, altering the client's access to money, curtailing the client's social activities, and changing the client's phone number. Involving significant others who are drug free in the treatment plans of clients during periods of high craving allows the significant other to provide support, monitor behavior, and encourage alternative activities to drug use.

The second goal of treatment is to prevent relapse. Well-accepted techniques for enhancing resilience to relapse include (1) predicting situations in which the risk to relapse is high, (2) rehearsing avoidance strategies, (3) changing lifestyle, (4) developing a drug-free network of social contacts, and, (5) developing memories of the negative consequences of drug abuse to counteract memories of drug euphoria, conditioned cues, and external stress reduction. Although such approaches appear to promote some control over certain substances (e.g., alcohol; see Marlatt & Gordon, 1980), their ultimate efficacy with crack cocaine is unknown. Given the apparently high rate of cocaine relapse, using medication to reduce intense craving in the early weeks of treatment may yield greater effectiveness (A. Stalcup, personal communication, October 30, 1989).

Treatment models, such as some of the OSAP programs, that incorporate a variety of rehabilitation services for adults before returning them back to their communities make sense. Malcolm (1989), in his article in the *New York Times*, quoted Salvatore di Menza, special assistant to the director of the National Institute on Drug Abuse:

> It may be more satisfying to think mainly of residential programs because the addict is put away somewhere safe. But we're going to need a range of strategies. For many addicts, for instance, it's not rehabilitation; it's habilitation. They don't know how to read or look for work, let alone beat their addiction. (p. 23)

Clients' psychosocial functioning may not be adequate to avoid relapse if they lack successful employment, self-esteem, parenting and coping skills, and educational and general life skills training. While drug taking may be statistically independent of environmental causes, it is highly interrelated with job productivity, life satisfaction, and life circumstances (Hubbard et al., 1989; Malcolm, 1989; Reed, 1987, Sutker, 1987). Hence, it appears that drug treatment programs need to be tailored individually and coordinated through various community agencies to provide specific needed services. Coordination of services across agencies has been a problem identified in social services since Mary Richmond, a social worker leader in casework, first discussed it at the National Conference of Charities (Leiby, 1978; Richmond, 1901). Strategies for coordinating social services, employment services, health, child care, and drug treatment continue to need exploration and evaluation.

Drug treatment programs are typically just one of the service pieces that a drug user needs. Drug treatment programs have, however, long existed independent of conventional agencies. Whereas social workers in a range of settings have gradually learned to refer clients to drug programs, many drug programs do not employ social workers to refer clients to allied services. Social workers must continue to improve their linkages to drug treatment programs, facilitate referrals, and evaluate their work. A variety of service components that assist clients in remaining drug free after treatment are needed and may include education, vocational training, medical services, and assistance to access other social services (e.g., AFDC, WIC food vouchers, social support, counseling and parenting and social skills training).

Even when drug treatment has been effective, clients have often not been integrated into the social and economic mainstream of society. This challenge is becoming still greater as businesses establish screening procedures and sanctions against subtance users. Programs need to include greater attention to family and employment needs of the client. The progress of the client in various services needs to be monitored to assure attainment of the clients' goals and objectives. Thus far, conventional programs that offer 1 month of residential treatment for drug users without follow-up services have not shown promising results, perhaps because they lack a mechanism for assisting clients with reentry. Most long-term residential programs (i.e., 3–18 months) have not incorporated a variety of habilitative services into their treatment. It may be propitious to experiment with a mix of short- and long-term programs. For instance, 30-day hospital-based programs may incorporate habilitative services such as education or vocational training and follow-up case management. Similarly, long residential programs may also include a range of services (treatment and habilitation), according to the needs of their clientele. Whereas group care arrangements for families in recovery are beginning to develop, they are not as affordable or flexible as foster homes that accept mother and child; these need development and evaluation. Under current social conditions and economic structure, alternatives that extend treatment and provide education and employment opportunities seem to be one of the ways to empower those who have drug problems and are also poor or unskilled. Additional efforts are needed to identify the feasibility of expanding the comprehensiveness of current programs and methods to minimize the difficulty in accessing services.

The research on drug treatment effectiveness is primarily limited to whether different kinds of clients benefit from different programs. The lack of randomized studies in the drug and alcohol field limit interpretation of findings. Research comparing the effectiveness of treatment models has not been conducted. It is apparent, however, that the length of treatment, not the type of treatment, is the better indicator of positive outcomes. Longer residential treatment for drug users (at least 3 months) improves 1-year abstinence rates. For alcohol users, no differences were found in treatment outcome between long- versus short-term programs and no single treatment approach was more effective than any other. Criminal activity decreases for both outpatient and inpatient drug programs, particularly when clients are in treatment. Methadone maintenance programs show positive treatment outcome for heroin users. Medications can reduce cocaine-related craving and anxiety, but their impact on long-range outcomes and their capacity to enhance other approaches is not clear. Treatment models that target life conditions warrant expanded use because returning clients to pre-use levels of functioning is inadequate if those clients lack the skills vital to maintaining a drug-free lifestyle.

Model treatment approaches to abuse of cocaine and other drugs, which include providing a variety of social services in the treatment program, remain to be tested empirically. We do not know what blend of social, cognitive, or medical intervention best reduces drug use. Accordingly, suggestions made in this section should be treated as working hypotheses. Developing sufficient evidence about what type of drug treatment or which model works best for clients must become a top priority for service providers and funders. The field's inattention to research or the inability to fund research has hampered the emergence of innovative approaches. The necessity or advantages of women-sensitive and culture-sensitive services need articulation through research.

While improving upon social conditions is needed and is an appropriate response for many persons with drug problems, some people do have adequate resources and social conditions and yet become addicts. The need, desire, or curiosity to alter mood, which has apparently characterized humankind from the beginning of time, remains a puzzle. We still do not know why persons become addicted to drugs or quit their addictions. Until we do, since short-term rewards of drug use exceed those of abstinence, the most effective drug treatment programs will endeavor to expose drug users to a wide range of rewarding and competing alternatives. The task of offering rewarding and competing alternatives is larger than what drug treatment programs—or even coordinated services—can accomplish. A cultural reorientation to focus on greater appreciation of long-term rather than short-term goals may be needed.

The breakdown of families, high divorce rates, short-term personal relationships, and environmental disregard characterize a culture that undervalues long-term goals. Turning drug users away from short-term goals and then returning them to a society that doesn't value long-term goals is destined to be difficult. Drug treatment programs that build in attention to the development of educational and vocational skills, in addition to attention to lasting personal and family needs, are more likely to bring the desired result, but even they will be constrained by our society's difficulty with integrating personal actualization and economic development (Ramos, 1981). In order to attain integration of a polarized personal and economic development, society at large may need to incorporate a substantive approach rather than just personal or economic means (Ramos, 1981). Effective drug treatment programs should be based on values that support belief in the individual's capacity for recovery, a commitment to keep families intact whenever possible, and social justice. Services should draw on the broadest range of health, social service, education, and drug treatment knowledge and resources.

Acknowledgments

The author is indebted to Richard P. Barth, PhD, Associate Director, Family Welfare Research Group and Associate Professor, School of Social Welfare, University of California at Berkeley, for offering this project and for his continual assistance and support. The author thanks Elizabeth Rahdert, Alex Stalcup, Lois Lowe, and Connie Weisner for their contributions to this manuscript. Maria Nunes-Dinis, MSW, is a doctoral candidate at the School of Social Welfare, a research associate for the Alcohol Research Group in Berkeley, and a research associate to the U.C. Berkeley Study of Services for Drug- and AIDS-Affected Families. The Zellerbach Family Fund, Wallace and Alexander Gerbode Foundation, and the Lois and Samuel Silberman Senior Faculty Fellow Award to Dr. Barth greatly assisted this effort.

Address correspondence to the author care of School of Social Welfare, University of California, Berkeley, CA 94720.

REFERENCES

California State Department of Alcohol and Drug Programs, Division of Administration, Data Management Services Branch. (1989, April). *Indicators of alcohol and drug abuse trends.* Sacramento, CA: Author.

Charney, D. S., Menkes, D. B., & Heninger, G. R. (1981). Receptor sensitivity and the mechanism of action of antidepressant treatment: Implications for the etiology and therapy of depression. *Archives General Psychiatry, 38,* 1160–1180.

Clark, W., & Midanik, L. (1982). Alcohol use and alcohol problems among U.S. adults: Results of the 1979 national survey. In *Alcohol consumption and related problems* (DHHS Publication No. ADM 82-1190, Monograph 1, pp. 3–52). Rockville, MD: National Institute on Alcohol Abuse and Alcoholism.

Clayton, R. R. (1985). Cocaine use in the United States: In a blizzard or just being snowed? In N. J. Kozel & E. H. Adams (Eds.), *Cocaine use in America: Epidemiologic and clinical perspectives* (Research Monograph 61, pp. 8–34). Rockville, MD: National Institute on Drug Abuse.

Crack mothers, crack babies and hope. (1989, December 31). *New York Times,* p. 17.

Dole, V. P., & Nyswander, M. E. (1965). The medical treatment for diacetylmorphine (heroin) addiction. *Journal of American Medical Association, 193,* 646–650.

Dole, V. P., Nyswander, M. E., & Warner, A. (1968). A successful treatment of 750 criminal addicts. *Journal of American Medical Association, 206,* 2708–2711.

Gawin, F. H., Byck, R., & Kleber, H. D. (1985, December 9–13). *Double-blind comparison of desipramine and placebo in chronic cocaine abusers.* Presented at the 24th Meeting of the American College of Neuropharmacology, Kaanapali, Hawaii.

Gawin, F. H., & Ellinwood, E. H. (1988). Cocaine and other stimulants: Actions, abuse, and treatment. *New England Journal of Medicine, 318,* 1173–1182.

Gawin, F. H., & Kleber, H. D. (1984). Cocaine abuse treatment: Open pilot trial with desipramine and lithium carbonate. *Archives General Psychiatry, 41,* 903–909.

General Accounting Office. (1990, September). *Drug abuse: Research on treatment may not address current needs* (Report to the Chairman, Select Committee on Narcotics Abuse and Control, House of Representatives, GAO/HRD-90-114). Washington, DC: Author.

Golwyn, D. H. (1988). Cocaine abuse treated with phenelzine. *International Journal of Addictions, 23,* 897–905.

Hilton, M. E. (1987). Drinking patterns and drinking problems in 1984: Results from a general population survey. *Alcoholism Clinical and Experimental Research, 11,* 167–175.

Hubbard, R. L., Allison, M., Bray, R. M., Craddock, S. G., Rachal, J. V., & Ginzburg, H. M. (1983). An overview of client characteristics, treatment services, and during-treatment outcomes for outpatient methadone clinics in the Treatment Outcome Prospective Study (TOPS). In J. R. Cooper, F. Altman, B. S. Brown, & D. Czexhowicz (Eds.), *Treatment research monograph series: Research on the treatment of narcotic addiction (state of the art)* (pp. 714–751). Rockville, MD: National Institute on Drug Abuse.

Hubbard, R. L., Marsden, M. L., Rachal, J. V., Harwood, H. J., Cavanaugh, E. R., & Ginzburg, H. M. (1989). *Drug abuse treatment: A national study of effectiveness.* Chapel Hill: The University of North Carolina Press.

Hurley, D. (1989, July/August). Cycles of craving. *Psychology Today,* pp. 54–58.

Institute of Medicine. (1990a). *Broadening the base of treatment for alcohol problems.* Washington, DC: National Academy Press.

Institute of Medicine. (1990b). *Treating drug problems: Vol. 1. A study of the evolution, effectiveness, and financing of public and private drug treatment systems.* Washington, DC: National Academy Press.

Khantzian, E. J. (1985). The self-medication hypothesis of addictive disorders: Focus on heroin and cocaine dependence. *American Journal of Psychiatry, 142,* 1259–1264.

Leiby, J. (1978). *A history of social welfare and social work in the United States.* New York: Columbia University Press.

Liu, S. J., & Wang, R. I. H. (1986). Possible mechanisms involved in the use and abuse of amitriptyline in methadone patients. In L. S. Harris (Ed.), *Problems of drug dependence, 1985. Proceedings of the 47th Annual Scientific Meeting, The Committee on Problems of Drug Dependence, Inc.* (Research Monograph 67, pp. 506–507). Rockville, MD: National Institute on Drug Abuse.

Malcolm, A. H. (1989, November 19). In making drug strategy, no accord on treatment. *New York Times*, pp. 1, 23.

Many unborn babies being exposed to drugs. (1988, August 30). *New York Times*, p. 1.

Marlatt, G. A., & Gordon, J. R. (1980). Determinants of relapse: Implications for the maintenance of behavior change. In P. O. Davidson & S. M. Davidson (Eds.), *Behavioral medicine: Changing health lifestyles* (pp. 410–452). New York: Brunner/Mazel.

Means, L. B., Small, M., Capone, D. M., Capone, T. J., Condren, R., Peterson, M., & Hayward, B. (1989). Client demographics and outcome in outpatient cocaine treatment. *International Journal of the Addictions, 24,* 765–783.

National Institute on Drug Abuse (1988). *National household survey on drug abuse: Main findings 1985* (DHHS Publication No. ADM 88-1586). Rockville, MD: Author.

National Institute on Drug Abuse. (1990). *National household survey on drug abuse: Highlights 1988* (DHHS Publication No. ADM 90-1681). Rockville, MD: Author.

National Institute on Drug Abuse/National Institute on Alcohol Abuse and Alcoholism. (1989). *Drug and alcoholism treatment unit survey (NDATUS): 1987 final report* (DHHS Publication No. ADM 89-1626). Rockville, MD: Author.

O'Brien, C. (1987, September 16). *Controlled studies of pharmacological and behavioral treatments of cocaine dependence.* Paper presented at the North American Conference on Cocaine Abuse, Washington, DC.

Ramos, G. A. (1981). *The new science of organizations: A reconceptualization of the wealth of nations.* Toronto: University of Toronto Press.

Reed, B. G. (1987). Developing women-sensitive drug dependence treatment services: Why so difficult? *Journal of Psychoactive Drugs, 19,* 151–164.

Richmond, M. (1901). Charitable co-operation. In I. C. Barrows (Ed.), *Proceedings of the 28th Annual Session of the National Conference of Charities and Corrections* (pp. 298–313). Boston, MA: George H. Ellis.

Rosecan, J. (1983, July 14–19). *The treatment of cocaine abuse with imipramine, L-tyrosine, and L-tryptophan.* Paper presented at the Seventh World Congress of Psychiatry, Vienna.

Schnoll, S. H., Karrigan, J., Kitchen, S. B., Daghestani, A., & Hansen, T. (1985). Characteristics of cocaine abusers presenting for treatment. In N. J. Kozel & E. H. Adams (Eds.), *Cocaine use in America: Epidemiologic and clinical perspectives* (Research Monograph 61, pp. 171–181). Rockville, MD: National Institute on Drug Abuse.

Sutker, P. B. (1987). Drug dependent women: An overview of the literature. In G. M. Beschner, B. G. Reed, & J. Mondanaro (Eds.), *Treatment services for dependent women* (Vol. 1, pp. 25–51). Rockville, MD: National Institute on Alcohol Abuse and Alcoholism.

Tennant, F., Jr. (1988). LAAM maintenance for opioid addicts who cannot maintain with methadone. In L. S. Harris (Ed.), *Problems of drug dependence, 1987. Proceedings of the 49th Annual Scientific Meeting, The Committee on Problems of Drug Dependence, Inc.* (Research Monograph 81, p. 294). Rockville, MD: National Institute on Drug Abuse.

Tennant, F. S. J., & Tarver, A. L. (1984). Double-blind comparison of desipramine and placebo in withdrawal from cocaine dependence. In L. S. Harris (Ed.), *Problems of drug dependence, 1984. Proceedings of the 46th Annual Scientific Meeting, The Committee on Problems of Drug Dependence, Inc.* (Research Monograph 55, pp. 159–163). Rockville, MD: National Institute on Drug Abuse.

Weisner, C. (1990). Coercion in alcohol treatment (Appendix D). In Institute of Medicine (Ed.), *Broadening the base of treatment for alcohol problems* (pp. 579–609). Washington, DC: National Academy Press.

Wesson, D. R., & Smith, D. E. (1985). Cocaine: Treatment perspectives. In N. J. Kozel & E. H. Adams (Eds.), *Cocaine use in America: Epidemiologic and clinical perspectives* (Research Monograph 61, pp. 193–203). Rockville, MD: National Institute on Drug Abuse.

Zangwell, B. C., McGahan, P., Dorozynsky, L., & McLellan, T. A. (1986). How effective is LAAM treatment? Clinical comparison with methadone. In L. S. Harris (Ed.), *Problems of drug dependence, 1985. Proceedings of the 47th Annual Scientific Meeting, The Committee on Problems of Drug Dependence, Inc.* (Research Monograph 67, pp. 249–255).

8

The Child's Developmental Path: Working with the Family

NIKA ST. CLAIRE

> If houses suitable for children do not exist, then let us build
> them.
>
> Maria Montessori

Working with children who are at risk of developmental delay demands recognition of the complex impact of the child and the parent on each other. A child's development unfolds within his or her relationship to a parent figure, and developmental and educational services must respect the essential role the family plays in any child's life. Drug-affected infants and children may have a multiplicity of needs, yet the importance of providing services to the child's parents and family may not be fully appreciated.

Most services have been child oriented over the last century. The move to a family focus has been more recent, yet child development and school personnel may be especially reluctant to provide services to the whole family when substance abuse is involved. They may believe that their responsibility is only for the child, or they may fear being unequipped or unreimbursed for interventions aimed at the mother or other family members. They may believe the many myths about addicted women, which may cause fear of them or uncertainty about how to establish rapport, and may believe that prenatal substance use equals child abuse and that biological families have therefore given up their right to be consulted about the child's welfare. Other personnel may have been influenced by misconceptions created by the media and may be consumed with a sense of hopelessness and despair, believing that these children and their parents are doomed and that interventions are ineffectual. They may also sense that they lack the training or expertise to meet the complex needs of chemically dependent women. Finally, developmental specialists and educators may simply not be aware of how much more potent interventions can be when the parents are included than when services are delivered only to children in a day program by even the most dedicated professionals. In addition, chemically dependent and recovering parents may have their own set of barriers, including low self-esteem, dual diagnosis, and lack of advocacy, that prevent them from accessing needed services.

It is critical for developmental specialists and educators to know that many drug-affected children, with appropriate early intervention, can lead normal healthy lives and will be able to succeed in school. Providers also need to be imbued with hope for the chemically dependent parent and to remember that recovery is possible and that interventions can and do make a difference for families (Lief 1980; Tittle & St. Claire 1989).

Despite our tremendous knowledge of child development, the lives of many of our young children are in grave jeopardy. We are increasingly aware of the child's capacities and vulnerablities yet continue to struggle with providing interventions that make a difference. Even when we know the interventions that can make a difference, we lack the commitment or the resources to provide them. To respond to the needs of drug- and HIV-affected children, there must be a determination to commit to interventions that are timely, comprehensive, coordinated, continuous, and able to address the real needs of that child within the family and community.

Infants born exposed to drugs and/or alcohol in utero have inundated the service system, and providers have scrambled to develop services sensitive to the needs of these infants and their families (Chira, 1990). The task is to evaluate which services have worked well in the past and make them specific to this population. A great deal of expertise and information about what children need already exists. Drug- and alcohol-exposed children may have more needs than other children, but service providers do not have to reinvent the wheel to serve them. They do need to look at those models that have been particularly effective with similar populations or similar symptoms and consider how to individualize programs for each infant and parent, without assuming they all have the same set of needs. For example, some drug-exposed infants do not need developmental intervention at all whereas other families need the full continuum of services. Interventions must be flexible, and providers must avoid dogmatic treatment approaches.

In this chapter I hope to provide a rationale for working with the family and a framework for understanding the array of developmental and educational services that must be made available for drug- and HIV-affected children. Beginning with consideration of the developmental needs of young children, this chapter reviews the effects of drug exposure in utero and looks at various assessment instruments currently being used. The chapter then discusses early intervention, provides a review of the spectrum of developmental services available, and looks at various model programs. Locating sources of funding is also discussed, focusing specifically at Part H of the Education of the Handicapped Act 1986 Amendments. The chapter further considers the effects of labeling and/or segregating drug-affected children from their peers, makes recommendations for programs, and addresses issues that relate to the older children of addicts and alcoholics.

INVOLVING FAMILIES

Every developing individual needs the opportunity to be raised by a loving and consistent figure who is capable of what Winnicott (1975) called "primary maternal preoccupation." Drug-affected infants and their parents need a consistent primary nurturing system that is capable of family preoccupation. According to Pawl (1989), "in terms of development, every child in the world deserves and needs a foundation of consistent, ongoing relationships that have as their hallmarks empathy, respect, mutuality, reciprocity and deep investment" (p. 1). Developmental and educational services must embody the same set of principles. Given the way the media and some legislators have presented the issue, there may be a desire on their part to rescue infants from "those drug mothers." This chapter stresses the vital role that mothers, even drug-dependent mothers, must play in promoting the optimal development of their children.

There exists a growing recognition that a family-centered approach to health care is particularly of benefit to those children who have special health needs (Hobbs, Perrin, & Ireys, 1985). Services to infants and children are often delivered through the family, and the family may have the greatest influence on the child's health. Children are dependent on their families not only for the basic necessities of life but especially for the emotional and intellectual environment necessary for healthy development. Family-centered approaches have long been recognized as the most effective practice for children with special needs (Dunst, Trivette, & Deal, 1988; Johnson, McGonigel, & Kaufman, 1989; McGonigel & Garland, 1988; Shelton, Jeppson, & Johnson, 1987). No single agency can match the family in the continuous day-to-day care that children require.

Providing services to young children with special needs and their families has led to the guiding principle of empowering families to be able to meet their own needs and maintain a sense of control. Dunst, Trivette, and Deal (1988) use the word *empowerment* to describe how service providers can enhance a family's strengths and abilities. It is necessary for all families to be able to maintain a sense of control, to have their skills and knowledge recognized, and to be able to meet their own needs as they increase their competencies. Since families with substance abuse and HIV issues may feel even more powerless than others, programs might need to be creative in finding ways to empower them. And since American families are changing, services aimed at families must increasingly expand their definition of who constitutes a family (Woodruff, Hanson, McGonigel, & Sterzin, 1990).

PROFILE OF THE DRUG-AFFECTED INFANT

There is no typical profile of a drug-affected infant; each child must be looked at individually to assess his or her particular strengths and vulnerabilities. Since Chapter 3 reviews how various substances taken by the mother during pregnancy may affect the developing child, it is only necessary here to remind ourselves of the general findings and salient features of research to this point, while recognizing that new information may continue to challenge our current knowledge and understanding. The long-term effects of narcotic (primarily heroin and methadone) exposure in utero beyond the perinatal period seems to include behavioral and perceptual difficulties and difficulties in organization (Finnegan, 1982; Kaltenbach & Finnegan, 1984; Rosen & Johnson, 1982; Wilson, McCreary, Kean, & Baxter, 1978). Exposure to alcohol may result in a pattern of abnormalities from full-blown fetal alcohol syndrome to fetal alcohol effect (Smith, 1977). In the absence of either of these diagnoses, infants exposed to alcohol in utero may demonstrate a number of long-term behavioral problems, including attention deficit disorders and decreased motor coordination. Exposure to cocaine also appears to be related to organizational difficulties, distractibility, attention deficits, and hypersensitivity to stimulation (Chasnoff & Schnoll, 1987; Zuckerman et al., 1989). PCP has also been recognized as having long-term effects, including borderline abilities in fine motor, adaptive, language, and personal and social development (Howard, Kropenske, & Tyler, 1986).

It would be unrealistic to set up separate and distinct programs for children exposed to either PCP, alcohol, heroin, or cocaine since most of the children are, in fact, exposed to multiple drugs. For the purposes of developing and providing services, some generalities can be drawn about drug exposure. Children who were drug exposed in utero may display attention deficit disorder, motor coordination, behavioral difficulties, and persistent problems in the process of organization. In research to date, we are not yet clear on the precise effects of a drug, independent of such variables as tobacco use, lack of prenatal care, environmental toxins, social isolation and related stressors, the caretaker's parenting abilities, and other medical and environmental factors. We are aware, however, that the real problems many of these children experience do need to be addressed.

ASSESSMENT OF THE DRUG-AFFECTED CHILD

Health professionals play a critical role in identifying and referring drug-affected children at risk for developmental delay. Developmental screening and assessment may often be the initial intervention. Glascoe, Martin, and Humphrey (1990) have underscored the importance of detection and referrals using standardized tests. They reviewed and rated 19 different screening tests in an effort to assist professionals in choosing from the wide array of instruments available. More complete assessment may follow the initial screening.

Interventions can only be effective if the assessment is broad enough to encompass the whole child and the family. Focusing on one aspect of the child, such as cognitive development, may narrowly focus interventions and decrease their effectiveness. Although there has been a proliferation of developmental tests, there continue to be questions in their appropriate use. Are they being used correctly by trained individuals who have demonstrated proficiency and are aware of normal child development? Or are assessors taking shortcuts? Do the outcome results reflect what the screening test was designed to measure? Frankenburg, Chen, and Thornton (1988) warn of the urgency of some of these concerns and recognize that "one can measure only a part of a child's developmental capacities at an early age, the more complete picture . . . not [being] evident until later" (p. 1111).

There continues to be debate on whether or not developmental tests can truly predict outcome (Meisels, 1989). If one wishes to attempt to predict later developmental status, using a risk model allows recognition that drug exposure may jeopardize developmental processes; however, one must at the same time recognize that organismic and environmental forces can contribute to positive developmental outcomes. Developmental outcomes are the product of both constitutional makeup and environment, and a dynamic transactional model is necessary (Sameroff & Chandler, 1975). One of the problems with early research on the effects of drug abuse on the developing child has been this failure to adequately control for potent postpartum environmental factors. Additionally, the use of a small aberrant sample often inflated the sensitivity of the measure, making effects appear more pronounced.

A number of developmental assessment instruments have been used to assess drug-affected infants and children and have provided useful information. It is beyond the scope of this chapter to review all those assessment instruments, but it may be helpful to review those most commonly used. The Brazelton or Newborn Behavior Assessment Scales (NBAS) (Brazelton, 1973) is a reliable and valid scale that assesses the infant's states and capacities within seven different behavioral clusters. Infants are assessed on their abilities with habituation, orientation, motor performance, range of state, regulation of state, autonomic regulation, and reflexes. Drug-exposed infants seem to evidence particular difficulty in their ability to orient themselves and to move smoothly from one state to another (Griffith, 1990); for example, these infants may go from deep sleep state to crying without any intervening states. Such problems are ameliorated by creating an environment in which the infant can respond to soothing techniques, including swaddling, use of a pacifier, vertical rocking, and modifying the stimulus intensity. T. B. Brazelton himself feels that conducting this test in the presence of the mother is a major intervention and may prove invaluable in assisting the mother with learning to read her baby (personal communication, November 13, 1991).

The Bayley Scales of Infant Development (Bayley, 1969) constitute an instrument used to assess the development of children aged 2 to 30 months, yielding a mental scale score, a motor scale score, and an infant behavior record. The test evaluates the child's perception, memory, learning, problem solving, vocalization, rudimentary abstract thinking, gross motor abilities, manipulation development, emotional and social behavior, attention span, and goal directedness. Chasnoff and Schnoll (1987) and Griffith (1990) have noted that by age 18 months there is little difference between drug-exposed infants and their drug-free peers, with members in both groups earning an average score of 100 on the Mental Development Index (MDI). They note, however, that the test itself helps these children by providing a structure that assists them in organizing. It would seem, then, that any assessment that is highly structured may overinflate the child's abilities. Practitioners often talk anecdotally of the child who can pass an item on a test yet whose quality of achievement is clearly distinguished from the non–drug-affected child's. Whether unstructured assessments fully capture the child's capacities remains to be seen. Despite the structure of a traditional assessment, however, drug-affected children still seem to have difficulty with language and the ability to organize. At age 12 months 35% cannot put a cube in a cup, and 35% do not babble as they should. At 18 months these difficulties are still evident: 70% cannot name one object and 33% cannot place one block in a cup because the item overstimulates them (Griffith, 1990).

Language delays persist in 42% of the children at age 3 (Griffith, 1990). Dixon (1990) also recognizes the persistent delays in language and recommends the use of the MacArthur Communication Inventory as an instrument that may be sensitive in the evaluation of a child's expressive and receptive language delays.

Assessment tools are less important than their application. An effort must be made to evaluate the whole child. The Connecticut Infant–Toddler Developmental Assessment Program (Provence, Palmeri, Erikson, & Epperson, 1986) is an assessment instrument that measures seven different areas of function and incorporates health factors and family factors that either support or interfere with the child's development. It also looks beyond the areas of cognition, motor development, and language to the areas of self-help; relationships to persons; and emotions, feeling states, and coping behavior and may be used with infants from 1 to 42 months of age.

FAMILY ASSESSMENT

Many programs focused their assessment almost exclusively on the child until the passage of Public Law 99-457, the Education of Handicapped Children Act Amendments of 1986. With this law early intervention programs are now mandated to assess family strengths and needs and to help families meet their needs.

Families with drug-affected children are often viewed as dysfunctional and the probable source of the problem, yet families can harbor great resources. Families differ in their levels of stress and resiliency, coping mechanisms, social supports, and personal skills. An assessment of the child should look carefully at the family's ability to function and at the parent–child interaction. As yet, there is no standardized approach to assess the drug-dependent family. Finding an appropriate instrument may be difficult since instruments used in research and clinical practice may not have been designed for formal assessment purposes. Some instruments may lack cultural sensitivity and sufficient respect for the privacy of the family.

Besides the lack of psychometrically proven measures, there is a limited theoretical basis on which to determine what family variables to assess. Some researchers (Gray & Wandersman, 1980; Ramey, Bryant, Sparling, & Wasik, 1984; Travers & Light, 1982; Weiss, 1983) argue for the importance of a more differentiated assessment despite the risks of lack of agreement on measures and theory. In response to the many criticisms of existing measures, Hanson and Lynch (1989) recommend the use of a family interview, which allows programs more flexibility in assessing and attempting to meet the needs of their families. Each program may develop its own set of appropriate questions to serve as a guideline in assessing the family's needs and strengths.

Bailey and associates (1986) believe information should be collected in at least the following three areas: (1) child variables that affect family functioning, (2) the family's needs for information, support, or specific training, and (3) parent–child interaction. Weiss and Jacobs (1988) developed an ecological schema for overall program evaluation focused on the following five levels: (1) child functioning, (2) parental functioning, (3) parent–child relationship, (4) family functioning, and (5) informal and formal social supports. They reviewed various programs' effectiveness across these five domains. A family assessment might also be organized around these five areas.

Assessing parent–child interaction is particularly critical for this population. Both the parent and the child may bring difficulties to the establishment of a relationship. Despite some limitations, Ainsworth's Strange Situation (Ainsworth, Blehar, Waters, & Wall, 1978), Sander's Model (Sander, 1962), Bromwich's Parent Behavior Progression Scale (Bromwich, Burge, & Khonkha, 1981), Barnard's Nursing Child Assessment Scales (Barnard & Bee, 1981), and Greenspan's Stages (Greenspan & Greenspan, 1985) are all possible assessment instruments for assessing parent–child interaction. A complete list of potential assessment instruments is available in the appendix of *Evaluating Family Programs* by Weiss and Jacobs (1988).

Any assessment requires skilled and highly trained staff. As family assessment is a relatively new technique, programs may need to invest in additional training for their staff. As programs become increasingly responsive to the family, the investment is likely to be worth the effort.

EARLY INTERVENTION

Early intervention services have developed considerably in the last 10 years. Evidence for the efficacy of early intervention for a wide variety of at-risk populations is presented by the American Psychological Association in a book entitled *Fourteen Ounces of Prevention* (Price, Cowen, Lorion, & Ramos-McKay, 1988).

Meisels and Shonkoff (1990) offer a good working definition of what early intervention is:

Early childhood intervention consists of multidisciplinary services provided for developmentally vulnerable or disabled children from birth to age three years and their families. These programs are designed to enhance child development, minimize potential delays, remediate existing problems, prevent further deterioration, limit the acquisition of additional handicapping conditions, and/or promote adaptive family functioning. The goals of early intervention are accomplished by providing developmental and therapeutic services for children, and support and instruction for their families. (p. xvi)

Since drug- and AIDS-affected children have widely diverse areas of vulnerability, services designed to meet those needs must be equally broad. Improving the developmental outcome of drug-affected children is an important task that cannot be achieved with minimal efforts. Every stage of a young person's life is critical; intervention demands a commitment to the principle of continuity of human development to have an impact. Family involvement may be the key to explaining the long-term benefits associated with early intervention. Some contend that early intervention programs have been successful not so much for what happens in the half day at school but because they encourage involvement by parents, who then feel more empowered and responsible throughout the whole days and years of the child's development.

The transactional model (Sameroff & Chandler, 1975) emphasizes the importance of continuous and progressive interactions between children and their environment. A child born with significant biological insult, such as drug exposure in utero, would be expected to develop more optimally in a supportive environment than in a poor caregiving environment. The purpose, then, of early intervention efforts is to create environments that nurture optimal development and prevent additional difficulties. It may be particularly true in the area of preventing additional difficulties that programs must support and enhance the caregiving environment and the caretakers themselves.

There are eight modes of early intervention (Bromwich et al., 1981) that may serve as a list of tasks associated with early intervention services: (1) listening empathically, (2) observing, (3) commenting positively, (4) discussing, (5) asking, (6) modeling, (7) experimenting, and (8) encouraging. Dunst and colleagues (1988) identified the following roles for the interventionist: empathetic listener, teacher/ therapist, consultant, resource, enabler, mobilizer, mediator, and advocate.

DEVELOPMENTAL SERVICES CONTINUUM

Appropriate developmental services may begin at birth and change over the course of time as the child's needs and capacities emerge. The child is endowed with innate growth capacities that unfold over a very long period of time. The infant has great plasticity, but there are limits to how he might respond to interventions. Each infant has tendencies that determine how, what, and, to some extent, when he will learn. Children's resilience or invincibility is remarkable (Anthony, 1974), and even in the wide spectrum of children exposed to highly potent risk factors it is unusual for half or more of them to develop serious disabilities or persistent disorders (Rutter & Hersov, 1985).

A drug-affected infant's developmental status may be further compromised by the risks of prematurity, the environment, or a long hospitalization in an intensive care nursery. Optimally, initial interventions in the hospital nursery begin with efforts to protect the infant from overstimulation by modifying the physical environment and staff interactions with the infant. Staff may lower the lights or noise levels and use swaddling, rolled blankets, bunting, or other means of containment for soothers and state stabilization. The mother may need a great deal of support at this time as she attempts to deal with the guilt and shame she may feel at having delivered a premature and drug-exposed infant. Parents need to know that they can make a difference and may, in fact, be equally as important as the technology available in promoting their child's healthy development. The mother also may be upset at not being able to hold, rock, and touch her child. And all too often, once the medical staff know that the mother used drugs and alcohol during pregnancy, she is made to feel less welcome in the nursery. It is critical that staff receive the education and supervision necessary to treat addicted women with compassion; otherwise, the mother's sense of failure will be confirmed.

Environmental factors, particularly family variables and parent–infant interactions, are significant determinants of ultimate developmental outcomes. Every effort must be made to help the mother read her baby's cues and respond more effectively to a possibly difficult child. This will help the child immediately as well as encourage the establishment of the critical mother–infant bond so important to the child's long-term development. O'Connor, Vietze, Sherrod, Sandler, and Altemeier (1980); Siegel, Bauman, Schaefer, Saunders, and Ingram (1980); and others have written compellingly of the importance of those first few hours and days of an infant's life in establishing attachment. When hospital staff create barriers to attachment, there may be very serious long-term effects. This may be especially important with a premature infant whose signals and responses are so different from those of the full-term baby. Drug-affected infants may need more help in attaining the "wisdom of the body" (Cannon, 1939), a marvelous description of the mechanism of self-regulation whereby the human body maintains an optimal equilibrium in its chemical constituents and physiological processes.

Primary developmental interventions must assist drug-affected infants in their ability to regulate themselves through sensory pathways. Some infants may be hyperarousable and overreact to normal levels of sound or light whereas others are hypoarousable, often described as floppy or lethargic. These infants may demonstrate other subtle effects: A bright, alert baby may become disorganized by sound, and a baby who uses vision and hearing to self-regulate may become irritable with gentle stroking and calmed only when held horizontally.

A new developmental intervention being piloted for drug-exposed infants in some intensive care nurseries is the modified Kangaroo Care method (Anderson, Marks, & Wahlberg, 1986). Originally used in Bogata, Colombia, for premature infants, the Kangaroo Care program responded to the economic constraints and infection problems in an underdeveloped country while at the same time recognizing the natural resource of mothers. In the Kangaroo Care method the mother holds the preterm baby skin-to-skin in an upright position between her breasts for extended periods. With the infant against the mother's body, the maternal heartbeat and breathing provide an immediate and continuous background stimulation that may be more effective than oscillating waterbeds (Korner, 1979) in reducing apneic episodes. Though infant outcome studies have not yet been done with preterm drug-exposed infants, clinical experience demonstrates clearly that the Kangaroo Care method is beneficial in developing and fostering the critical mother–infant bond (Klaus & Kennell, 1983). Researchers have reported dramatic reductions in infant morbidity, mortality, and parental abandonment (Rey & Martinez, 1983) in premature infants treated in this manner, although the infants in these studies were not identified as drug exposed.

After hospital discharge there are limited but growing opportunities for early intervention services for drug-affected infants. Some of these infants continue to have special health care needs that require specialized follow-up. Some will be sufficiently delayed to meet special education eligibility criteria in those states that provide such services to infants. Still others may be served through innovative model programs developed to meet the individual needs of these infants in interaction with their caregivers. Most of the programs have some significant aspects in common and they form a coherent basis for later recommendations.

INFANT MODEL PROGRAMS

The infant–parent psychotherapy model of Fraiberg and her colleagues (Fraiberg, Adelson, & Shapiro, 1975; Pawl, 1986) may hold promise for these troubled families. This model suggests that problems in the infant may come from the mother's unresolved problems with figures from her own past, who have been referred to as "ghosts in the nursery." Insight is gained by linking events in the present to events and feelings in the past. The Center of CARE (Chemical Addiction Recovery Efforts) Program at Children's Hospital, Oakland, California, has attempted to create an infant–parent psychotherapeutic model that is specific to the needs of drug-affected infants and their parents. The Center of CARE incorporates the woman's recovery and the infant's developmental needs into the basic psychotherapeutic model. Infant–parent psychotherapy embraces a program with three major components: concrete support, developmental guidance, and infant–parent psychotherapy accomplished through weekly home visits. The Center of CARE began with those basic components and has added center-based parent support groups to promote the women's recovery while also promoting the mother's capacities to enhance her infant's development. The Center provides comprehensive services and has an interdisciplinary team that supports the therapist providing direct support to the family. To promote the drug- or HIV-affected child's development, the focus must be on empowering caretakers. Enhancing the mother's capacities to care for her child throughout his or her life may be the single most important intervention possible. Traditional barriers to accessing services have also been addressed by providing transportation assistance (cab vouchers and bus tickets), on-site child care, and a daily lunch.

The following case study from the Center of CARE suggests some of the challenges in providing developmental services to a drug-affected infant. It also suggests how support to the family may directly affect the child's developmental progress. In this case, as the mother gained new skills, there was often a parallel advancement in the child's progress.

Case Study

Denzel was born prematurely at 34 weeks gestation, weighing 1,790 grams, and was transferred to Oakland's Children's Hospital intensive care nursery. He had bronchopneumonia and pulmonary atresia. His 31-year-old mother, Eleanor, used 30 to 40 dollars' worth of crack cocaine and drank one or two beers per day throughout the duration of the pregnancy. Eleanor was referred by the Intensive Care Nursery social work staff to the chemical dependency specialist at the hospital's infant development program for drug-affected children and their families. The specialist assessed the mother, referred her for drug and alcohol outpatient treatment, gave her information and literature about addictive disease, and invited her to the weekly parent support group for recovering mothers. Eleanor began attending the group regularly and sought support regarding various problems in her life: Denzel's father was abusive, she desired advocacy with Child Protective Services because she feared loss of custody as a known drug user, and she needed assistance in dealing with a relative who freely supplied her with drugs.

Eleanor presented like many mothers of drug-affected infants: She had low self-esteem and was a battered woman; she was the adult child of an addict, and had been neglected by her own mother. It became clear that the theme of abandonment would be a critical clinical issue to be explored and that Eleanor's guilt and her insecure attachment to her own mother might affect her ability to securely attach to Denzel. Eleanor focused on these issues for the first month of intervention until Denzel was scheduled for his first heart surgery and her concerns shifted to his survival. It was at this time that Eleanor mentioned for the first time that her own mother was dying.

Denzel's surgery was successful; he was discharged a month later to live with his mother, an 8-year-old sister, and his maternal grandmother. Eleanor's inability to protect herself and her infant from her abusive spouse was a grave concern, and all intervening agencies considered the family's safety a goal in the family's treatment plan. Eleanor was referred to a battered women's shelter and support services, encouraged to obtain a restraining order, and counseled regarding her feelings of depression and powerlessness. Although she admitted to continued binge use of cocaine at that time, she intermittently attended NA meetings and was able, with intense case management support, to keep all pediatric appointments. Denzel continued to receive at least weekly medical visits to monitor both his cardiac and his respiratory difficulties.

In order to promote Denzel's developmental progress while supporting the mother, the family was again referred to the service that would allow weekly home visitation. Eleanor seemed to be ambivalent about letting another helping professional in her life and was unable to follow through. Case management was transferred back to the cardiology social worker and the Child Protective Service worker, and Denzel was hospitalized twice for monthlong bouts with pneumonia. Upon discharge the family was again referred to the more intense service, but Eleanor canceled every home visit scheduled. Her ambivalence seemed to be related to the physical abuse by Denzel's father, her shame in allowing it to continue, and her fear that custody of Denzel would be removed from her if the system knew of the real predicament. After discussing her fears about this and being reassured that the original interventionist (the chemical dependency specialist) could be the one to make home visits, Eleanor relented, and nearly 9 months after the initial referral the family entered the home visitation program.

At the first home visit Eleanor relaxed upon hearing her fears and issues voiced and revealed that her mother was dying of AIDS. The family was being counseled once a week at the local AIDS center. The Center of CARE became the primary service coordinator and attempted to coordinate all involved programs to ensure a coordinated and comprehensive flow of services in response to the family's many needs.

The initial developmental assessment indicated that Denzel had significant delays in both gross motor and fine motor domains. After a careful evaluation of her and Denzel's needs, Eleanor was given suggestions about activities she might try at home. Home visits centered around supporting Denzel's developmental progress while exploring Eleanor's fears about her mother's impending death. Denzel's maternal grandmother had been an IV drug user nearly all her life and had left her daughter to be raised by a female relative. The issue of Eleanor's being abandoned for a second time by her mother was explored. Eleanor no longer used illicit drugs but continued to medicate herself with alcohol. Meanwhile, Denzel was progressing in developing his motor skills; the family was able to focus on his needs since they were experiencing support with their own needs. Eleanor was able to use the therapeutic relationship to meet some of her own needs and was then able to respond in a different way to Denzel. Working with the mother and infant together in their home gave the therapist many opportunities to observe and comment on natural interactions.

Several weeks after Denzel celebrated his first birthday, Eleanor, after being beaten by Denzel's father, decided to press charges against him and obtain a restraining order against his visitation. She was given emotional support to follow through with this, as well as concrete services such as transportation back and forth to the police station to file reports. The therapist, while continuing to provide consistent caring for Eleanor, made frequent comments on how much Denzel really looked to his mother to learn about his world and how important she was to him. As Eleanor's self-esteem improved and she was better able to protect herself and set boundaries, Denzel was then more able to use her as a stable base for his exploration and development. As his mother was able to take steps toward her own independence, Denzel learned to crawl and pull himself to a standing position.

Meanwhile, the maternal grandmother's physical condition worsened, and she began suffering from dementia. Eleanor was counseled regarding hospitalization as the grandmother became increasingly more difficult to care for in the home, and she was encouraged to express her feelings of guilt at now "abandoning" her mother. Denzel's father chose to ignore the restraining order and came to the home on several occasions, but Eleanor was firm in her stand. Within that week Denzel learned to walk.

Support to the family also included assistance with obtaining prescriptions and keeping the gas and electric turned on when Eleanor fell behind in her payments. She began to use the therapist for support when she needed it by asking for accompaniment to the hospital when the grandmother had to be transfused and inquiring about finding a suitable hospice. Eleanor made the funeral arrangements and began to plan for her mother's death. When her feelings became too intense, she would cancel the home visits as a way of staying in control of what she was willing to talk about. When the maternal grandmother died, Denzel was again hospitalized with pneumonia. Once again Eleanor had to sort through how torn she felt taking care of the needs of others. The therapist began to focus in on Denzel's language delays and found ways to encourage both the mother and the child to express themselves verbally. As Denzel approached his second heart surgery, Eleanor was able to increasingly ask the therapist for support.

STAFFING ISSUES IN WORKING WITH FAMILIES

One of the issues illustrated through the case study is the challenge in creating a therapeutic alliance with the primary caretaker. As Dr. Ewing discusses in Chapter 2, many chemically dependent women may have difficulty trusting the professional and establishing a relationship. Yet many of the suggestions for interventions will fall on deaf ears without this relationship. Children affected by drugs, alcohol, and HIV and their families have a multiplicity of needs that may require a broad range of disciplines working together to adequately meet them (de Yanez, 1988). How, then, can programs reconcile the need of such families for many professionals with the fact that many families have difficulty accepting support from even one?

Woodruff and colleagues (1990) have developed a "transdisciplinary" model that addresses this dilemma. The model suggests that each family be assigned one primary intervener, who may be an expert in one critical discipline but who will receive training and support from each of the other disciplines on the family's team. This leads to a kind of cross-fertilization whereby each team member develops some competence in the other disciplines. Family members can benefit from every member of the team without having to open their living room and their hearts to a parade of professionals.

The needs of drug- and HIV-affected children and their families dictates the inclusion of many disciplines. An appropriate team may include a developmental pediatrician, nurse, psychologist, child development specialist, teacher, social worker, drug and alcohol counselor, physical therapist, occupational therapist, speech therapist, and nutritionist. Staff composition should also attempt to reflect the rich and varied cultures and ethnicities of the families served. Children who have been identified as drug-affected infants are often children of color. Pediatric AIDS has also affected African-American and Hispanic children disproportionately. In order to make their interventions relevant, it is critical that service providers become "culturally competent" and understand the cultural beliefs and family values of the families they serve (Hopkins & Westra, 1989). It may also be helpful to have at least one recovering individual on staff. In addition to their ability to serve as a role model to chemically dependent women in the program, such individuals may immeasurably add to staff's sensitivity and competence in promoting recovery in the mothers.

Because the needs of families affected by drug use and HIV are complex and diverse, administrators should recognize the need for greater clinical supervision and ongoing support for the staff attempting to provide services to these families. They must build into their programs both the time and resources necessary to adequately support the staff.

MODEL PRESCHOOL PROGRAMS

In 1987 the Los Angeles Unified School District, Division of Special Education, created a pilot program for drug-exposed children aged 3–6 years at the Salvin Special Education Center. The Salvin pilot project consists of four classes, including a transitional kindergarten class, located on a regular elementary school campus. The staff, however, are the first to point out that they are not a "model" program and do not wish their program to be replicated because of their fundamental belief that drug-affected children should not be segregated from other children.

The Salvin project uses a team approach that includes a developmental pediatrician, psychologist, psychiatric social worker, four teachers, and five assistants; a support staff includes a physical therapist, a nurse, and a speech therapist. Each class has from six to eight students and operates for 3 hours and 20 minutes five mornings a week. Eligibility criteria require that children be of normal cognitive ability and eliminate children with disabilities, developmentally delayed children, and children on medication. The critical elements of the Salvin program include a family focus, interdisciplinary assessments, individualized programming, consistent teaching, and utilization of support staff. The primary goal is to facilitate the successful transition of drug-exposed children to a regular educational setting or to the least restrictive special education program placement. To that end, the Salvin School has begun an intensive dissemination program of technical assistance to teachers throughout the Los Angeles Unified School District, hoping to eliminate their own program by making every school capable of welcoming drug-affected children, even those identified with special needs.

The essential protective factors in the Salvin program include respect for the children, consistent routines and rituals, observation and assessment, a flexible room environment that reduces stimulation, transition-time plans, and a rich adult-to-child ratio. Special attention on keeping consistent, predictable routines and assisting children through transitions is indicative of the desire to respond to the persistent difficulties of drug-affected children.

The Salvin School has a developmentally appropriate, child-directed curriculum that emphasizes how children learn through play. The personnel evidence their recognition of the importance of the family through their commitment to a home–school partnership, offering many home visits and parent support groups. Additionally, they have created guidelines for teaching strategies in six areas, strategies that are presented in Appendix A (Callison, 1989). These strategies have been organized in the areas of learning, play, social/emotional development, communication, motor development, and home–school partnership. Recognizing that drug-affected children may be more easily distracted by sounds, people, and movement, the Salvin School staff offer concrete strategies, such as recommending that teaching staff provide support and emotional reassurance, that classroom interruptions be kept to a minimum, and that the number of objects in the room be limited. The teaching strategies in each area of development follow a description of normal development and the behaviors that place children at risk and have been adapted with permission from the *Child Development Subcommittee Report* (Callison, 1989), the California Foster Care Network, and the Children's Research Institute of California.

Project Headstart has provided comprehensive developmental services for low-income preschool children since its inception in 1965. Administered by the Administration for Children, Youth and Families in the Department of Health and Human Services, Headstart is based on the premise that all children share certain needs and that children of low-income families, in particular, can benefit from a comprehensive developmental program to meet those needs. Although Headstart was not created to meet the special needs of drug-exposed children (and certainly, drug-exposed children are found within every social stratum, not just low-income), it does have the critical components for success. Headstart embodies some of the same philosophy behind the Salvin School and other programs highlighted in this chapter, namely, the belief that children can benefit most from a program that is comprehensive and interdisciplinary and that takes into account family and community needs for involvement.

Each year 450,000 children throughout the country are served by Project Headstart, which has demonstrated remarkable improvement in the quality of life for its participants. The benefits are many: The children improve in performance on school achievement tests, there are gains in cognitive development, and fewer grade retentions and special class placements are needed. Headstart has also had a positive impact on the children's motivation, self-esteem, socialization, and development of socially mature behavior. Moreover, absenteeism from school is lower, and there are fewer cases of anemia reported, more immunizations, better nutrition, and better health in general compared to children who did not receive this intervention (Headstart, 1990). Headstart has also had a positive impact on the attitudes of parents toward their children and is associated with improvement in parental employment and educational status. Factors that seem to be most important to the success of Headstart include involvement of parents, quality of teachers, small group size and low child–staff ratios, and the availability of comprehensive services (education, parent, social services, health services, and special services).

The High/Scope Foundation's Perry Preschool Project in Ypsilanti, Michigan, strikingly demonstrates the effects of early intervention programs for poor children by showing that these programs have increased the percentages of persons who, at age 19, were literate, employed, and enrolled in postsecondary education while reducing the percentages who were school dropouts, labeled mentally retarded, and on welfare (Weikart, 1989). The Perry Preschool is part of a long-term study of 123 disadvantaged black youths that began in 1962. At the ages of 3 and 4, children were randomly divided into two groups, with one group going into the Perry Preschool and the other group receiving no special services. The High/Scope Curriculum at Perry is based on Piaget's theory of cognitive development and is organized around "key experiences" in eight categories of intellectual and social development. The program is child-centered in that it values child-initiated activities and is develomentally appropriate. The program staff believe it is critical to have teaching teams that are well trained, classes with two adults and less than 20 children, involved parents as partners, effective assessment and evaluation procedures, and strong administrative support.

DEVELOPMENTAL SERVICES FOR HIV-INFECTED CHILDREN

Young children with HIV infection vary widely in the severity of impairment; like all children with special needs, they require special services, including those that attend to their concurrent medical complications. It is also necessary to contend with the public's concern about transmission of the infection to others (Crocker, 1989).

Planning developmental and educational services for HIV-infected children is becoming increasingly important. Although the mortality rate is high, many more children with symptomatic HIV will be surviving longer because of the effective use of chemotherapies and immunomodulation (Diamond, 1989). In fact, some believe that "HIV infection promises to become the primary infectious cause of developmental disabilities and neurologic impairment in children" (Klindworth, Dokecki, Baumeister, & Kupstas, 1989, p. 292). Initial reports suggest that as many as 78%–93% of children with symptomatic HIV have central nervous system damage (Hopkins, Grozz, Cohen, Diamond, & Nozyce, 1989), which is often evidenced by developmental delay. Progression of the disease may result in the loss of developmental achievements, and staff may need more frequent assessments to determine if skills acquired earlier are still within the child's repertoire. As the child becomes more ill, his neurological development also becomes more impaired.

Families sometimes cannot avail themselves of desperately needed services. Many of the families described throughout this book are overwhelmed by poverty and their addictive disease, making it difficult for them to advocate for themselves. Through guilt and denial, parents may have difficulty accepting the implications of the diagnosis and may refuse services (Hopkins, 1989). Much of the challenge for service providers may be in simply engaging the family to accept services. Programs that recognize critical needs of families, such as transportation and child care, will be that much more accessible when this happens.

The threat of social isolation looms large for affected families. HIV-infected children and their families may be especially isolated, and the importance of play may be even more essential to the health of the family inasmuch as the HIV-infected child is, first and foremost, a child (Crocker & Cohen, 1988). Furthermore, segregating these children—the issue of mainstreaming infected children is still controversial (Fraser, 1989)—will not allow for the peer interaction that is so valuable in optimal social development. Woodruff and colleagues (1990) recommend that families be educated about how the body works; about how HIV is transmitted, prevented, and treated; and about empowerment and advocacy.

MODEL PROGRAMS FOR HIV-INFECTED CHILDREN

In the Bronx Municipal Hospital Center, the Albert Einstein Complex operates a special, exclusive day care center for HIV-infected children because its administrators believe that existing preschools and day care facilities are not able to meet the needs of the HIV-infected child (Hopkins, 1989). The program provides a safe yet stimulating environment for the children and addresses the needs of the family as well. Services include comprehensive medical and psychosocial case management of families; individual, family, couple, and group therapy; respite care; and referral to community support services.

The Project Star Mission is a collaborative effort of five well-established community agencies in Boston that serves children, families, minority ethnic and racial populations, and intravenous drug users. Its intent is to prevent the spread of AIDS and to provide innovative home- and center-based services to children who are at risk for or have been diagnosed with HIV infection and their families. The center-based program includes early intervention, therapeutic day care and drop-in respite care, individual and group counseling and education for caregivers, crisis intervention, and counseling and peer support for siblings. Community outreach workers and street counselors are also enlisted to provide education and counseling to hard-to-reach drug users and engage them in the program.

The Herbert G. Birch Residential Children's Center in Brooklyn, New York, is a model 10-bed home for developmentally delayed children, birth to 6 years old, who may be HIV-infected and who suffer drug-related impairments. In addition to comprehensive residential, medical, therapeutic, and educational services to all its residents, the program also has a center-based component for an additional 10 families in the community.

ADDRESSING THE CONTINUING NEEDS
OF DRUG-AFFECTED CHILDREN
AND THEIR FAMILIES

Although programs currently in place have only provided services to drug- and HIV-infected children in a continuous manner through kindergarten, the needs of these children will change as they grow older. It will be important to look at the literature of adult children of alcoholics for clues as to what those needs may be. Until very recently, little attention has been paid to the important needs of the 28 million individuals (or the one out of eight Americans) whose parents had alcohol problems. This group is at tremendous risk for alcoholism as well as other emotional, medical, and social problems (Booz-Allen & Hamilton, 1974). These are the persons for whom there was no early intervention.

Many children of addicts and alcoholics become responsible and mature far beyond their years by taking care of their parents and younger siblings. Children of alcoholics often are victims of delayed stress syndrome; they may feel depressed without a recent precipitating event and have feelings of emptiness and isolation because they are unable to trust. The inconsistent parenting in an alcoholic family interferes with the ability to establish trust. Many children of alcoholics become chemically dependent themselves, marry an alcoholic, or choose a helping profession such as social work or nursing, determined to give others what they tried to give their alcoholic parents.

Primary goals of therapy for children of alcoholics include expressing feelings and developing trust, which may be particularly difficult for those who took the role of the responsible one or the family hero (usually the oldest), that is, those who adjusted or enabled and were so busy negotiating the lives of others that they avoided directing their own lives. There have been several attempts to identify family roles in alcoholic and otherwise dysfunctional families. Wegscheider (1989) poses five different roles, besides that of the dependent person, that, in her experience, are often present in an alcoholic family: (1) the enabler (often the spouse), who steps in to protect the dependent from the consequences of drinking, thereby enabling the disease to progress; (2) the hero (usually the oldest son or daughter), who takes on the role of parent and is often a high achiever in school and later in business; (3) the scapegoat, the child who reacts by looking to peers for support and who may act out in school and the community; (4) the lost child (usually a middle child), who becomes withdrawn and isolated and may be very disturbed although unlikely to show it; and (5) the mascot (often a younger child), who reacts by clowning and other attention-getting devices.

Therapy may be needed for some families. Often, education about the disease and what is normal relieves people's anxieties and allows them to get on with their lives. The harm done may be subtle; it has been likened to the effect of water wearing away stone, that is, gradual but lasting. If interventions occur early in the child's life, the effects can be minimized.

There is convincing evidence that there is a genetic predisposition to at least some types of alcoholism (Goodwin & Guze, 1974). Tarter (1981) describes an association between early-onset severe alcoholism and retrospective evidence of childhood traits associated with childhood attention deficit disorder. Since so many of our drug- and alcohol-exposed children are now diagnosed with attention deficit disorder, the implications are frightening if these children do not receive education and support about their predisposition to the disease of alcoholism and treatment for their dysfunctional family roles. The Children of Alcoholics Screening Test (CAST; Jones, 1983) is designed for general use with children to evaluate their need for services and may be used in educational settings.

When children of addicts and alcoholics do not receive interventions, they may suffer lasting effects. It seems that our educational system has a role to play in expanding prevention efforts, providing information about alcohol and drugs, helping children understand the dynamics of alcohol use in the family and explore their role in the family, encouraging children to identify and accept their emotions, teaching practical survival skills where there may be danger, and clarifying personal and societal values regarding drinking. An intervener providing a consistent parental role model is also important. Persistence and predictability can help children begin to trust their world and its adults.

Group counseling may also be of benefit. Referrals to Al-Anon and Alateen are helpful if schools are unable to provide meetings on site. Al-Anon and Alateen are nonprofessional 12- step self-help groups analogous to Alcoholics Anonymous and Narcotics Anonymous. They are free of charge and open and accessible to everyone. Children learn that they are not alone, that they are not responsible for their parent's addiction, and that they can focus in on their own issues and recovery.

When addicts and alcoholics are in recovery-oriented treatment, their children have additional needs. Children may be frightened of hospitals or treatment facilities that seem like hospitals. They may wish to know what kind of treatment the parent gets. Many children even become frightened of the 12-step programs, with their slogans and rituals, and fear their parents have been taken over by some strange cult (Oliver-Diaz, 1988). Children also struggle with the emergence of the "new" parent, who may seem like a stranger; it may be necessary for parent and child to get reacquainted. Sometimes, there is resentment of the recovered addict because the parent may now place limits on the child. Ironically, children may feel even more abandoned when a parent enters a recovery program because there is less time together while mother or father attends daily meetings. The language of Alcoholics Anonymous and the rigorous adherence to a recovery plan may cause the child to ask, "Why can't we just be normal? Why can't we just move on in our lives and put this behind us?" With education and support, children can understand and participate in the recovery process. They can even develop pride in family recovery when they are involved in the process.

Children need to feel safe, secure, validated, and successful. It is important for them to feel that their parents can take care of them and that they don't have to be responsible for their parents. School programs should not rush forward offering services without first assessing when and how to speak to children about these issues; denial in children may be a reasonable and appropriate defense and is not to be treated like the denial of the addicted or alcoholic parent. This defense mechanism may be necessary to allow children to continue to function within their family. Children should receive information when they request it and when they can use it.

PROBLEMS WITH DIAGNOSIS AND LABELING

Inherent in the following discussion of how to use legislation and how to define drug-affected children is the more general problem of labeling. Drug exposure in utero is only another risk factor, not a diagnosis. Drug-affected children are not all alike, although some persons may be tempted to name or label as a way of believing they have explained, fully understood, or satisfactorily responded to a condition.

Arriving at the diagnosis or condition of drug exposure in utero is complicated by the fact that there are numerous possible symptoms that any one baby might exhibit. Clearly, it is inconceivable that all symptoms would be necessary to establish the condition, and it is unknown whether any single symptom is sufficient. It seems more reasonable, then, that we look at each child individually and treat each symptom accordingly, without undue emphasis on the etiology. Many of the drug-affected infants requiring services are children for whom the environment has been documented to be less than optimal. Many of the drug-affected children who are now being followed are the most serious cases. Often, they have had an average of three to four placements in their first few years, and the effects of multiple placement only exacerbate their organic compromises (Halfon & Klee, 1987). A specific diagnosis may be required only if remediation fails to help or when one solution leads to yet another academic problem.

Dr. Tyler of the Salvin School remarked most appropriately that "in drug prevention, the basic idea is to build self-esteem. . . . We aren't going to do it by sending [a child] through life labelled as a drug baby" (quoted in Sommerville, 1990, p. 9). The identification of a baby as drug exposed may be helpful in framing our efforts with children but not if the label is used to abridge an individual's rights and opportunities, such as by diminishing the expectations of teachers. We are well aware of the frightening potential for a self-fulfilling prophecy for these children, and we have already seen teachers diagnose children with behavior problems as drug exposed with little substantiating evidence. We need to be rigorous in our insistence that these children are not a biological underclass to be written off; they are children who are capable and ready to respond to our interventions as long as we meet our responsibility to make those interventions.

There is a need to be diligent in confidentiality protections, especially in school-based programs. Foster parents, biological parents, and adoptive parents may all need to become sensitive about whom to inform and must recognize that dispensing information may be detrimental to the child.

RECOMMENDATIONS

Many similarities can be seen among the model programs discussed in this chapter. They form the basis for recommendations to programs that seek success in dealing effectively with children who are affected by drugs, alcohol, and HIV.

1. Programs should be comprehensive and make available "one-stop shopping." Families have multiple needs and should not be asked to go to separate providers for their developmental needs, health needs, social service needs, and family support needs.

2. Early intervention services are effective and may significantly reduce later costs. All children from birth to age 3 should be regularly assessed by their pediatrician for their need for, and their ability to make use of, early intervention and prevention services.

3. Educational programs for children embrace individualized assessment and program planning that emphasize the development of self-competence, play, and discovery, not rote learning. Developmentally appropriate curricula respond to the child at his or her level rather than impose standards of competence. Children differ in their need for structure in their learning environments and social interactions.

4. Programs should be interdisciplinary and multicultural. Drug-affected children and their families present a complex set of needs that can best be served by a variety of providers in a sensitive team approach. Recommendations for an effective team might include a pediatrician, nurse, psychologist, child development specialist, teacher, social worker, chemical dependency consultant, physical therapist, occupational therapist, speech therapist, and nutritionist. Not every discipline will need to be involved with every infant and family. Transdisciplinary approaches through a primary intervener or a small intervention team work best.

5. The highest possible provider–child ratio should be established. Although the National Association for the Education of Young Children recommends an adult to child ratio of 1:10 for 3- and 4-year-olds, a 1:4 ratio may make more sense for children who may require more individual attention. Adult to child ratios will be even higher for infants and might be 1:2.

6. Enhancing the parent's capacities is the real goal. Programs can best support the child's competencies if they support the parent's competencies. Interventions aimed at the family will have an effect 24 hours a day, 7 days a week. No program can match that level of care or commitment. Integrating the chemically dependent parent's need for recovery services may be a challenging yet important goal for child providers.

7. Children affected by drugs, alcohol, or HIV should not be segregated; the goal must be to integrate them or place them in the least restrictive setting. Structured opportunities for peer interactions are vital normalization experiences for these children. Teachers and child care providers should receive training on sensitive strategies for promoting the healthy development of drug- and alcohol-

affected children in their classrooms. Providers acknowledge that some of these children may bring problems severe enough to limit their success in regular classrooms but not enough to land them in special education.

FUNDING SOURCES

One mechanism for funding early intervention services may be through Public Law 99-457, which established Part H of the Education of the Handicapped Act (EHA) Amendments of 1986 (Gallagher, Trohanis, & Clifford, 1989). This law recognizes the benefits of early intervention, provides assistance to states to enhance services, and recognizes the vital role of the family in the development of handicapped children. There are two major sections of the law that are critical to the expansion and improvement of the system's comprehensive services to infants, toddlers, and preschoolers: Title I—Program for Infants and Toddlers with Handicaps (birth through 2 years), and Title II—Preschools Grants Programs (ages 3 through 5 years). Public Law 99-457 provides financial help to states because it recognizes how important it is

> to enhance the development of handicapped infants and toddlers and minimize their potential for developmental delay, to reduce the educational costs to our society . . . by minimizing the need for special education and related services after handicapped infants and toddlers reach school age, to minimize the likelihood of institutionalization . . . [and] to enhance the capacity of families to meet the special needs of their infants and toddlers with handicaps. (Education of the Handicapped Act Amendments of 1986, PL 99-457, Sec. 671 [a]).

Part H of the EHA allows the establishment of a comprehensive interagency interdisciplinary service system to provide early intervention services to all eligible infants and their families. The law is intended to draw attention to and require states to address the needs of infants and toddlers who are experiencing developmental delays or a diagnosed condition with a high probability of an associated developmental delay (Hanson, 1989). States may choose to define and serve at-risk children, such as drug-exposed infants, under this act. One controversy that has arisen is how each state defines *handicapped* and whether that definition should include infants and toddlers defined as being at-risk, thereby using the law to provide needed services. Funds may be used for system planning, policy development, direct services to children who are not otherwise covered by public or private sources of funding, and expansion of existing services.

Title II creates enhanced incentives to states to provide to all eligible handicapped children between the ages of 3 and 6 a free appropriate public education, which includes the use of individualized education programs and recognizes the right to confidentiality, due process, and the least restrictive environment. Thus, Public Law 99-457 provides another opportunity for states to be proactive in meeting the needs of vulnerable children.

In the early phases of program development, 50% of the states included drug-exposed and other at-risk infants in their definition of developmentally delayed; yet when Part H was clarified as an entitlement, some states narrowed the eligibility criteria to exclude populations they considered to be only at risk. Part H is specifically designed to serve families that need a broad array of social and health care services—such as family counseling, transportation, respite care, training, and developmental services—that may not be paid for elsewhere. These services are essential if we wish to support infants and their families by removing some of the barriers they might otherwise face in achieving their potential. If states fail to serve infants at risk, children will only be able to receive these preventive measures if they already have demonstrated delays. Things may change dramatically, however, because Part H is up for reauthorization.

Although there may be problems with Part H, Part B of the EHA (Public Law 94-142) is yet another source of potential services. All 50 states accept federal special education funds. Public Law 94-142 created a structure for handicapped children to be guaranteed the right to a free, appropriate public education. Although existing research is not clear on the developmental status of drug-exposed children ages 3 and beyond, it does indicate enough to assume that many of the categories of handicapping condition can be the result of in utero drug exposure.

If drug-exposed children are not determined to be handicapped under either Part H or Part B of the EHA, it is possible that they meet the criteria under Section 504 of the Rehabilitation Act of 1973. According to these regulations, the definition of a handicapped person is anyone who (1) has a physical or mental impairment that substantially limits one or more major life activities, (2) has a record of such impairment, or (3) is regarded as having such impairment. The risk, of course, is in documenting eligibility and the problem of labeling drug-exposed children.

Developing ways to pay for early intervention and preventive education services seems critical. Drug-affected children will have a great impact on our schools, creating enormous demands. We will need our schools to be ready to provide these children with services they may both need and deserve. Early intervention and preventive service prior to school age may significantly reduce later special education costs. The challenges facing developmental and educational service providers are tremendous. Let us move forward, recognize the wonderful potential in all our children, and provide the necessary services with sensitivity, empathy, and compassion as if their very lives depend upon it. They do.

REFERENCES

Ainsworth, M. D. S., Blehar, M. C., Waters, E., & Wall, S. (1978). *Patterns of attachment.* Hillsdale, NJ: Erlbaum.

Anderson, G., Marks, E., & Wahlberg, V. (1986). Kangaroo care for premature infants. *American Journal of Nursing, 86*(7), 807–809.

Anthony, J. E. (1974). The syndrome of the psychologically invulnerable child. In J. E. Anthony & C. Koupernick (Eds.), *The Child in his family: Yearbook of the Interna-*

tional Association for Child Psychiatry and Allied Professionals (Vol. 3, pp. 529–544). New York: Krueger.

Bailey, D. B., Simeonsson, R. J., Winton, P. J., Huntington, G. S., Comfort, M., Isbell, P., O'Donnell, K. J., & Helm, J. M. (1986). Family-focused intervention: A functional model for planning, implementing, and evaluating individualized family services in early intervention. *Journal of the Division of Early Childhood, 10,* 156–171.

Barnard, K., & Bee, H. (1981). *The assessment of parent–infant interaction by observation of feeding and teaching.* Unpublished Manuscript, University of Washington School of Nursing and the Child Development and Mental Retardation Center, Seattle.

Bayley, N. (1969). *Bayley Scales of Infant Development.* New York: Psychological Corp.

Booz-Allen & Hamilton, Inc. (1974). *An assessment of the needs of resources for children of alcoholic parents.* Springfield, VA: National Institute of Alcohol Abuse and Alcoholism.

Brazelton, T. B. (1973). *Neonatal Behavioral Assessment Scale.* Philadelphia: Lippincott.

Bromwich, R. M., Burge, D., Khonkha, E. (1981). *Working with parents and infants: An international approach* (Vol. 8). Baltimore: University Park Press.

Callison, P. (1989). *Today's challenge: Teaching strategies for working with young children prenatally exposed to drugs/alcohol.* Los Angeles: Los Angeles Unified School District, Division of Special Education.

Cannon, W. B. (1939). *The wisdom of the body.* New York: Norton.

Chasnoff, I. J., & Schnoll, S. H. (1987). Consequences of cocaine and other drug use in pregnancy. In A. M. Washington & M. S. Gold (Eds.), *Cocaine: A clinician's handbook* (pp. 241–251). New York: Guilford Press.

Chira, S. (1990, May 24). Crack babies turn 5, and schools brace. *The New York Times,* p. A1.

Crocker, A. (1989). Developmental services for children with HIV infection. *Mental Retardation, 27*(4), 223–225.

Crocker, A., & Cohen, H. (1988). *Guidelines on developmental services for children and adults with HIV infection.* Silver Springs, Maryland: American Association of University Affiliated Programs for Persons with Developmental Disabilities.

CSR, Inc. (1985). The impact of Headstart on children, families, and communities. In *Project Headstart 25th Anniversary Information Kit.* Washington, DC: U.S. Department of Health and Human Services Administration for Children, Youth and Families.

de Yanez, N. (1988). A multidisciplinary approach to developmental delay in high risk infants. *Delaware Medical Journal, 60*(3), 159–163.

Diamond, G. (1989). Developmental problems in children with HIV infection. *Mental Retardation, 27*(4), 213–217.

Dixon, S. (1990, September). *Infants of substance-abusing mothers, demographics, and medical profile.* Paper presented at Babies and Cocaine: New Challenges for Educators Conference, San Francisco.

Dunst, C. J., Trivette, C. M., & Deal, A. (1988). *Enabling and empowering families: Principles and guidelines for practice.* Cambridge, MA: Brookline Books.

Education of the Handicapped Act (EHA) Amendments of 1986, § 102 [a], Public Law 99-457 (1986).

Finnegan, L. (1982). Outcome of children born to women dependent upon narcotics. In B. Stimmel (Ed.), *Advances in alcohol and substance abuse: The effects of maternal alcohol and drug abuse on the newborn* (Vol. 1, pp. 55–102). Boston: Haworth Press.

Fraiberg, S., Adelson, E., & Shapiro, V. (1975). Ghosts in the nursery: A psychoanalytic approach to the problems of impaired infant–mother relationships. *Journal of the American Academy of Child Psychiatry, 14,* 387–421.

Frankenburg, W., Chen, J., & Thornton, S. (1988). Common pitfalls in the evaluation of developmental screening tests. *Journal of Pediatrics, 113*(6), 1110–1113.

Fraser, K. (1989). *Someone at school has AIDS: A guide to developing policies for students and school staff members who are infected with HIV.* Virginia: National Association of State Boards of Education.

Gallagher, J., Trohanis, P., & Clifford, R. (1989). *Policy implementation and PL 99-457: Planning for young children with special needs.* Baltimore: Brookes.

Glascoe, F., Martin, E., & Humphrey, S. (1990). Consumer reports: A comparative review of developmental screening tests. *Pediatrics, 86*(4), 547–554.

Goodwin, D., & Guze, S. (1974). Heredity and alcoholism. In B. Kissin & H. Begleiter (Eds.), *The biology of alcoholism: Vol. 3. Clinical pathology* (pp. 37–52). New York: Plenum.

Gray, S., & Wandersman, L. (1980). The methodology of home-based intervention studies: Problems and promising strategies. *Child Development, 51*, 93–109.

Greenspan, S., & Greenspan, N. (1985). *First feelings.* New York: Viking.

Griffith, D. (1990, September). *The effects of perinatal drug exposure on child development: Implications of early intervention and education.* Paper presented at Babies and Cocaine: New Challenges for Educators Conference, San Francisco.

Halfon, N., & Klee, L. (1987). Health services for California's foster children: Current practices and policy recommendations. *Pediatrics, 80*(2), 183–191.

Hanson, M. (1989). *Early intervention: Implementing child and family services for infants and toddlers who are at risk or disabled.* Austin, TX: PRO-ED.

Hanson, M., & Lynch, E. (1989). *Early Intervention: Implementing Child and Family Services for Infants and Toddlers who are at risk or disabled.* Austin, TX: PRO-ED.

Hobbs, N., Perrin, J., & Ireys, H. (1985). *Chronically ill children and their families.* San Francisco: Jossey-Bass.

Hopkins, B., & Westra, T. (1989). Maternal expectations of their infants' development: Some cultural differences. *Developmental Medicine and Child Neurology, 31*(3), 384–390.

Hopkins, K. (1989). Emerging patterns of services and case finding for children with HIV infection. *Mental Retardation, 4*, 219–222.

Hopkins, K., Grozz, J., Cohen, H., Diamond, G., & Nozyce, M. (1989). The developmental and family services unit: A model AIDS project serving developmentally disabled children and their families. *AIDS Care, 1*(3), 281–285.

Howard, J., Kropenske, V., & Tyler, R. (1986). The long-term effects on neurodevelopment in infants exposed prenatally to PCP. In D. Clouet (Ed.), *Phencyclidine: An update* (pp. 237–251). Rockville, MD: National Institute on Drug Abuse.

Johnson, B. J., McGonigel, M. J., & Kaufman, R. K. (1989). *Guidelines and recommended practices for the Individualized Family Service Plan.* Washington, DC: Association for the Care of Children's Health.

Jones, J. W. (1983, April 5–6). *The children of alcoholics screening tests: Development, research and applications.* Paper presented at the Children of Alcoholics Conference, Springfield, IL.

Kaltenbach, K., & Finnegan, L. P. (1984). Developmental outcome of children born to methadone maintained women: A review of longitudinal studies. *Neurobehavioral Toxicology and Teratology, 6*, 271–275.

Klaus, M. H., & Kennell, J. H. (1983). *Bonding: The beginnings of parent–infant attachment.* St. Louis: Mosby.

Klindworth, L., Dokecki, P., Baumeister, A., & Kupstas, F. (1989, Winter). Pediatric AIDS, developmental disabilities, and education: A review. *AIDS Education and Prevention, 1*(4), 291–302.

Korner, A. F. (1979). Maternal rhythms and waterbeds: A form of intervention with premature infants. In E. B. Thoman (Ed.), *Origins of the infant's social responsiveness* (pp. 95–124). Hillsdale, NJ: Erlbaum.

Lief, N. (1980). The drug user as a parent. *International Journal of the Addictions, 20*(1), 63–97.

McGonigel, M., & Garland, C. (1988). The Individualized Family Service Plan and the early intervention team: Team and family issues and recommended practices. *Infants and Young Children, 1*, 10–21.

Meisels, S. (1989). Can developmental screening tests identify children who are developmentally at risk? *Pediatrics, 83*(4), 578–585.

Meisels, S., & Shonkoff, J. (Eds.). (1990). *Handbook of early childhood intervention.* New York: Cambridge University Press.

O'Connor, S., Vietze, P., Sherrod, K., Sandler, H., & Altemeier, N. (1980). Reduced incidence of parenting inadequacy following rooming in. *Pediatrics, 66*(2), 176–182.

Oliver-Diaz, D. (1988). How to help recovering families struggle to get well: What treatment centers need to know about helping children of alcoholics. *Focus, 11*(2), 20–21.

Pawl, J. (1986). Flexible intervention approaches with disturbed parent–child interactions. *Colorado's Children, 5*(3), 1–6.

Pawl, J. (1989, February). *Developmental issues in foster care.* Paper presented at California Conference for Foster Children, Oakland.

Price, R. H., Cowen, L., & Ramos-McKay, (1988). *Fourteen ounces of prevention: A casebook for practitioners.* Washington, DC: American Psychological Association.

Provence, S., Palmeri, S., Erikson, J., & Epperson, S. (1986). *The Connecticut Infant Toddler Developmental Assessment.* New Haven, CT: Yale University Child Study Center.

Ramey, C., Bryant, D., Sparling, J., & Wasik, B. (1984). A biosocial systems perspective on environmental interventions for low–birth weight infants. *Clinical Obstetrics and Gynecology, 27*(3), 672–692.

Rey, E. S., & Martinez, H. G. (1983). *Rational management of the premature infant.* Paper presented at the First Course of Fetal and Neonatal Medicine, Bogata, Colombia.

Rosen, T., & Johnson, H. (1982). Children of methadone maintained mothers: Follow-up to 18 months of age. *Journal of Pediatrics, 101*(2), 192–196.

Rutter, M., & Hersov, L. A. (Eds.). (1985). *Child and adolescent psychiatry: Modern approaches* (2nd ed.). Oxford, UK: Blackwell Scientific.

Sameroff, A. J., & Chandler, M. J. (1975). Reproductive risk and the continuum of caretaking of causality. In F. D. Horowitz (Ed.), *Review of Child Development Research* (Vol. 4, pp. 187–244). Chicago: University of Chicago Press.

Sander, L. (1962). Issues in early mother–child interaction. *Journal of the American Academy of Child Psychiatry, 1*, 141–166.

Shelton, T., Jeppson, E., & Johnson, B. (1987). *Family-centered care for children with special health care needs.* Washington, DC: Association for the Care of Children's Health.

Siegel, E., Bauman, K., Schaefer, E., Saunders, M., & Ingram, D. (1980). Hospital and home support during infancy: Impact on maternal attachment, child abuse and neglect, and health care utilization. *Pediatrics, 66*(2), 183–192.

Smith, D. W. (1977). Fetal Alcohol Syndrome: A tragic and preventable disorder. In N. Estes & M. E. Heineman (Eds.), *Alcoholism development, consequences, and interventions.* St. Louis: Mosby.

Somerville, J. (1990). Helping coke kids. *American Medical News,* 9–10.

Tarter, R. E. (1981). Minimal brain disfunction as an etiological predisposition to alcoholism. In R. Myer, B. Glucek, J. O'Brien, T. Babor, J. Jaffe, & J. Stabereau (Eds.), *Evalu-*

ation of the alcoholic: Implications for research, theory and treatment. Rockville, MD: U.S. Department of Health and Human Services.

Tittle, B., & St. Claire, N. (1989). Promoting the health and development of drug-exposed infants through a comprehensive clinic model. *Zero to Three, 9*(5), 18–20.

Travers, J., & Light, R. (1982). *Learning from experience: Evaluating early childhood demonstration programs.* Washington, DC: National Academy Press.

Wegscheider-Cruse, S. (1989). *Another chance: Hope and health for the alcoholic family* (2nd ed.). Palo Alto, CA: Science & Behavior Books.

Weikart, D. P. (1989). Quality preschool programs: A long-term social investment. In O. Sullivan (Ed.), *Occasional Paper Number Five* (pp. 1–28). New York: Ford Foundation.

Weiss, C. (1983). Ideology, interests, and information: The basis of policy positions. In D. Callahan & B. Jennings (Eds.), *Ethics, the social sciences, and policy analysis.* New York: Plenum.

Weiss, H., & Jacobs, F. (Eds.). (1988). *Evaluating family programs.* New York: Aldinede Grayter.

Wilson, G., McCreary, R., Kean, J., & Baxter, J. (1979). *The development of preschool children of heroin-addicted mothers: A controlled study. Pediatrics, 63*(1), 135–141.

Winnicott, D. W. (1975). Primary maternal preoccupation. In *Through pediatrics to psychoanalysis* (pp. 300–305). New York: Basic Books.

Woodruff, G., Hanson, C., McGonigel, M., & Sterzin, E. D. (1990). *Community based services for children with HIV infection and their families: A manual for planners, service providers, families and advocates.* Boston, MA: Author.

Zuckerman, B., Frank, D., Hingson, R., Amaro, H., Levenson, S., Kayne, H., Parker, S., Vinci, R., Aboagye, K., Fried, L., Cabral, H., Timperi, R., & Bauchner, H. (1989). Effects of maternal marijuana and cocaine use on fetal growth. *New England Journal of Medicine, 320,* 762–768.

Today's Challenge:
Teaching Strategies for Working
with Young Children at Risk
Due to Prenatal Substance Exposure*

VENETTA WHITAKER
Administrator
Division of Special Education

VICTOR SIGNORELLI
Director
Special Schools/Centers

EUGENE R. FERKICH
Coordinator
Special Education Student Services

FOREWORD

The purpose of this booklet, Today's Challenge: Teaching Strategies for Working With Young Children at Risk Due to Prenatal Substance Exposure, is to provide guidelines for the adaptation of preschool primary programs to serve these children. We gained our knowledge of these children by looking at them in an intensive specialized setting. One of the things we have become convinced of is that these children should not be grouped together solely on the basis of the prenatal substance exposure. The strategies are organized in the areas of learning, play, social/emotional development, communication, motor development, and home-school partnership. The strategies in each area follow a description of normal development and behaviors that place children at risk. The strategies have been adapted with permission from the *Child Development Subcommittee Report*, California Foster Care Network, Children's Research Institute of California.

This booklet is based on a review of the literature as well as the observations and experiences of the contributors, most of whom have worked with the PED Program for 3 years. Because the educational treatment of children exposed to drugs and/or alcohol is a relatively new field, the booklet cannot reflect research or data comparisons in this area.

*Los Angeles Unified School District, Division of Special Education, Prenatally Exposed to Drugs (PED) Program. Copyright © 1990 Los Angeles Unified School District.

Following in-services, it is hoped that staff will use their knowledge and experience and adapt the teaching strategies, as needed, to meet the individual needs of children.

PHILLIP T. CALLISON
Assistant Superintendent
Division of Special Education

ACKNOWLEDGMENTS

Appreciation is extended to the following individuals for their development of this booklet:

Carol K. Cole, PED Program Teacher
Vicky Ferrara, PED Program Teacher
Deborah J. Johnson, Psychiatric Social Worker, School Mental Health
Mary W. Jones, PED Program Teacher
Marci Blankett Schoenbaum, PED Program Teacher
Rachelle Tyler, M.D., District Physician's Services
Valerie R. Wallace, Special Education School Psychologist
Marie Kanne Poulsen, Ph.D., University Affiliated Program, Children's Hospital, Los Angeles
Nancy Lawrence, Specialist, Instructional Services.

CONTENTS

I. OVERVIEW

A. Statement of Problem

There is mounting concern at the rising incidence in the population of children who are born prenatally exposed to drugs/alcohol. The National Institute for Drug Abuse reports one out of ten pregnant mothers uses or has used drugs during pregnancy. Estimates from the State of California Department of Alcohol and Drug Abuse indicate that 72,000 births in California in 1988 involved infants prenatally exposed to drug substances, including alcohol. The total impact of prenatal drug exposure on society's ability to provide medical, social, and educational services has not yet been felt; the child who has been prenatally exposed to drugs/alcohol is at risk for developmental, behavioral, psychosocial, and learning problems. Schools must continue to prepare to meet the educational needs of these children.

B. Characteristics of Children Prenatally Exposed to Drugs/Alcohol

There is no typical profile of a drug-exposed child; each child must be educated as an individual with particular strengths and vulnerabilities. Because the effects of prenatal drugs/alcohol use on children are varied, the continuum of impairment can range from minimal symptomatology to severe impairment in all areas of the child's development. Characteristic behaviors include a heightened response to internal and external stimuli, irritability, agitation, tremors, hyperactivity, speech and language delays, poor task organization, processing difficulties, problems related to attachment and separation, poor social and play skills, and motor delays. While organic deficits caused by prenatal exposure to drugs/alcohol cannot always be remediated and while immunity against adverse child-rearing conditions cannot always be created, high-quality child/family intervention services can significantly improve a child's self-esteem, self-control, and ability to solve problems in the real world.

C. Description of the Prenatally Exposed to Drugs/Alcohol Program

The Los Angeles Unified School District, Division of Special Education, in cooperation with district psychological, health and school mental health services, created a pilot program at the Salvin Special Education Center. Four classes, including a transition kindergarten class, were located on a regular elementary campus at 75th St. School.

Children aged 3–6 and their families were served in the pilot program. Transportation was provided for the children, and they received support from a district speech and language specialist, adaptive physical education teacher, school social worker, school psychologist, school physician, and school nurse.

D. Goals of the PED Program

1. To develop a preschool program that incorporates a family focus, systematic interdisciplinary assessments, individualized programming, consistent teaching, support staff, and program evaluation
2. To develop effective strategies and provide structured learning experiences to promote the cognitive, communicative, psychosocial, and motor development of children prenatally exposed to drugs/alcohol
3. To identify preschool children who are at risk for behavioral and developmental learning problems due to prenatal drug/alcohol exposure
4. To facilitate the successful transition of PED children to a regular education setting or to the least restrictive special education program placement
5. To promote a better understanding of young children who have been prenatally exposed to drugs/alcohol and who are at risk for school failure

II. PHILOSOPHY OF PROGRAM

The behaviors seen in the preschooler prenatally exposed to drugs/alcohol are the result of a constellation of risk factors, including possible organic damage, early insecure attachment patterns, and, often, ongoing environmental instability. The child is particularly vulnerable to many stresses that impact daily living. The extremes observed in a child's behavior—whether passivity to hyperactivity, apathy to aggression, indiscriminate trust to extreme fear and suspicion—must be understood in the context of each child's experience.

Research has shown that the progress of a child at risk is more favorable when the child is placed in a predictable, secure, and stable environment. Intervention programs for the child must include the development of protective environments with defined structure, expectations, and boundaries, as well as the provision of ongoing nurturing and support. Early positive, responsive care is crucial for the child's emotional and cognitive well-being. Establishing a strong attachment with each child through understanding and acceptance is a teacher's major priority. Only in the context of a good attachment will a child's true potential be realized.

Intervention strategies must attempt to counteract prenatal risk factors and stressful life events. To accomplish this, the teacher must build in protective factors within the classroom environment and facilitate ways for young children to cope appropriately with stress. Self-esteem, self-control, and problem-solving mastery are best achieved when protective factors are coupled with a facilitative approach in the acquisition of better coping skills. These protective factors and facilitative processes are similar to those built into any good preschool program, but because children prenatally exposed to drugs/alcohol are more vulnerable, these program components are essential.

The following are protective factors to be built into a classroom for at-risk children:

A. Curriculum: Children at risk need a setting where curriculum is viewed as the children's total experience from the time they leave home until they return. A developmentally appropriate curriculum provides active learning through interaction, exploration, and play. Concrete experiences, decision making, and problem solving encourage competency and self-esteem and promote motivation for new learning.

B. Play: Children at risk need a setting that allows extended periods of play. Through play a child learns to learn, to explore and manipulate the environment, to cope with the perplexities of life experiences, to express feelings, and to become a symbolic thinker. Adults can facilitate a child's play by furnishing props, making suggestions, and asking questions to clarify and elaborate. When adults participate in a child's play, by sharing and encouraging, it reassures the child that the play is valid and meaningful and that the solutions reached during play are important.

C. Adult to Child Ratio: Children at risk need a setting in which the adult–child ratio is high enough to promote attachment, predictability, nurturing, and ongoing assistance in learning appropriate coping styles.

D. Flexible Room Environment: Children at risk need a setting in which classroom materials and equipment can be removed, to reduce stimuli, or added, to enrich the activity.

E. Transition Time Plans: Children at risk need a setting in which transition time is seen as an activity in and of itself and, as such, has a beginning, middle, and end. Special preparation is given to transition time, recognizing that it is one of the best times of the day to teach the child how to prepare for and cope with change and ambivalence.

F. **Routines and Rituals:** Children at risk need a setting that allows continuity and reliability through routines and rituals. Scheduling activities to occur in a predictable order over time strengthens a child's self-control and sense of mastery over the environment. Not all professionals (e.g., speech and language therapist, psychologist, social worker) come into the classroom on a weekly basis to interact with the children. These adults should develop a routine for reintroducing themselves and predicting for the children when they will appear again. Consistent personnel who help children understand the visiting adult's schedule enhance a child's sense of security.

G. **Classroom Rules:** Children at risk need a setting in which the number of explicitly stated rules are limited. By limiting classroom rules, children are encouraged to explore and actively engage in their social and physical environment. While it is possible to teach specific objectives by relying on rules to control the child, it may be at the expense of the child's intrinsic motivation, problem-solving capacity, and self-mastery.

H. **Observation and Assessment:** Children at risk need a comprehensive assessment. While monitoring skill acquisition in the areas of language, social/emotional, cognitive, and motor development is necessary, it does not constitute an adequate assessment of the child's progress. The manner in which the child uses these skills during play, at transition time, and while engaged in self-help activities is equally important. Close observation of a child's behavior at these times allows for an understanding of how the child experiences stress, relieves tension, copes with obstacles, and reacts to change. It provides valuable information on how the child uses peers and adults to meet needs and solve problems.

The following are facilitative processes to be built into a classroom for children prenatally exposed to drugs.

A. **Respect:** Children at risk need nurturing adults who are respectful of each child's work and play space and who do not make unrealistic demands or unpredictably appear or disappear.

B. **Attachment:** Children at risk need a teacher who accepts that each child comes with a history of both positive and negative experiences. It is assumed that a high-risk child may have a history of poor attachments and lack of trust. The degree to which a child comes to trust the world depends upon the extent to which the caregiver can respond to the developing child's special needs. When care is inconsistent, inadequate, or rejecting, it fosters mistrust, fear, suspicion, apathy, or anger toward the world and toward people in particular. These feelings will carry through to later stages of development.

C. **Feelings:** Children at risk need a teacher who accepts that children have negative and positive feelings, and who acknowledges that feelings are real, important, and legitimate. Children behave and misbehave for a reason, even if it cannot be figured out. In responding to a child's misbehavior, the first priority should be to acknowledge what the child seems to want before dealing with the misbehavior. Doing so allows the child to recognize that feelings are real and valid. Being understood facilitates self-esteem and promotes a willingness to function within prescribed limits. Different children respond to stress (internal and external) in different ways. Individual children show different responses to the same stressful events on different days. Teachers need to develop a sensitivity to the particular meaning different stressors have for the individual child and to avoid maintaining a predetermined set of expectations for or responses to child behavior.

D. Mutual Discussion: Children at risk need a teacher who acknowledges that children's behavior, feelings, and experiences are open to discussion. Talking about behavior and feelings (with empathy rather than judgment) validates the child's experiences and sets up an accepting atmosphere. Permission to have these feelings leads to the increased ability to distinguish between wishes and fantasies on the one hand and reality on the other. Verbal expression allows the child to integrate past and present events into a total experience. This integrating process leads the child's increased ability to modulate behavior, gain self-control, and express feelings.

E. Role Model: Children at risk need a teacher who understands that by establishing an individual trusting relationship the teacher becomes an important person to the child and that the behavior such a teacher models is more likely to be imitated.

F. Peer Sensitivity: Children at risk need a teacher who realizes that children become sensitive and aware of the needs and feelings of others only by repeatedly having their own needs met.

G. Decision Making: Children at risk need a teacher who recognizes that it is important that they be allowed to make decisions for themselves. Freedom to choose and to assume the responsibility for those choices gradually expands the child's physical, social, emotional, and intellectual growth and promotes self-esteem, problem-solving mastery, and moral values.

H. Home–School Partnership: Children at risk and their families are best served when the home is recognized as an essential part of the curriculum. Facilitating parent/caregiver goals helps to establish a close working relationship between home and school. Intervention strategies that strengthen the positive interaction between child and family increase parental confidence and competency.

I. Transdisciplinary Model: Children at risk and their families are best served when all professional interventions are coordinated. To accomplish this successfully, time must be allotted for teachers to meet and plan with assistants and for medical staff, social workers, psychologists, speech and language therapists, and adaptive physical education teachers to come together to develop a comprehensive plan to meet the special needs of the child and family.

III. TEACHING STRATEGIES

A. Learning

Learning occurs within a developmental framework. Development is an internal process in which the child is consistently organizing and reorganizing experiences within a continuum of stages. Movement through the stages is not an automatic passive activity. From birth a child who has not been exposed to drugs/alcohol has the potential to selectively attend and respond to stimuli and to take the initiative to explore and control the environment.

Competency to perceive and explore the environment can be damaged in the child prenatally exposed to drugs/alcohol. Concrete experiences, decision making, and problem solving within a nurturing environment, as well as positive interactive communication, help to build the foundation for development. This foundation promotes self-esteem, competence, and motivation for new learning.

Normal learning development	Learning behavior of at-risk children	Teaching strategies
The child	The child	Teaching staff
• Learns to focus on tasks in play situations	• May easily be distracted by sounds, people, and movement	• Recognize stressors in child's environment and attempt to minimize them
• Uses numerous problem-solving strategies	• May have poor visual scanning	• Provide support and emotional reassurance
• Shows sustained attention in individual and small group activities	• May show decreased trial-and-error learning	• Reduce classroom interruptions as much as possible
• Develops a sense of task completion	• May show decreased problem-solving strategies	• Limit number of objects in room
• Steadily progresses in the acquisition of skills	• May have decreased attention and concentration	• Establish classroom routines with minimum number of transitions
• Learns to delay immediate needs and to conform to the social expectations of the classroom	• May show perseverative behavior in problem solving	• Model alternative strategies
	• May show decreased task completion	• Direct child to watch another child who is using a successful strategy
• Is able to end a preferred activity and start a teacher-directed activity	• May need longer time to complete task	• Consider developmental level of child
	• May give up easily when confronted by problem-solving situations	• Recognize preschoolers may need to sit in adult's lap
• Demonstrates sporadic/intermittent mastery of skills in new learning situations	• May be easily frustrated and become irritable in problem-solving situations	• Recognize preschoolers may need to sit next to an adult
	• May be unable to do task previously mastered	• Use physical, concrete, and verbal cues to direct or redirect child in task or activity
• Acquires preacademic concepts through incidental learning	• May be unable to take turns	• Recognize and consistently praise child's attempts and accomplishments
	• May not remain seated in circle or at the table with the other children	• Ask child to verbalize steps of a task
	• May withdraw from a lack of social and environmental stimulation and may learn to become nonresponsive	• Provide verbal cues (talk the child through task) if child is unable to verbally give steps of task
	• May not have regular play/rest cycles or patterns	• Provide the child with an opportunity to take turns with peers and adults
	• May become upset with changes in routine	• Model taking turns
	• May have difficulty with changes/transitions	• Provide attention and time to children who are behaving appropriately

Normal learning development	Learning behavior of at-risk children	Teaching strategies
The child	The child	Teaching staff
	• May be unable to end or let go of preferred object or activity	• Protect child from the overstimulation of intrusive persons or noisy environments and from the understimulation of a bland social and environmental experience
	• May demonstrate sporadic/ intermittent mastery of skills over prolonged period of time	
	May not learn incidentally	• Provide the child a schedule of play and rest activities to help develop regular patterns
		• Alert the children routinely 1–2 minutes ahead of time that the activity will soon be over
		• Talk about the next activity before entering into the activity
		• Allow adequate time for the transition activity
		• Guide the child through the transition and into the next activity
		• Recognize stressors in child's environment and attempt to minimize them

B. Play

Play is the area where a child integrates experiences with communication, social, emotional, and motor skills. Through play children can learn to understand themselves and their relationships to others and the world. As a child grows and matures, play involves increased communication skills, attention, concentration, and concept development. Strategies for play are important because a child prenatally exposed to drugs/alcohol is at risk for poor play skills.

Normal play development	Play behaviors of at-risk children	Teaching strategies
The child	The child	Teaching staff
• Learns to organize own play	• May show decreased spontaneous play with increased aimless wandering	• Recognize stressors in child's environment and attempt to minimize them
• Can independently select materials and focus on them in an appropriate manner	• May not organize own play, may appear perplexed and confused, and cannot select materials and focus adaptively	• Give each child toys and/or areas in the classroom that are child's alone and do not have to be shared
• Engages in play that is functional, representational, and sequential		• Recognize that child may not have had consistent play objects in home environment
• Progresses from parallel to interactive play	• May be easily overstimulated by too many things and people and by too much noise, movement, and excitement	• Find out what is available for child in child's home

Normal play development	Play behaviors of at-risk children	Teaching strategies
The child	The child	Teaching staff
• Joins in play with other children	• May show delay, discontinuity, and disorder in representational play	• Decrease/regulate amount of toys for child
• Initiates interactive play	• May have difficulty joining others in play	• Will respond to and follow child's lead in play
• Takes part in and initiates dramatic play	• May not initiate appropriate interactive play	• Will model toy choices for child with correct verbal cues
• Is able to sequentially move through a play activity	• May not initiate dramatic play	• Verbally and physically model play with toys
		• Provide opportunities for child to play interactively in a safe environment with the adult available for assistance and reassurance
		• Provide child with opportunities to take turns with peers and adults
		• Provide time to model interactive play
		• Provide child with support and encouragement during play
		• Initiate and model dramatic play with child
		• Respond to child when child initiates dramatic play by verbal responses or by playing with the child

C. Social/Emotional Development

When interactions between the drug/alcohol-exposed infant and caregivers result in poor attachment or rejecting or inconsistent care, the child is at greater risk for developing mistrust, suspicion, and fear. These attitudes may carry through to later stages of development and manifest themselves behaviorally. Exaggerated behavior patterns are often the way a child copes with a situation that is overwhelming. Each child must be made to feel emotionally safe to attempt new learning. It is important to establish a responsive, nurturing environment conducive to active learning in which the child may build a positive self-concept.

Normal social/ emotional development	Social/emotional behavior of at-risk children	Teaching strategies
The child	The child	Teaching staff
• Develops and maintains healthy attachments	• May not use adults for comfort, play, approval, or object attainment	• Recognize stressors in child's environment and attempt to minimize them

Normal social/ emotional development	Social/emotional behavior of at-risk children	Teaching strategies
The child	The child	Teaching staff
• Separates from parent when trust has been established	• May go from one to another, showing no preference for a particular adult	• Provide opportunities for contact, mutual touch, and smiling throughout the day
• Learns to look for and respond to adult approval	• May not look to adult for recognition of a job well done	• Respond to specific needs of child with predictability and regularity
• Learns to respond to gestural/verbal praise and setting of limits by teacher	• May display negative feelings about self and abilities	• Need to address child by name, elicit eye contact, and/or touch child before giving verbal command
• Forms attachment to teacher	• May not respond in any way to verbal praise from adult	• Talk child through to consequences of child's actions
• Learns to socially signal desires and needs	• May ignore verbal/gestural limit setting	• Provide the child with explicitly consistent limits of behavior
• Learns to interpret and respond to social cues of adults	• May engage in negative attention-getting behavior	• Take every opportunity to develop teacher–child relations
• Learns to read and respond to social cues of peers	• May show decreased compliance with routine simple commands	• Use close proximity and gestures
• Shows broad range of emotions, including pleasure, anger, fear, curiosity, and assertiveness	• May show indiscriminate attachment to all adults	• Respond to muted signals and give child a verbal explanation of his or her behavior
• Shows a balance in emotions	• May display overly compliant behavior toward adults and peers	• Move close to the child, look at the child, and help the child read teacher's cues by explaining to the child what the teacher's look, body language, or gesture means
• Learns to regulate own inner-state	• May not signal desires by giving eye contact, gesturing, or vocalizing	• Label expression of emotions so child learns to identify those emotions
• Responds to emotions of others	• May not be able to read teacher's cue/look	• Use books, pictures, doll play, and conversation to explore and help child express a range of feelings
• Learns to develop an independent sense of self and responsible behavior, resulting in self-esteem	• May show a restricted range of emotion: Overreacts to "no" by total withdrawal; rarely smiles, laughs, or shows joy; lethargy, listlessness, flat affect, clingy behavior with adult	• Allow, identify, and react to child's expression of emotions, including pleasure, protest, excitement, anger, self-assertion, curiosity, depenency, love, and fear
• Develops a strong self-interest	• May not express/show feelings of fear, grief, worry, anger	• Model full range of emotions for child
	• May withdraw or seem to daydream	• Communicate with caregiver to determine if there has been an upset or any change of routine in the home or any family emergency or if the child's sleeping pattern has changed
	• May have poor inner controls	
	• May have difficulty modulating behavior (e.g., mood extremes, giggles turn to screams)	

Normal social/ emotional development	Social/emotional behavior of at-risk children	Teaching strategies
The child	The child	Teaching staff
	• May remain clingy and dependent on teacher for decisions and daily living activities for extended periods of time	• Assist child in gaining control by: establishing eye contact; sitting next to the child; giving verbal reassurance; providing physical comfort (i.e., teacher rubs child's back)
	• May overreact to separations from primary caregiver	• Use stories, puppets, and role play to help child develop empathy for others
	• May show some lack of self-awareness as an individual	
	• May not show concern or empathy toward others	• Provide daily opportunity for the child to practice independent feeding, dressing, bathing, toileting, and play skills and display tolerance for messiness and dawdling
		• Provide child with a daily opportunity to make small decisions and limited choices in play and/or self-help activities
		• Have activities centered around the child as an individual
		• Provide spaces (e.g., cubby with child's name) and objects in the classroom (e.g., personal toys from home and individual picture books) that are for each child

D. Communication

The child's capacity to communicate evolves from early mother–child interaction. The development of a child's language depends on the child's ability to receive, understand, integrate, and express meaningful experiences. The child learns to use gestures and words to express feelings, communicate wants, and describe experiences. A child learns language best through social interaction with significant individuals and through active exploration of the environment.

Normal communication development	Communication behaviors of at-risk children	Teaching strategies
The child	The child	Teaching staff
• Is able to follow directions appropriate for developmental level (simple commands, multiple commands)	• May have delayed receptive and expressive language	• Recognize stressors in child's environment and attempt to minimize them
• Learns to communicate simple wants and	• May be unable to follow directions that are appropriate for developmental level	• Create a stable environment in which child feels safe to express feelings, wants, and needs

Normal communication development	Communication behaviors of at-risk children	Teaching strategies
The child	The child	Teaching staff
needs, names objects, expresses feelings at appropriate developmental levels, and describes experiences and events	• May have prolonged infantile articulation at the preschool level	• Use "hands-on" activities to reinforce the child's language
• Is able to use pragmatic language	• May not use attained language to communicate feelings, wants, and needs	• Use eye contact, give simple one-step directions, and gradually increase the number of steps in a direction
• Learns to initiate appropriate interactions with peers	• May be unable to verbalize needs, wants, and fears and expresses them through behavior such as banging, stomping, and shouting	• Map language in the context of the activity
	• May show listlessness, passivity, and/or lack of social awareness	• Provide names of people, pets, food items, body parts, objects, feelings, and events in the process of conversation
	• May observe rather than verbally engage with peers in play	• Immediately respond to beginning attempts at verbal communication
	• May inappropriately initiate interaction with peers by hitting, pushing, biting, swearing, and negative verbal remarks	• Investigate child's behavior by asking child questions to discover what child needs, wants, or fears
		• Acknowledge the needs, wants, or fears of the child
		• Provide strategies to the child of how to appropriately express needs, wants, or fears
		• Acknowledge attempts by child to cooperate and interact with other children
		• Recognize that negative behavior may be a signal of child's unmet needs
		• Reflect child's feelings
		• Verbally direct child's behavior
		• Verbally cue child's attempts toward adaptive behavior
		• Ignore inconsequential verbal behavior
		• Verbalize expected behaviors
		• Redirect behavior
		• Remove child and help child calm self
		• Provide children with verbal language to use with each other
		• Will intercede with extra support for child who has used best de-

Normal communication development	Communication behaviors of at-risk children	Teaching strategies
The child	The child	Teaching staff
		velopmental skills to resolve conflict but without success
		• Set consistent limits on inappropriate behavior but allow for expression of feelings
		• Provide time to talk with child about emotions

E. Motor Development

Motor and spatial development stems from the interplay of a number of factors beginning prenatally and continuing through early childhood. Any major interferences along this continuum can result in motor/spatial impairment. As a result of prenatal exposure to drugs/alcohol, the child may exhibit varying degrees of fine, gross motor and spatial relationship delays that are neurologically based. A child's sense of autonomy over the environment is enhanced when given the opportunity to experiment and discover effective approaches in mastering activities.

Normal motor/spatial development	Motor/spatial behavior of at-risk children	Teaching strategies
The child	The child	Teaching staff
• Has awareness of body placement in relationship to the environment	• May trip or stumble without apparent cause	• Recognize stressors in child's environment and attempt to minimize them
• Has age-appropriate gross motor skills	• May have difficulty with gross motor skills (e.g., swinging, climbing, throwing, catching, jumping, running, and balancing)	• Verbally remind child of obstacles
• Has awareness of space relationships among objects in relationship to self	• May walk into stationary or moving objects	• Guide child through motor activities that emphasize rhythm, balance, and coordination
• Has awareness of space relationship among objects in relationship to each other	• May move too close or too far away from another object	• Model and guide child in learning to control the body through songs, games, and play
• Is able to manipulate objects at an age-appropriate level	• May show splaying of fingers and immature grasping skills	• Provide child with opportunities to experience spatial relationships through motor mazes and outdoor and indoor play
	• May have difficulty manipulating objects (e.g., stacking or stringing them) and cutting or drawing	• Provide a variety of tactile and fine motor activities (water and sand play, pegboards, puzzles, blocks, Legos, etc.)

Normal motor/spatial development	Motor/spatial behavior of at-risk children	Teaching strategies
The child	The child	Teaching staff
	• May exhibit tremors when stacking or stringing objects or drawing	• Observe child and note tremor occurrences and duration and how child compensates for tremors

F. Home–School Partnership

The home is recognized as an essential part of the curriculum. Research has indicated that early intervention programs are successful in producing long-term positive results only when parents/caregivers are part of the program design. Interactions between teachers and parents/caregivers must be professional, sensitive, and flexible. This relationship must be based on the expression of mutual concerns and goals.

Parents of children at risk may themselves have past and/or present experiences that can compromise their ability to effectively parent their child. Such factors as poverty, depression, a history of child abuse/neglect, family instability and violence, history of psychiatric problems, and drug abuse are taken into consideration when staff address the child's needs with the parent.

Children who reside in foster homes or are placed with extended family members are particularly vulnerable to the consequences of separation, loss, and poor attachments. These children require ongoing support and coordinated case management plans for the goal of maximizing their success within the home and in the school. The emphasis on strengthening the positive interaction between caregiver and child increases the caregiver's awareness and understanding of the child's individual needs and assists in promoting feelings of confidence and competency within the caregiver. This empowerment of the caregiver will benefit the child far beyond his or her formal school program. Teachers who have the knowledge of school/community resources and a genuine interest in the well-being of the parent/caregiver are essential to bridging the home–school partnership.

Healthy home environment	At-risk environment	Teaching strategies
The child	The child	Teaching staff
• Has a mother who received proper prenatal care	• With prenatal exposure to drugs/alcohol may: Be premature; be small for gestational age; go through withdrawal; suffer damage to gastrointestinal, endocrine, respiratory, genitourinary, cardiovascular, and/or central nervous systems	• Recognize stressors in child's environment and attempt to minimize them
• Has a consistent, responsive primary caregiver from birth		• Approach child and family history with professionalism and respect for confidentiality
• Has a predictable, safe, stable environment	• May have multiple home placements	• Identify family constellation and primary caregiver.
• Has regular eating and sleeping patterns	• May have multiple caretakers	• Develop relationship with the caregiver and open lines of communication with caregiver

Healthy home environment	At-risk environment	Teaching strategies
The child	The child	Teaching staff
• Has a mother/primary caregiver who sees herself as child's first teacher	• May live with other young children who are at risk	• Schedule ongoing visits in order to
• Is provided with established family rituals around daily living activities and special events	• May be abused and neglected	Obtain child's history (number of placements, medical history, family history, other agency involvement)
• Is provided appropriate developmental activities	• May receive inconsistent and intermittent nurturing	Identify current interventions used by caregiver
• Is encouraged to express feelings	• May have a caregiver who is emotionally unavailable	Discuss observations of child's behavior and progress
• Is encouraged to be self-sufficient and independent	• May have a caregiver who is overwhelmed or untrained in dealing with the child's emotional needs	Observe and discuss caregiver–child relationship
	• May be exposed to chaotic, unpredictable, and unstable environment	Identify parental concerns and assess family needs
		Develop individual family service plan
		Facilitate referral to other agencies as services are needed
		Encourage participation in parent education classes
		• Discuss and model the importance of predictability and organization
		By developing a transition plan with caregiver as child enters school (books, toys, expected parent attendance)
		By establishing regular patterns of communication with home (phone calls, classroom newsletter, informal notes, notebook back and forth)
		By anticipating, discussing, and integrating events at home and school (daily routine, special events)
		By discussing implications of prenatal exposure to drugs/alcohol (short-term and long-term effects)
		By promoting an understanding of psychosocial risk factors (abuse, neglect, and multiple caregivers and placements)

9

Family Support Services for Drug- and AIDS-Affected Families

GENEVA WOODRUFF
ELAINE DURKOT STERZIN

INTRODUCTION

Practitioners working with children with special needs and their families have learned that a single problem-oriented, client-focused approach has not been especially effective with families with many service needs. Delivering services to an identified client around a specific presenting problem without coordinating efforts with other involved providers has resulted in fragmented, piecemeal, narrow, rigid services that have often overlapped or missed addressing the real needs of the family. Not surprisingly, such isolated services have not always achieved their intended outcomes; in many cases they have inadvertently perpetuated families' problems.

Delivering services in this traditional mode has proven especially problematic and unsuccessful with families affected by drug use and AIDS. Most drug treatment programs have been designed to serve men and have not taken into account women's multiple roles and responsibilities—of wife, mother, family member, wage earner—necessary to sustaining the recovery process. The few treatment programs that have broadened their focus to help women with parenting and relational issues, life skills, or vocational training have noted that such support has strengthened recovery (Black & Mayer, 1980; Lief, 1985).

Similarly, counseling and educational services for children with special needs traditionally have centered solely on the child. Programs developed for children

were designed with the expectation that parents would carry out planned therapeutic and educational activities to help the child reach his or her maximum
potential. Any problems that the parents had in addition to the child's needs—
such as financial difficulties, substance addiction, marital discord, or mental
illness—were overlooked or ignored or were expected to be dealt with when the
family was referred to the "appropriate" agency for assistance. Drug-dependent
women involved in these programs feared, usually with good reason, that exposure
of their drug use would result in removal of their children from their care.
Therefore, they concealed their addiction, were reluctant to seek help, and did not
effectively use medical, social, or support services.

Dissatisfied with the ineffectiveness of single-focus service delivery, families as
well as providers have sought alternative approaches. In the 1970s and 1980s
practitioners and families developed family-centered models that focused on the
needs not only of the individual adult or child but of the entire family. These
approaches were found to be effective for families with multiple service needs,
especially families who had not previously benefited from traditionally delivered
services.

In this chapter, using case material to illustrate, we discuss the support service
needs of families affected by drug use and AIDS and describe how services can
be effectively provided using a family-centered and coordinated transagency
approach.

WOMEN, DRUG DEPENDENCE, AND AIDS:
A NATIONAL EPIDEMIC

The latest available national statistics document that over 5 million women of
childbearing age use illicit drugs; most use more than one kind of substance
(General Accounting Office, 1990). Dependence on drugs usually results in a
variety of health, psychological, social, emotional, and legal problems. Among
these problems is AIDS, which results from sharing needles or having unprotected
sex with an infected partner. AIDS has become a leading cause of death worldwide,
especially in the 19–35 age group; recent statistics indicate that the death of 1 out
of 5 women of reproductive age is caused by AIDS. This year more than 100,000
American women of reproductive age will be HIV-infected. Twenty-five to thirty
percent of the children born to these women also will be infected. As many as
20,000 American children under age 13 are thought to be infected as of this
writing. The World Health Organization predicts that 10 million children worldwide will be infected by the year 2000.

In America AIDS among women is, by and large, a minority issue. Eighty to
ninety percent of the women currently infected are African-American, Latina, or
Haitian. Many of these women were infected by their sexual partners. Of the newly
reported pediatric AIDS cases, most of whom were infected perinatally, over 85%
are African-American or Latino. Most of these women and children are poor. They

live in inner city areas torn apart by poverty, violence, and the urban drug wars. Most of the women are single parents who are dependent on welfare and other entitlement programs. They are, for the most part, undereducated and have few job skills. Many have been active drug users or partners of drug users for several years. Their access to services and adequate care is limited.

Depending on how frequently they use substances, the women may maintain a regular routine and competently care for their families or they may have unstable and unpredictable living arrangements. Homeless, moving among shelters, or staying with relatives or friends, without permanence or stability, they may be difficult to reach and engage in services. Their children may live with different relatives or friends; some may be in the care of foster families.

These women's behaviors may not be conducive to building intimate relationships based on trust with anyone; consequently, it is highly unlikely that they will be able to form a positive working relationship with a service provider. Their life patterns may be chaotic and crisis-ridden. Poor problem-solving skills result in poor decision making. As children, many were physically and sexually abused; reared in substance-abusing families where they had inadequate parental models, many are compromised in their ability to form and sustain relationships. Many shifted through a series of foster and group residential placements. As adults, they may be trapped in abusive, exploitative relationships with men. Chronic depression, anxiety, low self-esteem, low levels of trust, and high levels of guilt often result in self-destructive behaviors. Many women evidence a pattern of learned helplessness, similar to that of battered women, which often contributes to a continuing cycle of drug use and abuse (Reed, 1987).

Women who have been drug users since adolescence may know no other lifestyle and may feel that they are successful and belong only in the drug subculture. In spite of loving their children and wanting to do the best they can for them, the women may have difficulty understanding and accomplishing the tasks that are essential to creating a stable, predictable, and consistent atmosphere for their families. As long as they are in the grip of their addiction, they are developmentally ill-equipped and constitutionally limited in their ability to make sound decisions.

Addiction and living in the drug subculture results in changes in behavior and personality. The driving force and central focus of an addict's daily activity is acquiring drugs; addicts will do anything to ensure their supply. When compulsively using drugs, their behavior can be bizarre, impulsive, aggressive, hostile, self-defeating, and self-destructive. Low tolerance for anxiety or frustration leads to inconsistent, impulsive behaviors. The poor problem-solving skills of addicts result in poor planning and unrealistic expectations for themselves and their children. Addicts often are undependable, miss or are late for scheduled appointments, and forget to follow through on planned activities.

Even when drug use stops, problems with life adaptation and decision making remain. A clinical team at UCLA working with a group of women whose primary drug of choice was PCP, but who also regularly used a variety of drugs, reported that the women were limited in their ability to generalize information. They interpreted communication in a concrete and immature manner, and many had short-term memory problems. They also frequently got lost and were childlike in social situations. Although the women functioned better during recovery treatment, they continued to report difficulties with the tasks of daily living, thus demonstrating their impaired ability to provide a consistent routine for their children (Howard, Beckwith, & Rodning, 1989).

Many women with substance use histories do not live in traditional family settings and do not have the support of extended family members or partners. Rather than husbands or blood relatives, their supportive networks are "chosen family" members. Thus, a friend—often identified as a "cousin" or "sister" or a "godmother"—who is not actually related fulfills the role of a family member. Historically, kinship networks have regularly, as well as in times of crisis, provided a wealth of support for their members, including an exchange of child care and household tasks and emotional and financial help. This has been especially true in African-American, Latino, and immigrant families (Malson, 1983). Unfortunately, service providers have not traditionally recognized the central importance of chosen family members in their planning and delivery of services.

Hartman (1981) recommends an encompassing definition of family that includes persons who define themselves as family and who act toward each other as family members. To effectively make use of the supports and involvement of these chosen family members, practitioners must learn whom the family defines as belonging in its constellation and must acknowledge and respect the enduring importance of those relationships. In families where a parent is addicted or where there is an ill parent or child, it is crucial that the family determine whom they want to be involved in services. It is also critical that practitioners include alternative caregivers in their planning so as to ensure an uninterrupted flow of services when caregivers are absent for periods of time or when birth parents are too ill to care for their children.

When women become HIV-infected, yet another layer is added to their difficult lives. Already isolated and stigmatized by being a member of the drug subculture, many women believe that having AIDS will cause them to be completely ostracized from their families and neighborhoods. Some women have felt so overwhelmed with guilt and remorse for causing their child to be ill that they have left their children in hospitals or in the care of others and have escaped even deeper into the drug subculture (Lewart, 1988). Conversely, an AIDS diagnosis has often resulted in many women making a purposeful recovery from addiction and taking responsibility for themselves and their children. They work with diligence and determination to ensure that their children are loved, well cared for, and receive the medical and social services that will prolong their lives. They carefully plan for their children's future care and custody and advocate for their welfare. And they serve as supports to other women recovering from addiction or affected by AIDS.

However, it is difficult for these women to accomplish all that they need to do to care for themselves and their children alone. And it is also difficult for them to benefit from services delivered in traditional, single-client–focused methods. These approaches are inadequate, ineffective, and misdirected. To help women and children affected by substance dependence and HIV infection, the service community needs to expand its understanding of the dynamics of the addiction, recovery, and relapse process, as well as of how a chronic and debilitating illness affects how a family with limited resources functions. Drug treatment, medical care, and social service delivery must be reevaluated and realigned to meet family needs.

In order to meet the challenges of delivering services that support the woman's recovery, address the child's special medical and developmental needs, and promote healthy parent–child interactions, services to substance-using and HIV-infected women and their families must be radically expanded. Drug treatment services for women must take into account their many diverse roles and responsibilities and be tailored to strengthen their social and survival skills. Therapeutic and developmental services for drug-exposed children that are family-centered and community-based and that build on the strengths of the families must be created and implemented. Services must be coordinated, and service providers must collaborate in their efforts. From these component parts a seamless continuum of family support services must evolve.

Moreover, with AIDS disproportionately affecting people of color, it is important that service providers understand and respect the family's cultural belief system, values, traditions, and coping styles, as well as recognize how they respond to people from outside their culture and community. Services must be adapted to respect the cultural norms and language of clients. When possible, services should be delivered to a family by sensitive and caring workers from a similar culture, linguistic background, and ethnic group.

FAMILY-CENTERED SERVICE DELIVERY

The practice of delivering services with a family focus evolved in early intervention programs serving children with developmental disabilities and their families. Parents rebelled against being considered deficient and dependent by the "experts" in those programs. Recognizing parents' central importance to the child's health, well-being, and developmental outcomes and their own relative insignificance in the child's life, professionals in developmental programs began to collaborate with parents in planning the child's and family's service plan. Believing that their program efforts would be most helpful to the child and family as a whole if they were directed toward sustaining the parents in their caregiving roles, professionals began to work to support, rather than supplant, the parents' roles.

It was clear that unless families were offered services to meet their basic needs, other interventions would not be utilized by the family. A family living in an apartment that has no heat is not likely to give its full attention to working on their child's developmental intervention plan. A family that does not know where its next meal is coming from is not likely to be extraordinarily concerned about methods for weaning a toddler from the bottle. A family living in a cramped apartment in a dangerous neighborhood has more immediate and pressing concerns than helping their preschooler identify colors. Helping families to deal with their survival issues frees them to address the social, psychological, and developmental needs of their children.

Early intervention programs for children with special needs have identified service delivery that focuses on the child within the context of the family as "family-centered programming." Central to the concept of family-centered service delivery are the beliefs that all families want to do the best they can for their children and that they know more about their children than anyone else. There are eight key elements to family-centered care:

- Recognition that the family is the constant in the child's life while the service systems and personnel within those systems fluctuate
- Facilitation of parent/professional collaboration at all levels of care and intervention
- Sharing of unbiased and complete information with parents about their child's care on an ongoing basis in an appropriate and supportive manner
- Implementation of appropriate policies and programs that are comprehensive and provide emotional and financial support to meet the needs of the families
- Recognition of family strengths and individuality and respect for different methods of coping
- Understanding and incorporating the developmental needs of infants, children, and adolescents and their families into service delivery systems
- Encouragement and facilitation of parent-to-parent support
- Assurance that the design of service delivery systems is flexible, accessible and responsive to family needs. (Shelton, Jeppson, & Johnson, 1987, p. 71)

Family-centered services are provided for all family members, and families are "empowered" (Dunst, Trivette, & Deal, 1988) by maintaining a sense of control in working with service teams and meeting their own needs. The Lutheran Child and Family Service Program in Michigan defines empowerment as the "process of equipping families with the knowledge and skills necessary to provide for and protect their children, to transcend their dependency and to navigate and negotiate with systems that can provide needed support and resources" (undated). Services are determined in response to the family's strengths, needs, and priorities for services.

The literature on early intervention and early childhood programs for children with special developmental needs supports the concepts of addressing family needs and priorities as a starting point for service delivery and of involving caregivers in all aspects of program development, implementation, and evaluation. Family-centered service delivery has become a given as the best practice in the field (Dunst et al., 1988; Johnson, McGonigel, & Kaufmann, 1989; McGonigel & Garland, 1988).

The experience of parents and practitioners in early intervention led to legislation that recommended the delivery of family-centered services in programs for children with special needs. Public Law 99-457, passed in 1986, is a legislative acknowledgment that helping families to meet their needs is an essential prerequisite to helping them meet their children's needs. This law directs states to "develop and implement a statewide, comprehensive, coordinated, multidisciplinary, interagency program of early intervention services for handicapped infants and toddlers and their families" (Section 671[b]).

Family-centered service delivery was recognized as a way to flexibly respond to changing needs in families affected by AIDS by the Secretary's Work Group on Pediatric HIV Infection and Disease of the Department of Health and Human Services. The group recommended the development of family-centered, community-based, coordinated systems of care for HIV-infected children (Secretary's Work Group, 1988). Similarly, parents and caregivers of HIV-infected children have stated that the most helpful services for them and their children were those that were delivered in a coordinated and comprehensive manner and were responsive to the needs of all family members. These parents demonstrated that family members caring for children with HIV infection "frequently are able and willing to participate in planning services for their own children and, given proper support and assistance, to advise and advocate for services for other children as well" (McGonigel, 1988, p. 6).

Practitioners who have been delivering family-centered services cannot conceive of ever again delivering individually based and singularly focused services. However, those of us who have worked with families affected by drug addiction and AIDS are well aware that the realities of working with these families test the best abilities of the most experienced service providers. Not only are the families challenging, but medical and social service systems as they are presently organized do not support the delivery of family-centered services.

A CONTINUUM OF SERVICES

All families should have the right to receive a broad range of supportive services provided in the least restrictive and most normal environment consistent with the child's and family's strengths, needs, and resources. Because many families affected by drugs and HIV infection have complex and multiple needs, it is critical that they have access to a seamless continuum of services and supports and the ability to move from one service option to another, depending on their need, and to live "the most normal and dignified" life possible (Koop, 1987, p. 4). The service continuum should be part of the services readily available to all families and should build on the services already existing in the community. It should be family-centered, community-based, and part of an "organized network of integrated and coordinated services delivered locally" (Gittler, 1988, p. 3).

While the following list is by no means exhaustive, it gives a fair representation of the types of services families with an HIV-infected parent and child might need.

- Specialized medical care, preferably provided at the same facility and at the same time, for the child and other infected family members to help them deal with the effects of drug exposure and HIV infection
- At a minimum, primary health care from practitioners trained in drug and HIV treatment for the child and other infected family members; preferably, primary health care, including prenatal care for pregnant women, for the whole family
- Comprehensive, family-centered early intervention services for drug-exposed and HIV-infected children under the age of 5, including family support and education services
- Increased access to clinical trials integrated into the comprehensive care/treatment centers to assure up-to-date therapy and therapeutic research benefits for all HIV-infected adults, children, and youth
- Early childhood special education programs for infected children between the ages of 3 and 6, and regular special education services for children over the age of 6, including family support services
- Developmentally supportive child care for the infected child as well as for the noninfected children in the family
- Babysitting and respite child care
- Home health and homemaker support
- Readily available and accessible drug treatment programs, including those designed for women
- Emotional support for the family, such as grief and bereavement counseling for family members, support groups and counseling for uninfected brothers and sisters, and opportunities for family-to-family support
- Environmental and social support for the family, such as housing assistance; food stamps and other nutrition programs; employment assistance, when possible; and legal assistance, when necessary
- Specialized foster care for children or for mother/child pairs when the biological family is unable to care for them
- Adoption services for both infected and uninfected children when family members are unable to care for them or when they are orphaned by a parent's death
- Expedited procedures for extended families to obtain legal guardianship of orphaned children
- Stipends, as received by other foster families, for extended families caring for children
- Enhanced efforts to recruit culturally appropriate foster families
- Small, developmentally supportive, nurturing group homes to provide transitional or long-term care for those children who are in hospitals for nonmedical reasons and for whom foster care, adoption, or other permanent home arrangements are not immediately possible
- Subsidized transportation to allow families to use available services
- AIDS education and prevention programs for the entire community, with

special outreach to persons most at risk, including teenagers, intravenous drug users, and sexual partners of intravenous drug users

- Home-based hospice services for the child and family, as well as residential programs for both the infected parent and child
- Health and social services for undocumented aliens who are parents of HIV-infected children
- Life skills training and supported employment for those adults capable of working (adapted from Woodruff, Hanson, McGonigel, & Sterzin, 1990, pp. 19–20)

These services must be delivered in the community and coordinated. They must surmount the bureaucratic fragmentation and singularity of focus that prevent services from helping families to meet their needs. In order to succeed with families with multiple needs, programs must offer a broad spectrum of services; must cross traditional professional and bureaucratic boundaries; must be flexible; must see the child in the context of family and the family in the context of its surroundings; must be offered by people who care about their clients and respect them and by people they can trust; must offer services that are coherent and easy to use; must offer continuity of services from a small, committed team; must find ways to adapt or circumvent traditional professional and bureaucratic limitations, when necessary, to meet the needs of those they serve; and must be offered by professionals who are able to redefine their roles to respond to needs (Schorr & Schorr, 1988, pp. 257–259).

Services to drug-dependent women must focus on their recovery, parenting skills, and their life skills. Mothers' self esteem will improve with improvement in parenting skills. In a cyclic and self-reinforcing way, a mother gains necessary incentives for working on her recovery if she can feel good about her ability to care for her children (Black & Mayer, 1980). Services must be broad and address the many roles and responsibilities of the parent. Service delivery must also address the family's cultural issues and the woman's devalued role in society. Services must also take into account the importance of kinship and social networks and how they strongly influence the recovery process, especially of women (Reed, 1987). Grandmothers often provide key roles in childrearing and family support, and their central importance to family life cannot be underestimated.

Experts in the drug treatment and child welfare field believe that programs must "support the mother, protect the infant and promote positive mother–infant interaction and formation of a positive relationship" (Weston, Ivins, Zuckerman, Jones, & Lopez, 1989, p. 6). Programs that are preventive in focus and comprehensive in design and that involve prenatal care, drug treatment, and infant–parent support must be designed and implemented. Such a comprehensive approach to drug treatment helps women deal with many areas in their life in order to "unravel the strands of disorder and make possible a reasonably constructive design for living" (Lief, 1985, p. 74). Clearly, in dealing with a population of children with special medical and developmental needs and parents who are compromised in their ability to provide their children with the quality of caregiving they need, services that will be most effective will help both parents and children achieve their maximum potential.

A study conducted in eight centers across the country with children of low birth weight concluded that those infants who received early intervention, consisting of weekly home visits, child development groups, and bimonthly parent education and support, had significantly better cognitive development and better behavior than children who received only pediatric follow-up. Furthermore, children at greater risk because of social and environmental factors benefited most from early intervention services (Kong, 1990). This certainly supports the concept of intervening early and regularly with these children and families at risk and giving them a broad array of services.

However, traditionally delivered, fragmented services cannot appropriately meet the needs of the child and family in all cases. If a mother is using drugs, she may not be able to follow through in planning or delivering the care her children need. With drug treatment limited as well as inaccessible and with follow-up treatment virtually unattainable, substance-abusing women are having difficulty maintaining sobriety. Many of the child health services in the inner city are underutilized or used only episodically by these families; therefore, the children are not being seen consistently by the health professionals who could monitor their health and development. With inadequate home environments and parents who continue to use drugs, the children are exposed to potential abuse and neglect and the families are at high risk for dissolution.

Programs for substance-dependent women and their drug-exposed children have demonstrated that these families can be helped if services are designed to meet their special needs. In 1975 the Pregnant Addicts and Addicted Mothers Program (PAAM) started as a demonstration program in East Harlem. PAAM offered addiction treatment; obstetrical, pediatric, psychiatric, and general medical care; and counseling and child development services in one site on weekdays as well as weekends and had a 24-hour emergency telephone hotline. This intensive combination of services resulted in improved obstetrical outcomes, stability in recovery, improved developmental outcomes for children measured at 1 year, and improved family functioning (Suffet & Brotman, 1984).

A similar program currently operating at Boston City Hospital is showing comparable results in the maintenance of recovery and family integrity and in the reduction of behaviors that place women at high risk for HIV infection. The MOM's Project is a program designed to reduce women's risk for HIV infection through education. The project recruits women through an intensive outreach effort in the community conducted by culturally and linguistically compatible outreach workers. The outreach workers first help the women address their most pressing and immediate concerns, such as housing, food, addiction, abuse and violence, and legal or custody issues. They also work to empower the women in the program by conveying respect and helping them develop a positive sense of self (Amaro, 1990).

Two other community-based programs in Boston, Projects WIN and STAR, have demonstrated that family-centered services can help vulnerable families who had not previously benefited from services delivered by traditional methods. WIN (1986–1989) and STAR (1989–1993) use the transdisciplinary (TD) model to organize the direct services of a team composed of members from different disciplines. One service plan is developed with the family that encompasses family priorities and needs. Staffing for STAR includes social workers experienced in recovery treatment; child development specialists; physical, occupational, and speech therapists; and a nurse. In the TD team approach, all members of the team and the family plan and monitor child and family services, although all are not directly involved in delivering these services. Rather, services are delivered by one team member, who is identified as the family's primary service provider. Such an approach includes parents as decision-making team members, thus strengthening and reinforcing their caregiving roles. The model contributes to the development of a strong, trusting relationship between the family and one member of the team and, at the same time, offers the cushion of a less intense relationship with the rest of the team.

To coordinate the many services provided by the various community agencies involved with the client families, WIN and STAR employ the transagency (TA) model, which applies the rationale and principles of a transdisciplinary team based delivery to the community service system. In the TA model, practitioners from community agencies that directly serve the family form a team to develop and implement a coordinated cross-agency family service plan. This team defines the roles and responsibilities for each team member, schedules when and how interventions will take place, and determines how services will be monitored, and formulated into a single family service plan. The team selects one member to function as the case manager and gives that person the responsibility of monitoring and coordinating the activities of the service team.

The TA model also coordinates community services through the activities of a transagency board. Representatives from a variety of agencies in the community that serve the client families join together as a working board that meets on a monthly basis. Transagency board members are responsible for recommending services for children and families, advocating on families' behalf in the larger society, and overseeing the implementation of community services.

To illustrate the issues and needs of the families and to highlight how family-centered transagency services are delivered, we offer the following case.

CASE HISTORY

Diane, a 23-year-old woman of mixed racial background, and her son Dennis were referred for STAR services when Dennis was 6 months old. Diane is a recovering substance abuser, and both she and Dennis are infected with HIV.

As a child, Diane and her two siblings were removed from their mother's care on neglect charges; they spent 2 years in different foster homes before being returned home. Shortly after Diane returned home, she began using drugs and alcohol and missing school; she has smoked cigarettes and used marijuana, pills, and alcohol since the age of 11. Diane quit school and ran away from home at 14 after being sexually abused by her mother's boyfriend. She has not spoken to her mother for many years and has no idea of her father's whereabouts.

Diane came to Boston's combat zone as a runaway and, looking older than her age, worked as a dancer in nightclubs. Pregnant at age 17, she got married to an alcoholic, who abused her when he was drunk. Within 11 months they had two baby boys. After 2 years of fighting Diane's husband left, and she began going out to bars at night. At one of these bars, she met José, a 35-year-old heroin addict and drug dealer, who introduced Diane to heroin. Diane frequently left the children by themselves when she was with José. Neighbors reported Diane to the child welfare agency, claiming that the children were alone overnight. After several failed attempts to engage Diane in services the child welfare agency placed the boys in foster care on charges of neglect.

Once the boys were removed, José encouraged Diane to forget about them and concentrate on him. Diane has not seen the boys, now 5 and 4, since their foster care placement 3 years ago.

After the boys' removal Diane moved with José to a squalid, rat- and roach-infested condemned building that was also occupied by other drug users and dealers. Diane and José fought often, after which José returned to his wife and children. José beat Diane several times, including when she was pregnant with Dennis. He has thrown her possessions and the baby's furniture out on the street, hidden the keys to the car, and taken off for weeks at a time, leaving her and the baby stranded. Twice since Dennis's birth, Diane fled to a battered women's shelter. Each time José promised to change, and they reunited. During their separations, Diane paid for drugs through prostitution. She has been arrested at least three times for prostitution or shoplifting.

When she was 7 months pregnant with Dennis, Diane first entered methadone treatment. She has been inconsistent in following through with treatment and has had frequent positive urines and observable tracks. She has told the drug treatment counselor that transportation is a problem. José's car is unreliable and uninsured, and Diane does not have a valid license. When she drives to the clinic she takes roundabout routes through the city to avoid being stopped by the police. When the car is not available, she does not go to the clinic.

Although she was in drug treatment for her last 2 months of pregnancy, Diane still used heroin, and Dennis was born with positive screens for heroin and methadone. He suffered the effects of neonatal abstinence syndrome, including frantic and excessive sucking, irritability, and crying. Diane interpreted his sucking as hunger and fed him constantly during his early infancy; some days she would feed him almost twice the recommended number of ounces. Dennis has had frequent colds and ear infections, which Diane attributes to the inconsistent heat in their house; he has also had thrush and recurrent diarrhea. Diane has followed through with most of the baby's immunizations and early infant checkups, although each one was at a different neighborhood health center and usually later than the recommended time. No one pediatrician consistently followed the baby. For the first few months Diane had biweekly home visits from a visiting nurse, but she lost contact with her because of upheaval in her living arrangements.

A mandatory neglect petition was filed based on Dennis's positive drug screens. Diane was assigned a child protective case worker to determine whether she could adequately care for Dennis. This worker learned of Diane's experience with her other children and also knew José and his family very well because he supervised José's adolescent son's foster placement. The case worker was aware that José had children with several women; all of these families were involved with protective services. The case worker was strongly invested in giving Diane all the support she needed to care for Dennis. Unfortunately, within 2 months, he was reassigned to another unit; although Diane was assigned a new worker, her case was lost in the bureaucratic shuffle.

Because of her inconsistent attendance and drug use, Diane was discharged from the drug treatment program. Unable to get methadone and trying not to inject heroin, Diane experienced extreme fatigue and frequent night sweats, which she attributed to withdrawal or pregnancy. She finally went to City Hospital's emergency room because she felt so ill. A series of blood tests revealed that she is HIV positive but not pregnant. After her test came back positive, she decided to have Dennis tested as well; she has learned that he is also positive for HIV antibodies, although he will be retested at 15 months. This news has affected Diane deeply, and she states that she wants to stay clean and lead a healthy life off the streets. José disappeared after Diane told him the test results.

Diane was afraid to stay alone with the baby in the building she had occupied with José, so she moved in with Tessie, a woman in her late forties who is recovering from substance addiction, whom she met at an NA meeting. Tessie agreed to let Diane and Dennis stay with her until they find a place to live and offered to care for Dennis when Diane needed help. Diane and Dennis share a cramped bedroom and sleep together in a twin bed.

Diane took the necessary steps to get reinstated for methadone treatment and counseling at the city program. Her counselor referred her to STAR for help with housing and child development services for Dennis.

During her initial intake meeting with a STAR team member, which took place at the drug treatment center with the drug counselor present, Diane said that more than anything else she wanted to make a good home for Dennis. She talked wistfully about getting her other children back and about trying to get back together with José so they could be a family. She believed this could happen if only they both could stay away from drugs. Diane said she wanted to find a decent apartment and medical care at the same place for both herself and Dennis. Since she felt too tired to play with him, Diane wanted to find day care for Dennis so he could be with other children. The only women she knew who had babies were still using drugs, and Diane felt that she had to stay away from them to stay clean.

As part of the intake process, Dennis was assessed by the transdisciplinary team. He was a small, placid child with delays in speech and gross motor development and moderate tightness in his trunk and lower extremities. The team had concerns about the quality of his play and his manipulation of toys because he could not bring his hands to midline. The team believed Dennis could benefit from develomental intervention.

The information gained during the intake and assessment process was presented to the transagency board. Discussions among board members and STAR staff to develop the family's individualized sevice plan resulted in the following recommendations based on Diane's stated needs and priorities:

- Enroll Dennis in the STAR early intervention and day care program 5 days per week and provide transportation.
- Facilitate Diane's application for subsidized housing.
- Arrange primary and infectious disease care at City Hospital clinics for Diane and Dennis with coordinated medical appointments.
- Provide prevention education concerning safer sex and needle use.
- Support Diane's recovery by coordinating intervention with her drug treatment counselor.
- Help Diane bring closure to the custody issues of her sons in foster care.
- Help Diane deal with her relationship with José, and if she chooses to continue the relationship, work with José to help him enter drug treatment.
- Help Diane negotiate her living arrangements with Tessie until she finds her own apartment.
- Include Tessie in discussions concerning Dennis's care needs.
- Encourage Diane to participate in STAR's parent education and support groups, where she can make friends with other women working on recovery and AIDS-related concerns.
- Help Diane clear up outstanding warrants related to prostitution and shoplifting charges.
- Help Diane straighten out Medicaid and welfare benefits, which had lapsed in the confusion of her many moves.
- Look into social security benefits as an alternate means of support.
- Help Diane arrange taxi vouchers for her methadone treatment and other medical appointments.
- Call together the involved service providers, including a child protective worker, to form a transagency case management team.

The STAR case manager talked with Diane about meeting with the other service providers and was given permission to call them together. She called Diane's drug counselor, the AIDS clinic admissions coordinator, and the visiting nurse with whom Diane had a relationship. She also called the child protective agency to locate the assigned worker for Dennis and invited that worker to participate in the case conference. At this meeting it was agreed that the drug counselor would focus with Diane on recovery issues and would advise other members of the case management team on ways that they could support and reinforce Diane's recovery treatment; the visiting nurse would resume making home visits at least once a month and reinforce Diane's appropriate use of medical services at City Hospital; the AIDS clinic personnel would coordinate Diane's and Dennis's medical care, including retesting Dennis at 15 months; and the STAR worker would assume case management responsiblities for the team and help Diane with housing, parenting, management, and developmental and custody issues, as well as help her make use of the services provided by STAR. The STAR worker would work with Diane, Dennis, and Tessie at home as well as at the center. The case management team agreed to meet every 3 months to review how they were addressing and meeting family needs for the services.

Based on this case conference, the STAR case manager drafted an Individualized Family Service Plan (IFSP), including goals and objectives for the family. In order to not overwhelm Diane, the IFSP contained activities that responded to her immediate priorities, such as housing and Dennis's enrollment in day care. In addition to center-based services, the case manager also visited Diane, Dennis, and Tessie at home to work on activities.

Dennis adjusted very well to the STAR early intervention and day care program. Diane had him dressed and ready every morning when the bus arrived and helped to strap him in the car seat. On the mornings when Diane was at drug counseling, Tessie put him on the bus. Two mornings a week Diane came to the center and worked with Dennis in his early intervention group. During these groups she learned activities that help Dennis relax the tightness in his trunk and extremities and that help him manipulate objects. Dennis's gross motor skills improved, and he began sitting independently and crawling; he enjoyed being with other children and the staff, responding to them with smiles, coos, and gurgles. Diane took pleasure in his accomplishments and pride in her increased ability to better understand and care for him. She also enjoyed parent group meetings, where she talked with other mothers.

Diane spent a lot of time using the telephone at the center to track down apartments and complete housing applications with the STAR worker's help. Finding an apartment in a neighborhood that was safe and accessible to the hospital, STAR, and the drug treatment program, an apartment that was close to Tessie and not in the housing projects, was a formidable task. The STAR worker helped Diane get her name on housing lists at city agencies, complete applications, and register with apartment management companies. However, Diane was not encouraged that she would find housing in less than 3 years. The STAR worker talked with Diane and Tessie to help them work out compatible arrangements for sharing costs and household jobs.

Through the efforts of the child protective worker, Diane learned that her older sons had been released for adoption and were going to be adopted by their foster parents. Because neither Diane nor her husband had seen the boys since their placement and because neither had responded to correspondence from the department, the agency had applied for court permission to proceed with permanency planning for the boys. Diane was devastated by this news and felt that her attempts to change her life were futile. This setback seriously compromised her sobriety. With Diane's permission, the STAR worker contacted the drug counselor and the child welfare worker and together they worked out extra supports to help Diane cope. In addition, she helped Diane write a letter to the boys, which the child welfare worker delivered.

Dennis's retest indicated that he was HIV positive. Diane's worst fear was confirmed and was the source of great pain. Anticipating that this would be devastating, the STAR worker went with her to the AIDS clinic to learn the results. They had a lengthy discussion with the hospital nurse about options for Dennis's ongoing medical care and arranged for follow-up appointments. The STAR worker provided extra support at this time because she was concerned that the bad news might be a trigger causing Diane to slip. She felt that Diane might not be able to stay sober and continue working on her resolve to change her life because of the finality of losing the boys to adoption and Dennis's confirmed HIV diagnosis. In addition, José had been coming around again and tempting Diane with promises of their being together.

As feared, Diane slipped. Saying she was going out for a few hours, she left Dennis with Tessie on a Friday evening and did not return until after Tessie put Dennis on the bus Monday morning for the day care program. Diane was confused, upset, and full of remorse when she returned. Although she had spent the weekend with José and had gotten high, she also came to the conclusion that she could not go back to José without sacrificing her sobriety and Dennis. Diane talked with the STAR worker about the weekend, about her decision not to see José again, and about her resolve to increase her attention on her recovery and Dennis's care.

In the months that followed, Diane attended group counseling regularly and participated in group meetings at the STAR program. She became close to the other mothers in the program, receiving a lot of support from the group while also giving support. She and Dennis have had relatively stable health and have regularly attended both STAR and hospital appointments. Dennis's development is progressing, and Diane is proud of his accomplishments.

The service coordination team met every 3 months to review services. When Diane's stability and attachment to STAR increased, the visiting nurse reduced her contact to once a month. The team helped Diane coordinate hospital services and called in legal consultants to help her clear up her warrants and also write a will naming Tessie as Dennis's guardian. No progress was made in finding an apartment for Diane and Dennis. Tessie offered to let them stay with her indefinitely and even arranged to exchange apartments with a neighbor whose grown children had left home and who therefore had available room.

Summary

The high level of communication and coordination among the practitioners afforded by the transagency case management model provided the supportive services for Diane, Dennis, and Tessie that helped them stay together and function as a family. Diane was helped to acquire and use the services she needed, the quality of her and Dennis's life was improved, and she learned the skills she needed to continue caring for him. Without these coordinated, comprehensive supportive services, it is highly likely that Diane would not have been able to work on her recovery and Dennis would have become part of the foster care system. Using one person to help Diane coordinate services certainly has been a critical factor in the family's ability to benefit from services.

CONCLUSIONS AND POLICY RECOMMENDATIONS

Projects like STAR, WIN, PAAM, and the MOM's have demonstrated that it is possible to provide families the supports they need to function better, that is, to maintain progress in their recovery, to improve the health and development of their drug-exposed and HIV-infected children, to improve the ability of parents to care for their children, and to overcome the odds against them. These programs work to improve the immediate situations of families while also preventing the perpetuation of addiction, poverty, and child neglect. Programs that strengthen and support family functioning and programs that coordinate available services are investments in families' futures.

The noted pediatrician and vocal supporter of families, T. Berry Brazelton (1990) called the "anger and addictions of the impoverished . . . a national crisis" and exhorted the National Commission on Children to make families its top priority. However, in order to make families a top priority in this country, attitudes toward those who are impoverished, addicted, or afflicted by disability and disease must be changed. The design and delivery of services to families must be radically altered.

In order to widely implement programs that will help families, Lisbeth and Daniel Schorr (1988) believe that we must address six great challenges: knowing what works; proving we can afford it; attracting and training enough skilled and committed personnel; resisting the lure of replication through dilution; gentling the heavy hand of bureaucracy; and devising a variety of replication strategies (p. 267).

We have demonstrated that a family-centered, community-based approach works for families with multiple social, environmental, medical, and developmental needs. Now it is important to replicate this model and ensure that such practice becomes the norm. In order to accomplish this, we must have uniform policies of family support. We must also have sufficient and secure financial support from federal, state, and local governments as well as from private sources. We need to operationalize a comprehensive continuum of services, readily and universally available to families, based on their need. We need to reevaluate how services are funded and develop noncategorical criteria for family eligibility.

Revolutionary changes in how services are delivered can happen within existing structures. However, revolutionary changes cannot occur until the attitudes of funders, administrators, and service providers toward families affected by drug use and AIDS are changed. By investing now in services that support family functioning, we are ensuring the future growth and success not only of our nation's citizens but also of our nation.

REFERENCES

Amaro, H. (1990, August 12). *HIV prevention with pregnant women: Preliminary findings from the MOM's project.* Paper presented at the 98th Annual American Psychological Association Convention, Boston, MA.

Black, R., & Mayer, J. (1980). Parents with special problems: Alcoholism and opiate addiction. *Child Abuse and Neglect, 4,* 45–54.

Brazelton, T. B. (1990, September 9). Is our nation failing its children? *The New York Times Magazine,* pp. 49–90.

Dunst, C. J., Trivette, C., & Deal, A. (1988). *Enabling and empowering families: Principles and guidelines for practice.* Cambridge, MA: Brookline Books.

U.S. General Accounting Office. (1990). Drug-exposed infants: A generation at risk (No. GAO/HRD-90-138). Washington, DC: Author.

Gittler, J. (1988). Case management for children with special health care needs. In H. M. Wallace, G. Ryan, & A. C. Olgesby (Eds.), *Maternal and child health practices* (3rd ed., pp. 659–666). Oakland, CA: Third Party Publishing.

Hartman, A. (1981, January). The family: A central focus for practice. *Social Work, 26,* 7–13.

Howard, J., Beckwith, L., & Rodning, C. (1989, September). *Adaptive behavior in recovering female polysubstance abusers.* UCLA Department of Pediatrics, Los Angeles.

Johnson, B. J., McGonigel, M. J., & Kaufmann, R. K. (1989). *Guidelines and recommended practices for the Individualized Family Service Plan.* Washington, DC: Association for the Care of Children's Health.

Kong, D. (1990, June 13). Early programs found to help babies at risk. *The Boston Globe,* p. 4.

Koop, C. E. (1987). Keynote address made at Surgeon General's Workshop on Children with HIV Infection and Their Families. Philadelphia.

Lewart, G. (1988). Children and AIDS. *Social Casework: The Journal of Contemporary Social Work, 69,* 348–354.

Lief, P. (1985). The drug user as a parent. *The International Journal of the Addictions, 20*(1), 63–97.

Lutheran Child and Family Service (undated). *Empowerment.* Southfield, MI: Author.

Malson, M. (1983). The social-support systems of black families. *The ties that bind* (pp. 37–57). New York: The Haworth Press.

McGonigel, M. J. (1988). *Family meeting on pediatric AIDS* (Project No. MCJ-113 793, Maternal and Child Health, Health Resources and Services Administration, Department of Health and Human Services). Paper from the Family Meeting on Pediatric AIDS. Washington, DC: Association for the Care of Children's Health.

McGonigel, M. J., & Garland, C. (1988). The individualized family service plan and the early intervention team: Team and family issues and recommended practices. *Infants and Young Children, 1*(1), 10–21.

Reed, B. G. (1987). Developing women-sensitive drug dependence treatment services: Why so difficult? *Journal of Psychoactive Drugs,* 151–164.

Schorr, L., & Schorr, D. (1988). *Within our reach.* New York: Doubleday.

Secretary's Work Group on Pediatric HIV Infection and Disease. (1988). *Final report of the secretary's work group on pediaric HIV infection and disease.* Washington, DC: Department of Health and Human Services.

Shelton, T., Jeppson, E., & Johnson, B. (1987). *Family-centered care for children with special health care needs.* Washington, DC: Association for the Care of Children's Health.

Suffet, F., & Brotman, R. (1984). A comprehensive care program for pregnant addicts: Obstetrical, neonatal and child development outcomes. *International Journal of the Addictions, 19*(2), 199–219.

Weston, D., Ivins, B., Zuckerman, B., Jones, C., & Lopez, R. (1989). Drug-exposed babies: Research and clinical issues. *Zero to Three, 9*(5), 1–7.

Woodruff, G., Hanson, C., McGonigel, M., & Sterzin, E. D. (1990). *Community-based services for children with HIV infection and their families: A manual for planners, service providers, families and advocates.* Boston, MA: Author.

10

Drug-Exposed Infants and Their Families: A Coordinated Services Approach

MILDRED THOMPSON

One of the most challenging tasks facing professionals in the health care service delivery system is initiating and maintaining effective collaborative relationships with appropriate agencies. This is particularly challenging for those working with infants born exposed to drugs and AIDS. These cases require massive amounts of coordination, collaboration, cooperation, and consistent follow-up. It is impossible for a single agency to provide the range of services required by this population; therefore, it is essential that agencies and organizations that may never have worked together before become partners to meet these special needs.

This chapter presents a framework for assessing coordination needs of drug- and AIDS-exposed infants, discusses the reasons for coordination of services, indicates common barriers and consequences of the lack of coordination, and presents a structure for initiating a system of coordination. The primary focus is on providing services to drug-exposed infants during the first 3 years of life. References are made to resources within California, but most of those noted are available in other states.

NEED FOR COORDINATION

Outreach efforts to encourage pregnant substance-using women to receive prenatal care are often unsuccessful. Reluctance to seek health and social services is typical of this population. There may be fear of being discovered as a drug user or fear of law enforcement or child protective services, or there may simply be a lack of priority on the need for health care. As a result, some cities have been very creative in their outreach strategies.

Increasing the awareness of drug dealers about the effects of drugs on mothers and babies has been effective in some areas. There have been instances in which drug dealers have refused to sell to pregnant women. Some had wallet-sized referral lists with drug treatment phone numbers that they distributed. Even if the number of women reached was low, there was success in the ability to educate dealers about the impact of drugs on infants. Similarly, many churches have been active participants in providing outreach to members of their congregations and of their larger community. Many have acted as a service broker for troubled families by providing food, counseling, referrals for housing, drug treatment, and health care. Schools and child care centers also have been a source of referral for pregnant women who may be suspected of using drugs. The community is rich with people who want to help. As service providers, we may need to take the initiative in letting them know how to access our services.

In most instances, however, entry into the health care delivery system for women who deliver drug-exposed infants occurs when they arrive at the hospital. Often with no prenatal care and living in unstable situations or with inconsistent support systems, many substance-abusing women just show up in labor at the county hospital. In fact, labor may have been precipitated by drug use. Health professionals face their initial challenge during this point of entry because they have no medical, social, or drug history on the woman. Her ability or willingness to follow through on discharge recommendations is unknown. Essential information, such as length and type of drug use and prior history of children being removed, is missing.

Many hospitals have developed a protocol of performing a toxicology screen on all women who present in labor without prenatal care. Typically, the screen determines if opiates, cocaine, amphetamines, or barbiturates have been taken in the past 72 hours. Unfortunately, there are no universal follow-up requirements or standards if the toxicology screen is positive. Protocols vary in different hospitals, from immediately placing the child in child protective custody to discharging mother and infant without any required follow-up. Attempts should be made to provide some type of follow-up service for the infant and mother.

Many hospitals in California will refer the case to either Social Services, Public Health Nursing, or Child Protective Services (CPS). Generally, a psycho-social assessment is made of the mother's receptivity and ability to care for the baby. Attempts are also made to determine any prior CPS history and the extent of drug use. Ideally, this assessment is done within 24 hours of delivery of all drug-exposed infants or infants born to HIV-positive mothers. A discharge plan is developed on the basis of the assessment findings. Medical, social, and economic needs of the family are identified and appropriate resources sought. A case manager should be assigned to coordinate referrals and ensure that services are provided in a timely manner. If a case manager is not available, a social worker or nurse assigned to the nursery can perform some of these functions prior to discharge. Some of the services that may be required include the following:

- Identification of a pediatric provider
- Locating medical resources near mother's residence
- Scheduling of postpartum and family planning visits
- Referrals for Medicaid; Women, Infant, and Children Services (WIC); regional centers (agencies that serve the disabled and infants at risk for disabilities)
- Referrals for drug treatment and housing
- Referrals for HIV counseling and information

Many hospitals do not have enough staff to provide comprehensive follow-up for these special needs families. In those situations, it is important that someone take responsibility for initiating contact with the mother and referring her to an outside agency such as CPS, visiting nurses, or public health nursing. In some agencies, there are staff who work specifically with these families, maintaining a caseload of about 15 to 30 cases.

The Healthy Infant Program (HIP) of Highland Hospital in Oakland, California, provides case management and substance abuse services to drug-exposed infants and their families. Contact is made with women immediately following delivery of the infant. By initiating a relationship early between mother and health worker, there is a greater possibility of sustaining a more meaningful, lasting relationship. Case managers (social workers and public health nurses) provide follow-up for 1 to 2 years and work closely with substance abuse counselors, treatment programs, and hospital staff in coordinating required services.

In the first 3 years of the program 270 families were served. Compliance with pediatric appointments increased by 70%. Initially, case managers maintained a caseload of 45 clients; this number was reduced to 25 when it became apparent that other children in the home also required services. The intensity of the families' needs was too great for workers to effectively intervene with such a large number of cases. Extensive networking and collaboration were required to provide the range of services needed. Although a typical family may have been involved with health care providers, treatment counselors, the regional center, and other support programs, the primary worker involved was the case manager. Thus, soliciting the cooperation of the mother while she was still in the hospital was critical to ensuring that needed services were obtained.

It is crucial that a bond be established between the mother and worker prior to discharge for optimal follow-up to occur. Some hospitals require a contract to be signed by the mother to encourage compliance. The contract may include requirements for monthly home visits by the worker, attendance at drug recovery groups for the mother, and consistent pediatric visits. Some hospitals have agreements with CPS to enforce discharge plans and contracts. All agree that once the mother leaves the hospital without any agency being clearly responsible for monitoring the case, it is then almost impossible to provide appropriate services for the mother or the infant.

Even with a comprehensive approach, adequate staffing, a signed contract, and good coordination with CPS, a percentage of families will be "lost to follow-up," meaning that they are unable to be located. Women sometimes give wrong addresses and phone numbers. Many do not fear CPS consequences and have no intention of following through once they leave the hospital. Some also know which hospitals have tough policies for mothers of drug-exposed infants and therefore avoid them. There have been women who travel from county to county to deliver at the most "lenient" hospital.

Ideally, to best address the needs of this high-risk population, a hospital-based multidisciplinary team should be responsible for working with the mother and infant. Members would include social workers, nurses, substance abuse and HIV counselors, developmental psychologists, nutritionists, and medical providers. This team, with the cooperation of the family, should meet regularly to continue to assess the family's adjustment to the baby, provide support to the family, and ensure the smooth flow of services. Clearly, this requires the basic foundation of collaboration: a commitment from all the various agencies to work together.

Initiating this process of collaboration often has ethical and legal considerations. Determining who should have access to what information can be challenging. When working with families with infants who have been drug or HIV exposed, it is important to know the laws regarding confidentiality. For example, in working with HIV-positive infants, crucial background information may not be revealed to other service providers or to family members without the mother's consent. Signed consents must be obtained from the mother before referring to any of the various agencies—except CPS. Unless the infant receives follow-up services at the hospital where she or he was born, the pediatric provider may not even be aware of the drug exposure because of limited access to medical records; health professionals are not permitted to reveal this information without consent. As a result, the provider is operating under a disadvantage and the infant may not receive necessary services such as referral for developmental testing or more intensive medical exams.

Depending on the extent of drugs used during pregnancy, the infant may need special care prior to discharge. Those born with obvious medical problems may be transferred to the intensive care nursery of a tertiary care setting. Infants with symptoms such as irritability, excessive crying, and sensory sensitivities may be placed on a monitor and required to stay in the regular nursery for a longer period of time. Many infants born exposed to drugs require no special medical treatment. It is, however, important that they receive regular pediatric medical visits, obtain the required immunizations, and establish a relationship with one primary provider who can monitor their development. Because little is known about the long-range effects of drug exposure on the fetus, it is important that all infants born exposed to drugs receive regular pediatric follow-up services.

In a HIP study done by a staff psychologist on infants born exposed to drugs but with no outstanding medical problems, 41% were found to be developmentally delayed by 9 months of age (Stewart, 1990); the delay ranged from 1 to 4 months below normal standards. Because only limited research studies are available regarding developmental screenings of drug-exposed infants, no conclusive information is available on long-term effects. Whenever possible, these infants should be tested at least twice in the first year because they are at risk for developmental delay. Although there is debate in the professional community on whether the effects on the infants are solely the result of drugs or a combination of drugs and environmental factors, early intervention is essential in detecting and possibly preventing long-term consequences.

Convincing the mother of the need for ongoing pediatric follow-up is one of the first tasks of the worker assigned to the family. Because many of the women have not obtained prenatal care, they often lack an understanding of the need for preventive services. Many of the women enter pregnancy with a range of social and medical risk factors. The effects of poverty, poor nutrition, inadequate and transient housing, ineffective parenting models, mental health problems, and high-risk sexual practices all have an impact on pregnancy outcomes.

In addressing these issues, health care providers should involve the family in developing a plan of action. Workers must examine their own values and beliefs when working with this population. Many people feel a great need to reach out to babies born exposed to drugs and AIDS but feel some reluctance to reach out and sensitively engage the mother. In order for services to be effective, the family must feel a level of acceptance. This means that workers will need to spend more time understanding the dynamics of their clients' family systems and relationships. It means involving the father of the baby, if he is present. Many times, workers only focus on the identified client, failing to realize how easily their efforts can be sabotaged by a family member not involved in the planning and treatment process. The needs of the family must be addressed as well as the needs of the infants.

Organizations must provide training and support to those who work with these families. If the family feels reluctance or lukewarm acceptance, workers will find it even more difficult to establish the basic relationship that is needed for any effective plan of action to be accomplished. Social service agencies, hospitals, and treatment programs often have training sessions, seminars, and workshops for service providers of high-risk populations. Networking with these agencies is recommended.

Infants born to HIV-positive mothers require consistent medical attention and periodic testing. Intensive coordination must occur not only for adequate medical services to be provided but also for the vast amount of emotional and social support needed by these families. Agencies working with substance abuse clients may be the first to identify families at risk of AIDS. Thorough family health histories, including drug and alcohol use, are essential elements in initial screenings. Encouraging an at-risk client to get tested for HIV can be a challenge. If the client consents, support and encouragement are still needed to have the client obtain the test results.

Becky was a 35-year-old woman who delivered a cocaine- and opiate-positive baby. In the initial psychosocial assessment she readily admitted to a 15-year heroin habit, a 3-year occasional use of cocaine, and a 10-year prostitution history and to living with a former IV drug user who was recently released from prison. Clearly, there were risk factors for AIDS. Becky appeared to bond well with the infant and expressed a desire to change her lifestyle. She was, however, not interested in taking an HIV test or in having her newborn tested, admitting, "I just don't want to know." After working with Becky for several months and providing the concrete services she needed (bus tickets for keeping appointments, formula, diapers, counseling regarding the physical abuse), her case manager and her substance abuse counselor developed a trusting relationship with her. Becky finally agreed to HIV testing but refused to get the results. After several more months she agreed to get the baby tested. Three months after taking the test, Becky obtained her results; she immediately shared her positive test results with her workers. They provided tremendous support for her and assisted her with the next step: finding an agency to refer her to that would offer the range of support services she needed. Following the initial shock and depression, the positive test results gave Becky renewed motivation to make some of the changes she had talked about during her initial psychosocial assessment. She decided that she wanted to leave the abusive relationship. She was afraid to tell her partner of the test results and chose instead to go to a shelter that was 25 miles away. At the time of case closure, 18 months after initial involvement, Becky had stopped using drugs and alcohol and had initiated contact with her family. She was getting support from her family and the new friends she made at the shelter. However, her follow-through on HIV services remained inconsistent.

Although the client demonstrated an ability to follow through with some of the services recommended, it was not without consistent, supportive intervention. The evidence of a client's positive HIV status is difficult for workers. It is not unusual for them to share the anger, denial, hopelessness, and grief of their clients. Services, all too often, are lacking. Many HIV programs are not minority- or women-focused and have a limited capacity for meeting the needs of children born to HIV-affected women. Staff training is required to understand the range of client needs; emotional, legal, and medical issues are just a few areas that should be addressed following a positive HIV test. Agencies are challenged to find creative ways to integrate HIV education into their programs, provide staff support, and network with agencies providing testing, counseling, and support services to HIV-positive clients.

Agencies working with multiple-need families must accept the reality that a single agency cannot possibly meet all the client's needs. By actively collaborating with other agencies involved with the family, one common goal can be established: the health and well-being of the infant and its family. Coordination is defined as "the harmonious functioning of parts for most effective results" (*Webster's Seventh New Collegiate Dictionary*, 1971). Member agencies should acknowledge and appreciate their differences and work toward integrating these parts into a fully functional unit. When such collaboration works well, tremendous benefits—a sense of cooperation and accomplishment, teamwork, and the development of effective strategies and interventions—result, thus improving the outcomes toward which each agency strives: a healthy baby, a system that works, and a parent who is aware of the problems in her life, equipped with tools to deal with them.

BARRIERS TO COORDINATION OF SERVICES

How do we achieve this state of efficiency? What is involved in making this ideal real for our clients and agencies? One of the first steps is to critically examine the barriers to effective collaboration.

Organizational Barriers

Although the recent trend is toward mandating coordination and collaboration, many agencies have not fully accepted this idea. Many who have accepted the idea have not instituted practices that make it happen. Having administrative support for multidisciplinary planning is crucial. Administrative support begins with creating an atmosphere within the agency that validates the need for ongoing collaboration. Meeting with other administrators to delineate staff and agency tasks and roles is crucial. Endorsing the attendance of staff at planning meetings and allocating necessary funds are ways in which administrators can accelerate the collaborative process.

Some agencies naively believe that their agency alone can serve the needs of these complex clients. Some arrogantly insist that although they can't meet all the service needs of their clients, their agency is clearly superior and should have the lead in any case planning. There is often mistrust of other agencies and possibly a history of not relating well with needed agencies. In the past this reluctance to coordinate did not have such devastating effects because those clients had limited needs. Now, with a new set of clients who have numerous needs, it is crucial for agencies to collaborate and coordinate services to meet the multifaceted needs of their clients.

Regional centers are an example of agencies caught somewhat unprepared by the recent increase in referrals of drug-exposed infants. Because these infants are at risk for developmental delay, many are referred to regional centers. The usual role of these centers is to provide assessments, make referrals, provide case management, and seek other services necessary for developmentally disabled people. In many instances staff members are unsure of how to deal with this increasingly large number of at-risk babies. They have had to learn about other agencies and collaborate more. Many have instituted preventive programs geared to serve infants who have social or medical risk factors.

Communication between agencies about existing and new services is crucial in the collaborative process. In some instances organizations may not even be aware of services available at other institutions. There could be a reduction of expenses and energy and an end to duplication of services if the old "turf wars" were to cease. A beginning step for these organizations is the development of an effective network that would include primary organizations serving the same population. An agreement in the form of "memorandums of understanding" could be developed, outlining involvement by each representative; agency heads should be involved in this step because line staff cannot generate and enforce these agreements.

Client Barriers

In developing any effective plan for the family, agencies must understand the dynamics of the population being served. If agencies have been able to create positive working relationships among themselves and agree on a plan of intervention but fail to involve the family, they will not achieve optimal results. Being aware of the behavioral patterns of their clients increases the possibility of success. Understanding the culture and nature of addiction is critical in working with substance-using clients. Recognizing manipulative patterns, impulsive behaviors, and tendencies of relapse will prevent workers from falling into pitfalls of doing too much or giving up too soon. As mentioned earlier, these are not clients who tend to seek preventive services. Their lifestyles have precluded the type of planning professionals might expect of them. Their ability to follow through on plans, even well-developed and beneficial ones, will often fall short. In beginning a relationship with clients who are already suspicious and who are often not seeking intervention, it is important to ask clients what they see as their primary concerns and to concentrate on small goals first until a stronger relationship develops.

Jenny was a 23-year-old woman with four children; two were drug exposed and one was severely developmentally delayed. Jenny was short-tempered and had been known to hit her children. She was in a physically abusive relationship with a man who had been in prison for most of the previous year. After making a home visit and observing the small living quarters, lack of patience toward the children, and general lack of interest in following through on pediatric visits for her newborn, the social worker asked Jenny what she saw as her most pressing need. What Jenny wanted most was to get the developmentally delayed child out of the house and into a special program. She was not interested in drug counseling (although she was still using drugs), support groups, individual therapy, pediatric follow-up, family planning, parenting classes, or even having the social worker come to visit her every month. She accepted the social worker's visits only because a partnership existed between CPS and the social worker's agency. She was able to keep her newborn with her by cooperating with the social worker. Only after a program was found for the developmentally delayed child could the mother begin to hear some of the concerns raised by the social worker. Joint sessions were held with the parents about abuse of the mother and the baby. Jenny developed a relationship with her case manager and began attending a support group. She also realized that her anger toward her children was related to pent-up anger toward her boyfriend.

It would have been too ambitious for the social worker to address all these serious issues at once, especially without the mother's consent and cooperation. By focusing initially on what Jenny saw as important and actually delivering a tangible product (school placement), the first goal was accomplished. This established the framework for other goals to be met. It also created basic trust in the worker by a woman who was extremely guarded and distrustful.

In their zeal to rapidly intervene with families, workers sometimes ignore obvious family needs and barriers. The most common barriers identified by families in following through with medical and social services include access problems such as transportation, child care, and long waiting lines. If clients do not understand what services they should use, why they are asked to use them, and how to use them, their most immediate daily challenges will be certain to consume their attention and efforts.

If an infant has been transferred to a tertiary care setting, access issues are often a real problem. Because these hospitals may be far from a family's home, families often encounter difficulty in visiting the baby. One children's hospital was successful in obtaining funds to develop a large house for families who lived out of the area to stay in while visiting their child.

There is a taxi voucher and drop-in child care service for families enrolled in perinatal substance abuse programs at Oakland's Highland Hospital (a county hospital for Alameda County, California). Thus, parents can maintain necessary medical appointments and attend support groups without child care being a barrier.

Unstable housing is one of those everyday challenges many families in crisis must cope with. Because of their drug use, many clients have alienated close family members. The result is a pattern of transient living that leads to the client's being lost to follow-up. Many women who deliver drug- and AIDS-exposed infants continue to use drugs. Their primary focus may be on obtaining drugs and finding a place to live, *not* on following through with individual service plans. In the initial contact and in developing a plan for continued involvement, workers should obtain several phone numbers of people who may know how to contact the client if housing emerges as a primary concern.

Health professionals are forced to become increasingly creative in how they provide services to high-risk populations. Home visits are advisable, and providing several services in one setting, when possible, increases the likelihood of compliance. By making home visits, health professionals can obtain crucial information by observing mother–infant interactions in their own environment and by performing home assessments. With the latter information workers can determine who in the family establishes rules and makes decisions. In many instances a grandmother has more control than the mother over what services are accepted. If this decision maker is ignored, usually nothing meaningful will happen. When trying to introduce a new or unfamiliar service to the family, the home is often a safe place for the worker to begin.

The HIP program, for instance, made many unsuccessful attempts to get babies in for developmental assessments. Yet home visits by the psychologist resulted in far more receptivity and cooperation from clients. The psychologist had a wonderful opportunity to observe how the mother interacted with the infant. By involving the mother in the actual assessment process, not only was there a more cooperative testing environment but this opportunity served to demystify the assessment procedure for the family. Another technique used by this program was the inclusion of the mother in the Individual and Family Service Plan meeting. Surprisingly, many mothers welcomed the opportunity to participate in the planning of goals and services. This meeting involved the case manager, substance abuse counselor, and psychologist. At the end of the 2-hour meeting, everyone was clear about the next year's expectations and the role each person had in accomplishing the goals. The mother was made to feel more like a member of the team, rather than an observer or simply a recipient of preplanned goals and services.

RESULTS OF LACK OF COORDINATION

Frequently, families with substance abuse histories are involved with several agencies. Often, these families are in a constant state of crisis. If a mother who recently delivered a baby is required to go to 6 to 10 different agencies, she will usually not follow through. A specific agency may be unaware of plans being developed by other agencies for the family. Agencies may, in fact, conflict with each other in their expectations. The resulting confusion is reason enough for the family to drop out of the system until another crisis arises. Withdrawal from services is a serious consequence.

Duplication of services results when clients are being served by multiple agencies. It can be time-consuming, difficult, and frustrating for a family to go to three or four different places and to be asked the same questions. Many of these agencies want to do their own assessments and provide case management in their own programs. Fragmented services, duplication of services, and a lack of service responsibility result when efforts are uncoordinated. It is less frustrating for the family to have one body of professionals to deal with that represents the various organizations. This body should meet on a regular basis and decide who will do what and when.

This type of group collaboration does not mean that an individual agency must become passive or surrender total control of the client. It does mean becoming more aware of an agency's specific area of expertise, appreciating the expertise of others, and becoming an active and willing participant in effective case planning. It also means that caregivers must place the family and its needs above any interagency resistance.

INITIATING A COORDINATED APPROACH

Once a collaborative agreement has been reached among willing agencies, a coordination plan can be set. Some useful guidelines follow:

List all services the client is receiving. The agency initiating the coordination should write down all the organizations the client is involved in. Knowing the types of services received is essential in discussing which agency is more appropriate to provide a specific service. Clients should be involved in this process, indicating what they feel is most important among the many available services.

Establish a contact person within each agency. The person assuming primary responsibility for the client could be the contact person. This person would know of meeting times and other relevant client data.

Agree on a structure for the multidisciplinary planning group. The multidisciplinary planning group should set some guidelines on the planning process, such as frequency of meetings (e.g., monthly), location (e.g., share meeting sites), goals (e.g., focus on the first 6 months of child's life), who will be in charge of meetings (e.g., shared leadership). The purpose of the first meeting should be to address these basic issues.

Agree to meet initially to plan services for the client. Generally, the more specific you are the better. Representatives from each agency should indicate what they perceive to be the needs of the client and agree on an initial action plan.

Describe types of services being provided. To avoid duplications, each agency should describe what services it is providing. If there are duplications, a decision should be made on which agency is most appropriate to continue providing this service.

Do a needs assessment of infant and family. The group should decide on the overall needs of the family and determine which needs are most important. Next, the team should develop a plan with time lines. Any family member with major issues, not just the identified client, could be included in the decision-making process. After the needs are identified, agencies should decide who will be responsible for addressing them.

Identify the key agencies not represented. After the needs assessment, a list of agencies that should be represented is made. Someone could be assigned to solicit their involvement at a future meeting. A decision should be made regarding which agencies could be minimally involved and which ones would be required to attend more frequently.

Focus on the family and the development of the plan. Avoid spending a lot of time on administrative concerns. Many people become frustrated when supposedly client-centered meetings become places of bickering over policies or programs unrelated to the client. The one central reason for the meeting should not be forgotten.

Define roles and responsibilities of professionals and family members. Decisions should be made regarding who will play which role—that is, who will be case manager, who will provide primary medical follow-up—who will have access to what information, what the indicators of progress or failure will be, whether the family will be expected to attend some of the meetings, and who will communicate concerns of the group to the family.

Develop letters of agreement. The ability to formalize areas of responsibility is useful in making sure that agreed-upon services will be provided. Binding letters of agreements and memorandums of understanding outline specific areas of an agency's focus. A designated agency should sign the agreement.

Periodically evaluate effectiveness of the plan. It is important to review the plan of intervention, or family service plan, on a regular basis. Be sure that it remains relevant, that services are being obtained. Determine if a more immediate need is being experienced by the family. Regularly talk to the agencies involved about their perception on the attainment of goals or about any concerns that may have developed since the last meeting.

Identify funding sources or develop networks to support efforts. Some funding sources have realized the benefits of agency coordination plans. Planning monies are becoming increasingly available. Some funding sources, however, only pay for direct services or require coordination of services but fail to provide administrative support necessary for coordination and collaboration. Diverse funding to support high-risk programs in Oakland have included the Office of Substance Abuse Prevention, the State of California Department of Health, and Alameda County's Board of Supervisors (the governing board for Alameda County), as well as other federal, private, and community agencies.

Make the commitment to follow through. Reaffirming the goal of providing effectively coordinated services to special needs families should help sustain membership in these multidisciplinary planning groups when frustration and exhaustion surface and patience begins to run low. Keep in mind that expectations should not be too grand and that most clients *do* appreciate your efforts.

Organizations *have* chosen to become part of service coordination, the new wave of the future. They enjoy the benefits of shared ownership of the problem. "Shared planning, decision-making, evaluation, and leadership among partners creates a sense of ownership on the part of each participant" (Benard, 1989). Shared resources, improved communication, more effective program planning, and a heightened appreciation and respect for other agencies are just some of the organizational rewards. For clients, roles are clarified and there are more effective, efficient service delivery systems, less duplication of services, and, generally, increased compliance.

POLITICAL SUPPORT FOR COLLABORATION

In the last 10 years, political support has increased for coordination. Many funding organizations are requiring collaboration as a condition of receiving funds. Public and political pressure has resulted in several bills being introduced that mandate coordination of services for high-risk, medically fragile, and developmentally delayed infants and their families. In addition to national policies requiring collaboration, many state and county programs have chosen to establish coalitions, develop networks, and seek ways of improving coordination of services.

The Healthy Start Initiative, a federal program focusing on cities with a demonstrated high infant mortality rate, is an example of progressive use of public dollars. These funds allow for planning and implementation of services targeting high-risk populations, which requires active collaboration.

Public Law 99-457, instituted in 1986, "establishes a national policy on early intervention which recognizes its benefits, provides assistance to states to build systems of service delivery, and recognizes the unique role of families in the development of their . . . children" (Gallager, Trohanis, & Clifford, 1989).

This legislation has not only promoted the need for coordination but has also made it possible, by allocating funds in each state to be used for specific areas of collaboration. The bill expanded an earlier law, Public Law 91-230, which focused primarily on education of the handicapped child. The new legislation allows for children with developmental delay and those at risk for developmental delay to receive comprehensive services. Services provided under this law have clear criteria, including the following:

- The family must be involved in the process.
- Services must be free and include medical screening, case management, special instruction, and therapy.
- Standards must be set in the provision of services.
- A trained case manager must be assigned.
- Individual Family Service Plans are required.
- Periodic evaluation of the case is required.
- Services should be provided by a multidisciplinary team.

Although Public Law 99-457 provides a basis for the provision of coordination of services, the implementation of this law has not been without difficulty. Many states have not produced clear, easy guidelines for agencies to use in referring clients for services. There are inconsistencies in the definition of "at-risk children," and questions have been raised about the long-term consequences of this law when planning funds eventually are cut. The benefits, however, far outweigh the difficulties. This law paves the way for agencies, families, and political leaders to begin thinking about coordination as a natural component of service delivery.

The commitment to ensure that coordination, cooperation, and collaboration occurs is the responsibility of all who work with high-risk populations. Because these groups of clients tend to have less power, advocacy, and lobbying support than other gruops of social service clients, it is even more important that workers in the field of substance abuse and HIV be more sensitive to their needs. Efforts must be made to provide the extra support to families trying to find their way through the maze of an often-disorganized and inflexible system of services. Agencies will need to reshape some of their old approaches to meet the needs of these new sets of clients.

In addition to researching the resources within and among agencies, attempts should be made to mobilize communities. The concept of shared ownership of the problem and the solution has to include community leaders and established organizations. Parnerships *must* exist between the community, health care providers, educational institutions, social service agencies, and other relevant organizations. Services should be developed based on a family-centered approach, with active involvement by immediate and extended family members. The ultimate goal of services should be empowerment of clients, not dependency on service systems.

Maintaining collaborative relationships is an ongoing process. Once the motion is set, it must continue to be nurtured. Accepting this, we can begin the process of a fulfilling relationship with significant agencies and individuals. It does take time, effort, money, patience, negotiation, flexibility, and persistence, but the sense of group accomplishment that results is worth it.

RECOMMENDATIONS ON COORDINATED SERVICES

1. Personnel serving perinatal clients should be trained to take a thorough drug history, including frequency of alcohol use.

2. Staff should be trained in the basic concepts of substance abuse and learn how to identify and intervene with at-risk clients. They should also be familiar with community resources. Work load standards should be developed and implemented.

3. Services should be provided in a sensitive environment that is accessible to hard-to-reach clients. Transportation and child care needs must be addressed by service providers. Policies should be developed by agencies and legislative bodies that promote access to health and social services.

4. Efforts should be made to provide comprehensive services in one central location to ensure optimal outcomes. Funding on local and federal levels must be allocated to promote coordination activities among workers and administrators serving high-risk populations.

5. Infants born drug exposed or to women who are HIV positive should be provided with follow-up services for at least 1 year after birth. These services should be provided by a trained multidisciplinary team that meets at least quarterly. Some of these services, which should be coordinated by a case manager, include pediatric follow-up, HIV counseling, developmental assessments, substance abuse treatment, and any other services identified by the family or case manager.

6. Agencies should coordinate services and involve family members in the development of a service plan. Periodic home visits should be made. Administrative support is crucial in successfully implementing service plans and home visits.

7. Effective collaborative relationships should be developed and nurtured with child protective services, alcohol and drug programs, regional centers, child development centers, public health nursing, and hospitals delivering high-risk perinatal patients. One of the agencies should be designated as the lead agency and assume responsibility for coordinating monthly or quarterly meetings. These meetings would focus on case staffings, review of service plans, and broad program planning.

8. More pediatric providers, including nurse practitioners, should be recruited to work with these special needs infants and should be trained to provide intensive medical screenings on a more frequent basis. Pediatric standards should be developed specific to this high-risk population, which would include additional medical visits beyond the usual EPSDT guidelines (Early Periodic Screening and Diagnostic Treatment requires only 6 visits in the first year of life).

9. Developmental assessments should be made to determine if the infant is developing within normal limits. Timely referrals to regional centers or other centers specializing in developmental services should be made in cases where delays are discovered.

10. Substance abuse treatment programs, both residential and outpatient, should be involved in coordinating and planning meetings. Licensing regulations for residential treatment programs should be adapted to allow pregnant women and their children to remain together in treatment. Barriers that limit access to this population must be explored and adapted.

REFERENCES

Benard, B. (1989, October). Working together: Principles of effective collaboration. *Prevention Forum, 10*(1).

Gallager, J., Trohanis, P., & Clifford, R. (1989). *Policy Implementation and PL99-457: Planning for Young Children With Special Needs.* Baltimore: Paul H. Brookes.

Nefakare, S. (1990). *Developmental assessment report of Healthy Infant Program's drug-exposed infants.* Oakland, CA: Highland Hospital.

11

Child Welfare Services for Drug-Exposed and HIV-Affected Newborns and Their Families

DIANA ROBERTS

The recent rise in cocaine use by mothers and fathers has been accompanied by increasing numbers of young children and infants from these families becoming clients of public child welfare agencies. Ten million children are being raised by addicted parents and at least 675,000 children are seriously mistreated by a drug- or alcohol-abusing caretaker each year (National Committee for Prevention of Child Abuse memorandum, October, 1989).

The new population of substance-abusing parents challenges the creativity of child welfare practitioners and taxes the resources of agencies whose job is protection of abused, neglected, and abandoned children. Child protection units of local child welfare agencies have recorded a dramatic rise in the number of infants exposed prenatally to drugs and reported to these agencies for investigation and services. In New York City referrals increased by 268% over the 4-year period from 1986 to 1989; for the same period, referrals increased by 342% in Los Angeles and by 1,735% in Chicago (United States General Accounting Office, 1990). The problem is not limited to urban centers. The Oregon Children's Services Division reports a 400% statewide increase in reports of drug-exposed newborns during the same 4-year period (Oregon Children's Division, 1990).

The estimated demand for foster care nationwide has increased 29% from 1986 to 1989 (United States General Accounting Office, 1990). A 1988 study by the Oregon Children's Services Division estimated that in 78% of the families with preschool-age children in foster care substance abuse is a problem. Estimates of new child welfare cases each year involving drug abuse range from 50% in Illinois to 80% in Washington, D.C. (Feig, 1990). At three of the four hospitals in the United States General Accounting Office 1990 survey, 26% to 58% of the drug-exposed newborns required foster care as compared to 1% to 2% of non–drug-involved newborns.

Why has the influx in illegal drug use taken such a high toll on young families? Violence is great in cocaine-involved families, placing children of cocaine-addicted parents at high risk for abuse and injury. The acquisition and use of illegal drugs often leads to such additional criminal activities as prostitution, theft, and the selling and manufacturing of drugs at home. Moreover, parents who are attending to their drug habit all too often neglect the basic needs of their children for food, clothing, supervision, medical care, and protection from other drug users who visit in the home. In addition, when adults manufacture illegal drugs, such as methamphetamine in their homes, children are exposed to toxic chemicals.

Substance abuse during pregnancy involves dangers to babies. Some babies experience physical or cognitive damage with medical complications and developmental compromises. A secure attachment between the baby and parent is jeopardized when a drug withdrawing infant experiences irritability, poor sucking, and irregular sleep patterns. And incidents of infant mortality are on the rise among offspring of drug-abusing mothers. A 1988 review of child fatalities in New York City revealed that in 25% of the deaths the child had been born with a positive toxicology (Besharov, Dempsey, & Dudley, 1988).

Mothers of drug-exposed newborns have special care needs stemming from drug addiction, domestic violence, childhood sexual abuse, and limited healthy support systems. In a survey of twenty mothers enrolled in a follow-up clinic for their drug-exposed newborns, Howard (1988a) reported that 94% had used drugs for 5 years or more and that all abused more than one drug. Eighty percent of the mothers had chosen a partner who also abused drugs, and only 15% had a supportive relationship with the father at the time of delivery. Forty-five percent had other children in foster care, and 70% had been raised by parents who abused alcohol and drugs.

Traditional child welfare services become more complicated when they are provided to substance-abusing families with drug-exposed newborns who have multiple service needs. Effective services demand multiagency collaboration by practitioners as well as administrators. Caseworkers face danger by working in drug-involved neighborhoods and with families with high rates of violence and crime. Resources to help families maintain or regain custody of their children are grossly inadequate. Long waiting lists deny women easy access to drug treatment programs. Residential programs where mothers can live with their children are being piloted in only a few locations. Family preservation services demonstrate success in a few locations; however, these programs and their unique approaches are not widely available.

This chapter describes how a public child welfare agency can adopt policies and practices to most effectively provide both helping and protective services to families experiencing the birth of a drug-exposed or HIV-affected infant. The chapter suggests the use of specially tailored risk assessment tools, extensive multi-disciplinary collaboration, and the establishment of a cadre of specially selected and trained foster parents. The challenge to child welfare administrators is to use their leadership to establish a comprehensive community continuum of services for substance-abusing families.

RISK ASSESSMENT

Referrals for services for drug-exposed infants usually come to the attention of the child welfare agency through a report from a medical provider stating that a mother has delivered a newborn who is suffering from the deleterious effects of prenatal drug exposure. Hospitals identify such newborns through urine drug screens of babies and mothers, from mother's self-reported drug history, and from observations of babies and mothers that indicate drug exposure. Referrals can also come from a community complaint alleging child maltreatment due to parental drug or alcohol abuse or through a complaint of abuse and neglect that does not mention drug or alcohol abuse. In the past 2 years several states have added language to their child abuse–reporting statutes that require the reporting of infants suffering from fetal alcohol syndrome and those whose prenatal exposure to illegal drugs has been identified. However, most hospitals still use procedures that allow drug-exposed newborns to go undetected. Recent studies have found that uniform application of screening and testing of newborns results in identification of a much higher number of drug-exposed infants (United States General Accounting Office, 1990). All hospitals should use uniform protocols to screen infants for exposure to drugs. Test results should be used only to identify families in need of treatment and to make referrals.

Most hospitals evaluate psychosocial risk factors, as well as the medical care needs of the infant, and refer only the highest risk infants to child protective services (CPS). Hospitals in Contra Costa County, California, use standardized risk assessment tools to assess which infants should be referred to CPS. Some states or individual hospital protocols require that all babies with positive urine drug screens and babies showing signs of withdrawal be reported to CPS. Reporting of all babies with positive screens results in better tracking of incidence but does not necessarily initiate CPS investigation or services, because only the highest risk cases are opened by child welfare agencies.

Upon receipt of a report of a newborn exposed prenatally to drugs, the CPS worker's responsibility is to assess the risk of harm to the infant, arrange necessary services to assure the infant's safety, and assist the family to care for their baby. A positive drug screen is a factor in the assessment but is not used in and of itself as the sole basis for court action or involuntary removal of the baby from the parent's custody.

CPS units are advised to have specialized workers assigned to the investigation of reports of drug-exposed newborns. These workers must have knowledge about drugs, infant development, addiction, and the particular treatment needs of women addicts. They must network with other professionals who work with substance-abusing women and their babies. Also, CPS must utilize a risk assessment tool that is designed especially for this population and that elicits answers to the following questions:

> Which babies can go home from the hospital with no child welfare services but requiring provision of community services?
> Which families can use voluntary services and no court supervision?
> Which families must have juvenile court–ordered services?
> Which babies must be placed in substitute care, that is, with relatives or in foster care?
> What emergency services could ensure the baby's safety and preserve the family as a home resource for the infant?
> What high-risk behaviors and conditions must change to assure a safe and healthy home for the baby?
> Which families should be immediately referred for termination of parental rights?

In order to answer these questions and provide accurate information for multiagency case planning, the risk assessment worker studies the child's condition, the parent or other caretaker's functioning, and the family's physical and social environment. Most child welfare agencies use a standardized risk assessment tool for assessment of all reports of child abuse and neglect. However, assessment of potential harm to drug-exposed newborns requires evaluation of additional risk factors. The County of Los Angeles Department of Children's Services (1988a) has developed a risk assessment matrix for use with drug-exposed newborns and their families. The advantage of the tool is to standardize information gathering and assure fairness of treatment to all families.

The special factors used in assessing reports of drug-exposed newborns include the child's medical condition, drug withdrawal behaviors, special care needs, and necessary medical follow-up. Parents' drug use pattern and treatment history must be assessed along with their ability to care for their baby. The parent's level of cooperation; awareness of impact of drug use on the baby; physical, intellectual, and emotional abilities; parenting skills; responsiveness to the infant; history of previous abuse or neglect reports; and pattern of prenatal care can all provide clues to predict the parent's ability to adequately care for their drug-exposed newborn. The family's environment (including the drug involvement and impulse control of other people living in the home), the strength of family support systems, the functioning of siblings, and the physical safety of the home must also be studied. High-risk factors that interact together to raise the possibility of harm to a baby include the following:

> An infant with severe withdrawal symptoms
> An infant born prior to 36 weeks or one who is significantly handicapped or requires special equipment or frequent doctor visits

A caretaker who is currently using drugs more than twice a week or who uses crack or PCP

A drug-using mother who has never been in drug treatment

Absence of prenatal care or care begun only in the third trimester

Severe parental physical or mental handicap that interferes with ability to care for child

Uninterested, evasive, uncooperative parent

A parent who is unresponsive to the child's crying, who doesn't visit the child, who criticizes the child, or who lacks concern for the child

Previous abuse or neglect of another child

A father or parent substitute who is drug-involved

Lack of a healthy non–drug-involved support system

Siblings who are inadequately cared for

Unclean home with health hazards

Absence of preparation for new infant's arrival

Risk factors interact together to effect the risk of harm. Certain individual and family strengths indicate better functioning and greater likelihood that a mother will be able to successfully parent her infant living at home with her family. Family and individual strengths are indicated by the following:

A mother who is involved in drug treatment and is following through

A non–drug-involved partner who supports mother's drug treatment and who is cooperative with helping agencies and professionals

Absence of a criminal history

A parent who meets the educational, medical, and environmental needs of the other children in the family

A mother who sought early prenatal care and was consistent with follow-up

No member of household suspected to be drug involved (in either the sale, use, or manufacture)

Family and friends who are committed to help

No apparent medical or physical problems in the baby

No known history of abuse or neglect

Parent(s) who express concern about the drug's effect on the child and who are willing and able to work with professionals to help the family

MULTIDISCIPLINARY COLLABORATION

A high degree of community collaboration characterizes successful work with drug-exposed infants and their substance-involved families. The knowledge and skills of many disciplines must be made available to plan appropriate help. Health care providers, particularly those in public health, should take the lead in identifying and providing initial follow-up services to substance-exposed children. Child welfare agencies become the primary service provider for drug and HIV babies only when the child's welfare is in jeopardy and the parent is unable or unwilling to provide for the child.

Use of drugs is a lifestyle involving both the family system and the community. Successful intervention focuses on strengthening families, as the family is the primary teacher and natural support system for children. Drug-dependent mothers and fathers must be treated with respect and viewed as colleagues who have a major say in the planning of services for themselves, their babies, and their families. Families are a part of the multidisciplinary team that assesses needs, develops service plans, and oversees activities designed to establish and maintain healthy families and safe, nurturing homes for babies.

Services must be offered to the family in a fashion that makes sense to parents and is coordinated between professionals. This coordination can start at the hospital discharge planning meeting. The ideal response is a community case management model: This consists of a team of professionals identifying procedures that fit for their respective disciplines and then designing a coordinated community effort. Developing joint protocols, signing interagency agreements, holding regularly scheduled case discussion meetings, and assigning a case manager for each family are techniques to assist practitioners with service coordination. Such a multidisciplinary community approach results in a process of providing health, social, legal, and treatment services while ensuring the safety of the infant.

Local agency directors must set the expectation for multiagency coordination and direct time and agency resources to achieve true collaboration. At the practitioner's level, the first professional from any discipline who identifies a pregnant woman abusing drugs or identifies a drug-exposed or HIV baby should call a planning meeting, whose participants include the family and individual professionals.

The assessment process requires several different disciplines to gather specific information. The child protective services worker focuses on the family's psychosocial issues and support systems and on interagency linkages with law enforcement personnel, juvenile courts, parole/probation officers, and drug counselors. The pediatrician assesses the infant's medical, neurobehavioral, and developmental status. The public health nurse determines the adequacy of the home and the baby's medical and nutritional needs. The hospital nurse or social worker observes parental attachment behaviors, general functioning, and relationships with other adults. All this information is brought together to answer the risk assessment questions (as previously outlined) and lay the groundwork for an intervention plan. The hospital discharge planning meeting provides a forum for these professionals to meet with the family and complete a thoughtful assessment and effective discharge plan.

Additional key team members might include the mother's drug treatment counselor, a child development specialist, the parent's parole or probation officer, parents, and concerned family members. In many instances this group would be widened to include other critical professionals, such as the family's Aid to Families with Dependent Children (AFDC) caseworker, the baby's physical therapist, the infant's foster parents, the local coordinator for early intervention services for handicapped children, a law enforcement officer, and a juvenile court representative.

Agencies must continue to regularly coordinate services after the initial assessment and plan. The 1989 policy of the Florida Department of Health and Rehabilitative Services requires quarterly staff meetings (which include a CPS worker, a public health nurse, a drug counselor, a probation office, and other involved source providers and caretakers) concerning all infants and children with complex medical problems in order to assure integrated service delivery and provision of the most appropriate services. The staffing process results in the assignment of a lead case manager, from one of several agencies, who is responsible for writing up and tracking the activities identified on the required interagency individual/family service plan. All service providers, parents, and caregivers sign the plan.

The University of California at Los Angeles Family Services Project (Howard, 1988a) represents a very successful multidisciplinary model for the care of infants exposed prenatally to drugs. Collaboration with community agencies for 20 infants enrolled in the intervention program involved an average for each family of five agencies that addressed medical, social, and developmental problems. The five agencies represented social work; health, legal, and educational services, and substance-abuse treatment. Services included an average of one home visit per month, arrangements for a once monthly clinic visit, and six telephone contacts per month to each of the infant's caregivers. Information was shared freely between agencies and incorporated into individual plans, resulting in stabilization of each infant's placement. Infants involved in the UCLA Family Services Project averaged only two out-of-home placements annually, instead of the five out-of-home placements per year experienced by other drug-exposed newborns in the child welfare system (Howard, 1988a).

A second successful UCLA pilot program involved teams of public health nurses and child welfare caseworkers jointly managing cases of drug-exposed newborns placed in out-of-home care. The 1988 UCLA TEAMS project trained groups of public health nurses, child welfare caseworkers, and foster parents. The participating caseworkers became an informed interagency support network for drug-exposed newborns in out-of-home care, acquiring special skills and knowledge and educating others in what is becoming viewed as a specialty area. The TEAMS curriculum and videotapes are available to other agencies.

ASSESSMENT AND CASE PLANNING

Families involved with child welfare are likely to be the most troubled of the parents giving birth to drug-exposed newborns, since more functional parents will participate willingly in drug treatment and voluntarily participate in public health programs. An individual and family assessment precedes the case plan and requires at a minimum an evaluation of the following:

Potential for harm to infant and siblings, taking into account parental functioning and motivation to change

Characteristics of the child and home environment

Strengths and competencies of the family

Health needs of mother and baby

Developmental status of baby

Drug and alcohol use by family members

Support systems and community resources available to family

Possible placement resources

Risk of harm for mother from domestic violence, prostitution, and gangs

Risk of harm to professionals from involvement with family

The first step for case planning is the multidisciplinary staffing, which occurs as soon as perinatal substance abuse is identified. If this is not until the birth of the baby, then the hospital discharge planning conference is the first staffing time. The participation of the child protective services worker at this conference is essential if referral to CPS is likely. One or more CPS workers in a community should specialize in handling cases of drug-exposed newborns in order to develop special- ized knowledge and skills and form working relationships with hospital staff, public health nurses, substance-abuse treatment providers, and foster parents who most often work with these babies and their families.

To set a tone of mutual respect and cooperation, the first step in planning ser- vices for a mother and her baby, caseworkers should encourage the mother, father, and other supportive relatives or friends to attend staffings. The case planning process empowers the parents by encouraging their participation and providing choices, thus bringing out the strengths and competencies of families. Whenever possible, an advocate for the mother, either a relative or another friend, should be included in the meetings to intensively support the mother.

The case plan delineates activities and responsibilities of professionals and parents. It is important that the case plan not be so complicated that the parents are overwhelmed and feel doomed to failure. The CPS part of the case plan must result in a service agreement that is jointly developed with the parents. Service agreements focus both the client and the worker on time frames and required actions. The client knows what and when things need to be done and what the outcome will be. The worker can track progress, organize data, and compile reports with a clear frame of reference. The juvenile court can use the service agreement to monitor progress and hold both the family and agency accountable for specified activities.

Components of the service agreement will vary from family to family but usually are in response to the question "What can we do to help you?" The agreements address participation in and monitoring of drug treatment through referral, urinalysis, and reports; follow-up medical care for the baby; and visitation arrangements if the baby is in out-of-home care. Families might request case- worker assistance in locating drug-free housing, respite care, and transportation to medical appointments. These, too, become essential parts of the service agreement.

As parts of the service agreement are achieved, the agreement is reviewed and rewritten. Because most families are involved with the juvenile court, the service agreement can become part of the official court record. The service agreement may outline what results must be obtained for children to be returned to parents and wardship dropped.

The case plan must address the special care needs of mothers who give birth to drug-exposed newborns. These mothers often suffer from drug addiction, poor nutrition, domestic violence, poverty, inadequate housing, few vocational skills, and unresolved guilt and anger from childhood sexual abuse. Mothers must be provided not only drug treatment and parenting classes but opportunities to resolve issues about their own childhood traumas that significantly impair their ability to parent and protect their children. Mothers' safety must also be addressed, and shelter from domestic violence provided. The recently implemented federal Family Support Act can provide job training for mothers receiving AFDC.

Family treatment must also be considered in the continuum of care offered to families of drug-exposed newborns. All too often it is the attitude among drug and alcohol service providers that the primary concern is the addicted individual, not the family, that is a barrier to treatment for the family. According to Dr. Curtis Janzen, the substance abuse treatment community falls short of addressing the treatment process for the codependent in the addict's family because of a lack of understanding of what family therapy is, how it is done, and why it works (Janzen, 1987).

FAMILY PRESERVATION

Family preservation services encompasses a range of services that child welfare agencies provide either directly or by contract to maintain children in their own homes. These services typically include "hard" services—such as transportation, respite day care, and aid in obtaining food, clothing, heat, shelter, and emergency financial assistance—and "soft" services, including counseling, homemaking, sexual abuse treatment, parenting groups, family therapy, case management, and referral to other agencies. Child welfare agencies have successfully provided in-home services to substance-abusing families for more than a century (Gordon, 1988).

Limited research guides child welfare workers' predictions of which crack-involved families may be able to provide a safe home for their children. In families where the use of crack cocaine is less severe, family preservation services, such as Michigan's Families First, have established an impressive track record working with substance-abusing families. The Michigan Office of Children and Youth Services has contracted since 1981 with Families First (National Association of Public Child Welfare Administrators, 1990b), a program built on the Tacoma Homebuilders model. Families First workers have small caseloads, two families per worker, and are available 24 hours a day. The approach builds on family strengths and provides both hard and soft services, utilizing a process of breaking family problems into manageable tasks and assisting families to achieve these tasks. Intensive services are provided for 4–6 weeks. In addition to providing emotional support and counseling, workers help families access a variety of resources, including day care, foster care when the parent enters residential drug treatment, mental health services, parenting classes, and Narcotics Anonymous. The easy accessibility and immediate response to Families First workers helps families manage tasks that otherwise would be overwhelming.

Families First has developed a continuum of substance abuse to determine eligibility for their services. The continuum ranges from occasional use to daily use. Users whose involvement is frequent and long-term typically face such severe barriers to parenting their children that they are not referred to Families First. In a review of 97 Families First cases only 15 children were placed in foster care (15%), and 9 of those 15 were placed with family members. About 50% of the cases were closed by the state shortly after Families First intervention (Barth, 1990).

Family preservation programs can get families off to a good start as primary directors and participants in their own recovery and case planning. Additional services, such as those discussed previously, must be provided to assure the safety and good health of all children in the family.

FOSTER CARE

The living situation for a drug-exposed and HIV positive newborn ready to be discharged from the hospital requires careful consideration. In April 1990 Oregon studied the placement experience of the 532 drug-exposed newborns reported to the state Children's Services Division in 1989: Two hundred and seven (39%) of the infants experienced some placement in foster care or with relatives; 128 (24%) of the babies were still in care in April 1990; and 69 babies (13%) were in the process of being freed for adoption, had been adopted, or were placed with legal guardians.

Several factors influence the placement decision for a drug-exposed newborn. The previously discussed multidisciplinary risk assessment forms the basis for predicting the ability of the parents to safely and adequately care for their baby. The hospital discharge planning conference provides a format for all professionals and family members to share information and recommend the best course of action to the child welfare worker. Particular attention must be given to the history and severity of the mother's drug use, the mother's compliance with drug treatment, the parents' history of abuse or neglect of siblings, the existence of a healthy support system, and whether or not the parents can meet the special medical or care needs of their infant. If the baby's well-being might be seriously at risk by going home with the parents and no services can be immediately started to reduce the risk of harm, then an alternate placement with relatives must be considered.

A juvenile court petition is always filed if the state will be placing the child away from the parents and is usually filed when the child welfare agency supervises a drug-exposed newborn at home. Juvenile court review of child welfare cases ensures due process for families and establishes accountability for parents to the juvenile court judge. The court also holds the agency accountable to make reasonable efforts to reunite the family and to regularly review the service plan, the family's progress, and the agency's activities.

Drug-exposed infants are at high risk for attachment disorders. Babies who are withdrawing from drugs have difficulty being visually alert, and, according to Robson (1967), eye-to-eye contact is important in the development of attachment because it conveys a sense of a responsive social being. A mother who is having a difficult time soothing her withdrawing infant may feel ineffective as a mother and may lose confidence in herself, and the attachment and interaction between infant and caregiver can only occur when the caregiver responds appropriately to the infant's needs. Research at UCLA suggests that drug-exposed newborns reared in foster care are more securely attached than babies reared by mothers who continue to abuse drugs. The insecurely attached toddlers in the UCLA study showed significantly lower developmental scores than the secure drug-exposed babies (Howard, Beckwith, & Rodney, 1989). Close attention must be paid to caretaker–infant attachment behaviors, and special training in attachment and bonding should be given to the infant's caregiver.

After reaching the decision to place the infant away from the parents, the child welfare worker carefully assesses all relatives who are interested in caring for the baby. Because these infants are at high risk of medical and physical complications, the caregiver chosen for the infant must be capable and well prepared. Los Angeles County Department of Children's Services (1988b) utilizes a special assessment matrix for the release to a relative of an infant prenatally exposed to drugs. Child welfare workers are directed to assess the relative's drug/alcohol use; history of abuse, neglect, and violence; physical, intellectual, and emotional abilities; level of cooperation; parenting skills; responsiveness to the infant; relationship with the parents; ability to protect the child; access to medical resources; and living environment. The assessment findings are then ranked as signifying low, intermediate, or high risk. The matrix provides an objective basis for helping to decide if placement with a relative is best for the infant. If a suitable relative cannot be located, the child welfare worker seeks a specially trained foster parent.

The San Francisco Department of Social Services worked together with public health nurses to develop the "Baby Moms" project, which provides specialized foster care to infants with specific medical needs, including those who were exposed to drugs and are HIV positive. Foster parents who want to participate in the program undergo a comprehensive screening and training program. The foster parents must be willing to care for an AIDS baby, allow biological parents to visit their babies in the foster home, and work toward reunification; they have no children under age 6, demonstrate a high energy level, accept no work outside the home, and limit placement to two babies from this project. High reimbursement rates, between $1,300 and $1,800 and $350/month respite care, attract more providers (National Association of Public Child Welfare Administrators, 1990d).

The Baby Moms public health doctor works with the hospital to identify babies who are sick enough for this program. The staff public health nurse and hospital nurses develop the discharge plan appropriate to the baby's needs. Babies remain in the program until a permanent plan is realized. Monthly foster parent training is provided, along with a support network among caregivers and 50 hours per month of paid respite care.

Although few child welfare agencies are blessed with Baby Moms projects, all agencies utilize foster care for medically needy drug-exposed newborns. Special selection and training of foster parents is critical. Agencies are encouraged to implement foster parent support groups, provide respite care for children in foster homes to give foster parents relief time, and provide higher reimbursement for particularly needy children. A team approach between child welfare worker, foster parent, parent, and public health nurse will most quickly achieve a permanent plan. Foster mothers provide an invaluable service to biological mothers during visits by using that time to model and teach parenting and attachment behaviors, thus keeping mothers involved in their baby's development.

Several states have recently started programs where mothers and their children can live together while the mother is undergoing drug treatment. San Francisco's Phoenix House and Oakland's Mandela House are two examples. In rural Pendleton, Oregon, the Children's Services Division (of the Oregon Department of Human Resources)–funded Mutual Home is a successful pilot project for drug dependent mothers to live together with their children in a residential drug treatment setting. Caseworkers report preference for this type of residential family drug treatment approach.

CLOSING THE CHILD WELFARE CASE

Virtually no empirical research or protocol exists to guide the child welfare agency's decision to close a case involving an infant born exposed prenatally to drugs. When is it safe to close the case and leave the children at home with their parents? On the other hand, when should the agency abandon working with the parents and, instead, set a case goal of termination of parental rights? Certainly, many of the same risk assessment criteria used to decide to open the case apply to the case closure decision. In addition, case practice evolves as information about evaluating the success of drug treatment becomes available and as more becomes known about the developmental needs of drug-exposed newborns.

Child welfare workers report that decisions to close cases in which babies were born drug-exposed depend to a great extent on the parents' successful completion of drug treatment. Success is measured by clean random urinalysis for a number of months, usually 3 to 6, and reports of graduation from a drug treatment program. Other criteria for case closure include follow-through with parenting classes and medical appointments for the baby, stable and safe housing, the absence of other reports of abuse or neglect, and keeping the baby healthy and adhering to an immunization schedule. When cases are closed, either at intake or after a period of services, families are always tied into other community resources, including public health programs, after-care drug treatment, and Narcotics Anonymous.

Because of the flood of new cases, child welfare workers carry enormous caseloads and are under pressure to close cases as quickly as possible to make room for new, often higher risk, families. Child welfare workers worry because they must often close cases while parents are still resistant to services and continue to deny problems that may ultimately lead to relapse. Workers report now seeing second and even third cocaine-exposed babies being born to mothers reported previously to child welfare. Many child welfare professionals believe subsequent births of drug-exposed siblings will decrease only when drug treatment for mothers, together with their children, is widely available and easily accessed.

A study of 532 drug-exposed newborns reported to the Oregon Children's Services Division in 1989 (Oregon Children's Services Division, 1990) revealed that 179 (34%) of the cases were open for less than 30 days, the majority of them having been opened only for the purpose of recording the report. Another study of the 346 reports of drug-exposed newborns made to the Oregon Children's Services Division in 1988 revealed an average case life of 280 days. Disregarding the 140 cases that were opened solely for recording the report and not for services, the remaining 206 cases had an average case life of 470 days. The average case life for the 71 cases still open in August 1990 was 752 days.

Recovery from drug addiction can take many years. In some families a mother has abused drugs so frequently and for so many years that it is virtually impossible for her to complete drug treatment and develop the sort of skills, environment, and support systems that would enable her to parent and protect her own baby. Communities, child development specialists, and federal and state laws have established a child's emotional need and legal right to grow up in a permanent family and not linger for many years in temporary foster care. In situations where there is little hope of reuniting mothers with babies and legal grounds exist to terminate parental rights, the child welfare agency moves quickly to free the child for adoption.

The family's prognosis always determines the length of treatment. Laws and policies that set specific time frames for decisions to terminate parental rights solely because of substance abuse are inappropriate. An order from a juvenile court judge terminating parental rights or a parent signing voluntary relinquishment papers legally frees a child for adoption. Judges can also establish legal guardianship with a relative.

Child welfare workers report that termination of parental rights petitions are filed most often in families where the parents failed to get into treatment and also failed to visit their baby. In most states parents have 6 months to a year to demonstrate their capability to provide a home for their child. Any effort on the part of the parents will result in the court delaying termination of parental rights. Other significant factors influencing the decision to pursue termination of parental rights include the following: a jail term of the mother for an extended period; intellectual or mental impairment of the mother so significant that she would be unable to care for her medically fragile baby; the existence of other severely abused or neglected siblings.

In 1986, 76 cases of drug-exposed infants were reported to the Oregon Children's Services Division. By early 1990, 17 (22%) of these children were placed in adoptive homes or legal guardianship. Of the 17, 11 children were placed for adoption: 3 were adopted by relatives, 5 by new adoptive families, and 3 by the foster parents who had been caring for them. At age 3 to 4 years, the developmental status for five of the children was described as acceptable. The developmental status of the other six children included mild developmental delays, speech difficulty, fine motor delays, and asthma. Adoption subsidies of up to $517/month were provided to adoptive parents to defray the financial costs of adopting high-risk children, with most families receiving subsidies of $100–$200/month (Zimmerman, 1990).

Information from relapse studies can help child welfare workers understand the variables affecting recovery. The finding that approximately two-thirds of individuals completing treatment for alcohol, heroin, or tobacco dependence relapse within 90 days of discharge from treatment has led to the identification of variables critical to the relapse process (Catalano, Howard, Hawkins, & Wells, 1988). The variables related to relapse are particularly important in assisting child welfare workers in identifying which parents are most likely to remain drug-free, although caution is advised since most of the relapse studies were of male addicts. Catalano, Howard, Hawkins, and Wells (1988) report that severity of dependence prior to treatment and the degree to which the individual experiences pretreatment withdrawal symptoms predict the likelihood of relapse. In addition, the extent of pretreatment drug craving is an indicator of the likelihood of relapse in opioid dependence. The length of time an individual has been addicted also seems to predict the likelihood of relapse.

The severity of psychiatric symptomatology may be an important predictor of drug treatment outcome. In one study patients with low psychiatric severity improved in every treatment program while patients with high psychiatric severity showed almost no improvement in any treatment program. In addition, the use of drugs and involvement in crime during treatment have been associated with a higher relapse rate (Catalano et al., 1988).

Patients' experiences following treatment are also related to relapse (Hawkins & Catalano, 1985). Many studies have shown that family support is a strong predictor of an individual's successfully remaining drug-free. In one study people who quit using drugs without treatment reported strong ties to children and non-using lovers as reasons for quitting. Conversely, family and interpersonal conflict was identified as a trigger for a return to drug use. Other factors related to return to drug use include involvement in a peer group who are drug users, the social isolation accompanying unemployment, and a lack of leisure or recreational activities. Clinical depression and physical discomfort, such as headache, allergies, and insomnia, during the posttreatment phase were also related to a return to alcohol and drug use.

OPPORTUNITIES FOR CHILD
WELFARE ADMINISTRATORS

The challenge of finding and providing appropriate helping services for drug-exposed newborns and their drug-dependent families presented itself to child welfare agencies about 5 years ago in the areas of the country hardest hit by illegal cocaine and methamphetamine. As crack cocaine became more widly available, many other areas began to identify drug-exposed newborns and file reports with child protective services units of child welfare agencies. As more hospitals adopt protocols to identify infants exposed prenatally to drugs and as states pass new laws requiring reports to child welfare and public health agencies, the demand for extensive multiagency services increases.

Prevention, intervention, treatment, and recovery require multidisciplinary coordination by individuals and agencies. Local and state child welfare administrators must take leadership positions in advocating necessary services from various disciplines and identifying the most appropriate child welfare services for families of the drug-exposed newborns who have become part of their agency's caseload. Child welfare administrators are advised to develop a strategy for obtaining optimal services from their own agency and for working together with other agencies to establish comprehensive substance abuse treatment programs, including residential treatment where mothers and babies can live together.

The first step involves renewing the commitment to the philosophical framework and values of the child welfare agency to protect children, strengthen families, and avoid the temptation to punish. Many agencies experience pressure from law enforcement and district attorneys to take a punitive approach to substance-abusing parents. Laws, regulations, or policies that respond in a primarily punitive manner result in inappropriate intervention strategies. Law enforcement is not an effective prevention program. The only known successful intervention with drug-addicted women is the development of a treatment alliance between the mother and the service provider and the incorporation of consequences if she does not follow through with her treatment plan. The family resource model is being adopted by many child welfare agencies as a positive, effective family-centered approach to practice. The family resource model helps family members find and build on their own strengths. It provides a welcome alternative to the conventionnal approach that revolves around the removal of children and reunification with them.

In the face of growing caseloads and a paucity of resources, child welfare administrators must communicate that they understand the problem of drug use in pregnancy and the difficulties faced by their staff working with these families. There are many ways to do this and support staff. Administrators can forge new partnerships with agencies' directors and with the professionals who are responsible for various parts of the continuum of services. For example, administrators can work with hospital administrators and neonatologists to help hospitals adopt protocols for the identification and reporting of drug-exposed newborns. Administrators can also make specialized CPS workers available to attend hospital discharge planning conferences and can encourage the hospital to include parents in these conferences. Communicating with the directors of local alcohol and drug treatment programs can result in setting the highest priority on drug treatment services for pregnant women and women whose children are at risk of foster care placement. In addition, child welfare administrators can encourage drug treatment providers to develop programs where mothers and children can reside together. Administrators can ask the local and state interagency coordinating councils (ICC), formed under Public Law 99-457, to focus early intervention policy and resources on the developmentally delayed babies born to drug-abusing mothers. This would effectively open the door for new kinds of collaboration, advocacy, planning, and implementation. Public welfare agency administrators can be lobbied to use vocational, educational, and day care resources available under the 1988 Family Support Act to assist women completing drug treatment to develop successful after-care plans.

Strengthening the partnership with local and state public health administrators represents the most critical linkage. Public health agencies should take the lead to identify and provide initial follow-up services to substance-exposed children. Child welfare agencies should plan for and make available those services identified by public health administrators. Public health nurses are the most appropriate helpers for mothers who take their drug-exposed newborns home from the hospital. As long as a public health nurse is available, many of the families never need to enter the child welfare system. For a family in the system, a public health nurse is an essential part of the team, along with the child welfare worker, drug treatment counselor, and parole or probation officer, that works with the family and the foster parents.

Support by child welfare administrators for the multidisciplinary approach to cases can be communicated through the expectation that collaboration is the rule, through formal interagency agreements, by making time available for staff to attend interagency meetings, and by advising workers with whom to network. Interagency team training results in workers sharing a common theoretical and practice base. Personnel of courts and human service and law enforcement agencies should be jointly trained in identification and appropriate intervention with substance-abusing families and drug-exposed newborns.

Cases of drug-exposed newborns are expensive to administer. A higher percentage of these babies go into foster care compared to those in other child protective services cases, and a significant number move into adoption with a subsidy to the adoptive parents. A recent Oregon study of 11 children born drug-exposed in 1986 and subsequently adopted revealed total costs of $428,167 or $39,000 per child for casework, foster care, medical expenses, and adoption and legal costs over a 4-year period (Zimmerman, 1990). The adoption of these children will ultimately save the child welfare agency a minimum of $50,000 per child over the cost of long-term foster care. The average cost of neonatal newborn care for drug-affected infants, according to data reported by Los Angeles County, was more than $40,000 per baby. A residential drug treatment program for a woman and her child costs $23,000 per year (California Department of Alcohol and Drug Programs, 1990). Thus, it is cost-effective for child welfare administrators to advocate for prevention and residential treatment services. Administrators must also advocate within their own agency for higher reimbursement rates for foster parents who care for medically fragile infants. Creative ways can be found to finance new programs. The San Francisco Baby Moms foster program was funded as a pilot by the state legislature, as was the Pendleton, Oregon, Mutual Home. The Michigan Families First family preservation program was financed by redirecting foster care money to in-home services.

Supporting staff translates into providing the tools needed to do the job. Administrators must provide risk assessment tools specialized for drug-exposed newborns and their families, such as the one developed in Los Angeles. Agencies are advised to develop guidelines for multidisciplinary staffing and practice handbooks to assist with case decision making. Staff should be provided with reliable hardware, such as cars equipped with phones for the safety of workers who must enter dangerous neighborhoods. Caseloads should be specialized so that a few staff members develop extensive expertise and build relationships with others who specialize in working with the families of drug-exposed and HIV infants. And, of course, current literature should be available to staff.

Administrative attention aimed at worker safety will pay off. Large caseloads have left workers with little time to plan their actions in advance. When they walk into a potentially dangerous situation, they are often mentally unprepared to take action. Because of overload, workers hesitate to ask other staff members to accompany them. Many workers employ defense mechanisms and denial when it comes to the dangers in their work. The prevalent attitude all too often is "It won't happen to me." Actions that administrators can take to help make workers aware of the risks they face include education on how to interview a drug-abusing client and survival skills on how to gain entry to a home, what to say, when to leave, and how to deal with hostility (National Association of Public Child Welfare Administrators, 1990a). In addition, administrators can develop a risk assessment for staff safety and write policies that address worker safety and support. Administrators must make sure that any worker who does not want to visit a family alone will be accompanied by another staff person or by law enforcement personnel.

A final area for child welfare administrators to address is the critical need for data. Information that is useful to policy makers is scarce. The American Public Welfare Association encourages administrators to collect, at a minimum, the following information: the number of drug-exposed infants reported and the number placed in foster care, the number of children in families of substance-abusing parents, and the number of children placed in foster care due to parental substance abuse (National Association of Public Child Welfare Administrators, 1990c).

REFERENCES

Barth, R. P. (1990). *Family preservation services to drug-using families.* Unpublished manuscript.

Besharov, D. J., Dempsey, P. L., & Dudley, R. G. (1988). *Report of the child fatality review panel.* New York: The City of New York Human Resources Administration.

California Department of Alcohol and Drug Programs. (1990, June). *Preliminary fact sheet on perinatal drug and alcohol use.* Sacramento: California Department of Alcohol and Drug Programs.

Catalano, R. F., Howard, M. D., Hawkins, D. J., & Wells, E. A. (1988). Relapse in the Addictions: Rates, determinants, and promising prevention strategies. In *Surgeon General's Report: The Health Consequences of Smoking: Nicotine Addiction* (pp. 20–21, 26). Washington, DC: U.S. Government Printing Office.

County of Los Angeles Department of Children's Services. (1988a). Assessment for infants prenatally exposed to drugs. In *Drug-exposed infants and their families: Coordinating responses of the legal, medical, and child protection system* (pp. 115). Washington, DC: American Bar Association Center on Children and the Law.

County of Los Angeles Department of Children's Services. (1988b). Assessment matrix for release to relative for infants prenatally exposed to drugs. In *Drug-exposed infants and their families: Coordinating responses of the legal, medical, and child protection system* (pp. 117). Washington, DC: American Bar Association Center on Children and the Law.

Feig L. (1990, January). *Drug-exposed infants and children's service needs and policy questions.* Washington, DC: U.S. Department of Health and Human Services.

Gordon, L. (1988). *Heroes of their own lives: The politics and history of family violence: Boston 1880–1960.* New York: Viking Press.

Hawkins, D. J., & Catalano, R. F. (1985). Aftercare in drug abuse treatment. *International Journal of the Addictions, 20*(6, 7), 918–920.

Howard, J., Beckwith, L., & Rodney, L. (1989). The development of young children of substance-abusing parents: Insights from seven years of intervention and research. *Zero to Three, 9.*

Howard, J. (1988a). *A multi-tiered approach to intervention with infants exposed prenatally to drugs.* Unpublished manuscript.

Howard, J. (1988b). *Project TEAMS: Muting the needs of infants exposed prenatally to drugs.* (Final Report, Grant Number: 90-CA 1194). Washington, DC: National Center on Child Abuse and Neglect.

Janzen, C. (1987, July–August). Alcohol Health and Research World. In Hyatt, L. L. Confronting the system's denial. *Focus on Family and Chemical Dependency* (pp. 15).

National Association of Public Child Welfare Administrators. (1990a, April). Danger in the field: A caseworker's tale. *Network, 6,* 3–4.

National Association of Public Child Welfare Administrators. (1990b, April). "Families First" becomes motto in Michigan. *Network, 6,* 5.

National Association of Public Child Welfare Administrators. (1990c, April). Critical need for national data. *Network, 6,* 5.

National Association of Public Child Welfare Administrators. (1990d, July). Public health. *Network, 6,* 3–4.

National Committee for the Prevention of Child Abuse. (1989, October). *Memorandum.* Chicago: Author. P.O. Box 2866, Chicago, IL 60690.

Oregon Children's Services Division. (1990). *A task force report on alcohol and drug abuse among pregnant women and mothers with young children.* Salem, OR: Author.

Robson, K. S. (1967). The role of eye-to-eye contact in maternal–infant attachment. *Journal of Child Psychology and Psychiatry, 8,* 13–25.

State of Florida Department of Health and Rehabilitative Services. (1989). Staffing process for infants and children with complex medical problems. In *Drug-exposed infants and their families: Coordinating responses of the legal, medical, and child protection system* (pp. 90–96). Washington, DC: American Bar Association Center on Children and the Law.

United States General Accounting Office. (1990). *Drug-exposed infants: A generation at risk.* Washington, DC: Author.

Zimmerman, J. (1990). *Drug-exposed infants: Preliminary cost tracking.* Unpublished manuscript, Oregon Children's Services Division.

12

Shared Family Care: Child Protection Without Parent-Child Separation

RICHARD P. BARTH

From the outset this nation's explicit public policy objective for child welfare services has been to avoid the separation of mother and child unless absolutely necessary for the protection of the child. Yet placement of children in out-of-home care has been a common practice for the last 50 years and is again on the rise, in good part because of increased homelessness and parental drug abuse. The often unacceptable risks of leaving an abused or neglected child in a dangerous situation with minimal supervision from a child welfare worker results in nearly 200,000 new episodes of out-of-home care each year in the United States (Tatara, 1990). Group care for infants is an increasingly common response. Intensive home-based family preservation programs, which place a social worker in the home for a brief period, are an emerging alternative to separation of mother and child. Although these programs can effectively serve some drug-affected families, they have their limits (Sudia, 1990). Across the nation these home-based family preservation programs probably serve less than 20,000 children, and their ability to significantly reduce the placement of children is not certain (Frankel, 1988; Yuan, 1990). They may be least effective with families suffering from mental illness (Berry, 1992), chronic neglect (Nelson, 1991), drug abuse (Spaid & Fraser, 1991), and problems with older children's behavior.

Further, programs to reunify children with their families after placement in foster care appear to return home quickly no more than 30% and another 30% of children who are returned home will have experienced a failed placement and will end up back in foster care (Goerge, 1990; Wulczyn, 1991). The search for methods

272

to protect children and preserve families continues. Given the anticipated shortage of foster parents and the more intense demands for the care of drug-affected, medically troubled, and HIV-infected children by their similarly affected parents, alternatives to foster care that maintain the mother–child connection and ensure adequate supervision are much needed.

This chapter describes programs that fall under the rubric of shared family care. Kufeldt and Allison (1990) use the expression *shared care* to refer to a broad phenomenon in which "the principle of shared care reinforces the notion of support of the family to maintain the child at home. Where a child does have to be taken into care, this principle establishes the basis for an inclusive orientation to foster care" (p. 10). I will use *shared family care* more narrowly to describe the *"planned provision of out-of-home care to parent(s) and children so that the parent and host caregivers simultaneously share the care of the child and work toward independent in-home care by the parent(s).* This narrower definition only encompasses out-of-home care arrangements and intends to (1) make the review of shared family care programs a manageable task and (2) encourage readers to make the conceptual leap to understanding that there can be both in-a-home and out-of-home services. In shared care, then, the living arrangement crosses the traditional precipice between "supportive" and "substitutive" child welfare services (Kadushin, 1971); shared family care arrangements provide both.

This narrower definition excludes *respite care* and *family reunification* arrangements, which may be quite prolonged and eventually lead to the independent care of a child by his or her birth parent (e.g., when a relative becomes a foster parent until the birth parent is ready to resume the care of the child). Such arrangements are important and common, but they involve parent–child separation and lack any structural characteristics that directly promote the birth parent's capacity to share the care of the child.

THE RATIONALE FOR SHARED FAMILY CARE

The trend toward family-centered residential care goes back several decades (e.g., Simmons, Gumpert, & Rothman, 1973; Whittaker, 1978). Kadushin and Martin (1988) argue that "residential institutions must provide opportunities for parents to interact with institutional staff, to engage their children, and to serve the institution itself. Parents are to be included in the daily activities of the agency; their participation is not to be limited to occasional visiting" (p. 699). Yet they aptly report that "many institutions continue to severely restrict the parents' role and to closely control the amount of contact they have with their own children." Critchley and Berlin (1981) express the commonly held conviction that "previous work with the child alone and parents alone usually has not altered the parents' capacity to deal with the child in the home setting" (p. 153).

Whereas efforts have been made by residential care providers to involve parents in their programs, in the United States few child care institutions allow parents to reside with their children. Parents are generally allowed the right to visit with the child in residential care during the daytime, to attend family treatment, and, occasionally, to spend evenings (but not nights) with the child. Family-centered approaches to child care that involve parents in a variety of activities regarding the child care center and their children can certainly result is considerably more parent–child contact than in traditional residential care or in foster care (Oxley, 1977). Yet they do not avoid the confusion and distress of parent–child separation or structure significant parent education experiences. Even "5-day foster care," a version of family-centered care that aimed to assist parents by placing the children in professionally supervised foster homes during the week and returning them to their own parents during weekends, holidays, and vacations, does not meet these tests of protection and parent education without separation. That program ostensibly closed because few families were troubled enough to need foster care but well enough to have their children at home over the weekend (T. Hanrahan, personal communication, February 28, 1991).

Shared family care goes beyond family-centered approaches. Littauer (1980) has described strategies for working with families of children in residential treatment that demonstrate effective parenting techniques. The opportunity to observe such techniques is more available to families residing in residential care than to those operating in isolation from other children and caregivers. Krona (1980) argues for discussing all major disciplinary decisions about children in child care with the children's parents. Simmons, Gumpert, and Rotham (1973) hold such discussions in collaborative meetings between parents, social workers, and children. Although sharing some similarities with shared care arrangements, these approaches seem too limited to help our more distressed families.

The need to rapidly develop arrangements that prevent separation of parent and child and promote parental capacity to care is not just a matter of fairness to parents. Also demanding action is the compelling evidence that parental involvement—indeed parental improvement—is central to the successful return of a child to the family. When children are young and there are many of them and when parents are chronically ill or substance-involved or have a history of neglect, these improvements are hardest to achieve (Landsman, Nelson, Saunders, & Tyler, 1990). These are increasingly the parents whose children enter and stay in foster care.

MODELS OF SHARED FAMILY CARE

At least five types of shared family care living arrangements have evolved to keep parent and child together. These are (1) child care homes (residential treatment programs for children) that also offer residence and treatment for their parents; (2) drug and alcohol treatment programs for adults that also offer treatment for children; (3) drug treatment programs for mothers and children; (4) residential programs expressly developed to offer care to pregnant and parenting mothers; and (5) foster homes that offer care of parent and child. The parameters of each type of program are described and at least one example of a program is presented. To learn about these programs, the reader must be willing to follow the discussion across the

United States and to Europe (especially Sweden, where I have done field research), where the practice of opening one's home to unrelated adults goes back centuries.

Child Care Homes for Families

"It would be appropriate to say that, here [Sweden], a silent revolution has indeed taken place. In the space of a few decades the [child care] homes have developed from institutions exclusively intended for children to establishments capable of catering to whole families with progressive social and mental disturbance" (Arnhoff, nd, p. 1). Approximately 100 child care programs in Sweden now offer treatment and residence to families. Of those homes, about 50 also offer care to unaccompanied children. (Homes that do not also offer care for unaccompanied children more often care for families where severe parental mental illness is the primary cause of the need for placement.) These institutions care for 509 children, from birth to age 12, with more than half in care with at least one parent (to be exact, 267 children with 156 parents). The law and the National Board of Health and Welfare are "supporting and promoting the kind of institutional care which allows a child to be with his/her parents during his stay at the home" (Arnhoff, nd, p. 4), that is, shared family care. This section describes three very different Swedish programs and one American example.

Barnhyn Ska

Children's Village at Ska, Sweden, may be the originator of shared family care programs to care for parent and child together (Borjeson, 1974). For more than a century the children's village cared only for children. Once a conventional child care institution, Children's Village at Ska began to involve families in the 1970s and now houses up to 13 guest families. Families with parents who are suffering from mental illness and who have neglected or abused their children can live at Ska. Families are also often referred to the village as a result of parental substance abuse, but, unlike conventional therapeutic communities in the United States, residence at Ska does not require abstinence from drugs or alcohol. The philosophy and operation of the program is as follows:

> As soon as a family moves in they become citizens of Children's Village. As such they have the same rights and obligations as they would in any other community. The same laws and rules apply. . . . The fact that a family has problems and has moved here in hope of finding some help does not change the basic principles of civic rights. Employed experts have the added duty to assist families. We have, however, no right or authority to decide how the families should live their lives. Social control is everybody's responsibility and concern. (Lorentzon, 1986, p. 2)

The Children's Village at Ska is a unit within Stockholm Social Services. The community life of families at Ska dominates the professional structure. Everybody takes part in the daily running of the village, but the emphasis is on shared residential responsibility. Families not taking part in the program and the everyday running of the village must rethink their decision to live in that community. As a last resort, the Decision Group (which discusses all families moving in or out) may recommend that they leave the village (the final decision is the staff's). The children's village is not, however, just a place to live; a program of change is in force. Lorentzon views the program as a kind of "school for families" (p. 7) and hopes that it will one day be recognized as a college. Education includes adult education classes, therapy groups and psychodrama, decision-making groups, "talks" between professional staff and family (as often as three times a week), and planning sessions about work and finances.

The successfulness of the children's village is not well documented by standard measures of outcome at discharge and recidivism. The village does, however, offer theoretical grounds for success. Neglecting families are known to have small, dense support networks that often consist only of relatives, paramours, and formal service providers (Gaudin, 1990) and are often nonreciprocal (Crittendon, 1990). The children's village community is a dense network of relationships. Children meet other children and adults; they learn and get help from their new contacts. Adults meet other adults—guest parents and staff members. Like most shared family care arrangements, Children's Village at Ska seeks to stimulate and support parents so that they will feel that they want to become good enough parent figures themselves. By refraining from becoming parent figures, staff endeavor to support parental independence (Lorentzon, 1986).

Eurenii Minne Barnheim

Other children's homes that now care for families offer a briefer residence for diagnosis and treatment. Eurenii Minne Barnheim (EMB; Eurenii Children's Home) in Johanneshov, Sweden, began to serve families in 1981 (after 61 years of serving young children), when a mother was allowed to extend her visiting hours at the home, then stay over a few nights, and, finally, reside there. Although the mother's problems were so severe that she never did resume the care of her child, involving her in the life of the home made theoretical and practical sense. The staff believed that they were better able to assess her capacity for parenting, help her to determine that she could not care for her child independently, and develop alternative placement plans. The 1982 reforms of Swedish child welfare law that stressed voluntary and family-centered treatment supported this practical effort, and this program's involvement with families began to grow. At first resident families were distributed throughout the three traditional children's units, but the staff later concluded that it was best to have families separate from unaccompanied children in order to have unambiguous structures that allowed parents, children, and staff alike to know what to expect. The home serves 10 families at a time. The same number of staff members were retained as originally needed for the unaccompanied children's program, but new staff members with experience serving both adult and child clientele were recruited.

About half the families include a father figure in residence, and most families stay for about 6 weeks. Families with an actively psychotic parent cannot be included, but parents who are depressed or who are drug abusers, child molesters, or alcoholics are the typical clientele. Drug-testing is required for parents who are identified as drug users. If they receive a positive test, they are not automatically excluded from the program, but the issue is brought to the meeting of family, social worker, and staff for resolution. Few parents have jobs when they come to the program, so reintegration of families into their adult lives is not so difficult; some do continue going to off-campus drug treatment programs while in the home. Aftercare services that help the families transfer their new family living skills to their old environments are modest and ad hoc but may continue as long as 6 months.

The EMB program has diagnostic and treatment goals. Primary responsibilities are to inform the social services bureau of the appropriateness of family reunification and to develop a services plan. The brevity of the stay is, in part, to be sure that the social worker stays involved with the family while in residence. This is also accomplished by having weekly meetings between the family, social worker, and residence staff. According to the director, the recommendation is seldom to separate families at the conclusion of their stay. When that is the recommendation, it is usually agreed to by the mother, who may be given additional time in the home with her child to work through that separation and develop a suitable alternative for her child. The director indicates that most of the families entering Eurenii Children's Home are required to go there by the court and notes that she can see no difference in the outcomes for voluntary and involuntary families. "Usually, we can be the turning point," she says.

The intervention aspects of the program are based on milieu and family therapy. The same staff who work with the family in their daily living also provide family therapy during three weekly meetings. Given the brief stay, the Eurenii program has modest goals regarding teaching skills for independent living. Developmentally disabled parents do not do well there. The staff prepares lunch and dinner, although the staff and families clean together. Unlike Ska, the Eurenii Children's Home program does not encourage shared child care among parents and does not emphasize network building among clients.

Barnhemmet Solsidan

Barnhemmet Solsidan Socialvardsnamnden in rural Skaraborg, Sweden, was transformed into a shared family care home between 1985 and 1990. The change to shared family care resulted from the debate in Sweden on the importance of family centered care and from an ideological commitment to provide the optimum chance to families to remain together. The home's capacity is three adults (they have not allowed fathers or boyfriends to reside in the homes, but they are welcome to visit) and eight children. Because it has large quarters it is able to allow the mothers to come without decreasing the number of children it has in its care. The home also accepts unaccompanied children and plans to maintain this capacity in order to be able to accommodate those occasions when a child comes to the residence before the parents are willing or able to join the child or when a parent leaves the residence before the child does. As with Eurenii Minne Barnheim, the program transition to shared family care was quite gradual, required some staff retraining but no increase in staff, and was done without fiscal incentives, regulations, or significant consultation or contact with other programs simultaneously undergoing this evolution. Leif Andersson, the program's director, believes that his program can provide an opportunity for "the most unmotivated and unable parents who cannot be reached by services at home" (personal communication, October 1, 1990).

The treatment approach is based on the milieu. Each mother has an appointed therapist from the milieu staff, but no scheduled therapeutic hours are set. The approach also emphasizes the demonstration of skills and routines. As an example, a mentally disturbed mother who came to stay with her two children had no experience with providing them a bedtime routine or with toilet training or diapers (which she said she could not afford). As a result, her 3- and 5-year-old constantly wet their clothes and bed (or wherever else they fell asleep for the night). The staff helped the mother develop a routine of bedtime and toileting. The family was ultimately able to become involved in child care and other supportive services and to return to community life.

No drugs and alcohol are allowed (nor are intoxicated residents allowed to stay in the home during their inebriation), but no drug testing is required. Mothers maintain their own apartments and may continue to work during this time. This home does have regularly scheduled aftercare visits during the first 3 months after discharge, but families come to expect that they can call the home at later points if they are in crisis. The program has no official time limits, but for most families a decision is made within 3 months if they will be able to remain together and intact families move out within 6 months, with a completed posttreatment plan.

Andersson has no precise figures on the outcomes of the program, although he asserts that even when families cannot stay together and he must go to court to argue for their separation, the subsequent foster placement proceeds more smoothly because the birth mother is more likely to understand that even under these very supportive circumstances she cannot care for her child. In such cases, she is helped to determine the role that she can play to assist the foster parents in the upbringing of her child. Although Swedish child welfare services do not all share identical philosophies or structure, shared family care has been adopted as the policy and program goal.

Texas Baptist Children's Home

To date, there exists only one written description of a shared family care program hosted by a child care agency in the United States. For more than a decade the Texas Baptist Children's Home (TBCH) has operated a 24-hour child care facility that provides residential service for single mothers and their children (Gibson &

Noble, 1991). The intent of the program is to "prevent the separation of mother and child if at all possible but not at all costs" (Nelson Nagle, personal communication, May 23, 1991). Maximum capacity in each of the two family cottages is eight residents; each cottage can serve a maximum of three client families at a time (each has a staff family living in it in addition to the client families). The average length of stay is a little more than 3 months. The three full-time staff members provide role modeling and coaching of appropriate child guidance and discipline procedures, effective communication skills, leisure time planning, meal preparation, and techniques to assist children in school readiness. Each family has personal living space of at least one bedroom and a personal kitchen and eating area. Group and individual counseling sessions are provided. Day care is provided for each family while the mother is applying for employment, making appointments, working, and/or receiving respite care. Individual service plans are developed with each mother.

Children are not taken into protective custody at the outset. Among the 20 resident parents who entered TBCH at that time and who indicated that placement of their children in substitute care was imminent, only 2 families ultimately required the placement of their children. The residential stay helps families get started on public housing waiting lists, in job and educational training, and in getting child support or protective restraining orders from fathers and boyfriends. Approximately 75% of the mothers become employed or return to school full-time while in the program. Aftercare lasts for 1 to 2 years and consists of two to three contacts per month and some financial assistance. (TBCH also serves families in their own home.)

The current cost of this approach is less than $30 per day per person and "the program is significantly less expensive than residential care, since mothers, rather than staff members, provide much of the child supervision" (Gibson & Noble, 1991). In this way the program averts licensing regulations around staffing. Staff costs are limited to social services. (Under this arrangement, TBCH is not eligible for Title IV-E foster care reimbursement, but mothers can keep their Aid to Families of Dependent Children payment.) The program is aimed at clients with very limited income, little access to housing, and few parenting skills.

Residential Adult Programs with Provisions for Children

Residential drug treatment programs for adults are beginning to address the needs of families. In Sweden roughly 10% of all children in out-of-home care are in treatment homes for adults with drug or alcohol dependency problems (Arnhoff, nd, p. 4). Certainly, many fewer children are in such programs in the United States. While parents are involved in groups and rehabilitation training, children are in day care or school or are provided care on site. The general aim of these programs is to establish sobriety to improve parenting (although some of these programs do have parent support groups, many may not have parenting classes), whereas programs that are expressly for mothers and children are more likely to emphasize responsible parenting as a route to sobriety.

Residential programs for adults are typically more committed to the recovery of the mother than concerned about the children. These programs may lack the facilities for weekend and evening coverage for children if parents are absent without making arrangements for their children. The concept of residential programs stems more from the women's movement and the drug treatment culture than from the child welfare community. Yet child welfare workers, too, are beginning to face the inseparability of these issues.

Indeed, battered women's shelters have long provided shared care in the United States. They have evolved over the years from shelters with a nearly exclusive emphasis on women to those that have some children's programming and perhaps a children's coordinator to ensure appropriate activities for them. Certainly, battered women's shelters have been arenas in which the issues of substance abuse, family violence, and child protection merge. (Residential drug treatment providers who are affiliated with programs exclusively for adults and who are considering the transition into residential family care might do well to look to their colleagues in the woman's shelter movement for consultation.)

The Rectory

The Rectory, in Vallejo, California, is a program that has evolved from a women's alcohol treatment program into one that also accommodates children. It is an eclectic program (although it emphasizes a social model) involving self-help, a sober living environment, and a program that shifts from very structured to quite unstructured as the woman and child's stay lengthens. The residents write recovery plans that are facilitated by staff. The Rectory, like most homes for drug-using mothers and children, typically restricts the number of children (to one) and the age of children (to under 6) in its care. The assumption is that the more children the mother must care for, the slower her recovery (Albione Becnel, director of the Rectory, personal communication, January 19, 1990). The program does not accept pregnant women. A 6-month follow-up of women enrolled voluntarily in the program showed eight of thirteen women sober and drug free. Out of five enrolled involuntarily due to children's protective services (CPS) referral, one is sober and drug free.

The Whale's Tale

Whale's Tale Family Treatment Center in Pittsburgh, Pennsylvania, is operating under an Office of Substance Abuse Prevention (OSAP) grant and uses a therapeutic community approach to services. The program runs from 6 to 12 months and is funded by grant money and by copayment from the mothers (who turn their AFDC over to the program). Program staff conduct random drug testing weekly; a woman may be tested more often on a random basis if she goes out. If a woman uses drugs that are brought into the house by someone else, she is given a more structured contract; if she brings drugs into the house, she is kicked out. The staff conduct their own drug treatment program. Relapse prevention is fostered by parenting skills training; the sharing of alcohol and drug information; membership in women's groups, encounter groups, and Cocaine Anonymous, Narcotics Anonymous, and Alcoholics Anonymous meetings; and by women taking responsibility for cooking, cleaning, and child care. The director of the Whale's Tale succinctly underscores the program's philosophy: women are the clients, not the children.

Mother and Child Group Homes

Homes for mothers and children have traditionally cared for teenagers from pregnancy through a few months postpartum, when the mother relinquished her child for adoption or returned to the community. The number of these homes has dropped sharply in the United States in the past two decades because of greater acceptance of adolescent and single motherhood. Yet these programs are still available for a few women who would otherwise be without housing.

Florence Crittendon Homes

Residential programs for pregnant adolescent mothers and their newborns were immensely popular in the United States in the 1950s and 1960s. By the 1970s, however, "policy analysts began to recommend alternatives to the costly, cloistered, segregated residential institutions" (Sedlak, 1982; p. 458) in favor of community-based settings and services. Legal barriers to integration of the pregnant adolescents into the public schools were largely overcome through Title IX of the 1972 Education Amendments. This victory has, however, been at the cost of reducing access to the option of residential care. At this time, Florence Crittendon homes continue to provide residential services to pregnant adolescents and, for a short time, to their newborns if those women would otherwise be incarcerated or in foster care. There are approximately 25 homes (about half are in the South) and a small proportion of them have begun to provide substance abuse treatment services (Florence Crittendon, 1991).

Theodor-Wenzel-Haus

The western part of Germany has approximately 70 "mother and child houses" available for troubled mothers to care for their children in a cooperative setting. These residences are as small as 6 apartment units (each with its own kitchen) and as large as 50; many of the residences are loaned by the church. Mothers must be 16 years old (if they are younger, they are strongly encouraged to stay with their own families of origin) and may be referred because of actual or potential problems in parenting resulting from developmental disabilities, substance abuse, and/or previous child abuse. Approximately 1,000 units (which house mother and one or two children) are available in these mother and child houses, and many of them also include aftercare services. The monthly cost in the Theodor-Wenzel-Haus in Hamburg is approximately $3,000 per mother and child dyad (in 1990 dollars). Mothers stay a minimum of 6 months and may stay for a year. The staff for a 12-

unit house is three social workers, three early childhood educators, and one nurse. One-fifth of the mothers are there because of a child protection court order. The staff prefers that the mothers arrive during pregnancy—preferably at around the 8th month of pregnancy. Mothers are involved in group work one day a week and in individual therapy twice weekly. Each day they receive some parenting classes from the nurse (usually conducted in groups), and each week they prepare the equivalent of one day's meals together to learn food preparation techniques.

Drug Treatment Group Homes for Women and Children

The need for drug treatment homes expressly designed for women and children is great. Several new programs have been developed under federal, state, and local initiatives. Yet at the end of 1990 New York State had only one residential treatment facility for women and children and Pennsylvania had just three (Dinis, Chapter 7, this volume).

Mandela House

Mandela House is one of America's first programs expressly serving drug-addicted (primarily crack-addicted) pregnant women. As of 1990, nearly 70% of the residents use crack cocaine as their primary drug of choice, and 25% use two other drugs regularly (Redmond, 1990). Nearly two-thirds of the women have two or more children upon entry to Mandela House, and 29% have four or more children. These children cannot join their mothers at Mandela House but reunification is a primary program goal.

Mandela House embraces an abstinence model program, and even the staff are prohibited from using drugs or alcohol 24 hours before their shift begins (Thomas, 1989). The program is designed for a stay of 12 to 18 months, with a commitment by the client to stay for at least a year (one third of the women leave within the first 3 months). Residents are expected to begin seeking housing in their 8th month in the facility. During its first 2 years of operation, Mandela House admitted 28 residents. More than half remained 6 months or more, and a third remained the full year until graduation (Redmond, 1990). The program initially focuses on breaking ties to drug use and does not endeavor to support contacts between mothers and their social support systems: visits are only allowed after the first 90 days and with advanced approval by the program manager. Visitors must stay in public and visible rooms in the house and are subject to searches. Parenting sessions are mandatory; leaving a baby unattended and threats of violence or physical punishment are not allowed. Infants are cared for by the staff during psychoeducational classes. The program expressly seeks information about the mother's other children, who do not reside at Mandela House and may be in foster care. Visits can be arranged for the children to stay overnight and over the weekend. All visits are supervised by the staff.

Mandela House has not had a formal evaluation but has been judged successful enough by the community of service providers and funders to warrant expansion to a second home. The first nine graduates left in December 1988, the last one in December 1989. As of June 1990 most were living independently in their own apartments, four had steady jobs, five were in training programs at junior colleges, and one was, according to the director, "waffling a bit." Aftercare is central to this success. The graduates meet with the director every fourth Saturday at one of the women's homes, and they stay in touch with her frequently by phone. Also, when there are free beds in the nursery, alumnae can drop off their babies for respite care. The first 21 infants born to mothers in the program were full-term and full birth weight. Although a few infants were initially hyperactive and a few seemed to catch a lot of colds, there were no reports by staff of children with small head size, abnormal muscle tone, irregular sleeping patterns, increased heart rates, inappropriate responses to cuddling, or developmental delays (a more rigorous evaluation of infant outcomes is under way). This healthy start for newborns may have more than offset the $25,000 per year per mother–infant dyad program cost even if the mothers do not complete the program.

Moringen

Begun in 1985, Moringen is the oldest of Sweden's homes for drug-using mothers and their children. Clients are typically women older than 18 who use multiple drugs, including amphetamines, heroin, and alcohol, and who are pregnant or have recently given birth. Women are usually sent to Moringen by their social workers and by Stockholm hospital's special prenatal and maternity care service for drug-using women. Often, a woman enters the program voluntarily since she knows that her social worker can recommend involuntary placement in a foster home or residential treatment program and placement of her newborn in foster care if she does not go to Moringen or if she leaves before 6 months without social worker and court approval. (Some women do, indeed, come to Moringen rather than enter a locked unit for drugs users.)

While the women are at Moringen, the social worker continues to be involved with them and meets with them as often as weekly to try to ensure that they are gaining the educational, job preparation, and housing opportunities to which they are entitled. If the mothers were working prior to the birth of their child, they can claim the year's maternity pay all Swedish mothers are entitled to and are guaranteed the return of their old jobs. Women who are on methadone are eligible for the program, although all the women who entered Moringen to date have gone through detoxification and are not using methadone.

The superordinate goal of the program is to give the baby a good start during the first year of life. Thus, the program stresses parenting issues first and drug abuse second. It does, however, require random and routine drug tests for clients and their partners if these men are going to visit them. If the women are very involved with their husbands, the staff recommends that the family go to a residential program for families rather than to Moringen, which is primarily for single women. It also argues that the more children a mother must care for, the more difficult her recovery is; therefore, the program is limited to mothers with single newborns. The program has a relatively unstructured day; mothers are expected to spend most of their time parenting their child and going out to get the services they need. The staff does not want to bring all the services to the mothers for fear they will not develop skills for independent living. Moringen has experienced considerable turmoil in recent years and even closed down for a 2-year period as a result of heavy staff turnover.

The Johansson Home

The Johansson Home, a Swedish group home that was once a foster family home for drug addicts, is run by two women; the executive director worked in a drug day treatment program for a decade, and the other is a former client of that day treatment program. Although initially a foster home, over the years the Johansson Home has become more like a group home. At first the executive director had just one or two clients and continued her full-time work at the day treatment center. She soon realized that she needed to be on the premises more and quit her other work to be full-time at home. To make this financially possible, she expanded the number of residents in the home to three and hired a staff.

The executive director believes that the clients best suited for the program are those who are younger and not too heavily involved in criminal activity. She no longer accepts residents who apply to live in her home as an alternative to jail; she only accepts those who have avoided prison or who have completed prison terms. The structured schedule reflects the executive director's experience in drug treatment and includes a daily morning meeting to plan the day, a scheduled "family meeting" three times a week to discuss issues of family living, and exercise three times a week.

The meetings and milieu work are used to model the larger society; residents are expected to communicate about their relationships and to respect each other's rights. Staff and residents agree that there is less confrontation here than in a day treatment program but that it does occur and is more natural in this family living situation. Each resident meets with his or her social worker and the family home staff about once a week; this has also evolved into a group meeting, and each resident is expected to attend each meeting. This keeps all residents aware of the treatment issues for all other residents and helps them identify ways that they can assist each other in the recovery process.

The program has firm guidelines: No one goes out of the home alone during the first 5 months; if there is suspected drug use, the residents must take a urine test. Testing positive calls for a meeting with the social worker and a revised treatment plan. Clients who are successful in their early months begin to go to outside therapy; in their transition back to the community they live and work part of the week away from the residence and return on weekends. (The family home is fully reimbursed for the care of the residents even during this transition to independent living.)

Current residents include two adult male drug abusers and a heroin addict and her daughter, who was less than 1 year old when they arrived. Few special provisions are made for the mother and daughter in the home. Everyone assumes that the mother is responsible for her child at all times unless she asks for assistance. The home is not child-centered per se, and treatment discussions are rarely about parenting. Indeed, staff and residents needed some prompting to move beyond their adult-to-adult kitchen table discussions to include the child (who attends family day care during the day).

Foster Care for Families

Foster family care has been provided for adults who are identified as developmentally disabled, mentally ill, and frail (Sherman & Newman, 1988). The practice of opening one's home to unrelated dependent adults has been in operation for centuries in Europe. In this country the first foster family care program for mentally ill adults dates back more than one hundred years. Yet, these programs have been neglected by the social work community and other professions as well; they remain unknown and largely unavailable throughout most of the United States (Oktay, 1987; Sherman & Newman, 1986). Indeed, in Oktay's review of adult foster care in the *Encyclopedia of Social Work* there is no mention of foster family care for families.

Children's Home and Aid Society of Chicago

The Children's Home and Aid Society (CHAS) of Chicago has been operating a program for 2 years that provides shared family care for minor mothers. These mothers may enter the program as foster youth who get pregnant or as parents of small children who come to the attention of the agency as a result of child abuse and neglect.

CHAS's innovative Adolescent Mothers' Resource Homes Program to care for adolescent mothers and their children in out-of-home care. Foster parents undergo 8 weeks of training. Black foster parents are more likely than white or Latino foster parents (CHAS calls them "resource parents") to complete the training and join the program. Resource parents are typically single women who have raised their own children. Many are employed, but flexible employment is a must. Most are not experienced foster parents. The role seems to appeal to a distinct population who are particularly interested in supporting these young mothers (perhaps because they themselves once had a need for such support). The foster care rate as of March 1991 was $930 per month (which covers mother and child); this is roughly twice the adolescent rate but below a group home rate.

All mothers are dependents of the child welfare system. CHAS builds a placement agreement with every young mother, her significant others (including her current beau, the baby's father, and the grandparents), the social worker, and the foster parents. All parties clarify what they are willing to do. The plan also specifies ways that the mother will use other agencies; some mothers are involved with as many as three outside agencies. The plan also clarifies that if the mother is not happy with the resource parents, she is expected to give 30 days' notice that she intends to leave. Social workers meet with the mothers weekly and then biweekly. Young mothers can continue on in the program until they reach the age of 21.

According to the guidelines for the responsibilities of resource parent and mother, the mother must take full responsibility for the child; resource parents are encouraged to support but not supplant the mother. They may provide babysitting but are encouraged to exchange it for something else. Still, much is unwritten, and many understandings have to be hammered out on the anvil of everyday living.

The program is currently serving 22 mothers and their children and is now staffed by three social workers, who will ultimately each serve 10 mothers and their children (three of the mothers have more than one child). A maximum of two mothers may reside with each resource family. Mothers cannot be so drug-involved that they cannot function as parents. Yet no drug testing is required, and the program is well prepared for the fact that these adolescents—like all other adolescents—will "screw up." This is not reason for dismissal from the program. There has only been one placement termination initiated by the agency in 2 years (because the mother was bringing drug dealers into the home). "There is an unlimited number of girls you could place," says the program director Sheila Merry (personal communication, April 21, 1991).

The outcomes to date are impressive. Thirty mothers and more than 33 children have been served. Only one child has been referred to CPS through the child abuse hot line. Of the young women who left the program, four ran away (and did so before CHAS instituted the 30-day notice strategy) and one moved in with her boyfriend. Only three girls have graduated so far, but they do continue to connect with their resource parent. Still, the program director worries about the adequacy of parenting: "Lots of our kids are getting substandard parenting" (Sheila Merry, personal communication, April 21, 1991). The program will add individual child assessments and derivative parent education to their next budget. Organizations in eight other states have contacted the program to express interest in developing a similar program (Children's Home and Aid Society, 1991).

Project Demand

Project Demand in Minneapolis uses shared care arrangements in two ways. Substance-abusing women and up to three of their children can live in an apartment cluster with supervision and across-the-street day care and substance abuse treatment (Margie Clay, program coordinator, personal communication, May 8, 1991). Families reside in 12 apartments in the complex, with the 13th occupied by staff (only staff can admit outsiders to the apartment). The apartment approach helped Project Demand avoid zoning law requirements that often preclude group residences with on-site treatment services.

Arrangements are developed with resource families who provide residence to the mothers and their children after the mothers graduate from this program (after one year of operation, the graduation rate is 55%). The mothers pay for their own board and care from their paycheck, AFDC payment, or other available funds.

Since AFDC-foster care funds are not used for this purpose, the payments that resource families receive vary and are generally not as high as the special foster care rate provided by CHAS homes and are only a fraction of the cost of drug treatment group homes.

The Swensons

In Sweden more than 200 drug abusers in recovery are cared for in foster care. Many are parents. The Swensons met in a drug treatment program (the mother had been at Barnbyn Ska as a child) and were child care workers and certificated substance abuse counselors before becoming foster parents. They had taken in children and adults individually and then were asked by a social worker to take in a mother and her three children. Now, 5 years later, the mother is nearly blind— from HIV infection from her husband; the children continue to come twice a month for the weekend and may reside with the Swensons permanently upon the mother's death.

The Swensons share their kitchen and living room with guests. Although they say that "the difficulties of shared space has never stopped us from caring for guest families," they did recently build two cottages on their grounds to better accommodate the "guests" in their own spaces. They seek to have guests feel like family members, yet they have rules: no drugs in the home and none on weekends. Residents can come back, however, if they relapse or go AWOL (even though there is a long waiting list for the program); one resident has gone AWOL about 15 times but is now on methadone and doing very well. The Swensons have regular meetings with social workers and "guests." The foster parents contend that when guests are taking drugs everyone can see it; therefore, they have no urine tests. They expect the client to work toward a job, therapy, good spare time activity, and ordinary relationships. This is the treatment plan. The Swensons believe that a 12-step program is not necessary. There is one social worker for all the foster homes caring for families in recovery in the local district. When clients leave their program, the Swensons help them make the transition to a social district flat; they pay half and the client pays half, and then it becomes the client's flat in a year.

Although providing foster care to drug addicts would seem like a risky business in any society, in 5 years the Swensons haven't locked their doors once; only two bracelets have disappeared. The insurance company forced them to buy an expensive burglar alarm system, but they never activate it. Only once have the Swensons had to call the police: when a guest became increasingly paranoid and threatening and began to fight with other residents, eventually ending up in a neighbor's living room in the middle of the night (the foster family was not there that night). The guest was a 25-year-old man who had abused his grandmother, his girlfriend, and the staff at a treatment program. He started to use drugs every weekend and was getting worse and worse. By the time the Swensons came home, he had left. They then arranged a three-way meeting with the social worker and the drug addict, and it was amicably decided that the man should leave. He was placed in a more intensive setting.

UNIQUE ASPECTS OF SHARED FAMILY CARE

In practice, there is infinite variation in the configuration of shared family care arrangements. Foster family homes differ in principle from supervised apartments in providing more personal and more extensive social support; they differ from group homes in that group homes use shifts of paraprofessionals and professionals to provide supervision and treatment. Again, in theory, group homes should be able to accommodate families who need considerable intervention and oversight whereas foster family homes may not provide as much habilitative clout. In practice, this conclusion cannot be so readily drawn. Although we often assume it to be true, we do not know that the high structure (and cost) of group homes is necessary for habilitation of substance-involved mothers and their children.

Shared family care serves the same purposes as intensive family preservation services (which are much more widely known in the United States than in Europe). Yet critical differences call for the mutual use of shared care and family preservation. Intensive family preservation services are typically briefer than shared family care. Certainly, there are few 1-month-long shared family care arrangements, but many last no longer than a few months. The cost per month appears to be higher for family preservation services, although the service period is much longer for shared care arrangements.

Shared care is a particularly helpful program when the parents live in environments that are not conducive to their recovery—on the street, in transitional hotels, or in neighborhoods imbued with drugs and crime. Family preservation programs are little used in such situations; when they were applied in places like the south Bronx of New York, the struggles with horrid housing and neighborhoods were sometimes demoralizing to staff and overwhelming to families. Given Crittendon's (1990) findings that many of the most chronic neglecting families do not receive services because none are available or the family cannot get to them or the social worker does not fulfill the service agreement because of his or her combined pessimism and fear, shared care arrangements may be the only way to deliver services to some families.

SUCCESSFUL ELEMENTS OF SHARED CARE

Because there are virtually no outcome data on these shared care arrangements, unabashed speculation about the program elements that seem most critical is necessary and forgivable.

Homelike Setting

Public Law 96-272 calls for providing social services in the most family-like setting, the one least disruptive to parent and child. Ideally, services would be provided in the family's own home. Alberta (Canada) Family Support Services (1990) has developed a program that uses trained child care staff working in the family's home to create a "residential care bed at home" (p. 10). Shared family care, conversely, creates a home within residential care. Although not every shared family care program is able to provide the atmosphere of home, the mother, father, and child should have some sense of belonging and some privacy. In many cases the residential setting is more homelike than the settings in which families formerly resided—especially in the United States, where housing shortages are a critical contributor to the need for out-of-home care (Pelton, 1989). As Nelson Nagle, the director of the Baptist Children's Home program, said, "If they had a home, we would have provided the services there" (personal communication, May 23, 1991). Families living within the milieu of another family have the opportunity to maintain their relationships while learning or relearning effective patterns of interacting. Relief from the pressures of protecting themselves from homelessness and violence may allow for the development of alternatives to substance abuse and child abuse. The routines of the residence may help families who have long forgotten the rhythms and responsibilities of home to transfer them to an independent living situation.

Myriad Teachable Moments

Shared living provides innumerable opportunities for observation and support. The most intensive in-home service programs may include 10 to 30 hours a week for 6 to 10 weeks (Alberta Community Services, 1990). Most typically, intensive in-home services include no more than 50 hours. Shared family care arrangements, on the other hand, can include 140 hours of direct contact with families in just the first 2 weeks. Families can observe other families and receive feedback about their parenting styles at all hours and across many and diverse parenting tasks. These programs, with most of the work occurring in the milieu, may not be intensely therapeutic, but the opportunities for direct and indirect teaching are enormous.

Structure

A successful shared family care arrangement seeks to match the demands of the setting to the client's ability to respond to them. The shared family care arrangement must strike the proper balance for "maximizing motivation for excercise of skills" without "overstepping the individual's limits of tolerance for stress" (Sherman & Newman, 1988, p. 29). Drug treatment providers often assume that a structured environment that includes a constant schedule of skill-building activities, self-help groups, and chores is the best antidote to drug involvement. Foster family providers cannot offer such a demanding structure; it exceeds the boundaries of family life. Only innovation and evaluation will tell whether the recidivism rate is significantly different for clients in more or in less structured settings.

Community Integration

Community integration has been a traditional goal of adult foster family care (Segal & Aviram, 1978). Community integration involves using community resources and developing or renewing lasting connections to prosocial institutions (e.g., adult education, church, work, extended family). Yet much remains unknown about the approach and timing of efforts to reintegrate substance-involved parents into the community. Crack is considered to have the capacity to pull women out of residences and into deep and dangerous substance abuse if given the smallest opportunity; yet that opportunity may result from the very efforts of drug treatment personnel to increase a client's integration into the community. Still, community integration must occur at some point in recovery. For the most addicted women, the transition to independent living may require stepping down from less permeable arrangements (e.g., group care) to more permeable ones (e.g., foster family care or transitional housing programs). The shared family care provider is clearly a link between the client and the social community. Group home providers may have greater opportunity to organize group trips into the community whereas foster family providers may do more to include their guest families in informal religious and social events that allow for greater connectedness to the community. Either way, planned transitions back to the community will foster success.

CONCLUSIONS

The reader might wonder if these proposals to preserve families through placement in residential care are necessary in an era when successful models of intensive family preservation services that help families in their own homes are available. Certainly, community-based family preservation efforts are—all other things equal—more likely to be more cost-effective because they are brief and do not require the transition from the residential setting back to the community, which has been such a challenge to residential care providers. But, simply stated, all things are not equal. Some families have totally inadequate housing and need an alternative. Some are characterized by problems that make failure with family preservation services likely, for example, having more children, more poverty, and more years of welfare dependency. Other families do not succeed in family preservation programs because they are too short-lived. This may be particularly true for very young mothers and drug-involved mothers who may experience relapses; they may look successful at 3-month termination and 3-month follow-up but are not successful after a year. Some children require more protection than can be provided by social workers even if social workers are in the home for as many as 10 hours per week.

Any mention of residential care also conjures up concerns about costs. Certainly, residential care is not cheap. Yet Swedish providers who had converted from conventional child care to family care consistently indicated that the costs were no greater than those for children alone. They did not change their budget totals as a result of beginning to include parents in their programs. Texas Baptist Children's Home found the cost to be considerably less; the cost savings are partly attributable to the ingenuity of service providers in finding ways to include parents in activities in the home that needed to be done so that their participation could yield a net contribution to the operation of the agency. This makes the Texas Baptist Children's Home's program for families one-third the cost of its child care program.

Whittaker's (1978) precise articulation of the purpose of residential care captures the logic and challenge of shared family care: "The basic purpose of residential and day programs for troubled children should be to function as a family support system rather than to treat the child in isolation from his family and home community" (p. 25). Shared family care supports the family and prevents isolation of the child. It does not, however, prevent isolation from the home community. We do not yet know much about how to promote the transition from shared family care to the community.

Barriers to developing shared family care arrangements can be surmounted. Developing group homes is clearly the most difficult because of zoning laws and fire codes. Ironically, this seems like the favored approach. Existing child care agencies may have an easier time developing group homes. Apartment arrangements like those of Project Demand require no zoning waivers, nor do CHAS's resource homes. Perhaps the foremost deterrent to effective involvement in residential programs will probably continue to be staff beliefs about drug-involved parents and about their own ability to work with these parents. When staff and parents do interact on a long-term basis, a more helpful attitude often develops (Littauer, 1980; Van Hagen, 1983).

Residential care is intended to help a family find the best possible solution to its difficulties. This may call for a range of program designs. Numerous residential treatment programs have drawn on their child care and family treatment skills to develop family preservation programs. (Indeed, a growing number of programs simultaneously host residential treatment, day treatment, and family preservation programs.) Staff in residential programs have shown the capacity to engage with families and children in a range of ways; perhaps including families in residential care will be the next.

Many alternative shared family care arrangements now exist. Parson's Children's Center in Albany provides continued care for mother and child if the young mother is a group home resident who becomes pregnant, and the center's subacute adolescent facility allows families to stay on the unit as needed. Parson's foster family treatment cluster has child care support and has rooms to accommodate parental visiting on a case-by-case basis (Nadia Finkelstein, personal communication, February 11, 1991). Oregon's Multonomah County Alcohol and Drug Addiction Prenatal Treatment (ADAPT) program provides cluster housing for women recently released from jail. Case managers coordinate a weekly support and problem-solving group for participants and a full-time staffer provides monitoring and life skills assistance for apartment residents. These programs differ from shared family care insofar as they are not expressly designed to provide significant modeling of parenting skills and to provide services to the whole family.

Although the types of shared care arrangements described in this chapter all have common features (among the most important of those being their relative unavailability), they are certainly not equivalent. Foster care represents the most flexible program since it operates at a lower cost, can operate under conventional fire and safety regulations (e.g., they require installing smoke detectors but not a water-sprinkling system), and can expand or contract as the demand fluctuates. Its capacity to help heavy drug users is not clear, however. Mother and child homes have the longest history in the United States but have fallen out of favor lately and generally do not care for drug-involved women. Drug treatment programs that have expanded to include children may have trouble focusing on them—especially when the parents are not reliable parents. Residential children's centers have great capacity for shared family care arrangements but may have the greatest barriers to change.

There is the greatest need for each of these program types to respond to substance-abusing families. If they cannot, we will continue to see increases in the foster care and group home care of children. Yet there are at least two assumptions of foster care for drug-involved families that require analysis. The first is that parents can improve their functioning without an on-site social model treatment program. Clients are assumed to be able to benefit from living in a safe and well-managed environment, from working through a variety of milieu arrangements with foster parents (but without getting professional counseling on-site), and from attending auxiliary programs outside the foster family. The second assumption is that foster families will come forward and make themselves available to provide care for drug-involved or recently detoxified parents and children. Certainly, the horror stories in the media about the crack cocaine epidemic will not encourage such voluntarism, nor will the conventional pay rates that all but make foster parenting a form of voluntarism. Indeed, the lack of financial pay for conventional . foster parents is supposed to be offset by the pleasures of having another child around the hearth, but low pay rates would not be so readily offset by the additional responsibility and inconvenience of having another adult in the home. Supplemental board rates will probably be necessary but may not need to be extraordinary.

At the same time, we know that the next decade will see a continuation of the trend toward having multiple generations under one roof. This is especially true for people of color. Making room for one or two more kin in need is not uncommon; whether families would be willing to open their doors to strangers is another question. Certainly, it has been done and is being done in Minnesota and Chicago. The promise is there. Foster family care does not have the built-in drug treatment that many professionals (especially Americans) believe to be essential to recovery. It may need it.

The currently favored strategy of developing group homes for pregnant or parenting substance-abusing women deserves continuation but appears fraught with difficulty. One very successful program has recently received funding to open two other residences, but it has taken nearly 18 months to get the first one going because of difficulties with various regulating bodies (e.g., the fire department). The third residence may open in an industrial area because it is more feasible to situate it there. Another program that has managed to put out the welcome mat may not stay full because women are limited to bringing one child. Another proprietor of a group home for women that takes pregnant and parenting women also has some difficulty keeping her beds full and admits that she knows more motivated professionals than clients. However, staff of other such programs indicate that they have long waiting lists; still, when they do have a vacancy they may not have anyone on the waiting list who is ready to enter. The intensive staffing of such programs makes any vacancies prohibitively expensive. Less costly, more flexible alternatives await development.

RECOMMENDATIONS FOR THE DEVELOPMENT OF SHARED CARE

1. Children and parents have a right to remain together as long as the children's right to a safe family life is preserved. To date, however, the vast majority of drug-using women are separated from their children even when such separations are avoidable.
2. Family preservation programs and case management services to drug-involved mothers at home have shown some promise and warrant additional implementation and evaluation. Profiles of families who can remain at home together during the recovery period must be drawn by evaluation researchers. Home based services should be available to them.
3. The recovery of drug-using women is also facilitated by providing residential programs. At least five types of residential programs that protect children and preserve families are possible. The availability of the first three options should be increased, and pilot testing of the latter options should be commenced.
   a. Residential drug treatment programs designed for women and their children are a promising option, especially for women who need housing and intensive intervention programs.
   b. Established residential drug treatment programs can and should become more effective in providing services to women and their children.
   c. Homes for adolescent mothers and children are part of a strong but waning tradition in America. These have largely been eliminated as school-based programs and case management have grown. The reasons for rebuilding this capacity are strong.
   d. Placement of mothers and children in residential child care facilities has also been successful in other countries and deserves exploration. Residential child care facilities are expert at developing new programs and finding funding for them. They should use their expertise to develop programs for mothers and their children.
   e. Foster family care for children can be expanded to include women and children together. Because this model has been successful in other countries and can offer a flexible, community-based approach, pilot programs should be developed to test its efficacy. Barriers to such programs resulting from AFDC regulations, and licensing should be waived to enable these pilot projects to proceed.

Acknowledgments

Field work for this chapter was begun while the author was a Senior Fulbright Scholar at the University of Stockholm, School of Social Work. Preparation of this article was supported by a Senior Faculty Fellowship award from the Lois and Samuel Silberman Fund at Berkeley and grants from the U.S. Department of Health and Human Services, Children's Bureau, Abandoned Infants Assistance Services Program.

REFERENCES

Alberta Family Support Services. (1990). *Home-based, family-centered treatment for children* (Annual Report). Alberta, Canada: Hull Community Services: Author.

Arnhoff, Y. (nd). *Children in treatment homes for alcoholics and drug users and adults in child-care homes or family care institutions.* Unpublished manuscript. Stockholm: National Board of Health and Welfare, Division for Social Therapy.

Berry, M. (1992). An evaluation of family preservation services: Fitting agency services to family needs. *Social Work, 37,* 314–321.

Borjeson, B. (1974). *Reestablishing an identity: Family treatment of Ska Children's Village.* Stockholm: Child Welfare Board.

Children's Home and Aid Society. (1991, April 1). *Final report to the Chicago Community Trust on CHAS's adolescent mothers: Resource homes.* Chicago: Author.

Critchley, D., & Berlin, I. (1981). Parent participation in milieu treatment of young psychotic children. *American Journal of Orthopsychiatry, 51,* 149–155.

Frankel, H. (1988). Family-centered, home-base services in child protection: A review of the research. *Social Service Review, 62,* 137–157.

Gaudin, J. (1990, September). *Social networks of neglecting families.* Paper presented at the 8th Annual International Congress on Child Abuse and Neglect, Hamburg, Germany.

Gibson, D., & Noble, N. N. (1991). Creative permanency planning: Residential services for families. *Child Welfare, 70,* 371–382.

Goerge, R. M. (1990). The reunification process in substitute care. *Social Service Review, 64*(3), 422–457.

Hill, E. P. (1957). Is foster care the answer? *Public Welfare, 15*(2), 67–72, 77–78.

Kadushin, A. (1971). *Child welfare services.* New York: Macmillan.

Krona, D. (1980). Parents as treatment partners in residential care. *Child Welfare, 59,* 91–96.

Kufeldt, K., & Allison, J. (1990). Fostering children, fostering families. *Community Alternatives, 2,* 1–18.

Landsman, M., Nelson, K., Saunders, E., & Tyler, M. (1990, fall). New research: Chronic neglect in perspective. *The Prevention Report,* p. 4.

Littauer, C. (1980). Working with families of children in residential treatment. *Child Welfare, 59,* 225–234.

Lorentzon, L. (1986). *Children's village at Ska, Sweden.* Unpublished manuscript.

Nelson, K. E. (1991). Populations and outcomes in five family preservation programs. In K. Wells & D. E. Biegel (Eds.), *Family preservation services: Research and evaluation* (pp. 72–91). Newbury Park, CA: Sage.

Oktay, J. S. (1987). Foster care for adults. In A. Minahan (Ed.), *Encyclopedia of Social Work* (Vol. 1, 634–638). Silver Spring, MD: National Association of Social Workers.

Oxley, G. B. (1977). Involuntary clients' responses to a treatment experience. *Social Casework, 58,* 607–614.

Pelton, L. H. (1989). *For reasons of poverty alone.* New York: Praeger.

Redmond, S. P. (1990). *Mandela House: Residential treatment programs for substance-abusing pregnant women.* San Francisco: Zellerbach Family Fund.

Sedlak, M. W. (1982). Youth policy and young women, 1870–1972. *Social Service Review, 56,* 448–499.

Segal, S. P., & Aviram, U. (1978). *The mentally ill in community-based sheltered care.* New York: Wiley.

Sherman, S. R., & Newman, E. (1988). *Foster families for adults: A community alternative to long-term care.* New York: Columbia University Press.

Simmons, G., Gumpert, J., & Rothman, B. (1973). Natural parents as partners in child care placement. *Social Casework, 54,* 224–232.

Spaid, W. M., & Fraser, M. (1991). The correlates of success/failure in brief and intensive family treatment: Implications for family preservation services. *Children and Youth Services Review, 13,* 77–99.

Sudia, C. (1990). *In-home services for crack-using mothers in Detroit.* Washington, DC: DHHS.

Tatara, T. (1990). *Child abuse reports and foster care.* Unpublished report. Washington, DC: American Public Welfare Association.

Thomas, M. (1989). *The Solid Foundation's Mandela House: Admissions and operations policies and guidelines.* Unpublished manual available from Mandela House, Hayward, CA.

Van Hagen, J. (1983). One residential center's model for working with families. *Child Welfare, 62,* 233–241.

Whittaker, J. K. (1978). The changing character of residential child care. *Social Service Review, 52,* 22–35.

Wulczyn, F. (1991). Caseload dynamics and foster care reentry. *Social Service Review, 65*(1), 133–156.

Yuan, Y-Y. T. (1990). *Evaluation of AB 1562 in-home care demonstration projects* (Vols. 1 & 2). Sacramento, CA: Walter R. MacDonald & Associates.

IV

LEGAL, ETHICAL, AND POLICY ISSUES

13

Pediatric HIV Infection and Perinatal Drug or Alcohol Exposure: Legal Issues and Legal Advocacy

ABIGAIL ENGLISH

INTRODUCTION

Thousands of children are born each year who have been infected with the Human Immunodeficiency Virus (HIV), the virus that causes Acquired Immune Deficiency Syndrome (AIDS), or exposed to drugs or alcohol. These children and their families require a broad range of services from the public health care and child welfare systems. Although some of these children and families are covered by private health insurance or receive services through private child welfare agencies, the vast majority are dependent to a significant degree on services provided through publicly financed sources of health care and public child welfare agencies.

While infants who have been infected with HIV or exposed to drugs or alcohol often arouse sympathetic responses, they are also at particular risk of being denied essential services because of discrimination and societal ambivalence about them and their families. Moreover, the existing structure and funding of health care and child welfare services do not meet the needs of children born exposed to drugs or alcohol or infected with HIV and their families in a comprehensive way. This population will only obtain adequate and appropriate services through vigorous advocacy by health care and child welfare professionals, educators, and attorneys.

This chapter explores a framework for advocacy to secure essential health care and child welfare services for drug- or alcohol-exposed and HIV-infected children and their families. The first section provides a three-part overview of the context in which health care and child welfare services are provided by, first, reviewing the epidemiologic data concerning perinatal drug or alcohol exposure and HIV infection; second, describing the service needs of drug- or alcohol-exposed children and their families; and, third, discussing the new burdens for the health care and child welfare systems associated with the increasing numbers of infants born exposed to drugs or alcohol or infected with HIV. The second section outlines strategies for identifying children born exposed to drugs or alcohol or infected with HIV in ways that will facilitate rather than impede access to appropriate services for them and their families. The third section of the chapter explores strategies for increasing access to essential health care and the fourth examines strategies to promote delivery of appropriate child welfare services. The last section concludes with recommendations for improving legal advocacy for children born infected with HIV or exposed to drugs or alcohol and their families.

BASIC ASSUMPTIONS

The analysis contained in this chapter rests on the following set of basic assumptions about children who are born exposed to drugs or alcohol or infected with HIV and their families, all of whom share many characteristics with one another:

- Perinatal drug or alcohol exposure and HIV infection are health problems that may have serious economic, social, physical, psychological, and developmental effects on children and families.
- The impact of HIV infection and perinatal drug or alcohol exposure varies among children and families.
- Many families affected by perinatal drug or alcohol exposure or HIV infection are capable of caring for their children with the assistance of appropriate support services.
- Acute illness or other problems associated with either HIV infection or drug/alcohol use sometimes interfere with parents' ability to provide adequate care for their children.
- Children and families affected by perinatal drug or alcohol exposure or HIV infection need a range of health care and child welfare services and other social supports that are provided in a comprehensive and coordinated manner.
- HIV-infected children and families and those affected by drug or alcohol exposure are often at serious risk of discrimination and denial of necessary services.

Drug- or alcohol-exposed and HIV-infected children and their families also share many of these characteristics and needs with other children and families who require services from the public health care and child welfare systems, including children and families with chronic illnesses and disabilities and those who have multiple complex needs and are at high risk of having those needs go unmet because of physical, psychological, social, or economic circumstances. Thus, new approaches to ensuring essential services for children and families affected by drugs, alcohol, or HIV can serve as a model in providing services for other children and families as well.

THE ROLE OF LEGAL ADVOCACY

Legal standards governing health care and child welfare services should facilitate delivery of services to children with drug or alcohol exposure or HIV infection and their families. However, current legal standards sometimes impede delivery of appropriate care to this population. Inadequate implementation of existing mandates also deprives this population of the health care and child welfare services they need. Improvements in health care and child welfare services for these children and families can occur through advocacy efforts to change existing legal standards, to secure appropriate judicial interpretations of those standards, and to fully implement existing mandates.

CURRENT CONTEXT FOR PROVIDING SERVICES

An understanding of the context in which health care and child welfare services are currently being delivered to children with drug or alcohol exposure or HIV infection and their families is essential to developing effective advocacy strategies. This context includes the epidemiology of HIV infection and drug exposure, the service needs of drug-exposed and HIV-infected children and their families, and the new burdens associated with caring for these children in the health care and child welfare systems.

Epidemiology

A comprehensive understanding of the epidemiologic issues is essential for advocates trying to improve access to services and address legal issues for the population of children and families affected by drugs, alcohol, or HIV infection. The number of children and families affected as well as the impact on them of exposure or infection bears directly on both the services needed and the legal issues requiring advocacy.

Incidence and Effects of Perinatal Drug and Alcohol Exposure

No completely reliable figures are currently available that establish either the number of women of childbearing age who use drugs or alcohol or the number of births of drug-exposed infants. Estimates of the number of infants born exposed to drugs each year are based on a small number of efforts to gather data nationally and on information and estimates compiled in some local communities. Comprehensive data based on longitudinal studies establishing the long-term effects on children of perinatal exposure to drugs is also unavailable at this time. Moreover, the accuracy of the data that is available—both as to numbers and effects—may be limited by a number of confounding variables (Lockwood, 1990b): inaccurate self-reports concerning drug use; false positive and false negative results of toxicology tests; limited applicability of animal studies; impact of prenatal factors such as nutrition, prenatal care, and coexisting diseases; impact of postnatal factors such as social and physical environment and availability of health care and other services; demographic differences between public and private hospital populations; poly-drug use; and variation in effects of different drugs (Lockwood, 1990a). In addition, journalists, advocates, and officials who use the data often fail to identify clearly the specific substances included in various estimates of exposure or to differentiate between the effects of different substances.

The National Association for Perinatal Addiction Research and Education (NAPARE) has estimated, on the basis of a survey of 36 hospitals nationwide, that 11% of women are using one or more of a variety of drugs (not including alcohol) during pregnancy, resulting in the birth of 375,000 drug-exposed infants annually (National Association for Perinatal Addiction Research and Education, 1988). The Institute of Medicine has reported that between 350,000 and 625,000 infants are exposed each year to one or more illegal drugs (Institute of Medicine, 1990) and the National Association of State Alcohol and Drug Abuse Directors (1990) has reported that an estimated 40,000 babies are born each year at increased risk of fetal alcohol syndrome or fetal alcohol effects due to their mothers' drinking during pregnancy.

Some of the available estimates have been criticized for flaws in methodology, which may lead to estimates that are either too low or too high (Weston, Evins, Zuckerman, Jones, & Lopez, 1989), but "there appears to be a consensus at the state and national level that the 11% figure reflects a base line estimate of overall incidence of substance exposure at birth" (Senate Select Committee, 1990). Clearly, it is the perception of health care providers (Miller, 1989) and child welfare personnel (Feig, 1990; Senate Office of Research, 1990) that whatever the actual numbers are, they are increasing rapidly.

The service needs of these children and their families depend at least in part on the short-term and long-term effects of perinatal drug or alcohol exposure. While considerable data is available concerning the short-term effects of prenatal exposure to certain drugs, such as cocaine (Fink, 1990), more limited information is available concerning their long-term effects (Zuckerman, 1991). Often individual case reports, studies based on small sample sizes, or even anecdotal evidence are used to generalize about the effects on infants of perinatal exposure to crack cocaine or other drugs (Kandall, 1991). Such inferences may be inappropriate because not all infants react in the same way to the same drug: the nature and intensity of their reactions vary (Weston et al., 1989). However, exposure to any one of a range of different drugs, including legal substances such as prescription drugs, tobacco, and alcohol, certainly causes serious harm to some infants.

Incidence and Effects of Pediatric HIV Infection

In terms of absolute numbers, the scale of magnitude is significantly smaller for pediatric AIDS and HIV infection than for drug exposure. However, because the vast majority of pediatric AIDS cases have thus far been concentrated in a small number of communities and because the cost of providing health care for these children has imposed substantial burdens on certain hospitals, the relatively small number of cases belies the overall scope of the problem. Moreover, the number of cases of perinatal HIV infection is growing rapidly (Gittler & McPherson, in press).

The total number of cases of pediatric AIDS is known from data gathered by the Centers for Disease Control (CDC), but only estimates are available to suggest the total number of infants who are born infected with HIV. As of January 1992, a total of 209,693 AIDS cases had been reported to the CDC. Of these, 3,522 were pediatric AIDS cases occurring in infants and in children under age 13 (Centers for Disease Control, 1992). More than 80% of these cases are attributable to perinatal transmission (Oxtoby, 1990). Pediatric AIDS cases so far have been heavily concentrated in a small number of states (Centers for Disease Control, 1992), but the epidemic is spreading to new areas of the country (National Research Council, 1990). Minority children are disproportionately affected (Charlottesville Report, 1988).

Pediatric AIDS case statistics do not include either children who are infected with HIV but remain asymptomatic or those who are ill but do not meet the CDC AIDS case definition. Estimates of the total number of HIV-infected children vary. One panel of experts estimated in 1988 that 10,000 to 20,000 children in the United States would be infected by 1991 (Charlottesville Report, 1988). More recent data collected by the CDC suggest that approximately 6,000 infants were born to women with HIV infection in 1989 (Gwinn et al., 1991), of whom it is likely that between one-quarter and one-third were actually infected with the virus (Oxtoby, 1990).

The clinical manifestations and course of HIV infection is different for infants than for adults. Infection tends to progress more rapidly in infants (Ammann, 1988), and they suffer from certain bacterial infections and lung diseases that do not normally appear in adults (Cooper, Pelton, & LeMay, 1988; Novello, Wise, Willoughby, & Pizzo, 1989). Of all pediatric AIDS cases reported to the CDC, more than half of the children have died (Centers for Disease Control, 1992). Although certain opportunistic infections are a major cause of early mortality for some infants with HIV infection (Oxtoby, 1990), it is not yet known to what extent new advances in early intervention will successfully prolong the life expectancy of some infected infants. Already, some children remain healthy or suffer only mild symptoms for several years, and a few perinatally exposed children have been diagnosed with AIDS as late as age 11 (Oxtoby, 1990).

Service Needs of Children and Families

The public has responded to infants with HIV infection or drug or alcohol exposure with a curious mixture of compassion and fear, believing that these children are innocent victims but apprehensive that they have the capacity to harm others. These attitudes appear to rest on the premise that infants who have been exposed to drugs or who are infected with HIV are, in some profound way, different from other children (Anderson, 1990; Kandall, 1991). In fact, children born exposed either to drugs or alcohol or to HIV share more characteristics with other children than many of the public images indicate and public reactions acknowledge. While these children have some special needs related to their HIV infection or drug or alcohol exposure, they and their families also require many of the same services as other children and families.

Numerous experts have recognized that children and families affected by drugs, alcohol, or HIV infection need access to a broad range of services (Halfon, 1989). Special panels and task forces have recommended that needed services be provided on a comprehensive and coordinated basis (Senate Select Committee, 1990). A few model programs have been providing comprehensive services to families affected by perinatal drug or alcohol exposure or HIV infection or both (Jameson & Halfon, 1990; Tittle & St. Claire, 1989; Woodruff & Hanson, 1990; Woodruff, Sterzin, & Hanson, 1989). Recent efforts have been made to incorporate mandates for comprehensive and coordinated services for these populations into legislation at the state (Senate Bill No. 2669, 1990) and federal (Ryan White CARE Act, 1990) level, but thus far they have met with only limited success, frequently due to limited appropriations and budgetary constraints.

Most services for children and families affected by drug or alcohol exposure or HIV infection continue to be available, if at all, through fragmented, uncoordinated, "categorical" programs that provide funding for a particular category of service rather than on the basis of a child or family's overall needs (Feig, 1990; Halfon, 1989). Thus, at the present time, efforts to ensure that these children and their families receive needed services must focus at least some attention on the existing categorical services, working either to implement them to the maximum degree possible or to modify them in targeted ways most likely to meet this population's needs. Inasmuch as the service needs of children with HIV infection and drug or alcohol exposure and of their families cannot be viewed in isolation from those of other children and families, especially those with special health care needs, analysis of the legal issues involved in providing services for these children necessarily involves an examination of the overall framework for providing health care and child welfare services to needy children and families.

Burdens on the Health Care and Child Welfare Systems

Although the total number of children who are born exposed to drugs or alcohol or infected with HIV is not known and the prognosis for these children is uncertain, sufficient data are available to conclude that pediatric HIV infection and perinatal drug or alcohol exposure pose major challenges for the child welfare and health care systems. Many thousands of children are born exposed to drugs or alcohol or infected with HIV each year. Even though the impact of drug exposure or HIV infection varies among individual children, these children and their families often require extensive medical care. Most require a range of social support services; many are reported to child protective services, triggering investigations; and a substantial number need foster care or other out-of-home placements. Because of the significance of health issues in the lives of these children and families, ensuring that they receive adequate care requires close coordination between the health care and child welfare systems.

Health Care

The costs of providing health care for drug-exposed and HIV-infected children and their families are enormous (Hellinger, 1991; Makadon, Seage, Thorpe, & Fineberg, 1990; Scitovsky, 1989; Senate Select Committee, 1990). The average annual hospital cost for each child with HIV infection is between $35,000 (Andrulis, Weslowski, Hintz, Parrott, & Brady, 1990) and $50,000 (Oleske, 1990), and a recent estimate suggested that by 1991 children with HIV infection would be occupying one-tenth of the 40,000 pediatric hospital beds in the United States, at a cost of nearly $1 billion (Oleske, 1990). As opportunities for early medical intervention expand for HIV-infected infants, the costs will be substantial (Fox, 1990; Scitovsky, 1989). Assuming approximately 6,000 seropositive babies are born and identified each year (Gwinn et al., 1991), the cost of providing monitoring and treatment for these infants for a 2-year period has been estimated at more than $30 million (Arno, 1990). There are no specific data on the medical care costs for women with AIDS or HIV infection (Scitovsky, 1989). However, the hospital costs for adults generally have been lower than for children (Andrulis et al., 1990), while estimates of early medical intervention costs for adults appear to be somewhat higher than for children (Arno, Shenson, Siegel, Franks, & Lee, 1989).

The costs of health care associated with perinatal drug exposure are also huge. For example, California estimates suggest that delivery and initial hospitalization costs for children born exposed to drugs may total between $2.1 and $2.6 billion per year, with average costs for individual infants of $40,000 (Senate Select Committee, 1990). In comparison, the cost of residential treatment for women and children is approximately $23,000 per year (California Department of Drug and Alcohol Programs, 1990), and nonresidential community-based care is even less expensive (National Institute on Alcohol Abuse and Alcoholism [NIAAA], 1987). Comprehensive data on the long-term costs of providing health care services for drug-exposed children are not available because the long-term effects of drug exposure have not yet been adequately documented. Data concerning the costs of providing effective drug treatment for women are limited, in part because appropriate services for this population are currently limited, although studies have suggested that expenditures for substance abuse prevention and treatment are cost-effective (National Institute on Alcohol Abuse and Alcoholism, 1987).

Child Welfare

In order to provide adequate care for drug- or alcohol-exposed and HIV-infected children and their families, child welfare agencies will need to develop some new targeted services and to adapt existing services for this population. Family support services designed to prevent family separation are needed for those HIV-infected or drug- or alcohol-exposed children who could safely live at home if their families received assistance. For those children who cannot live with their biologic parents, appropriate out-of-home placements must be guaranteed through recruitment and training of foster parents and more extensive financial and social support for substitute families (Child Welfare League, 1992).

Child welfare agencies are already mandated to provide these services for children and families generally, but adaptation of these services for drug-exposed and HIV-infected children and their families involves extensive program planning and development efforts, coordination with other agencies, and substantial costs (Woodruff & Hanson, 1990). These new burdens for child welfare agencies are occurring at a time when their ability to meet the needs of children and families has already been undermined by a variety of social problems in the 1980s, such as the growth of poverty among children, the increase in the number of homeless families, and the dramatic rise in the number of child abuse and neglect reports (Allen, 1988).

STRATEGIES TO FACILITATE
APPROPRIATE IDENTIFICATION

In order for drug-exposed and HIV-infected children and their families to receive necessary care, they must be identified and referred to appropriate service providers (U.S. General Accounting Office [GAO], 1990). The existing system of services for children and families is fragmented and has no single entry point. Therefore, any contact between children and families and the health care or child welfare services system should trigger a process with the greatest possible likelihood of providing an effective link to appropriate services. This process may be triggered in numerous ways, including a family's request for services, clinical assessment and diagnosis by health care providers, and reports and referrals to child welfare agencies.

The specific procedures currently used to identify children who are drug- or alcohol-exposed or HIV-infected and their families—such as drug testing, HIV testing, and mandatory child abuse reporting—have been the subject of considerable controversy. Identification of women and children through drug testing and HIV testing carries a risk of stigma and discrimination. In addition, in some states positive drug tests are being treated as a basis for mandatory child abuse reports and for removal of children from parental custody (Larsen, Horowitz, & Chasnoff, 1991). Moreover, in more than a dozen states, women have been subject to criminal prosecution based on drug use during pregnancy (Paltrow & Shende, 1990). These factors may deter many women from seeking health care and social services.

Because access to appropriate services is so limited by availability and financing (U.S. General Accounting Office, 1990), other barriers and deterrents should be minimized as much as possible: standards and criteria for drug testing, HIV testing, and child abuse reporting, as well as other procedures for assessment and referral, should be carefully crafted to promote rather than inhibit clients' access to health care and related support services.

Safeguard Integrity of Testing Process

The performance of an HIV test or a drug test is appropriate when it will facilitate delivery of necessary medical care or related health and social services in a nonpunitive context. Although the medical procedures involved in testing for HIV or for drugs are relatively noninvasive physically, they carry profound legal and social significance. To increase the likelihood that testing will provide a linkage to appropriate services and to minimize the likelihood that it will result in punitive responses or in unnecessary invasions of privacy, clear standards are needed to safeguard the integrity of the testing process. These standards should include protections to ensure accurate test results, to limit discriminatory testing, to obtain appropriate consents, and to maintain the confidentiality of medical information. Although different approaches have been taken toward drug testing and HIV testing of pregnant women and newborn infants, there are strong reasons for applying similar standards.

Ensure Accuracy of Tests

Any testing for drugs, alcohol, or HIV should be conducted in such a way as to ensure the highest standards of accuracy, and every effort must be made to avoid false positive and false negative results. Significant variation exists among the different procedures available to test for drugs, alcohol, or HIV, both in their degree of accuracy and in the implications of a positive or negative result. Legal standards and policy guidelines for testing should require use of the most accurate tests and should limit use of the results to purposes for which the tests are reliable.

Testing for Alcohol and Other Drugs. The most frequently used method of testing women and infants for drugs is the urine toxicology test or "tox screen," while for alcohol a blood or breath test is more common (Larsen et al., 1991). Analysis of a newborn infant's first stool, or meconium, is also used to determine intrauterine exposure to drugs (Ostrea et al. 1992). The accuracy and reliability of the results of these tests vary depending on the methods of analysis, the skill and experience of the technicians, and the procedures used by laboratories to avoid errors (Larsen et al., 1991). In addition, the procedures used by courts to establish "chain of custody" and otherwise verify the accuracy of test results can affect the reliability of test results as evidence (Larsen et al., 1991). Positive results from procedures such as the enzyme multiplied immunoassay technique (EMIT), which is inexpensive but yields less accurate results, should always be confirmed by more accurate procedures such as gas chromatography (GC) and mass spectrometry (MS) (Larsen et al., 1991). In addition, the implications of a positive test vary among different procedures. Urine tox screens performed on an infant, for example, only indicate drug exposure within the previous few hours or days whereas meconium testing may provide evidence covering a period of 2 or 3 months (Larsen et al., 1991).

There is a particular risk of inaccurate results with tox screens because the standard of accuracy varies greatly among different laboratories and technicians (California Advocates, 1990; Senate Select Committee, 1990). Moreover, mistakes can occur in the handling of samples (California Advocates, 1990). Because positive tox screens are sometimes used either in civil or criminal proceedings to remove a child from parental custody or to punish the mother, some advocates recommend that the results of any blood or urine test for alcohol or drugs should be admitted as evidence only if forensic standards of testing prevail in the laboratory and the chain of custody of the sample is established (California Advocates, 1990).

Testing for HIV. There are two primary issues related to accuracy and reliability of HIV test results for women and children: first, the need to ensure that the test itself is an accurate one and, second, the need to establish definitively the presence or absence of HIV infection in infants who test positive at birth. The HIV antibody test remains the most common procedure for determining whether an individual is infected with HIV. In order to ensure against the risk of false positive and false negative results, experts recommend that confirmatory procedures be used (San Francisco Department of Public Health, 1990).

Virtually all infants of HIV-infected mothers are HIV positive at birth because maternal antibody is transmitted across the placenta. This means that an HIV antibody test of an infant at birth usually reveals the serostatus of the mother rather than the infant (Cooper et al., 1988). At the present time the child welfare agency policies of very few states provide for confirmatory tests (Teare, English, Lockwood, & Clark, in press). However, experts recommend retesting of infants at intervals up to 18 months and the use of procedures—such as a viral culture, a p24 antigen assay, or a polymerase chain reaction—that are capable of detecting the virus itself rather than the maternal antibodies (San Francisco Department of Public Health, 1990).

Discourage Exclusive Reliance on Testing

In view of the risk of false positive and false negative results and the other limitations of information obtained as a result of testing alone, exclusive reliance on tox screens or HIV antibody tests for making important decisions, such as removal of an infant from parental custody or foster care placement of a child, is rarely appropriate. The use of HIV antibody tests, tox screens, and other tests for drugs or alcohol should be limited to those situations in which they can further an important diagnostic or therapeutic purpose.

Limit Discriminatory Testing

A major dichotomy exists between the view that universal testing or screening is appropriate and the view that testing should only occur on the basis of an individualized assessment of risk conducted according to a behavior-based profile. Wide variation currently exists in the criteria used to make decisions about who should be tested for drugs or for HIV. At minimum, criteria and practices that are discriminatory should not form the basis for testing.

Advocates of universal testing, whether for HIV infection or for alcohol or drug use and exposure, assert that it is too difficult to obtain reliable information upon which to base an accurate assessment of risk. Studies have suggested that women do not always acknowledge their risk behaviors when giving a health history (Ostrea, Brady, Gause, Raymundo, & Stevens, 1992). Therefore, advocates argue, without universal testing or screening too many children will not be identified who are exposed to drugs or alcohol or infected with HIV. As a result, these children will not be adequately protected and their families will not receive adequate services. Others favor universal testing for the protection of others (in the case of HIV infection) or for punitive reasons (in the case of drug use during pregnancy) rather than for the benefit of the infant or the mother.

Proponents of individualized determinations generally assert that testing should be limited to those who are actually at risk and would therefore be most likely to benefit from identification. They also maintain that individualized determinations of risk can help avoid both the unnecessary costs associated with testing individuals who are not at risk and the harms associated with false positive test results and that they can at the same time involve the individual whose risk is being assessed in an educational process (California Advocates, 1990).

Few states have laws specifying the criteria to be used in selecting the pregnant women or infants who will be tested for alcohol, drugs, or HIV. A small number of states have enacted statutory criteria for drug testing of pregnant women or newborn infants, and the public child welfare agencies in some states have adopted HIV policies that articulate the basis for HIV testing of children under agency jurisdiction. For the most part, however, the criteria are developed at a local level by agencies, hospitals, or individual physicians (Larson, 1991).

While a more universal approach to testing for drugs, alcohol, or HIV can avoid the use of discriminatory criteria, universal testing should not be implemented unless access to necessary health care can be assured. Identification of women and children without protection from punitive responses and a link to essential health care and related services does not increase trust in the health care or social service systems and is likely to be harmful rather than helpful for children.

Testing for Alcohol and Other Drugs. No state requires testing of all pregnant women or all newborn infants for drugs or alcohol (Larson, 1991). A recent Minnesota statute requires physicians to test newborns if, as a result of a medical assessment of the mother or the infant, there is "reason to believe" the infant has been exposed to drugs (Minnesota Statutes Annotated, Section 626.5561(1), 1990). A Wisconsin statute permits, but does not require, testing if the physician determines that there is a "serious risk" that the infant was exposed (Wisconsin Legislative Service, 1990). The Wisconsin statute also authorizes hospital health care workers, social workers, or foster care intake workers to refer infants to physicians for testing. However, parental consent is required for the test to be performed.

Wide variation exists in the criteria hospitals use to decide which pregnant women and infants to test for alcohol or other drugs (Senate Office of Research, 1990). Criteria used include clinical symptomatology, public patient status, inadequate prenatal care, young age, and neighborhood of residence (Chavkin, 1990a). Lack of prenatal care is often the basis for testing, although access to prenatal care is so limited for many poor women that there is a high likelihood that use of this factor alone would have a discriminatory effect (Moss, 1990). Advocates have recommended that hospitals apply uniform standards for use of tox screens and other tests for alcohol and drugs in order to avoid intervention in patients' lives that is arbitrary or due to class and race prejudice (California Advocates, 1990). One group has recommended that a "chemical dependency assessment" is a better diagnostic and treatment tool than a tox screen (California Advocates, 1990). To the extent that all women in prenatal or obstetric care received a chemical dependency assessment, the risk of discriminatory testing could be reduced.

Testing for HIV. No state law mandates testing of all pregnant women or newborn infants for HIV infection, and formal recommendations have not been issued for universal HIV screening of pregnant women or newborn infants. However, experts, including a recent committee of the Institute of Medicine (IOM), have recommended *voluntary* HIV screening of all pregnant women in areas of high seroprevalence (Hardy, 1991; San Francisco Department of Public Health, 1990). Some have also recommended that all pregnant women be informed about HIV infection, risk behaviors, modes of transmission, and risk reduction (Hardy, 1991) while others have suggested that for all women and adolescents of childbearing age the health history include questions about risk behaviors (San Francisco Department of Public Health, 1990). One rationale offered for a more universal approach is that it avoids the risk of discriminatory testing based on a woman's racial or ethnic background that can occur with selective risk-based testing (Hardy, 1991).

In contrast, recommendations for testing newborn infants have relied primarily on assessment of the mother's risk factors and HIV status, rather than on a universal approach (San Francisco Department of Public Health, 1990). The IOM committee (Hardy, 1991) found that universal screening of newborns for HIV was not warranted at this time due to the present uncertainty concerning the benefits and risks of early intervention for asymptomatic HIV-infected infants. These recommendations could change, however, as more is learned about treatment of asymptomatic infants and young children.

Obtain Appropriate Consents

Except in an emergency, any medical procedure ordinarily requires the consent of the patient or, in the case of a minor child, of a parent. At the present time, however, pregnant women are frequently tested for drugs without their express informed consent and newborn infants are also often tested for drugs without the informed consent of a parent (Senate Office of Research, 1990). Similarly, both pregnant women and newborn infants are tested for HIV without express informed consent (Faden, 1990). While few statutes expressly address the issue of informed consent for drug testing of pregnant women or infants, approximately two-thirds of the states have enacted statutes requiring informed consent for HIV testing (Albert, Eisenberg, Hansell, & Marcus, 1992). All states must now require informed consent for HIV testing as a condition of receiving federal HIV funds under the Ryan White CARE Act (1990). Nevertheless, practice often varies from statutory requirements.

Indiscriminate testing of women without informed consent may violate their constitutional right to bodily integrity (Moss, 1990). It may also constitute medical malpractice, under an evolving legal standard for informed consent that requires disclosure of any risks that would be material to the patient's decision (*Cobbs v. Grant*, 1972). Neither the drawing of blood for an HIV antibody test nor the procuring of a blood or urine sample for an alcohol or drug test involves serious medical risks, but the tests do involve substantial social and psychological risks. Thus, it can be argued that informed consent should be obtained and the process should include giving information to the client about such risks as the possibility of discrimination or the likelihood of being reported to child protective services (Moss, 1990). While this is the practice in some settings for HIV testing, it is not universal (Faden, 1990; Levine & Dubler, 1990); and for drug testing it appears to be the exception rather than the rule (Senate Office of Research, 1990).

If a parent refuses consent for a drug or HIV test on an infant, a court order should usually be obtained (Connolly & Marshall, 1990; Moss, 1990). In other than emergency circumstances, court orders authorizing surgical procedures over the objection of parents ordinarily may only be issued when the court has exercised limited jurisdiction to take custody of the child. Some experts have suggested, however, that the generalized consent form signed by a pregnant woman on entering the hospital may be sufficient to authorize a drug test for her infant (Connolly & Marshall, 1990), although this is less frequently suggested in the case of an HIV test.

Maintain Confidentiality of Medical Information

One of the major concerns with respect to drug testing and HIV testing is the harm that may occur if confidentiality is broken. The obligation to maintain confidentiality derives from numerous sources in law and professional ethics (Rennert, 1991). The primary purpose of confidentiality requirements is to encourage candor between physician and patient. This goal is especially pressing in the case of drug or alcohol use and HIV infection because pregnant women fear loss of custody, criminal sanctions, and discrimination if their test results are disclosed (Levine & Dubler, 1990; Moss, 1990).

Many states have enacted specific statutes requiring confidentiality for HIV test results (Albert et al., 1992; Rennert, 1991), and states are now required to have adequate guarantees of confidentiality in place as a condition of funding under the Ryan White CARE Act (1990). Despite these requirements, breaches of confidentiality frequently occur.

The confidentiality of information resulting from drug tests performed on pregnant women and newborn infants is even less clear, however. Federal regulations contain detailed and strict requirements for confidentiality of information in any drug or alcohol program that receives federal funds (Legal Action Center, 1988) but permit disclosure for the purpose of mandatory child abuse reporting under state law (42 U.S.C.A. §§ 290ee-3(e), 1991). Most states' child abuse reporting statutes waive certain medical confidentiality requirements, such as the physician-patient and psychotherapist–patient privileges, for purposes of reporting pursuant to the statute, although there is significant variation among states' legal requirements concerning whether or not positive drug tests are considered reportable under child abuse reporting laws (English, 1990). At least one appellate court in California has determined that health care providers do not violate legal requirements of medical confidentiality by reporting the results of a positive toxicology test performed on a newborn infant to a child protective services agency (*In re Troy D.*, 1989).

Facilitate Referrals for Health Care and Child Welfare Services

The primary purpose of any effort to identify children and families who are affected by drugs or alcohol or HIV should be to ensure that children are safe and that children and families receive the services they need. To the extent that pregnant women and new mothers are deterred from seeking health care, including prenatal care, drug or alcohol treatment, and HIV testing and treatment, this purpose will not be served. In order to further the goal of making services accessible to those who need them, standards for child abuse reporting should be clarified, punitive interventions should be limited, and appropriate assessments and linkages to services should be encouraged.

Clarify Standards for Child Abuse Reporting

A growing number of states explicitly require the reporting of prenatal drug exposure to child welfare and law enforcement authorities under their child abuse reporting laws (English, 1990). Some of these states have adopted an "addictive model," mandating reports in cases in which children are born dependent on an addictive drug or controlled substance (Florida Statutes Annotated, 1989; Massachusetts General Laws Annotated, 1989; Oklahoma Statutes Annotated, 1988).

Others expressly require the reporting of positive toxicology results (Illinois P.A., 1989; Minnesota Statutes Annotated, 1990; Wisconsin Statutes, 1990). Statutes based on the addictive model and on the "positive tox" model are both overinclusive and underinclusive. Both models can result either in the reporting of children who do not actually require protection by a child welfare agency and in the failure to report children who do.

In addition to the problems associated with the accuracy of test results discussed previously, there is also the potential for discrimination based on race, ethnicity, and socioeconomic status in reporting. A recent study in Pinnellas County in Florida found that although use of illicit drugs is common among women, regardless of race and socioeconomic status, black women were reported to child protective services at approximately 10 times the rate for white women (Chasnoff, Landress, & Barrett, 1990).

Mandatory reporting to child protective services of all positive toxicology tests on newborn infants is not necessary to ensure either the safety of children or the provision of services. Existing standards for child abuse reporting are adequate to trigger reports in appropriate cases. Health care professionals must consider, as they are already required to do, all the information available to them concerning the child and must determine, on the basis of their professional training and experience, whether they reasonably suspect that the child is abused or neglected. If they suspect abuse or neglect, they are mandated to make a child abuse report; otherwise, they need not do so.

Encourage Appropriate Assessments and Linkages to Services

Recent legislation in California has established a new approach to the reporting of positive toxicology tests (California Statutes, 1990). The new law amended California child abuse reporting requirements in two significant ways. First, the statute makes clear that a positive toxicology screen alone is not to be the basis for reporting. Second, when a report based on all available facts is made, the report is to be made to the child welfare agency and not to law enforcement. In lieu of mandatory child abuse reporting, the new legislation establishes a system of assessments to determine the needs of the child and family and whether a referral to child welfare is warranted. These new requirements provide an appropriate framework for adequately protecting children needing state intervention while avoiding the risk of both unnecessarily broad reporting and unduly punitive intervention.

Limit Punitive Interventions

Fear of punitive intervention by child welfare and law enforcement agencies is a major factor in deterring women who are dependent on drugs or alcohol or at risk of HIV infection from seeking the care they need (Chavkin, 1990a; U.S. General Accounting Office, 1990). The adverse effects of punitive approaches to women who use drugs during pregnancy has been extensively debated in the media and addressed in the literature (McNulty, 1987–1988; Moss, 1990).

Several states have used the criminal law to prosecute women who use drugs during pregnancy (McNulty, 1987–1988; Moss, 1990). These prosecutions have been initiated under the authority of various criminal statutes penalizing conduct such as homicide, criminal child neglect, child endangerment, child abuse, criminal child support, delivery of drugs to a minor, and assault with a deadly weapon (ACLU, 1990). Although most of these cases have been dismissed or have not resulted in convictions, the threat of prosecution may nonetheless have a deterrent effect on women seeking drug treatment, prenatal care, or hospital delivery. Further, these prosecutions have no direct or indirect benefit for the health of infants and carry a significant risk of harming infant health (Committee on Substance Abuse, 1990).

STRATEGIES TO INCREASE ACCESS TO ESSENTIAL HEALTH CARE

There are dozens of federal (and state) benefit programs that provide funding or direct services to meet the health care needs of children (Select Committee on Children, Youth, and Families, 1987). Knowledge of the legal requirements, including eligibility rules and scope of benefits, for these programs is essential in order to advocate effectively to increase access to health care for drug- or alcohol-exposed and HIV-infected children and their families. However, it is also important for advocates to develop an understanding of some of the threshold barriers that may impede access to health care for this population and to formulate strategies that will be effective in overcoming these barriers. Some recent federal initiatives provide opportunities for targeted advocacy to expand access to health care for these children and families.

General Approaches

In the effort to ensure access to essential health care services, advocates must, at minimum, work to promote utilization of prenatal care, to expand access to drug treatment for women, to expand access to HIV treatment for women and children, and to expand access to nonmedical health-related services. In doing so there are numerous specific barriers that must be overcome or avoided.

Promote Utilization of Prenatal Care

Prenatal care can be a critically important opportunity to protect the health of both the pregnant woman and the infant and can provide linkages to other services. Research has shown that while prenatal care cannot eliminate health problems for drug-exposed infants, it does improve birth outcomes for infants even if their mothers continue to use drugs during pregnancy (Larsen, 1990; MacGregor, Keith, Bachicha, & Chasnoff, 1989). Also, to the extent that appropriate drug treatment is available, a prenatal care provider who is trusted by the pregnant woman may have a good opportunity to make an effective referral. Access to prenatal care is also critical for women with HIV infection because it can provide an important link to early intervention services for HIV disease for the woman and, potentially, for the fetus as well (Faden, 1990).

However, poor pregnant women's limited access to prenatal care has been well documented (Alan Guttmacher Institute, 1987; McNulty, 1987–1988), and women with HIV infection, many of whom use drugs as well, also experience difficulty in obtaining access to reproductive health services, including prenatal care (Levine & Dubler, 1990). Moreover, women with HIV infection are subjected to various explicit and subtle forms of coercion in their reproductive choices (Chavkin, 1990b; Levine & Dubler, 1990). Such experiences are likely to contribute to mistrust of health care providers among many women and may thus discourage them from seeking prenatal care as well as drug treatment and/or HIV care.

Expand Access to Drug Treatment for Women

Access to drug treatment for pregnant women and women with children is even more severely limited than access to prenatal care. One of the most serious limitations to access results from the refusal of existing programs to admit women (Chavkin, 1990a), even though these exclusionary practices may in some cases be subject to legal challenge based on state public accommodation laws, state equal rights amendments, or hospitals' community service obligations under the federal Hill-Burton laws (McNulty, 1989). Many experts have recommended that priority for drug treatment be given to pregnant women, to women and families with substance-exposed infants, and to women and families with children who have been removed or are at risk of being removed from their custody (Senate Select Committee, 1990) and that drug treatment programs be redesigned to meet women's needs (Smith, 1990).

Ultimately, however, access to drug treatment for pregnant women and women with children will depend on the availability of adequate funding, not just for drug treatment in general but for services that are appropriate for women. Medicaid provides little or no coverage of some preferred drug treatment approaches, although several recent developments with respect to Medicaid coverage of drug treatment appear promising (English & Gates, 1991; Gates, 1991). Other sources of substantial funding for drug treatment for women include the federal Alcohol, Drug Abuse, and Mental Health Administration (ADAMHA) and its Office for Substance Abuse Prevention (OSAP). Sources of more limited amounts of funding may include the federal Health Resources and Services Administration (HRSA) (Gates & Beck, 1990), the federal Maternal and Child Health Bureau's Special Projects of Regional and National Significance (SPRANS) (Title V, 1991), and possibly even the Adoption Assistance and Child Welfare Act (AACWA). (At least one lawsuit—*Doe v. Reeves*, 1990—has been filed to require a child welfare agency to provide funding for residential drug treatment for a mother based on its obligation under the AACWA to make reasonable efforts to keep families together.) Advocates must work aggressively to ensure that women receive the full benefits of any funding that may be available through these sources.

Expand Access to HIV Treatment for Women and Children

Although for the past few years HRSA has funded Pediatric AIDS Demonstration Projects (Conviser, 1991) to encourage the delivery of comprehensive, coordinated family-centered care for women and children with HIV infection, access to HIV treatment for these groups remains limited (English & Gates, 1991). Thus far, access to drugs and therapies for HIV infection has occurred to a significant degree through clinical trials from which women have been largely excluded (Anastos & Marte, 1989; Chavkin, 1990b; Levine, 1990). Moreover, many women at risk for HIV have extremely limited access to primary care in general (Levine, 1990), which impedes their access not only to clinical trials but also to any other specialized HIV-related care.

Children also encounter barriers that impede their access to HIV treatment. For example, foster children in most states have great difficulty in gaining access to clinical trials, although a few states have developed procedures for enabling them to participate (Martin & Sacks, 1990). Less than 2% of foster children with HIV infection were reported to be in clinical trials by state child protection agencies responding to a survey; seven states have a policy addressing the issue and six additional states without a formal policy reported having a mechanism to facilitate participation (Martin & Sacks, 1990).

Expand Access to Nonmedical Health-Related Services

There is widespread agreement among experts that many nonmedical services are essential components of delivering appropriate comprehensive health care to families and children affected by drugs, alcohol, or HIV. Nevertheless, funding for these services is often severely limited. Even when funding is available, it is frequently through demonstration programs, pilot projects, or grants that do not create any entitlement to services for individual children or families. In order to ensure that any health care children and families receive is effective in meeting their needs, advocates must work to promote the inclusion of appropriate nonmedical health-related services to the maximum degree possible under various funding sources. This may be an option under programs specially targeted to children and families affected by drugs, alcohol, or HIV such as the OSAP model programs within the Alcohol Drug, Abuse, and Mental Health Block Grant or the Ryan White CARE Act (English & Gates, 1991). It may also be possible under certain new provisions of the federal Medicaid statute (DeWoody, 1991; English & Gates, 1991; Halfon & Klee, 1991).

Recent Federal and State Initiatives

Within the past decade action by Congress and by state governments has resulted in new initiatives with the potential to increase access to health care for drug- or alcohol-exposed and HIV-infected children and their families. Some of these initiatives were designed to benefit poor children and families generally but can be used to advantage for those who are drug- or alcohol-exposed or infected with HIV; others are targeted programs specifically created to provide drug treatment or HIV care. These initiatives include expansions of the federal Medicaid program; amendments to the Early and Periodic Screening Diagnosis and Treatment (EPSDT) program; the Medicaid waiver programs; the Alcohol, Drug Abuse, and Mental Health Block Grant; the Ryan White CARE Act; and the Maternal and Child Health Block Grant.

General Medicaid Reforms

The federal Medicaid program (Title XIX, 1992) is the largest single publicly funded source of health care for poor women and children (Congressional Research Service, 1988). As such, Medicaid is a critically important resource for funding health care for drug-exposed and HIV-infected children and their families. The Medicaid program has at least one major advantage in that it, unlike other programs that fund services for this population, operates as an entitlement program. That is, individuals who meet federal eligibility requirements are entitled to receive whatever services are covered under their state's Medicaid plan. The program also has many disadvantages in that, generally, only individuals with extremely low incomes can establish eligibility (Congressional Research Service, 1988), many providers are unwilling to participate in Medicaid owing in part to low reimbursement rates, and coverage of appropriate nonmedical services related to substance abuse or HIV is limited. Recent amendments to the Medicaid program have addressed some of these barriers.

Eligibility Expansions. Beginning in 1986 Congress enacted a series of provisions expanding eligibility for Medicaid beyond those groups that have traditionally been eligible (Medicaid Amendments, 1990). Under the federal Medicaid program, eligibility is guaranteed for those individuals, among others, who are eligible for Aid to Families with Dependent Children (AFDC), for Supplemental Security Income (SSI) (in all but nine states), or for federal foster care maintenance or adoption assistance payments (Title IV-E) (Perkins & Melden, 1991). These amendments initially targeted pregnant women and infants and more recently have included older children, thus providing greater geographical uniformity in eligibility for Medicaid and dramatically expanding the population of eligible women and children. The most recent of these amendments are contained in the Omnibus Budget Reconciliation Act of 1989 (OBRA-89) (Medicaid Amendments, 1990) and the Omnibus Budget Reconciliation Act of 1990 (OBRA-90) (Medicaid Amendments, 1991). Based on these new mandates, states are now *required* to provide Medicaid coverage for pregnant women and children up to age 6 in families with incomes at or below 133% of the federal poverty level and, effective in July 1991, for children between ages 6 and 19 on a phased-in basis, one year at a time, in families with incomes up to 100% of the federal poverty level (Medicaid Amendments, 1991). States also have the *option* to provide coverage for pregnant women and infants up to 185% of the federal poverty level, although, as required by OBRA-89, the 20 states that had already adopted higher levels were required to maintain them (Medicaid Amendments, 1990).

Provider Participation Requirements. Recognizing that the lack of adequate numbers of Medicaid providers is a serious obstacle to care for poor children and families, Congress included in OBRA-89 a statutory mandate applicable to all Medicaid providers and services and codifying an earlier regulation, known as the "equal access" regulation, that requires states to provide sufficient payments to ensure that Medicaid recipients have access to health care to the same extent as others in their geographic area with third-party coverage (Medicaid Amendments, 1990). At least one federal court has already issued an order enforcing this provision with respect to dental care *(Clark v. Kizer,* 1991).

In addition, Congress included in OBRA-89 a provision requiring states to specify on an annual basis in their Medicaid plans the payment rates for obstetrical and pediatric services so that rates will be sufficient to enlist the participation of enough obstetricians and pediatricians to ensure equal access to care for pregnant women and children. This provision also may be enforceable through litigation, since the Supreme Court has held that hospitals and nursing homes may sue states for higher Medicaid reimbursement rates on the basis of the provision that requires states to provide rates that are "reasonable and adequate" *(Wilder v. Virginia Hospital Association,* 1990).

Early and Periodic Screening, Diagnosis, and Treatment (EPSDT) Program

Congress included in OBRA-89 additional Medicaid provisions directly targeted at improving health services for children (Children's Defense Fund, 1990). These were major reforms of the Early and Periodic Screening, Diagnosis, and Treatment (EPSDT) Program (42 U.S.C.A. §§ 1396d(a)(4)(B) and 1396d(r), 1991), which provides critically important preventive and treatment services for poor children (Medicaid Amendments, 1990). Since 1967 states have been required to offer, as part of their Medicaid programs, EPSDT services for all Medicaid-eligible children under age 21 (Perkins & Melden, 1991). The OBRA-89 reforms not only enacted into statute many of the federal requirements previously contained in regulations—thereby making clear both that they were mandatory and that they expressed the intent of Congress for implementation of the program—but also added important new mandates.

Pursuant to federal EPSDT requirements, each eligible child must be provided with comprehensive health assessments as well as with vision, dental, and hearing services. The assessments must include a health and developmental history, physical examination, immunizations, and laboratory tests. They must also, as a result of the OBRA-89 reforms, include health education and anticipatory guidance (Children's Defense Fund, 1990).

The periodicity schedules (i.e., the frequency with which these services must be provided) are to be determined by the state in consultation with recognized professional medical and dental organizations involved in child health care. The program also includes an outreach component, requiring the identification of eligible children and measures to ensure that they receive the preventive and remedial benefits of the program.

The new changes require states to pay for "interperiodic" screens whenever a health problem is suspected and make clear that providers may be reimbursed for partial screens (Children's Defense Fund, 1990). Most significant of all is a provision that states must now provide for EPSDT-eligible children any federally reimbursable Medicaid services—mandatory or optional—that are medically necessary to diagnose or treat illnesses and problems identified in an EPSDT assessment, whether or not those services are generally available to other Medicaid recipients under the state's plan (Children's Defense Fund, 1990; Medicaid Amendments, 1990).

Taken together, the new mandates and the newly codified requirements provide an important opportunity to advocate for expanding health care services to vulnerable populations of children (DeWoody, 1991; Halfon & Klee, 1991). For example, children who are born exposed to drugs or alcohol or who are infected with HIV may be especially likely to need certain services (such as rehabilitative services and case management) that are optional Medicaid services. Under OBRA-89 mandates, states must now provide these services for EPSDT-eligible children if they are medically necessary to address a problem identified in an EPSDT screen.

Medicaid Coverage of Drug Treatment

Coverage for substance abuse treatment under Medicaid has until now been extremely limited largely because most services do not fit the medical model required by Medicaid (Gates, 1991). Outpatient treatment services may be covered if they are hospital-based or are provided in a clinic treatment facility that provides medical care under the direction of a physician (Gates, 1991). Thus, treatment provided by means of peer counseling and group support or primarily by laypersons usually would not be covered (Gates, 1991). Some inpatient treatment services, including detoxification, are covered, but there are significant limitations. For example, treatment in an institution for mental disease (IMD) is excluded from Medicaid coverage for anyone under age 65 and the Health Care Financing Administration (HCFA) has interpreted substance abuse as a mental disease. In addition, HCFA has taken the position that Medicaid cannot cover room and board costs without express statutory authorization. However, new options are emerging for expanding this coverage (Gates, 1991).

In addition to those general provisions previously mentioned that provide a basis for expanding Medicaid coverage of nonmedical services such as rehabilitative services and case management, Congress included in OBRA-90 a specific provision designed to expand Medicaid coverage of nonmedical substance abuse treatment services. The following language was added to the Medicaid statute: "No service (including counseling) shall be excluded from the definition of 'medical assistance' solely because it is provided as a treatment service for alcoholism or drug dependency" (42 U.S.C.A. § 1396d(a), 1991). This provision could be useful in arguing, for example, that Medicaid coverage of rehabilitation services, which were added as an optional Medicaid service by OBRA-90, should be available to cover nonhospital residential drug treatment services (Gates, 1991).

Moreover, there is substantial interest in Congress in further eliminating some of the most serious barriers to Medicaid coverage of appropriate substance abuse treatment services for women and children. In 1990 four bills—H. R. 5536 (Towns), S. 3002 (Moynihan), S. 2559 (Kohl), H.R. 5750 (Durbin)—were introduced in Congress that would have expanded Medicaid coverage of nonhospital residential treatment for women and children. No action was taken in 1990, but these bills may be reintroduced (Gates, 1991). Finally, at least two states—Illinois and Pennsylvania—have chosen to provide Medicaid coverage of nonhospital substance abuse treatment entirely with state funds (Gates, 1991).

ADAMHA Block Grant, Drug Abuse Demonstration Projects, and the OSAP Model Programs

Special funding for drug treatment for pregnant women and mothers with children is available under the Alcohol and Drug Abuse and Mental Health Services Block Grant (42 U.S.C.A. §§ 300x et seq., 1991), the Model Projects for Pregnant and Post Partum Women and their Infants (42 U.S.C.A. § 290aa-13, 1991), and the Drug Abuse Demonstration Projects of National Significance (42 U.S.C.A. § 290aa-14, 1991). At least 10% of each state's total allotment under the ADAMHA Block Grant must be set aside to be used specifically for drug and alcohol treatment programs and services, including residential treatment for women, with a particular emphasis on pregnant women and women with children. Because the total appropriation for the ADAMHA Block Grant for fiscal year 1991 was more than $1.2 billion, the 10% set aside represents substantial funding for targeted services for women. The OSAP Model Projects were designed to fund drug abuse prevention, education, and treatment and are expressly targeted for pregnant and postpartum women and their infants, with priority given to low-income women and their infants and to innovative programs for drugs such as crack cocaine. The Drug Abuse Demonstration Projects of National Significance include pregnant and postpartum women and their infants among their target populations. Although none of these projects provides an entitlement to services for individual women and children, they nevertheless afford significant opportunities for advocacy to increase access to services for this population.

Medicaid Waivers

Beginning in 1981 Congress established authority for the states to seek "waivers" of some of the federal requirements for the Medicaid program to allow greater flexibility in fashioning programs to meet the needs of particular groups who would otherwise be unable to obtain essential care under Medicaid (English, Jameson, & Warboys, 1988; Fox, 1990). Several states have elected to establish

"AIDS Waivers" under the Section 2176 waiver authority (42 U.S.C. § 1396n(c), 1991), which is designed to enable states to provide broader home- and community-based services to the target population than to the general Medicaid population in the state. In addition, Congress has granted authority to states to seek waivers to provide services to young children who are born HIV positive or exposed to drugs (Dunn-Malhotra, 1990).

Waiver for Drug-Exposed and HIV-Positive Foster Children. The Waiver for Children Infected with AIDS or Drug Dependent at Birth (42 U.S.C.A. § 1396n(e), 1991) would authorize states to provide Medicaid coverage for a range of services, including medical treatment and health-related services such as respite care, home nursing, and transportation. To qualify for services, children must be born drug-dependent or HIV-positive, must be younger than age 5, and must be eligible for federal foster care or adoption assistance payments (Title IV-E, 1991). In addition, however, they must be sick enough to require care in a nursing facility or hospital (Dunn-Malhotra, 1990). This new waiver provides states with great flexibility to provide noninstitutional services, with federal reimbursement, albeit for a limited population of drug-exposed and HIV-positive children. Nevertheless, as of 1990 no state had applied to the Health Care Financing Administration (HCFA) for such a waiver (Dunn-Malhotra, 1990) and no such waivers had been granted (DeWoody, 1991).

AIDS Waivers. One reason cited by some states for not applying for a waiver for drug-dependent and HIV-positive foster children is that they already have the ability to provide similar services to this population under other auspices, usually an "AIDS waiver." However, AIDS waivers have one clear limitation in comparison with the waiver for drug-dependent and HIV-positive foster children: drug-exposed children are not eligible for services under an AIDS waiver unless they have also tested positive for HIV. By late 1989 six states had approved waiver programs for persons with HIV infection and other applications were pending (Fox, 1990). Because each state has the discretion to design its own waiver program within federal limits, the degree to which these programs meet the needs of children may vary significantly from state to state.

Advocates must carefully examine waiver applications to determine whether children will be able to meet eligibility requirements and whether the services offered are appropriate for a pediatric population. For example, a foster care supplement in California's AIDS waiver might not be available to children placed in the homes of relative caretakers unless they meet stringent federal and state foster care eligibility requirements or unless the waiver application contains its own definition of foster care (Dunn-Malhotra, 1990).

Ryan White CARE Act

In 1990 Congress enacted the Ryan White Comprehensive AIDS Resources Emergency (CARE) Act. The act authorizes funding for cities, states, and other public and private entities to provide essential services to individuals and families affected by HIV (English, 1991). Although the system of comprehensive care envisioned by Congress in designing the legislation is ambitious, the initial level of funding available to implement the law falls far short of its promise. Congress authorized a total $875 million to be appropriated for the three major programs included in the act: the HIV Emergency Relief Grant Program; the Care Grant Program; and Early Intervention Services. However, barely one-quarter of that amount, $221 million, was actually appropriated for fiscal year 1991, which will place severe constraints on the ability of the programs to meet the needs of HIV patients (Hilts, 1990).

Nevertheless, the Ryan White CARE Act contains several provisions that can be used by advocates to expand services for women and children with HIV infection. For example, one-half of the funds under the HIV Emergency Relief Grant Program are disbursed according to a formula to cities hardest hit by the HIV epidemic; the remainder of the funds are awarded as supplemental grants to areas that provide assurances that their use of funds will include appropriate allocations for infants, children, women, and families (English, 1991). The purpose of these grants is to provide outpatient services for individuals and families, including case management and comprehensive treatment (English, 1991). Under the Care Grant Program, block grants are provided to states to provide a continuum of care to individuals and families, and at least 15% of these funds are to be used for health care and supportive services to infants, children, women, and families with HIV disease (English, 1991). Title IV of the act also authorizes demonstration grants both for clinical research on therapies for women and children with HIV disease and for providing outpatient health care to patients who participate in such research and their families (English, 1991).

STRATEGIES TO INCREASE ACCESS TO NECESSARY CHILD WELFARE SERVICES

The child welfare system has the potential for facilitating access to a complex array of services for children and families who are affected by drugs, alcohol, or HIV. However, many families mistrust the child welfare system because they fear the coercive authority of child protective services to remove children from parental custody and place them in foster care. Nevertheless, the child welfare system can assist children and families, helping to meet their special needs for health care and related social, educational, and developmental services and financial support. A legal framework for ensuring that this occurs is already in place, but frequently child welfare agencies do not fully meet their obligations. Thus, better implementation of existing mandates could dramatically improve services for children and families affected by drugs, alcohol, or HIV as well as for other vulnerable children and their families who are within the jurisdiction of the child welfare system.

General Approaches

During the past two decades several general principles to guide reform of the child welfare system have been defined and incorporated into state and federal law. These principles include the importance of supporting the integrity of the biologic family, the necessity of ensuring that children who are placed outside of their own homes receive appropriate care, the need to secure permanent homes for children who cannot return to biologic families, and the value of promoting comprehensive and coordinated services. These very principles can effectively guide advocacy on behalf of children and families affected by drugs, alcohol, or HIV.

Support Biologic Family Integrity

Support for the integrity of biologic families is a central tenet of the Adoption Assistance and Child Welfare Act of 1980, federal child welfare reform legislation enacted more than a decade ago. The right to family integrity is also recognized under the Constitution, which limits state intervention unless it is necessary to protect the life, health, or safety of the child (Developments, 1980). Consistent with principles of family integrity is the principle that children should only be removed from their biologic family homes when they cannot safely remain even with the provision of supportive services (Wald, 1976).

Children and families affected by drugs, alcohol, or HIV should not be considered an exception to this approach because many of these families can safely care for their children (Child Welfare League, 1992). Advocacy to support the integrity of these families must, at minimum, address both the criteria for removal of the children from parental custody and the specific services that are essential to enable families to care for their children safely.

Ensure Appropriate Out-of-Home Care

Some children who are born exposed to drugs or alcohol or infected with HIV cannot remain with their biologic families and require placement out of their own homes. These children must receive out-of-home care that is appropriate to their special needs. Too many infants born exposed to drugs, alcohol, or HIV remain in hospital settings or other inappropriate placements. For many children, placement with an extended family member may provide the best likelihood of appropriate care, but these relatives must receive adequate financial and social support. Other families providing foster care for drug- or alcohol-exposed or HIV-infected children also must receive the support necessary to care for them appropriately. Advocates must explore the diverse strategies available under existing law to promote appropriate placements and adequate support for children who need placement in out-of-home care.

Facilitate Essential Permanent Placements

Some children will not ever be able to return to their biologic families. For these children a permanent placement should be secured, consistent with the philosophy of permanency planning underlying the child welfare reforms of the past decade. In working to ensure adoption, guardianships, or other permanent placements for children born exposed to drugs or alcohol or infected with HIV, advocates must address the special issues, such as access to health care and financial support, that exist for this population.

Promote Comprehensive and Coordinated Services

The value of comprehensive and coordinated services for children and families affected by drugs, alcohol, and HIV has been widely recognized. Child welfare agencies are in a position to promote access to services on a comprehensive and coordinated basis for children and families who are within their purview. To do so, child welfare personnel must be familiar with the requirements of a diverse range of federal and state programs offering services needed by these children and families; and advocates must consider ways in which existing legal requirements can be used to promote comprehensive and coordinated care for this population.

Requirements of Federal and State Law

"Reasonable Efforts"

The federal Adoption Assistance and Child Welfare Act requires states, as a condition of receiving federal foster care and adoption assistance funds, to make "reasonable efforts" to prevent the necessity for removal of children from their homes and to reunify families from which children have been removed. The act also requires that juvenile courts make determinations in individual cases of whether reasonable efforts have been made (Allen, Golubock, & Olson, 1983; National Council, 1987; Ratterman, Dodson, & Hardin, 1987; Shotton, 1989–1990). The obligations of public child welfare agencies to make reasonable efforts are not diminished because children are born exposed to drugs, alcohol, or HIV (Grimm, 1990).

Congress did not define "reasonable efforts" in the act, and the federal regulations do not contain much additional specificity. In addition, only a few states have included definitions in state law (Shotton, 1989–90). One state's statute defines "reasonable efforts" as "the exercise of due diligence by the agency to use appropriate and available services to meet the needs of the child and the child's family" (Minnesota Statutes Annotated, 1990). Another state refers to "reasonable diligence and care" (Florida Statutes Annotated, 1991), and a third speaks in terms of "utilizing all available services related to meeting the needs of the child and the child's family" (Missouri Statutes Annotated, 1990). One state specifies criteria for courts to use in making reasonable efforts determinations, namely, whether the services are relevant to the child's safety and protection; adequate to meet the child's and family's needs; culturally appropriate, available, accessible, consistent, timely, and realistic under the circumstances (Minnesota Statutes Annotated, 1990).

One court in a major metropolitan area has developed a protocol for dependency cases that could promote the delivery of services to enable chemically dependent women to care for their children and thereby avoid unnecessary foster care placements (Boland & Henning, 1990). In other cities specific models have been developed to deliver intensive community-based support and home-based family preservation services to families affected by drugs or HIV (Foundation for Children with AIDS, 1991; Jiordano, 1990; Woodruff et al., 1989).

In order to comply fully with their reasonable efforts obligations under federal law, child welfare agencies should develop protocols for providing services that directly meet the needs of families affected by drugs, alcohol, or HIV. At minimum, a child welfare agency failing to make reasonable efforts may be unable to claim federal reimbursement for the child's foster care placement. Although the United States Supreme Court recently held that children cannot sue in federal court to enforce the reasonable efforts requirement (*Suter v. Artist M.*, 1992), the mandate continues to provide a basis for advocates to argue for expanded services in individual cases, in state legislatures, and at the administrative level with state and county agencies.

Standards for Dependency Jurisdiction and Removal

Many states include in their juvenile or family court statutes provisions that enable courts to assume jurisdication of children as dependents on the basis of problems associated with their parents' drug use. However, as a result of growing attention and concern about drug-exposed infants, a few state courts have addressed the question of whether prenatal exposure to drugs alone is sufficient to support dependency jurisdiction.

In a small number of cases, courts either have held that drug exposure alone may be the basis for dependency jurisdiction, independent of any other evidence of parental unfitness or harm to the child, or have defined exposure to drugs in utero as harmful to the child. A California appellate court recently held that a child could be declared a dependent based on evidence that he "was born with opiates in his urine and displayed symptoms of drug withdrawal . . . so that it was necessary to medically treat his withdrawal symptoms" (*In re Stephen W.*, 1990). A New York appellate court held that a child could be declared a dependent if the mother admitted drug use during pregnancy, the child tested positive for cocaine, and the mother failed to enroll in a drug treatment program (*In re Stephanel Tyesha C.*, 1990). Other courts have found that prenatal exposure is a relevant factor, although not sufficient to support dependency jurisdiction without additional evidence (Grimm, 1990; *Matter of Baby X.*, 1980).

The preferred approach should be to require evidence other than the single fact of prenatal exposure to drugs to establish dependency jurisdiction. Whether the child is exposed to drugs or alcohol or infected with HIV or both, the determinative factor should be the parent's ability and willingness to provide appropriate care for the child. The decision of whether or not dependency jurisdiction should be sought by the child welfare agency or granted by the court generally requires a determination of whether the child has suffered or is in imminent danger of suffering serious harm (e.g., California Welfare and Institutions Code §300, 1991). This determination necessarily involves an assessment of risk to the child. Although assessing risk is a difficult task, it is the same assessment that child welfare agencies and juvenile court must make whenever they are called upon to decide whether to remove children from their homes or to make them dependents of the court (Wald & Woolverton, 1990). The specific factors that child welfare personnel should look to in making these difficult decisions must be carefully developed and articulated for families affected by drugs, alcohol, or HIV (Wightman, 1991).

Case Plans

When a child is removed from the custody of a parent and placed in foster care, the federal Adoption Assistance and Child Welfare Act of 1980 requires the development of a case plan. The case plan must be designed to ensure placement in the least restrictive setting in close proximity to the parents and consistent with the special needs of the child (42 U.S.C.A. §675(5)(A)). The Abandoned Infants Assistance Act (1988), recent federal legislation enacted to prevent drug-exposed and HIV-infected children from languishing in hospitals as "boarder babies," also requires that case plans that meet the criteria established by the Adoption Assistance and Child Welfare Act be developed for each child placed in foster care by a recipient of Abandoned Infants Assistance Act funds.

The case plan requirement for placement in the least restrictive setting should provide a basis for arguing that children born exposed to drugs, alcohol, or HIV should not remain as boarder babies in hospital settings (*Baby Angel v. Koch*, 1989; *Baby Jennifer v. Koch*, 1987; Bussiere & Shauffer, 1990). It may also provide a basis for arguing that the child should be placed together with the mother while she is in a residential drug or alcohol treatment program if that arrangement would best serve the child's special needs.

Foster Parents and Relative Caretakers

Foster parents and relatives caring for children born exposed to drugs, alcohol, or HIV require, at minimum, adequate foster care payments, including "special needs" payments, where necessary; respite care and other support services; and training in the care of children with special medical needs. Although some states and some specialized programs currently meet these needs, there are many situations in which adequate financial support, social support, or training is lacking.

Federal law provides cash assistance in the form of foster care maintenance payments for children who meet federal eligibility requirements under Title IV-E of the Adoption Assistance and Child Welfare Act of 1980. Cash benefits are also available under the federal Supplemental Security Income (SSI) program for low-income children who qualify as disabled (Matthews, 1991; *Sullivan v. Zebley*, 1990). Children who qualify for Title IV-E or SSI benefits are also entitled to coverage under the Medicaid program. These cash assistance and medical benefits are available to children living with relatives as well as those living with unrelated foster parents. However, many children born exposed to drugs, alcohol, or HIV do not meet federal eligibility requirements for either the IV-E or the SSI program. If they are living with unrelated foster parents, they can generally receive state-funded foster care payments. Some states, however, continue to deny state foster care benefits to children living with relatives. Recent litigation challenging these exlusions has not been successful *(Lipscomb v. Simmons, 1992)*.

Many states do provide increased rates for foster care benefits for children with special needs. In some states these higher rates are only available to children with drug exposure or HIV infection while in other states they are available generally for medically fragile children. Eighteen states have specialized rates for children who are HIV positive or who have AIDS; and eight states have specialized rates for "drug-addicted" infants (WMCP, 1990).

Comprehensive support services are not available for children with special needs whether they are with relatives or unrelated foster parents (Baughman, Morgan, Margolis, & Kotler, 1989). Even for children with HIV infection or AIDS, who are widely acknowledged to need intensive support services if they are ill, such services are severely limited. For example, in only a small number of states do the HIV policies of the public child welfare agencies specify that supportive services other than specialized payments—that is, services such as counseling, respite care, medical consultation, day care, homemaker services, or transportation—will be provided to foster parents (Teare et al., in press).

Nor do all states provide for training of foster parents in caring for children with special medical needs. In response to a licensing problem that impeded the placement of medically fragile children in foster care, at least one state has enacted legislation to facilitate such placements (Bussiere & Shauffer, 1990). The new California statute requires individualized health care plans for foster children with special health care needs and training of foster parents by health professionals (California Welfare and Institutions Code §§ 17730 et seq., 1991).

Adoption

For those children who cannot return home and need permanent placements with adoptive families, ongoing financial support and access to medical care is critical. The Adoption Assistance and Child Welfare Act of 1980 provides for adoption assistance subsidies for children with special needs. The children must satisfy two basic requirements: the federal definition of "special needs" and eligibility for other federal benefits (IV-E foster care or SSI). Many children born exposed to drugs, alcohol, or HIV would meet these requirements and qualify for adoption assistance. Those who do would be eligible not only for a cash adoption assistance subsidy but also for continued Medicaid coverage (Bussiere & Segal, 1988).

CONCLUSION

Strategies for Advocacy

In order to meet the needs of children and families associated with the continuing incidence of perinatal drug and alcohol use and the increasing incidence of HIV infection, effective advocacy efforts must be addressed to issues such as the identification of women and children and their access to essential health care, related services, and appropriate child welfare services.

Strategies to promote the identification, in appropriate circumstances, of women and children who are affected by alcohol or other drugs and/or HIV infection must include efforts to safeguard the integrity of the testing process and to facilitate necessary referrals for health care and child welfare services. In order to safeguard the integrity of the testing process, accuracy of test results must be assured, exclusive reliance on testing must be discouraged, discriminatory testing must be limited, informed consent must be obtained, and the confidentiality of medical information must be protected. In order to facilitate appropriate referrals for necessary health care and child welfare services, child abuse reporting standards should be clarified to limit reporting based solely on positive toxicology screens, punitive interventions should be eliminated to avoid discouraging women from seeking health care, and comprehensive assessments by health care providers should be encouraged as the basis for linkage to appropriate services.

Strategies to increase access to essential health care must be based on several general approaches, including efforts to promote access to prenatal care, to expand access to drug and alcohol treatment for women, to expand access to HIV treatment for women and children, and to expand access to nonmedical health-related services such as home-based care and early intervention services. Some recent federal initiatives provide opportunities for advocates to expand access of women and children to publicly funded services. These include general Medicaid reforms expanding eligibility for women and children and requirements for improving provider participation, reforms of the Early and Periodic Screening, Diagnosis, and Treatment (EPSDT) program, new options for Medicaid coverage of drug treatment, funding opportunities under the ADAMHA Block Grant and OSAP model programs, Medicaid AIDS Waivers and Waivers for Drug-Exposed and HIV-Infected Foster Children, and the Ryan White CARE Act.

Strategies to increase access to appropriate child welfare services must be based on several general approaches, including supporting biologic family integrity, promoting comprehensive and coordinated services, ensuring appropriate out-of-home placements for children who need them, and facilitating permanent placements for children, when necessary. Implementing these strategies will require working to ensure that children and families receive the various benefits they are entitled to under provisions of state and federal law and that other legal provisions are interpreted to benefit rather than harm these children and families. The reasonable efforts requirements of the Adoption Assistance and Child Welfare Act must be interpreted to ensure the provision of services specifically appropriate to assist families and children affected by drugs, alcohol, or HIV. Standards for dependency jurisdiction and removal of children from their homes should not be based solely on drug or alcohol exposure or HIV infection. Foster parents and relative caretakers should receive adequate financial benefits and related support services to enable them to provide proper care, and adoption assistance should be available to ensure that children who are adopted receive adequate financial support and continued Medicaid eligibility.

Guiding Principles for Advocacy

Ten general principles may provide guidance for advocates who pursue one or more strategies to improve services and protect the rights of children and families affected by drugs, alcohol, or HIV infection.

1. Testing for drugs and alcohol or HIV should occur only when necessary to facilitate medical diagnosis and referral for appropriate social or health care services for the child or family.

2. Procedures used in performing tests for drugs or HIV must ensure the highest standards of accuracy, and confirmatory procedures or repeat tests must be used whenever necessary to ensure reliable results.

3. Testing for drugs or HIV should occur only with written informed consent, unless a test is necessary in an emergency situation for the purpose of medical diagnosis.

4. Neither drug or alcohol use or exposure nor HIV infection should be the sole basis of a mandatory report under the child abuse reporting laws. Such reports should be made when mandated reporters have a reasonable suspicion based on all available facts that a child has been abused or neglected. Referrals to child welfare agencies should be based on uniform risk assessment protocols to avoid the risk of discriminatory reporting.

5. HIV test results and drug or alcohol test results should be disclosed only with the informed consent of the subject of the test or, when an infant is tested, with the consent of the child's parent or guardian or the juvenile court.

6. Criminal prosecution, incarceration, civil commitments, and restrictions on reproductive decision making should not be imposed upon pregnant or postpartum women who are HIV-infected or who use drugs or alcohol.

7. Recent amendments to the federal Medicaid and EPSDT program enacted by Congress that would improve the ability of families affected by drugs, alcohol or HIV infection to obtain essential health care services should be fully implemented at the state level.

8. HIV infection or drug or alcohol use or exposure should not be the sole grounds for the dependency jurisdiction of the juvenile court or for removal of children from parental custody and placement in foster care. As in other cases, dependency jurisdiction and removal should be reserved for cases in which the child cannot safely live with his or her own family even when supportive services are provided and reasonable efforts are made.

9. Reasonable efforts to prevent family separation should include a broad range of services designed to meet the needs of families affected by drugs, alcohol, or HIV infection. Legal time limits on preventive or reunification services should be extended, if necessary, to enable a parent who is willing to complete a treatment program and to recognize the issues associated with successful recovery from chemical dependency to do so when such behaviors would enable a child to continue or return to living safely with his or her own family.

10. For children with HIV infection or drug exposure whose health requires either temporary or permanent placement apart from their families, placement procedures should be designed to ensure that they are placed as quickly as possible in the least restrictive, most family-like setting appropriate to their special needs and that specialized supportive services and cash payments are made available to ensure their adequate support.

Acknowledgments

The author gratefully acknowledges the generous support of the David and Lucile Packard Foundation, the Gerbode Foundation, the San Francisco Foundation, and the Zellerbach Family Fund. The author also gratefully acknowledges the research assistance of Stacie Sheelar, M.S.W.

REFERENCES

42 U.S.C.A. § 290aa-13 (West 1991).
42 U.S.C.A. § 290 aa-14 (West 1991).
42 U.S.C.A. § 290ee-3(e) (West 1991).
42 U.S.C.A. §§ 300x et seq. (West 1991).
42 U.S.C.A. § 1396d(a) (4) (B) (West 1991).
42 U.S.C.A. § 1396d(r) (West 1991).
42 U.S.C.A. § 1396n(c) (West 1991).
42 U.S.C.A. § 1396n(e) (West 1991).
42 U.S.C.A. § 675(5) (A) (West 1991).
45 C.F.R. §§ 1355-1357 (1989).
Abandoned Infants Assistance Act, Pub. L. No. 100-505, §§ 1,2, 101-301, 102 Stat. 2533 (1988).
ACLU Reproductive Freedom Project and ACLU Women's Rights Project. (1990). *State by state case summary of criminal prosecutions against pregnant women.* New York: ACLU.
Adoption Assistance and Child Welfare Act of 1980, Pub. L. No. 96-272, 42 U.S.C. §§ 620-628 and §§ 670–677 (West 1991).
Alan Guttmacher Institute. (1987). *Blessed events and the bottom line: The financing of maternity care in the United States.* Washington, DC: author.
Albert, P., Eisenberg, R., Hansell, D. A., & Marcus, J. (Eds.). (1992). *AIDS practice manual: A legal and educational guide* (3d ed., updated). San Francisco: National Lawyers' Guild AIDS Network.
Allen, M. L. (1988). Foster care, child welfare, and adoption reforms. Joint Hearings Before the Subcommittee on Public Assistance and Unemployment Compensation of the House

Committee on Ways and Means and the House Select Committee on Children, Youth, and Families, 100th Cong. 1st Sess.

Allen, M. L., Golubock, C., & Olson, L. (1983). A guide to the Adoption Assistance and Child Welfare Act of 1980. In M. Hardin (Ed.), *Foster children in the courts* (pp. 575–611). Boston: Butterworth Legal Publishers.

Ammann, A. J. (1988). Immunopathogenesis of pediatric Acquired Immunodeficiency Syndrome. *Journal of Perinatology, 8,* 154–159.

Anastos, K., & Marte, C. (1989). Women: The missing persons in the AIDS epidemic. *Health/PAC Bulletin 19*(4), 6–13.

Anderson, G. (Ed.). (1990). *Courage to care: Responding to the crisis of children with AIDS.* Washington, DC: Child Welfare League of America.

Andrulis, D. P., Weslowski, V. B., Hintz, E., Parrott, R. H., & Brady, M. (1990). Pediatric AIDS and hospital care in the U.S.: Report on the 1987 U.S. Hospital Pediatric AIDS Survey. *Pediatric AIDS and HIV Infection: Fetus to Adolescent, 1,* 33–41.

Arno, P. S. (1990, July). *The economics of early intervention in pediatric HIV disease.* Paper presented at Surgeon General's Pediatric Workshop, Washington, DC.

Arno, P. S., Shenson, D., Siegel, N. F., Franks, P., & Lee, P. R. (1989). Economic and policy implications of early intervention in HIV Disease. *Journal of American Medicine, 262,* 1493–1498.

Baby Angel v. Koch, No. 89 Civ. 4770-VLB (S.D.N.Y. filed July, 1989).

Baby Jennifer v. Koch, No. 86 Civ. 9676-VLB (S.D.N.Y. amended complaint filed, Mar. 10, 1987; stipulation and order of settlement approved June 4, 1987).

In the Matter of Baby X., 97 Mich. App. 111, 293 N.W.2d 736 (1980).

Baughman, L. N., Morgan, C. H., Margolis, S., & Kotler, M. (1989, Sept. 14). *Infants and children with HIV infection in foster care.* (Report of the Assistant Secretary for Planning and Evaluation, U.S. Dept. of Health and Human Services).

Boland, P. (1990, Jan. 12). Decision-making Protocols for Drug-related Dependency Cases, Juvenile Department, Superior Court of Los Angeles County, California.

Bussiere, A., & Segal, E. C. (1988). Adoption assistance for children with special needs. In J. H. Hollinger (Ed.), *Adoption Law and Practice* (pp. 9–67). Oakland, CA: Matthew Bender.

Bussiere, A., & Shauffer, C. (1990). The little prisoners. *Youth Law News, 11*(1), 22–26.

California Advocates for Pregnant Women. (1990, July/August). A model for advocacy and treatment: The role of perinatal toxicology testing. *California Advocates for Pregnant Women Newsletter,* p. 3.

California Department of Drug and Alcohol Programs. (1990, June). *Preliminary fact sheet on perinatal drug and alcohol use.* Sacramento, CA: Author.

California Statutes, S.B. 2669, Chapter 1603 (approved Sept. 30, 1990).

California Welfare and Institutions Code § 300(b) (West 1991).

California Welfare and Institutions Code §§ 17730 et seq. (West 1991).

Centers for Disease Control. (1992, February). *HIV/AIDS surveillance.* Atlanta: Author.

Charlottesville Report: Report of the Second Public Health Service AIDS Prevention and Control Conference. (1988). *Public health reports, 103,* 88–98.

Chasnoff, I. J., Landress, H., & Barrett, M. (1990). The prevalence of illicit drug or alcohol use during pregnancy and discrepancies in mandatory reporting in Pinellas County, Florida. *New England Journal of Medicine, 322,* 1202–1206.

Chavkin, W. (1990a). Drug addiction and pregnancy: Policy crossroads. *American Journal of Public Health, 80,* 483–487.

Chavkin, W. (1990b, Spring). Preventing AIDS, targeting women. *Health/PAC Bulletin*, 20(1), pp. 19–20.

Chavkin, W., & Kandall, S. (1990). Between a "rock" and a hard place: Perinatal drug abuse. *Pediatrics*, 85, 223–225.

Child Welfare League of America. (1992). *Children at the front: A different view of the war on alcohol and drugs*. Washington, DC: Author.

Children's Defense Fund. (1990, January). *Report on 1989 maternal and child health federal legislation*. Washington, DC: Author.

Clark v. Kizer, 758 F. Supp. 572 (E.D. Cal. 1990).

Cobbs v. Grant, 8 Cal. 3d 229 (1972).

Committee on Substance Abuse, American Academy of Pediatrics. (1990). Drug exposed infants. *Pediatrics*, 86, 639–642.

Congressional Research Service. (1988). 100th Cong. 2d Sess. Report to the Subcommittee on Health and the Environment, Committee on Energy and Commerce. *Medicaid Source Book*. (Comm. Print).

Connolly, W. B., & Marshall, A. B. (1990). Drug addiction, pregnancy and childbirth: Legal issues for the medical and social services communities. In *American Bar Association Center on Children and the Law. Drug exposed infants and their families: Coordinating responses of the legal, medical, and child protection system* (pp. 29–50). Washington, DC: American Bar Association.

Conviser, R. (1991). *Caring for families with HIV: Case studies of pediatric HIV/AIDS demonstration projects*. Washington, DC: Maternal and Child Health Bureau, Health Resources and Services Administration, U.S. Public Health Service, Department of Health and Human Services.

Cooper, E. R., Pelton, S. I., & LeMay, M. (1988). Acquired Immunodeficiency Syndrome: A new population of children at risk. *Pediatric Clinics of North America*, 35, 1365–1387.

Developments in the law: The constitution and the family. (1980). *Harvard Law Review*, 93, 1156–1383.

DeWoody, M. (1991). *Medicaid and supplemental security income: Options and strategies for child welfare agencies*. Washington, DC: Child Welfare League of America.

Doe v. Reeves, CA 90-1700 (E.D. Pa. 1990).

Dunn-Malhotra, E. (1990). Medicaid waivers promising for some drug-exposed children; Don't help most. *Youth Law News*, 11(1), 27–31.

English, A. (1990). Prenatal drug exposure: Grounds for mandatory child abuse reports? *Youth Law News*, 11(1), 2–8.

English, A. (1991). New federal law may help children and adolescents with HIV. *Youth Law News*, 12(2), 1–5.

English, A., & Gates, D. (1991). Drugs and AIDS: Meeting the health care needs of women and children. *Clearinghouse Review*, 24, 361–374.

English, A., Jameson, E., & Warboys, L. (1988). Legal issues in pediatric and adolescent AIDS. In C. Hockenberry (Ed.), *AIDSLaw* (pp. 235–238). San Francisco: AIDS Legal Referral Panel.

Faden, R. R. (1990). HIV infection, pregnant women, and newborns: A policy proposal for information and testing. *Journal of the American Medical Association*, 264, 2416–2420.

Feig, L. (1990, January 29). *Drug exposed infants and children: Service needs and policy questions*. Washington, DC: U.S. Department of Health and Human Services, Office of Social Services Policy, Division of Children, Youth and Family Policy.

Fink, J. (1990). Effects of crack and cocaine on infants: A brief review of the literature. *Clearinghouse Review, 24*, 460–466.

Florida Statutes Annotated, § 415.503(8) (a) (2) (West Supp. 1989).

Florida Statutes Annotated, § 39.41(4) (b) (West Supp. 1991).

Foundation for Children With AIDS, Inc. (1991). Substance abuse programs and HIV services forming a therapeutic alliance. *Children with AIDS, 3*, 1, 6–7.

Fox, D. M. (1990). Financing health care for persons with HIV Infection: Guidelines for state action. *American Journal of Law and Medicine, 16*, 223–247.

Gates, D. (1991). *An overview of federal funding programs for the prevention and treatment of alcoholism and drug dependency.* Washington, DC: National Health Law Program.

Gates, D., & Beck, D. (1990). Prevention and treatment: The positive approach to alcoholism and drug dependency. *Clearinghouse Review, 24*, 472–489.

Gittler, J., & McPherson, M. (in press). HIV infection among women of reproductive age, children, and adolescents: An introduction. *Iowa Law Review.*

Grimm, B. (1990). Drug-exposed infants pose new problems for juvenile courts. *Youth Law News, 11*, 9–14.

Gwinn, M., Pappaioanou, M., George, J. R., Hannon, W. H., Wasser, S. C., Redus, M. A., Hoff, R., Grady, G. F., Willoughby, A., Novello, A. C., Petersen, L. R., Dondero, T. J., & Curran, J. W. (1991). Prevalence of HIV infection in childbearing women in the United States. *Journal of the American Medical Association, 265*, 1704–1708.

Halfon, N. (1989). *Born hooked: Confronting the impact of perinatal substance abuse.* Statement presented in hearing before the House Select Committee on Children, Youth, and Families, 101st Cong. 1st Sess. U.S. House of Representatives.

Halfon, N., & Klee, L. (1991). Health and development services for children with multiple needs: The child in foster care. *Yale Law and Policy Review, 9*, 71–96.

Hardy, L. M. (Ed.). (1991). *HIV screening of pregnant women and newborns: A report of a study by a commission of the Institute of Medicine.* Washington, DC: National Academy Press.

Hellinger, F. J. (1991). Forecasting the medical care costs of the HIV epidemic: 1991–1994. *Inquiry, 28*, 213–225.

Hilts, P. J. (1990, October 24). Panel approves large cut in AIDS Relief Bill. *New York Times,* p. A11.

Illinois P.A. 86-659 § 3 (approved Sept. 1, 1989).

Institute of Medicine. (1990). *Treating drug problems.* Washington, DC: National Academy Press.

Jameson, W., & Halfon, N. (1990). Treatment programs for drug-dependent women and their children. *Youth Law News, 11(1)*, 20–21.

Jiordano, M. (1990, November). Intensive family preservation services to crack-using parents: Hope and help in preserving the family. In *Family Preservation: Taking Stock and Moving Ahead* (conference materials). New York: Edna McConnell Clark Foundation.

Kandall, S. (1991). Physician dispels myths about drug-exposed infants. *AAP News, 7(1)*, 11.

Larsen, J. (1990). Creating common goals for medical, legal and child protection communities. In *American Bar Association Center on Children and the Law. Drug exposed infants and their families: Coordinating responses of the legal, medical, and child protection system* (pp. 1–18). Washington, DC: American Bar Association.

Larsen, J., Horowitz, R. M., & Chasnoff, I. J. (1991). Medical evidence in cases of intrauterine drug and alcohol exposure. *Pepperdine Law Review, 18*, 279–317.

Larson, C. (1991). Overview of state legislative and judicial responses. *The Future of Children, 1*, 72–77.

Legal Action Center. (1988). *Confidentiality: A guide to the new federal regulations.* New York: Author.

Levine, C. (1990). Women and HIV/AIDS research: the barriers to equity. *Evaluation Review, 14,* 447–449.

Levine, C., & Dubler, N. D. (1990). Uncertain risks and bitter realities: The reproductive choices of HIV-infected women. *Millbank Quarterly, 68,* 321–351.

Lipscomb v. Simmons, 60 U.S.L.W. 2697 (9th cir., Apr. 27, 1992).

Lockwood, S. (1990a). *Throwing away the key: The trend toward criminal sanctions against drug-abusing pregnant women.* Unpublished master's thesis, University of California, Berkeley.

Lockwood, S. (1990b). What's known—and what's not known—about drug-exposed infants. *Youth Law News, 11(1),* 15–19.

MacGregor, S. N., Keith, L. G., Bachicha, J. A., & Chasnoff, I. J. (1989). Cocaine abuse during pregnancy: Correlation between prenatal care and perinatal outcome. *Obstetrics and Gynecology, 74,* 882–885.

Makadon, H. J., Seage, G. R., Thorpe, K. E., & Fineberg, H. V. (1990). Paying the medical cost of the HIV epidemic: A review of policy options. *Journal of Acquired Immune Deficiency Syndrome, 3,* 123–133.

Martin, J. M., & Sacks, H. S. (1990). Do HIV-infected children in foster care have access to clinical trials of new treatments? *AIDS and Public Policy Journal, 5,* 3–8.

Massachusetts General Laws Annotated, Ch. 199, § 51A (West Supp. 1989).

Matthews, M. (1991). Children's disability benefits: A new resource for severely ill and disabled infants. *Newsletter of the Clearinghouse for Drug Exposed Children, 2(4),* 1–3, 7.

McNulty, M. (1987–1988). Pregnancy police: The health policy and legal implications of punishing women for harm to their fetuses. *N.Y.U. Review of Law and Social Change, 16,* 277–319.

McNulty, M. (1989). Combating pregnancy discrimination in access to substance abuse treatment for low-income women. *Clearinghouse Review, 23,* 21–25.

Medicaid Amendments. (1990). In An analysis of OBRA-89: The Omnibus Budget Reconciliation Act of 1989. *Health Advocate* (Special issue). Los Angeles: National Health Law Program.

Medicaid Amendments. (1991). In The Omnibus Reconciliation Act of 1990: An analysis of health related provisions. *Health Advocate* (Special issue). Los Angeles: National Health Law Program.

Miller, G. (1989). Addicted infants and their mothers. *Zero to Three, 9(5),* 20–23.

Minnesota Statutes Annotated, § 626.5562(1) (West Supp. 1990).

Minnesota Statutes Annotated, § 260.012(b)(West Supp. 1990).

Missouri Statutes Annotated, § 211.183(2)(Vernon Supp. 1990).

Moss, K. (1990). Legal issues: Drug testing of postpartum women and newborns as the basis for civil and criminal proceedings. *Clearinghouse Review, 23,* 1406–1408.

National Association for Perinatal Addiction Research and Education. (1988). *A First Look: National Hospital Incidence Survey.* Chicago: Author.

National Association of State Alcohol and Drug Abuse Directors (NASADAD). (1990). *Treatment works: A review of 15 years of research findings.* Washington, DC: Author.

National Council of Juvenile and Family Court Judges, Child Welfare League of America, Youth Law Center, and National Center for Youth Law. (1987). *Making reasonable efforts: Steps for keeping families together.* New York: Edna McConnell Clark Foundation.

National Institute on Alcohol Abuse and Alcoholism. (1987). *Program strategies for pre-*

venting fetal alcohol syndrome and alcohol related birth defects. Washington, DC: Author.

National Research Council, (1990, July). AIDS moving into new groups, rates increasing, panel stresses. *Nation's Health,* p. 1.

Novello, A. C., Wise, P. H., Willoughby, A., & Pizzo, P. A. (1989). Final report of the United States Department of Health and Human Services Secretary's Work Group on Pediatric Human Immunodeficiency Virus Infection and Disease: Content and implications. *Pediatrics, 84,* 547–555.

Oklahoma Statutes Annotated, tit. 21 § 846(A) (West Supp. 1988).

Oleske, J. (1990). The medical management of pediatric AIDS: Intervening in behalf of children and families. In G. Anderson (Ed.), *Courage to care: Responding to the crisis of children with AIDS* (pp. 27–38). Washington, DC: Child Welfare League of America.

Ostrea, E. M., Brady, M., Gause, S., Raymundo, A. L., & Stevens, M. (1992). Drug screening of newborns by meconium analysis: A large-scale prospective, epidemiologic study. *Pediatrics, 89,* 107–113.

Oxtoby, M. (1990). Perinatally acquired Human Immunodeficiency Virus infection. *Pediatric Infectious Disease Journal, 9,* 609–619.

Paltrow, L., & Shende, S. (1990, October 29). *State by state case summary of criminal prosecutions against pregnant women and appendix of public health and public interest groups opposed to these prosecutions.* New York: ACLU.

Perkins, J., & Melden, M. (1991). *An advocate's guide to the Medicaid program.* Los Angeles: National Health Law Program.

Ratterman, D., Dodson, G. D., & Hardin, M. (1987). *Reasonable efforts to prevent foster care placement: A guide to implementation.* Washington, DC: American Bar Association.

Rennert, S. (1991). *AIDS/HIV and confidentiality: Model policy and procedures.* Washington, DC: American Bar Association.

Ryan White Comprehensive AIDS Resources Emergency (CARE) Act of 1990, Pub. L. No. 101-381, 104 Stat. 576 (1990), 42 U.S.C.A. §§ 300ff et seq. (West Supp. 1991).

San Francisco Department of Public Health, Perinatal AIDS Project. (1990). *Women and infants at risk for HIV infection: Guidelines and protocols for prevention and care.* San Francisco; Author.

Scitovsky, A. (1989). Studying the cost of HIV-related illness: Reflections on the moving target. *Milbank Quarterly, 67,* 318–344.

Select Committee on Children, Youth, and Families, 100th Cong., 1st Sess., *Federal Programs Affecting Children, 1987* (Committee Print 1987).

Senate Bill No. 2669, Calif. Leg. (introduced March 1, 1990).

Senate Office of Research, California Legislature. (1990, July 16). *California's drug-exposed babies: Undiscovered, unreported, underserved: A county-by-county survey.* Sacramento, CA: California Legislature, Joint Publications.

Senate Select Committee on Children and Youth and Assembly Committee on Human Services, California Legislature. (1990, November). *Final report of the task force on substance abused infants.* Sacramento, CA: California Legislature, Joint Publications.

Shotton, A. (1989–1990). Making reasonable efforts in child abuse and neglect cases: Ten years later. *California Western Law Review, 26,* 223–256.

Smith, B. V. (1990). Improving substance abuse treatment for women. *Clearinghouse Review, 24,* 490–492.

In the Matter of Stephanel Tyesha C. and In the Matter of Sebastian M., 157 A.D. 2d 322, 556 N.Y.S. 2d 280 (1990).

In re Stephen W., 221 Cal. App. 3d 629, 271 Cal. Rptr. 319 (1990).

Sullivan v. Zebley, 493 U.S. 521 (1990).

Suter v. Artist M., 60 U.S.L.W. 4251 (Mar. 25, 1992).

Teare, C., English, A., Lockwood, S., & Clark, K. (in press). *HIV/AIDS policies and guidelines: State child welfare agencies.* Iowa City, IA: National Maternal and Child Health Resource Center and National Center for Youth Law.

Title IV-E, Social Security Act, 42 U.S.C.A. §§ 670 et seq. (West 1991).

Title V, Social Security Act, 42 U.S.C.A. § 701(a)(2) (West 1991).

Title XIX, Social Security Act, 42 U.S.C.A. §§ 1396 et seq. (West 1992).

Tittle, B., & St. Claire, N. (1989). Promoting the health and development of drug-exposed infants through a comprehensive clinic model. *Zero To Three, 9*(5), 18–20.

In re Troy D., 263 Cal. Rptr. 869 (Cal. App. 4 Dist. 1989).

U.S. General Accounting Office. (1990). *Drug-exposed infants: A generation at risk.* Washington, DC: U.S. Government Printing Office.

Wald, M. (1976). State intervention on behalf of "neglected" children: Standards for removal of children from their homes, monitoring the status of children in foster care, and termination of parental rights. *Stanford Law Review, 28,* 623–706.

Wald, M., & Woolverton, M. (1990). Risk assessment: The emperor's new clothes? *Child Welfare, 69,* 483–511.

Weston, D., Ivins, B., Zuckerman, B., Jones, C., & Lopez, R. (1989). Drug exposed babies: Research and clinical issues. *Zero to Three, 9*(5), 1–7.

Wightman, M. (1991). Criteria for placement decisions with cocaine-exposed infants. *Child Welfare, 70,* 653–664.

Wilder v. Virginia Hospital Association, 110 S.Ct. 2510 (1990).

Wisconsin Legislative Service, Act 122 of the Biennial Session, section 61r (West 1990).

Wisconsin Statutes § 146.0255(2) (West Supp. 1990).

WMCP 101-29, Staff of Committee on Ways and Means, 101st Cong. 2d Sess., Overview of Entitlement Programs: 1990 Green Book, Background Material and Data on Programs within the Jurisdiction of the Committee on Ways and Means (Comm. Print 1990).

Woodruff, G., & Hanson, C. R. (1990). *Community-based services for children with HIV infection and their families: A manual for planners, service providers, families, and advocates.* Brighton, MA: South Shore Mental Health Center.

Woodruff, G., Sterzin, E. D., & Hanson, C. R. (1989). Serving drug-involved families with HIV infection in the community: A case report. *Zero To Three, 9*(5), 12–17.

Zuckerman, B. (1991). Drug-exposed infants: Understanding the medical risk. *The Future of Children, 1,* 26–35.

14

Toward More Effective and Efficient Programs for Drug- and AIDS-Affected Families

RICHARD P. BARTH
MALIA RAMLER
JEANNE PIETRZAK

Since work on this volume began, the worlds of substance abuse and HIV have changed, yet the urgent need for a coherent service response has not. In inner-city hospitals the number of children born exposed to drugs appears to be decreasing, but those children who are born substance-exposed are likely to be the second or third drug-affected child in the family. The word about the dangers of drug use during pregnancy seems to have reached recreational users, but intervention and outreach efforts are not influencing women with more intractable problems before they have multiple drug-affected pregnancies. For example, during the first 3 months of this year referrals of drug-exposed newborns to child protective services decreased by 17% in San Francisco (DelVecchio, 1991) and 95% of all cases of infant drug exposure involved women who had given birth to drug-exposed babies in the past. This is an increase from the 62% repeat figure for all cases in the prior year. Across the bay, in Oakland, the percentage of newborns with traces of cocaine in their urine declined from 15% to 9% but "hard-core addicts continue to have babies at levels only slightly below those of 1988 and 1989" (DelVecchio, 1991, p. A13).

HIV disease is increasingly becoming a disease of people of color, of persons who are involved with drugs, and of women and children. In 1988 there were less than 7,000 reported cases of AIDS among adolescent and adult women and just over 1,350 cases of children with AIDS. Three years later, in August 1991, the

Centers for Disease Control (CDC) reported more than 40,000 cases of women with AIDS and 3,250 cases of children with AIDS; 73% of those women and 78% of those children are persons of color. The link between drug use and HIV continues to grow: Nearly one in five clients at a municipal New York City clinic for sexually transmitted diseases (STD) tested seropositive (Chirgwin, DeHovitz, Dillon, & McCormick, 1991) with crack cocaine use highly associated with HIV. The findings point to an "increasing efficiency of sexual transmission of HIV" in the drug-using population (p. 1576). This chapter considers the findings and conclusions of the authors of this volume in the light of predictable changes in drug and HIV epidemiology and responses.

COMMUNITY-BASED PREVENTION OF PERINATAL DRUG AND ALCOHOL USE

Individual behavior is profoundly influenced by community norms and behaviors as well as by public policies and the environment in which alcohol and drug use takes place. Therefore, reaching people and making a change in their behavior requires a broad effort that addresses the social, economic, and political climate in which alcohol and other drug use occurs. Prevention strategies must address the supply and demand for drugs and alcohol and be targeted to the community and public policy as well as the individual; otherwise, they will fail.

Prevention programs should recognize and consider targeting women who are known to be at high risk, namely, those living in a chemically dependent environment (children or partners of a chemically dependent person); survivors of incest, sexual assault, or other violence; those in transition (e.g., divorce, returning to the work force, pregnant, or newly parenting); and adolescents. Prevention programs should recognize the strong influence of male partners and family members on women's drinking and drug use and should direct prevention efforts to these partners as well. Women who use crack cocaine are most likely to have begun their use with male friends or family members (Boyd & Mieczkowski, 1990). Because women are at high risk of contracting HIV from drug-abusing lovers, outreach to prevent HIV transmission must also include men. Efforts in Seattle to change norms to support increased condom use among homosexual males appear to be paying off (Hinman, 1991); these may serve as a prototype for community approaches to increase heterosexual condom use.

Where legal drugs (e.g., alcohol, tobacco) are concerned, prevention strategies should aim at advertising, sales packaging, and pricing. Since alcohol is the superordinate gateway drug, a ban on all ad campaigns, promotions, and advertising of alcohol would be the first step. Additionally, more pronounced and legible warning labels on liquor packaging should be required and the tax on alcohol and tobacco products should be increased (which has been shown to reduce demand).

Communities also need statutory and fiscal support to reduce the availability of drugs. Citizen's groups in Berkeley and Oakland, California, are finding ways to shut down crack and heroin houses: Neighbors used civil suits in small claims court to pressure landlords to evict drug house tenants ("Cracking Down," 1991). They risked only the small fees required to file suits and had, as of July 1991, received a quarter of a million dollars in small claim judgments from landlords. More than 50 drug houses have been shut down in the first year of operation. A how-to handbook is now available (Wetzel, 1991).

PRENATAL SERVICES

Early intervention efforts begin with prenatal care. Policy makers should be aware of the special opportunity prenatal care offers for early intervention in alcohol and drug problems and HIV infection. Early detection and successful intervention with pregnant women using drugs can substantially improve maternal health, pregnancy outcomes, and child well-being. The stigma associated with drug problems and HIV infection currently hampers the delivery of prenatal care. Ongoing training of providers of prenatal care is critical. Training should address providers' knowledge and attitudes so that they can most effectively reach and assist pregnant alcoholics and drug users. Staff should be trained to understand the disease concept of addiction, and patients who deny their alcohol or drug use. Staff need to project hope and acceptance and to be advocates for women and children.

Staff also need to know the value of HIV testing to HIV-positive and negative men and women and how to counsel HIV-positive women. A recent randomized trial showed that clients at an STD clinic who received AIDS education, HIV antibody tests, and test results were significantly more likely to talk to their partners about their HIV status, worry about getting AIDS, and use a condom than clients who only received AIDS education (cited in Hinman, 1991). Whereas this information-based approach is not a total solution, it suggests that AIDS testing and counseling can promote skill development and HIV prevention.

DEVELOPMENTAL OUTCOMES AND SERVICES

Predicting the developmental and behavioral consequences of alcohol and drug exposure for infants is fraught with difficulties, as is isolating the effect of a particular drug. While some scientific knowledge exists about the effects of exposure to cocaine, opiates, alcohol, and marijuana, individual drugs have not been shown to cause a *specific* developmental dysfunction (the exception to this is fetal alcohol syndrome). Advances in meconium analysis for drugs promise highly sensitive and specific tests for perinatal drug exposure and indicate that conventional tests of infants' urine may significantly underestimate drug exposure (Ostrea, Brady, Gause, Raymundo, & Stevens, 1992). Given the relative unavailability of this method, it is seldom possible to know with any accuracy the amount, frequency, and duration of prenatal drug exposure; moreover, polydrug use may have interactive effects. Other risk factors, such as genetic influences and poor nutrition, may also come into play. Most clearly, the postnatal environment can either mitigate or compound biological developmental vulnerabilities. Given the difficulties in parenting caused by involvement with drugs and alcohol, drug- and alcohol-exposed children are undoubtedly at risk for developmental and behavioral problems. Early intervention models that include accessible and nonstigmatizing drug and alcohol treatment and support for the mother and family must be made more widely available.

Estimates of the likelihood that HIV-infected women will pass the virus to offspring has dropped steadily from 50% in the early years of the epidemic to 25% in 1992 (Squires, 1992). When AIDS is acquired, it affects children's development through associated medical complications (e.g., brain tumor, stroke, general malaise, and malnutrition due to illness). A minority of children with symptomatic HIV infection have central nervous system damage. Since most HIV-infected children have also been drug exposed, they may suffer from the adverse consequences of prenatal drug exposure and a drug-using caretaking environment. The most distinctive aspects of children with AIDS, compared to children prenatally exposed to drugs, is a progressive central nervous system dysfunction.

Although parents involved with substance abuse are likely to be reluctant to participate in voluntary long-term social services, they may do so if day care, counseling, and similar advantages accompany this voluntary status. Especially appealing to mothers is a mixture of in-home and center-based developmental services that help them learn how to care for their children. Several service providers indicate that case management that includes the option of in-home developmental services is the key element in retaining drug-involved women in programs (see Chapters 8 and 10). Recent reports on a 3-year-long and a 4-year-long in-home early intervention program with high-risk families indicate continuation rates of 93% and 89%, respectively (Infant Health and Development Program, 1990; Martin, Ramey, & Ramey, 1990).

Generalizations and stereotypes about the prognoses for drug-exposed children (and the prognoses of their effect on society) are neither useful nor accurate. Children must be assessed on an individual basis. Some children will have little or no effect, and others will be severely harmed; most will fall into the middle range. New evidence indicates that children who test positive for drugs and whose mothers admit to drug use will have greater perinatal complications than mothers who test positive but do not admit to drug use (Ostrea et al., 1992). They may also have greater developmental vulnerability.

Children affected by drugs or alcohol or infected with HIV should be placed in the least restrictive educational setting consistent with their needs and should have the opportunity to play, learn, and interact with other children. Teachers and child care providers should receive training in integrating children who are affected by drugs, alcohol, and/or HIV in their classrooms and in promoting their health and development.

MEETING FAMILIES' NEEDS

A comprehensive perspective explicitly recognizes that the early intervention and educational needs of children exposed to alcohol or other drugs or infected with HIV are key in the overall approach to the needs of families. Early intervention services are defined as multidisciplinary services provided for families with developmentally vulnerable or disabled children from birth to age 3. The programs are designed to enhance child development, minimize potential delays, remediate existing problems, prevent further deterioration, limit the acquisition of additional handicapping conditions, and/or promote adaptive family functioning. Some of the best programs for families of these children include therapeutic child care and drop-in respite care, education for caregivers, crisis intervention, counseling, and peer support for siblings. Models for these services exist but are not yet routinely available.

The evidence for the outcome of prenatal drug exposure is unclear (Barth, 1991). This, however, is a welcome contrast to the common view held a few years ago, namely, that these children were missing part of their humanity and were doomed. We now believe that the variation in long-term outcome for drug-exposed children is produced through habilitative family and school environments (Zuckerman, 1991): The fewer the services, the less the positive variation; and the later the services, the less the positive variation. Public Law 99-457 offers the clearest avenue for providing early intervention services for children from birth to age 3 and their families. The services that could be generated through PL 99-457 are not, however, uniformly in place, and they are largely not available to families with substance-exposed newborns (unless a severe developmental disability is evinced). The majority of drug-exposed children—even if they begin life under the protection of child welfare services—will fall into the chasm in developmental services that exists between the delivery hospital and Head Start. In-home child welfare services do not ensure appropriate developmental assessments and interventions. These must be done by health and education professionals. At least those children who are enrolled in hospital-based perinatal follow-up services will benefit from well-baby visits and pediatric screening during their first year, and for them the gap in care will be less. Without perinatal follow-up programs, the degree of pediatric medical monitoring among drug-exposed children is only a fraction of what it could be (see Chapter 10).

Children born exposed to drugs and their families have a complex set of needs that can best be served by a variety of providers functioning as a team. Potential team members include a pediatrician, nurse, psychologist, child development specialist, teacher, social worker, chemical dependency consultant, physical therapist, occupational therapist, speech therapist, and nutritionist, although not every discipline would need to be involved with each infant and family. Building such teams requires effective collaboration among child protective services, alcohol and drug programs, regional centers, child development centers, public health nursing, and hospitals delivering high-risk perinatal patients. One agency should have primary responsibility for coordinating quarterly meetings.

These agencies should provide a comprehensive continuum of care for pregnant and parenting chemically dependent women and their children, preferably in a single location. This continuum of care should include health care services for women and children, social services, alcohol/drug treatment and recovery services, individual and family counseling, and parenting skills training. These services should be family-centered and community-based, build on the strengths of families, recognize that the family is the constant in the child's life, and support parents' wish to do the best they can for their children. Agencies should provide emergency financial and practical assistance when necessary. Whenever possible, services should be delivered by people of the same ethnicity, culture, and language as the families served.

Child care services are the bedrock of developmental services and essential to the protection of children living at home. That the absence of child care is a barrier to successful drug treatment is widely known: Studies have shown that less than 10% of drug treatment programs provide child care (Chavkin, 1991; Portis, 1991; Magjaryi, T, 1990). Women in alcohol and drug treatment should receive priority status on waiting lists for subsidized child care. Women who have subsidized child care slots should be allowed to keep them when they enter residential treatment with or without their children. Child care is equally critical to the success of in-home child welfare services. In many areas of this country this is not the case and there are no child care allowances for mothers in child welfare programs.

Meanwhile, more ambitious efforts to develop 24-hour child care and crisis nurseries providing greater protection for children and their families are emerging. Crisis nurseries, respite care, and "child centers" provide therapeutic interventions and a home away from home for drug-exposed children. These are vital resources to families and professionals who, at best, visit with families every 2 weeks (or, more typically, every month) even during the short spells when the cases are active.

ALCOHOL AND DRUG TREATMENT

Prevention and effective treatment of pregnant and parenting women's drug and alcohol use requires an understanding of their circumstances. Unfortunately, this group has received little attention until recently. Many experts are now coming to recognize that women tend to have different biological, psychological, and cultural vulnerabilities than men in respect to complications of alcohol and drug use. Moreover, women who use drugs often have children and poor support systems and life skills outside the alcohol and drug culture.

Women require different intervention approaches from those developed for a predominantly male clientele. Women often need "habilitation," education, and support in such basic areas as economic survival, relationships, securing housing, job training, and time and household management. They need assistance in overcoming attitudinal and administrative barriers to participation in health care and alcohol and drug treatment. In addition, women who are parents require help with transportation and child care and assistance with parenting at-risk children.

Women-specific alcohol and drug treatment services are rarely offered or evaluated. Still, what little research exists offers some useful conclusions. No single treatment approach is more effective than any other. The previously reported results from studies on men—namely, that longer treatment appears to improve 1-year abstinence rates (see Chapter 7)—squares with our experience with women. Clinical consensus posits that group therapy for women with alcohol problems is more effective than individual and family therapy, that female therapists are more effective with women than male therapists, and that supportive approaches are more successful than confrontational ones.

Treatment models that target life conditions warrant expanded use, because clients returning to pre-use life circumstances are at great risk for recidivism if they lack the skills necessary to maintain an alcohol-free and drug-free lifestyle. It is critical to acknowledge the strengths of drug-involved mothers and to support their maternal instincts and concern for their babies. Focusing on the family helps to address the health and psychosocial needs of other key family members and may include parenting education, support groups, and family planning.

A COORDINATED SERVICE APPROACH

Families affected by drugs, alcohol, and/or HIV, with their multiplicity of health and social service needs, create challenging opportunities for collaboration among public health, alcohol and drug treatment, child welfare, and developmental service providers. Interagency collaboration, when managed effectively, affords clients and providers a rational, multifaceted, and integrated treatment approach. This is in sharp contrast with the fragmented, conflicting, and duplicative services, confusion, lack of service responsibility, and client attrition that result when efforts by multiple service providers are uncoordinated.

Earnest attempts at interagency collaboration can go awry, however, when insufficient attention is paid to strategic, contextual, and structural factors. Integrative linkages, the mechanisms that maintain interagency coordination, can be characterized as occurring at two levels of organizational structure: direct service and administrative. Direct service linkages tie the provision of services to specific clients while administrative linkages tie the management of service providers together (Gans & Horton, 1975). In order to be truly effective, agency efforts need to be made at both junctures. Additionally, "interpretive" and "contextual" factors may impede or facilitate coordination at each of these levels. The former are attitudes, values, and perceptions of personnel, and the latter include structural variables of the organization and the larger environment (Halpert, 1982). Experience has shown us the necessity of actively involving family members in the development of their family service plan, as well as designating a lead agency to serve as primary case manager for the family and catalyst for the interagency meetings.

An evaluation of interagency coordination associated with the Maternal and Child Health High-Risk Infant Follow-Up Projects served to isolate some of the variables responsible for successful collaboration (Jeremy & Korenbrot, 1987). The authors found that the following elements were required to ensure successful interagency collaboration: an explicit, formal charge to local agencies to increase interagency coordination; funds to support interagency activities by underwriting administrative costs, staff time, and parents' time; interagncy coordination at the state level among departments to remove categorical barriers prior to coordination at the local level; and authorization for local interagency coordinating bodies to make binding decisions and recommendations to local agencies participating in the decision making.

The ideal situation for interagency collaboration would be one in which there is personal commitment and intent on the part of the agency representative, personal endorsement from the agency administrator, and an allocation of agency resources that is supported by funding, authorization, and interdepartmental collaboration.

In the final analysis, practitioners and researchers alike remind us that interorganizational coordination is not an end in itself but, rather, a means to desired outcomes. Thompson (Chapter 10, this volume) cautions providers not to lose sight of the primary concern—the client—and to place the family and its needs above any and all interagency issues. The ultimate goal of services, integrated or not, should be the empowerment of the client, not his or her dependency on service systems.

CHILD WELFARE

The recent rise in the use of crack cocaine and methamphetmine presents a new set of challenges for child welfare workers. In the face of these challenges, and in the face of public demands for punitive approaches to drug-using mothers, child welfare professionals must remain staunch supporters of approaches that strengthen rather than disrupt families. Child welfare service providers are moving away from the presumption that every alcohol- and drug-exposed child should be removed from parental care and toward the presumption that family preservation can be achieved for most families. Heavy drug use has been a common contributor to the rationale for out-of-home care for decades (Fanshel, 1975). In contrast, the majority of the children of drug-using parents who now come to the attention of child welfare service providers will not enter foster care. These children will typically receive services at home, and these services will be quite brief. It is our thesis that we can and must do better at maximizing the potential of these very young children during the period of their greatest vulnerability. The brevity of child welfare services does not coincide with the fact that the resolution of drug treatment is typically a year or two or with the fact that drug-exposed children create great demands on parents or that drug users' capacity to parent may be compromised. Whereas some parents have failed to maintain their formerly successful roles as parents and providers and largely need drug rehabilitation, many drug-involved parents need habilitation and must—for the first time—learn to become effective parents and providers. Until they do, their children are in double jeopardy.

Decision making about protecting the future of drug-exposed children and preserving their families is becoming more studied. Risk assessment matrixes specific to drug-involved families have been developed (in Los Angeles County, among many places) and instituted. Wightman (1991) has clarified the assessment domains among child welfare workers making placement decisions in Illinois. As Roberts (this volume) has pointed out, case closings and transfer to permanent placement programs that all but preclude reunification with families are particularly difficult decisions for child welfare workers. A decision-making protocol for assessing the likelihood of a child's return home has been shown to be highly accurate in its predictability. This tool (Katz & Robinson, 1991), while addressing drug involvement in several ways, is designed for families with a range of presenting problems and deserves more testing with a cohort of drug-involved families.

Even as recently as 1990, an estimated 80% of drug-exposed children encountered by the child welfare system entered foster care—usually to stay (Feig, 1990). The foster care census rose swiftly across the country from 1988 to 1990. After the initial shock to state and local foster care programs and budgets, the criteria for accepting families into the child welfare system began to tighten in 1991 and 1992. By 1991 only 1 of 12 child abuse reports in California resulted in any formal child welfare services beyond investigation. Indeed, during recent years—despite the crack epidemic—the likelihood of a child receiving ongoing child welfare services beyond investigation decreased in California from 23% in 1985 to 8% in 1990. These data reflect national trends. It appears that the initial impulse to serve every drug-involved family has given way to a more profound decade long tendency to reduce service availability to vulnerable children.

Few drug-involved families receive family preservation services, with most of these services provided in the farm belt and in the Pacific Northwest, where heavy drug use is not as pervasive as elsewhere. Still, there are specific efforts to provide family preservation services to drug-affected families, at least, in the Bronx, Detroit, and Miami, and they have begun to show their effectiveness with a somewhat select group of voluntary clients (Barth, 1991). Intensive family preservation programs are making more of an effort to link their families with other resources, extend the length of services, and facilitate contingency plans with drug-using mothers regarding the protection of their children should they resume using drugs. Ideally, such services, which typically last 4–6 weeks, should be welded to longer-term, continuous developmental and case management services. Families First in Detroit, Michigan provided intensive family preservation service to 444 families during its first 16 months of operation; 246 of those families had at least one adult family member with a substance abuse problem (typically, crack cocaine). At least 80% of the families were intact at follow-up up to a year after completion of service, with parents caring safely for their children. Of these families, Blythe, Giordano, and Kelly (1991) write:

much of what we have learned in working with these families is counter to the beliefs of professionals and the lay population about parents who use drugs. . . . While crack cocaine can have devastating effects on families, Families First therapists have found that it is as treatable as any drug problem, perhaps even more so. The key factor appears to be the manner in which a client's drug use is addressed. When approached respectfully with options, drug-using parents are motivated to seek help and are willing to change to make their lives and the lives of their children better. (p. 13)

Conventional in-home services, whether voluntary or involuntary, are typically limited to 6 months, with the possibility of extensions to a year. One social worker on a special unit to provide in-home services to parents of drug-affected newborns commented, "Six months isn't even hardly enough. It isn't even a minimum amount of time. We are talking about a program that needs to run a year to eighteen months. If they go live in a group home they get to stay that long and it costs three times as much. Why shouldn't they get eighteen months of service at home, too?" (In a few areas, supervision extends beyond a year; New York City and Los Angeles have recently developed special units that will provide services to drug-involved families beyond 1 year.) The typical expectation is that families in drug treatment will participate in testing and will be subject to the conventional requirements of families in the child welfare system, for example, parenting training and maintaining the home in a safe condition. In some cases the court order requires that the parent bring the child to a day care program and that a social worker check with the family and the child care center (at first weekly, then biweekly, and finally monthly).

In-home services are often continued after a child is reunited with drug-involved parents, although not always. Regrettably, thousands of children return to their parents' homes and have their cases closed simultaneously. Drug testing and drug treatment are also usually discontinued at this time, a fact that many drug treatment specialists find disheartening.

Despite our best efforts, short- and long-term foster care will be needed by many children born to drug-using parents. The majority of these children will find homes with relatives. Although these kinship foster parents will provide much familial and cultural identity that children can benefit from, they are also less skilled than nonkinship foster parents at using the services of health and human service providers (Fein, Maluccio, & Kluger, 1990). They may need additional assistance in locating and approaching a variety of providers who can benefit their children. Many programs have sprung up in the last few years that offer these relative caregivers practical services and emotional support.

Much needed is the expansion of foster care arrangements for drug-involved mothers and their children (e.g., cluster housing or supervised living arrangements). The Children's Home and Aid Society of Chicago is pioneering foster care for mothers and children together; Project Demand in Minneapolis uses apartment clusters, and when mothers are discharged back into the community, they and their children are placed with resource families. This should be just a beginning; both programs have replicated the long experience of the Europeans. Providing foster care for drug-involved families can be done: The resource/foster families can be recruited, and recovery can be achieved. When it is not achieved (and the mother returns to heavy drug use or is afflicted with AIDS), at least the children have some continuity of care with the resource family. Resource families may become like relatives and offer children the commitment and advocacy they need.

Adoption is, by law, the option of first choice for drug-affected and HIV-infected children who will not return home and cannot find homes with relatives. Parents in California who adopted drug-exposed children between 1988 and 1989, when queried about their experience 2 years later, reported no more or less satisfaction with the adoptions than parents whose adopted children were not drug exposed (Barth, 1991). Consistent with adoptive parents' similar satisfaction ratings was the lack of difference reported in temperament, behavior problems, or school performance for drug-exposed and non–drug-exposed adopted children. HIV-infected children are also being adopted successfully. The Leake and Watts child care agency in New York has placed more than 65 HIV-positive children in adoptive homes during a 3-year demonstration project. The greatest impediment to the adoption of drug- and HIV-affected children is fear about the level of care that they require. Although some of these children do require high levels of care, many parents find that the rewards of caring for and interacting with them outweigh the burden of caregiving.

As the HIV epidemic claims the lives of increasing numbers of women, HIV orphans will become a greater part of child welfare caseloads. We are challenged to maintain families where there is an ill parent for as long as possible and to engage parents with AIDS in long-term planning for their children. Shared care arrangements and support for relative foster care and respite care are all needed.

FINANCING OF SERVICES

Women should be guaranteed access to prenatal care through such avenues as presumptive eligibility for Medicaid and extension of insurance coverage to families without maternity benefits. New reimbursement packages for health services should cover the costs of women-specific services that facilitate participation in prenatal care and in drug and alcohol treatment and recovery programs. Reimbursement packages should cover services such as child care, transportation, parenting and child development classes, home visits, outreach, and case management. Creative approaches to financing services for children and families affected by drugs, alcohol, or HIV must be developled. Existing options for expanding services and maximizing federal financial participation under programs such as Medicaid and EPSDT should be fully implemented. Additional flexibility in long-term funding for programs to meet the needs of these families and children must be developed at the federal, state, and local level. Prevention as well as treatment efforts can be fairly funded by, among other mechanisms, increasing alcohol and tobacco excise taxes and by earmarking revenues for services to women affected by drugs, alcohol, and/or HIV and their children.

POLICY

States are being called upon to clarify the stance of public health, child welfare, and law enforcement agencies with respect to perinatal substance use. Different areas have taken different approaches—from efforts to incarcerate women who use drugs throughout their pregnancies, to calling drug use during pregnancy prima facie evidence of child abuse, to placing the problem primarily in the domain of public health (as does the California legislative effort Senate Bill 2669, an approach we support). SB 2669 dictates that evidence of drug or alcohol use alone is not sufficient grounds for mandatory child abuse reports but should be a trigger for a comprehensive risk and needs assessment.

The complex mix of services required by drug- and HIV-involved families presents a challenge to create enduring fundings streams that support coordination rather than generate categorical regulatory and fiscal barriers. Personnel of programs emerging under newly created sources of funding (e.g., the Abandoned Infants Assistance Act, the Ryan White CARE Act) must look for opportunities for collaboration and guidance from health and social services personnel who have years of experience with similar programs, such as Title V maternal and child health programs for children with special medical needs. Efforts at coordination are more successful when there is an explicit expectation that it will occur and when funds are allocated specifically for both the administrative costs of administering an interagency council or board and for release time for staff to attend meetings (Jeremy & Korenbrot, 1987). Coordination requires the cooperation of local agency staff as well as the will of state and federal administrators to create legal interagency agreements that allow for the sharing of resources.

As Abigail English details in this volume (see Chapter 13), modifications in entitlement-based funding streams, such as Medicaid and EPSDT, that promise expanded access to health care for drug- and HIV-involved women and children must be fully utilized.

It may also be incumbent upon policymakers to clarify the privacy rights of women who use drugs or who have HIV infection by establishing guidelines for informed consent to and disclosure of results of toxicology screens and HIV tests for both women and their children. While some states have created specific protections around HIV testing, they are not universal, and very few protections are in place with regard to toxicology screens, which are routinely administered without consent, despite the potential for serious consequences. Testing for drugs or HIV should occur only with written informed consent unless a test is necessary in an emergency situation. In the case of an infant, written informed consent should be obtained from the mother or legal guardian.

LEGAL ISSUES

Perinatal alcohol and drug use must be recognized as a public health issue rather than a criminal justice issue. Evidence of HIV infection or perinatal drug or alcohol exposure in infants, including positive urine toxicology or HIV test results, should not be the sole basis for criminal prosecution, a mandatory child abuse report, dependency jurisdiction of the juvenile court, or removal of children from their home.

Families' rights to services and privacy should be protected to maximize the participation of drug- and HIV-affected families in health and social services. Clinical protocols should be developed that require a woman's informed consent for testing her or her newborn for exposure to drugs or HIV and that maintain the confidentiality of sensitive medical information. Test results must be used only in the context of comprehensive health assessments for medical diagnosis and referral to essential health and social services.

Professional schools and licensing boards should require initial and continuing education in perinatal drug and alcohol use and HIV infection, including such topics as addiction and the life cycle of treatment and recovery; resources for treatment and recovery; HIV risk; HIV risk reduction education techniques; drug, alcohol, and HIV risk screening; and intervention methods.

Professional organizations can work together to develop a standard of care incorporating education, screening, intervention, and referral for drug and alcohol use and HIV risk into all services—family planning; school health; and obstetric, gynecologic, pediatric, family practice, and sexually transmitted disease programs—that reach women of childbearing age.

CONCLUSIONS AND RECOMMENDATIONS

The current system, when it is working optimally, can promote the well-being of HIV- and drug-affected children and parents. The first wave of services to an affected family would involve a year or more of in-home follow-up services by the public health or child welfare service system. These services could continue as Family Services Plan under PL 99-457, which directs the child's developmental care until age 3. They might then be supplemented by Head Start and other early childhood educations that prepare children for school and support their transition to school. If children affected by drugs, alcohol, and/or HIV had this array of services strung together, they would have the opportunity to make the most of their potential. At this time, no such system exists, and the service cloth is full of holes. The following and final recommendations of this book are intended to patch some of those holes.

1. If we think of prevention merely as placement prevention or of prevention of some untoward outcomes for an existing drug-exposed child, then we are shortsighted. Every program—whether it provides residential or in-home services—should emphasize prevention of subsequent unwanted pregnancies via family planning messages. Programs must have the license and resources to ensure that women who want to use oral, surgical, or implanted contraception, and are medically fit to do so, receive that contraception. Abortions must also be available upon request.

2. Intensive family preservation services are a partial response to the needs of drug-involved families. Although intensive family preservation services are designed to address short-lived family crises rather than chronic lifestyles of drug use, the evidence suggests that these services can be helpful for drug-involved families. Anecdotal evidence indicates that the frequent companionship and tangible assistance provided through intensive family preservation services can help families who basically need brief rehabilitative services rather than long-term habilitative services.

3. Child welfare, drug treatment, and child care providers suggest the importance of continuous case management for families of heavy drug users. Services should be provided to the children of most heavy drug users regardless of whether the child protective services case is open or closed. This continuous coordinated case management can be offered through PL 99-457's Individualized Family Services Plan or through a mechanism such as the voluntary case management system for families proposed by the National Commission on Children (1991) and the National Commission on Child Welfare and Family Preservation (1991).

4. We must find a way to pay for women and their children to reside, when they need it, in shared family care together. At this time such an arrangement is not possible under the foster care program and it is not reimbursable under conventional child welfare services. In the meantime, provision of residential care services for mother and children may be the best alternative.

5. PL 99-457 is not currently providing significant services to the children of the majority of heavy drug users. Although the service mix reflects the spirit of federal law, the client eligibility criteria, driven by fiscal constraints that various states have developed, appear to be ruling out these services for drug-involved families. Although we do not have any evaluations of how those services might benefit the children of heavy drug users, the accumulated evidence from Head Start, Perry High Scope, and the recent Robert Wood Johnson Study on early intervention with low and very low birth weight children (Infant Health and Development Program, 1990) strongly suggests that much good could come out of these services at this time. Indeed, the evidence is increasingly clear that interventions must begin early (i.e., often within the first year) if they are going to help overcome long-term effects associated with the more extreme sequelae of drug exposure like subnormal head size associated with very low birth weight (Hack et al., 1991).

6. Child care for children at risk must be ensured so that every eligible family has access to it. Child care providers can develop the kind of relationship to the child that will protect the child in the future. When all the other fancier services fail a child, child care providers are there.

7. Although in-home services should be more enduring, child welfare services should not be extended merely to prolong the oversight of drug-involved families. Ideally, child welfare services should end with a family service plan that guarantees referral and retention in community-based and developmentally focused services. These services providers should ensure, in turn, that they will inform child welfare services if they suspect child maltreatment, whereupon voluntary or court-ordered

case supervision would be resumed. Upon case reopening, child welfare services should have the option to provide services and supervision for an additional 12 months. Permanency planning time frames should be maintained even with families receiving services at home. Although we view family maintenance as the most desirable option for children, fiscal, rather than statutory, constraints often limit services to less than 3 months. Allowing family maintenence services to go on longer does not substantially decrease the likelihood of adoption for children. Few children who begin in family maintenance are then pulled out and moved to adoption. Although adoption of drug-exposed children is desirable and very successful (Barth, 1991), there are thousands of children already in foster care waiting for homes. Providing longer periods of protection with in-home services should prevent child abuse and the accompanying harms and costs and improve developmental outcomes and may, if family planning is incorporated into the service, reduce repeat pregnancies.

8. Human service professionals must not perpetuate the notion that the best interests of the mother and of the child are at odds. Adversarial stances between those who view themselves as child advocates and those who view themselves as parent advocates are counterproductive and even harmful. Policy and program efforts must strive to help both mother and child by viewing and helping them as a family.

9. We must acknowledge that addiction and recovery are different for women than for men. Prevention and treatment policy must reflect our understanding of those differences and of the many roles (mother, family member, partner, wage earner, etc.) that women must fulfill.

10. Drug- and HIV-involved families have the paradoxical need both for a multiplicity of services and for a minimum number of interveners, so that they do not become overwhelmed and withdraw. The solution to these conflicting needs seems to be increased efforts at interagency coordination and the selection of a primary agent. Training across disciplines can reduce service workers' resistance to coordination and also enhance everyone's ability to intervene early for treatment and secondary prevention.

11. Social service and law enforcement interventions that separate families must be the option of last resort. Substance misuse and HIV disease are primarily public health problems, and therefore child protection professionals should only be involved when there are additional indicators of risk or evidence of maltreatment. Law enforcement interventions are a significant cause of family disruption and must be redesigned to provide rehabilitation and parenting preparation.

12. Standards and criteria for drug testing, HIV testing, and child abuse reporting, as well as for other procedures for assessment and referral, should be carefully crafted to promote rather than inhibit access to health care and related support services. At minimum, criteria and practices that are discriminatory and/or punitive should not form the basis of testing. Identifying women and children without protecting them from punitive responses does not increase trust in the health care or social service systems and is likely to be harmful rather than helpful to children.

We are learning that drug-exposed children are generally not doomed to educational and social failure and that most can succeed in their endeavors if given a boost. Nor are crack-using parents hopelessly beyond control and rehabilitation. These truths present us with a heavy responsibility: The children of drug users are going to need protection and support from family and community to avoid the outcomes we most dread. Because these children and their parents are more similar to than different from other children and parents we have been concerned about for a long time, we have many of the program models already in place to serve them. The unique aspects of providing services to drug- and HIV-affected women and children are also spurring new ideas; many of them are presented in these pages, and many more are still in the minds of service providers. Now we must ensure that these occasional programs become routinely available and that promising new ideas are translated into additional services.

REFERENCES

Barth, R. P. (1991). Adoption of drug-exposed children. *Children and Youth Services Review, 13*, 323–342.

Barth, R. P., & Berry, M. (1990). A decade later: Outcomes of child welfare reform. In J. Kroll & J. Anderson (Eds.), *A review of child welfare reform*. Minneapolis: North America Council on Adoptable Children.

Blythe, B. J., Giordano, M. J., & Kelly, S. A. (1991). Family preservation with substance-abusing families: Help that works. *The Child, Youth, and Family Services Quarterly, 14*(3), 13–14.

Boyd, C. J., & Mieczkowski, T. (1990). Drug use, health, family, and social support in "crack" cocaine users. *Addictive Behaviors, 15*, 481–485.

Chavkin, W. (1991). Drug addiction and pregnancy: Policy crossroads. *American Journal of Public Health, 4*, 483.

Chirgwin, K., Dehovitz, J. A., Dillon, S., & McCormack, W. (1991). HIV infection, genital ulcer disease, and crack cocaine use among patients attending a clinic for sexually transmitted diseases. *American Journal of Public Health, 81*(12), 1576–1579.

DelVecchio, R. (1991, June 3). Bay Area crack baby epidemic declines. *San Francisco Chronicle*, p. A13.

Fanshel, D. (1975). Parental failure and consequences for children: The drug-using mother whose children are in foster care. *American Journal of Public Health, 65*, 604–612.

Feig, L. (1990). *Drug-exposed infants and children: Service needs and policy questions*. Washington, DC: U.S. Department of Health and Human Services.

Fein, E., Maluccio, A. N., & Kluger, M. (1990). *No more partings: An examination of long-term foster-family care*. Washington, DC: Child Welfare League of America.

Gans, S. P., & Horton, G. T. (1975). *Integration of human services*. New York: Praeger.

Hack, M., Breslau, N., Weissman, B., Aram, D., Klein, N., & Borawski, E. (1991). Effect of very low birth weight and subnormal head size on cognitive abilities at school age. *New England Journal of Medicine, 325*, 231–237.

Halpert, B. P. (1982). Antecedents. In D. L. Rogers & K. A. Whetten (Eds.), *Interorganizational coordination: Theory, research and implementation*. Ames: Iowa State University Press.

Hinman, A. R. (1991). Strategies to prevent HIV infection in the United States. *American Journal of Public Health, 81,* 1557–1569.

Infant Health and Development Program. (1990). Enhancing the outcomes of low-birth-weight, premature infants: A multisite, randomized trial. *Journal of the American Medical Association, 22,* 3035–3042.

Jeremy, R., & Korenbrot, C. (1987, June 30). *Final report evaluation of MCH high-risk infant follow-up project: Interagency coordination.* San Francisco: University of California, Center for Population and Reproductive Health Policy Studies, Institute for Health Policy Studies.

Katz, L., & Robinson, C. (1991). Foster-care drift: A risk-assessment matrix. *Child Welfare, 70,* 347–358.

Magjaryi, T. (1990, March 6). Prevention of alcohol and drug problems among women of childbearing age: Challenges for the 1990s. Paper presented at the Office of Substance Abuse Prevention conference Healthy Women, Healthy Infants: Emerging Solutions in the Face of Alcohol and Drug Problems, Miami.

Martin, S. L., Ramey, C. T., & Ramey, S. (1990). The prevention of intellectual impairment in children of impoverished families: Findings of a randomized trial of educational day care. *American Journal of Public Health, 80,* 844–847.

Ostrea, E. M., Brady, M., Gause, S., Raymundo, A. L., & Stevens, M. (1992). Drug screening of newborn infants by meconium analysis: A large-scale prospective epidemiologic study. *Pediatrics, 89,* 107–113.

Portis, K. (1991). Intake and diagnosis of drug-dependent, pregnant women. Workshop presented at the National Institute on Drug Abuse National Conference on Drug Abuse Research and Practice: An Alliance for the 21st Century. Washington, DC.

SDSS. (1990). *Pre-placement prevention services: Emergency response and family survey of selected characteristics for cases closed during January 1989.* Sacramento, CA: Author.

Senate Office of Research. (1990). *California's drug-exposed babies: Undiscovered, unreported, underserved.* Sacramento, CA.

Squires, J. (1992, January 10). Risk of transmitting HIV-virus from mother to child. Paper presented at the Women and HIV/AIDS Conference, Fort Worth, Texas.

Wetzel, M. (1990). *Handbook on civil suits to shut down crack houses.* Berkeley, CA: Author.

Wightman, M. J. (1991). Criteria for placement decisions with cocaine-exposed infants. *Child Welfare, 70,* 653–664.

Zuckerman, B. (1991). *Drug-exposed infants: Understanding the medical risk. Future of Children, 1*(1), 26–32.

Name Index

Subject Index

362.1989
B284

LINCOLN CHRISTIAN COLLEGE AND SEMINARY

86929

362.1989 Families living with
B284   drugs and HIV

86929

DEMCO